MW01620651

# SHAKESPEARE AND EARLY MODERN RELIGION

Written by an international team of literary scholars and historians, this collaborative volume illuminates the diversity of early modern religious beliefs and practices in Shakespeare's England, and considers how religious culture is imaginatively reanimated in Shakespeare's plays. Fourteen new essays explore the creative ways Shakespeare engaged with the multifaceted dimensions of Protestantism, Catholicism, non-Christian religions including Judaism and Islam, and secular perspectives, considering plays such as *Hamlet*, *Julius Caesar*, *King John*, *King Lear*, *Macbeth*, *Measure for Measure*, *A Midsummer Night's Dream*, and *The Winter's Tale*. The collection is of great interest to readers of Shakespeare studies, early modern literature, religious studies, and early modern history.

DAVID LOEWENSTEIN is Helen C. White Professor of English and the Humanities at the University of Wisconsin-Madison. He is the editor and author of many publications, including *John Milton, Prose: Major Writings on Liberty, Politics, Religion, and Education* (2013), *Treacherous Faith: The Specter of Heresy in Early Modern English Literature and Culture* (2013), *The Cambridge History of Early Modern English Literature* (coeditor, Cambridge, 2002), and *Representing Revolution in Milton and his Contemporaries: Religion, Politics, and Polemics in Radical Puritanism* (Cambridge, 2001), which won a James Holly Hanford Distinguished Book Award.

MICHAEL WITMORE is Director of the Folger Shakespeare Library in Washington, D.C. He is the author of *Landscapes of the Passing Strange: Reflections from Shakespeare* (with Rosamond Purcell, 2010), *Shakespearean Metaphysics* (2008), and *Pretty Creatures: Children and Fiction in the English Renaissance* (2007). He is also the editor of *Childhood and Children's Books in Early Modern Europe, 1550–1800* (with Andrea Immel, 2006).

# SHAKESPEARE AND EARLY MODERN RELIGION

EDITED BY

DAVID LOEWENSTEIN

and

MICHAEL WITMORE

**CAMBRIDGE**
**UNIVERSITY PRESS**

University Printing House, Cambridge CB2 8BS, United Kingdom

Cambridge University Press is part of the University of Cambridge.

It furthers the University's mission by disseminating knowledge in the pursuit of education, learning and research at the highest international levels of excellence.

www.cambridge.org
Information on this title: www.cambridge.org/9781107026612

© Cambridge University Press, 2015

This publication is in copyright. Subject to statutory exception and to the provisions of relevant collective licensing agreements, no reproduction of any part may take place without the written permission of Cambridge University Press.

First published 2015

*A catalogue record for this publication is available from the British Library*

*Library of Congress Cataloguing in Publication data*
Shakespeare and early modern religion / edited by David Loewenstein, Michael Witmore.
pages cm
ISBN 978-1-107-02661-2 (hardback)
1. Shakespeare, William, 1564–1616 – Religion. 2. Religion and drama.
3. Drama – Religious aspects. 4. Religious tolerance in literature. 5. Cultural pluralism in literature. 6. Religion in literature. 7. England – Religion – 16th century.
8. England – Religion – 17th century. I. Loewenstein, David, editor. II. Witmore, Michael, editor.
PR3011S31 2015
822.3′3–dc23
2014044212

ISBN 978-1-107-02661-2 Hardback

Cambridge University Press has no responsibility for the persistence or accuracy of URLs for external or third-party internet websites referred to in this publication, and does not guarantee that any content on such websites is, or will remain, accurate or appropriate.

# *Contents*

# *Illustrations*

# *Notes on contributors*

DAVID BEVINGTON is the Phyllis Fay Horton Distinguished Service Professor Emeritus in the Humanities at the University of Chicago. His books include *Shakespeare: The Seven Ages of Human Experience* (2005), *This Wide and Universal Theater: Shakespeare in Performance, Then and Now* (2007), *Shakespeare's Ideas* (2008), *Shakespeare and Biography* (2010), and *Murder Most Foul: Hamlet Through the Ages* (2011). He is editor of *The Complete Works of Shakespeare* (7th edn., 2013) and a senior editor of *The Cambridge Edition of the Works of Ben Jonson* (2012).

BRIAN CUMMINGS is Anniversary Professor of English at the University of York. He has published widely on early modern religion and literature, including *The Literary Culture of the Reformation: Grammar and Grace* (2002) and *Mortal Thoughts: Religion, Secularity & Identity in Shakespeare and Early Modern Culture* (2013). He is also editor of *The Book of Common Prayer* (2011).

MICHAEL DAVIES is Senior Lecturer in English at the University of Liverpool. His research focuses on the literary and religious cultures of early modern England, from Elizabethan Protestantism to Restoration Nonconformity. He is the author of *Graceful Reading: Theology and Narrative in the Works of John Bunyan* (2002) and *Hamlet: Character Studies* (2008). He is also coeditor of *Literature and Authenticity, 1780–1900* (2011).

MATTHEW DIMMOCK is Professor of Early Modern Studies at the University of Sussex. His publications include *New Turkes: Dramatizing Islam and the Ottomans in Early Modern England* (2005), *Mythologies of Muhammad in Early Modern English Culture* (2013), and (as editor) of *William Percy's Mahomet and his Heaven: A Critical Edition* (2006).

EWAN FERNIE is Chair and Professor at the Shakespeare Institute, Stratford-upon-Avon (University of Birmingham). His latest book is

*The Demonic: Literature and Experience* (2012), and he is general editor, with Simon Palfrey, of Arden's Shakespeare Now! series.

BEATRICE GROVES is the Research Lecturer in Renaissance English at Trinity College, Oxford. She is author of *Texts and Traditions: Religion in Shakespeare, 1592–1604* (2006) and *The Fall of Jerusalem in Early Modern Literature* (forthcoming, 2015).

FELICITY HEAL is an emeritus Fellow of Jesus College, Oxford. Her books include *Hospitality in Early Modern England* (1990), *The Gentry in Early Modern England and Wales* (with Clive Holmes, 1994), *Reformation in Britain and Ireland* (2003), and *The Power of Gifts* (2014).

PETER LAKE is Distinguished University Professor of early modern English History at Vanderbilt University. He is the author of *The Antichrist's Lewd Hat: Protestants, Papists, and Players in Post-Reformation England* (with Michael Questier, 2002). He is currently working on a book about Shakespeare's history plays and the politics of the 1590s.

DAVID LOEWENSTEIN is Helen C. White Professor of English and the Humanities at the University of Wisconsin-Madison. His publications include *Representing Revolution in Milton and his Contemporaries: Religion, Politics, and Polemics in Radical Puritanism* (2001), *Treacherous Faith: The Specter of Heresy in Early Modern English Literature and Culture* (2013), and (as coeditor) *The Cambridge History of Early Modern English Literature* (2002). He is editing *Paradise Lost* for the Oxford *Complete Works of John Milton.*

PETER MARSHALL is Professor of History at the University of Warwick. His books include *Beliefs and the Dead in Reformation England* (2002), *Mother Leakey and the Bishop: A Ghost Story* (2007), and *Reformation England, 1480–1642* (2nd edn., 2012).

RICHARD MCCOY is Distinguished Professor of English at Queens College and the Graduate Center at the City University of New York. He is the author of *Sir Philip Sidney: Rebellion in Arcadia* (1979), *The Rites of Knighthood: The Literature and Politics of Elizabethan Chivalry* (1989), *Alterations of State: Sacred Kingship in the English Reformation* (2002), and *Faith in Shakespeare* (2013).

ALISON SHELL is Professor of Early Modern Studies at University College, London and has written widely on early modern literature and religion. She is the author of *Catholicism, Controversy and the English Literary*

*Imagination, 1558–1660* (1999), *Oral Culture and Catholicism in Early Modern England* (2007), and *Shakespeare and Religion* (2010).

PAUL STEVENS is Canada Research Chair in Early Modern Literature and Culture at the University of Toronto. He is author of *Imagination and the Presence of Shakespeare in "Paradise Lost"* (1985) and is coeditor of *Early Modern Nationalism and Milton's England* (2008). He is presently working on two book projects: *Milton Imagining England* and *Sola Gratia: English Literature and the Secular Ways of Grace*, for which he was awarded a Guggenheim Fellowship.

ADRIAN STREETE is Senior Lecturer in the School of English, Queen's University, Belfast. He is author of *Protestantism and Drama in Early Modern England* (2009), editor of *Early Modern Drama and the Bible: Contexts and Readings, 1570–1625* (2011), and coeditor of *The Edinburgh Companion to Shakespeare and the Arts* (2011) and *Filming and Performing Renaissance History* (2011).

MICHAEL WITMORE is Director of the Folger Shakespeare Library in Washington, D.C. His publications include *Culture of Accidents: Unexpected Knowledges in Early Modern England* (2001), *Pretty Creatures: Children and Fiction in the English Renaissance* (2007), *Shakespearean Metaphysics* (2008), and (as coauthor) *Landscapes of the Passing Strange: Reflections from Shakespeare* (2010).

# *Acknowledgments*

We are deeply grateful to Sarah Stanton and Rosemary Crawley, our editors at Cambridge University Press, for their invaluable advice and their patience. We greatly appreciate Sarah Stanton's encouragement of this project from its inception. We also thank the superb staff of the Folger Shakespeare Library for their assistance as this book was developing. Michael Gadaleto, our attentive research assistant, provided essential help, including with stylistic matters, as we prepared the final manuscript for press. Finally, we are grateful to all our contributors for their patience and professionalism and for their creative and rigorous critical thinking which, we hope, will generate further insights into and debates about Shakespeare and early modern religion.

We also thank the Bodleian Library, Oxford for permission to reproduce the woodcut in John Foxe, *Actes and Monuments* (London, 1570), depicting the persecution of early Christians.

# *Introduction*

*David Loewenstein and Michael Witmore*

## I

*Shakespeare and Early Modern Religion* contains contributions from both literary scholars and historians of religion; as such, it is a cross-disciplinary volume that illuminates Shakespeare's plays and the early modern religious beliefs that circulated in Shakespeare's England. Most notably, this volume explores Shakespeare's creative engagement with early modern religious culture, but it does so without assuming that Shakespeare can himself be aligned with any specific doctrinal beliefs, religious group, or confession. The chapters in this book thus eschew firm or reductive assertions about Shakespeare's personal religious convictions. Instead, contributors focus on his imaginative recasting of different currents of early modern religious culture and beliefs in their great variety, an array of perspectives that was at once contradictory, competing, and deeply contested.

Like the Cambridge University Press volume on *Shakespeare and Early Modern Political Thought* edited by David Armitage, Conal Condren, and Andrew Fitzmaurice,[1] this book offers fresh interdisciplinary perspectives on a large topic that has generated much critical controversy. In doing so, it is likely to generate more discussion, since it does little to resolve the vexed question of Shakespeare's confessional position or positions. This volume is timely, however, because both literary scholars and historians of early modern religion contribute their particular insights into religious matters and debates in relation to Shakespeare's plays. We have attempted, in bringing together historians of religion and literary critics, to engage both specialists and more general readers of Shakespeare, including student readers – anyone interested in tracing Shakespeare's imaginative engagement with the variety of religious beliefs and practices that characterizes early modern English culture.

[1] David Armitage, Conal Condren, and Andrew Fitzmaurice (eds.), *Shakespeare and Early Modern Political Thought* (Cambridge University Press, 2009).

How do Shakespeare's plays give dramatic, imaginative, and provocative expression to diverse early modern religious perspectives and faiths – some of them contradictory, paradoxical, and dissonant – without resolving them? This volume attempts to address this question in relation to the religious complexities and changing culture of Shakespeare's England. Shakespeare gives dramatic expression to both Protestant and Catholic perspectives in his plays, a reminder that he lived in an age marked by tumultuous religious change and divisions brought about by the cataclysm of the Reformation that shattered western Christendom. Henry VIII's England, in which Shakespeare's father was born, was predominantly a Catholic nation, albeit a nation riven with tensions and instabilities generated by the evangelical culture of the Reformation.[2] Catholics were still widespread during the early years of Elizabeth's reign,[3] but by the time Shakespeare was thriving as a playwright in London – in the late 1580s, the 1590s, and the first twelve or thirteen years of the seventeenth century – England was predominantly a Protestant nation, Elizabeth herself having been excommunicated and deposed in a papal bull of 1570 for "usurping monster-like the place of the chief sovereign of the church of England" and prohibiting "the exercise of true religion" and the Roman Church.[4] To be sure, there were plenty of ambiguities and inconsistencies within the Elizabethan religious settlement (which "wedded an essentially Calvinist theology to an essentially Catholic institutional structure, minus the pope"),[5] although Elizabeth identified herself as a Protestant ruler.

These tensions persisted over the course of Shakespeare's life, as Elizabeth's successor – James I, the patron of Shakespeare's King's Men – self-consciously presented himself in print as a major Protestant exegete and theologian (the figure of "Religio" appears prominently on the 1616 title page of his *Workes*). The English Reformation, although long and partial, was ultimately, in the words of Diarmaid MacCulloch, a "howling

[2] See Alec Ryrie, *The Gospel and Henry VIII: Evangelicals and the Early English Reformation* (Cambridge University Press, 2003); Peter Marshall and Alec Ryrie (eds.), *The Beginnings of English Protestantism* (Cambridge University Press, 2002).

[3] See Chapter 2 below, p. 42.

[4] See *Regnans in excelsis*, in Robert S. Miola (ed.), *Early Modern Catholicism: An Anthology of Primary Sources* (Oxford University Press, 2007), pp. 486–8; quotations from p. 487.

[5] Benjamin J. Kaplan, *Divided by Faith: Religious Conflict and the Practice of Toleration in Early Modern Europe* (Cambridge, MA: Harvard University Press, 2007), p. 136. See also Diarmaid MacCulloch, *The Later Reformation in England, 1547–1603*, 2nd edn. (Basingstoke: Palgrave Macmillan, 2001), pp. 28–30.

success,"[6] even as Protestant anxieties about the presence of Catholics (as Chapters 2 and 3 by Peter Marshall and Felicity Heal remind us) were never assuaged, including in King James's London, and even as Elizabethan England remained religiously divided and mixed (as Chapter 2 likewise makes clear).[7] Yet the degree to which Shakespeare himself can be characterized as a Protestant – was he a more moderate one tolerant of different faiths in religiously diverse London? – continues to provoke scholarly debate and conjecture. Likewise, the degree to which he can even be characterized as a religious playwright remains subject to debate. *Shakespeare and Early Modern Religion* challenges and complicates one-sided attempts to attribute to Shakespeare himself firm or rigid religious identifications, affiliations, or sets of religious practices (e.g., Shakespeare-as-Catholic or Shakespeare-as-Calvinist). Instead, the chapters in this volume stress the ways Shakespeare's plays explore, by giving voice to, a wide range of religious beliefs, practices, and confessional positions circulating in Shakespeare's England.

*Shakespeare and Early Modern Religion* addresses a number of major questions about Shakespeare's plays in relation to the religious culture, divisions, allegiances, and intellectual history of early modern England and Europe. How orthodox or mainstream are the religious perspectives dramatized in Shakespeare's plays? How experimental and daring are Shakespeare's plays, especially the tragedies, when it comes to representing early modern religious thought, experience, speculation, and anxieties? Do Shakespeare's plays implicitly endorse, question, challenge, or complicate Protestant orthodoxy and the widespread belief in providentialism in early

6 Diarmaid MacCulloch, "The Impact of the English Reformation," *Historical Journal*, 38 (1995), 152. See also Alexandra Walsham, *Providence in Early Modern England* (Oxford University Press, 1999), p. 4; Peter Marshall (ed.), *The Impact of the English Reformation, 1500–1640* (London: Edward Arnold, 1997); Patrick Collinson, *The Religion of the Protestants: The Church in English Society, 1559–1625* (Oxford: Clarendon Press, 1982), and *The Birthpangs of Protestant England: Religious and Cultural Change in the Sixteenth and Seventeenth Centuries* (New York: St. Martin's Press, 1988).

7 On Catholicism as an ongoing topic of intense political discussion and anxiety throughout the span of Shakespeare's career (and beyond), see also Alexandra Walsham, *Church Papists: Catholicism, Conformity, and Confessional Polemic in Early Modern England* (Woodbridge: Boydell & Brewer, 1993); Alison Shell, *Catholicism, Controversy and the English Literary Imagination* (Cambridge University Press, 1999); and Michael C. Questier, *Catholicism and Community in Early Modern England: Politics, Aristocratic Patronage, and Religion, c. 1550–1640* (Cambridge University Press, 2006). For the creative blending of Catholicism's visual emphasis with Protestantism's focus on the Word, see especially Beatrice Groves, *Texts and Traditions: Religion in Shakespeare, 1592–1604* (Oxford: Clarendon Press, 2007). Studies arguing for Shakespeare's relation to Catholicism include Richard Dutton, Alison Findlay and Richard Wilson (eds.), *Theatre and Religion: Lancastrian Shakespeare* (Manchester University Press, 2003); Richard Wilson, *Secret Shakespeare: Studies in Theatre, Religion and Resistance* (Manchester University Press, 2004); David N. Beauregard, *Catholic Theology in Shakespeare's Plays* (Newark, DE: University of Delaware Press, 2008); and Phoebe Jensen, *Religion and Revelry in Shakespeare's Festive World* (Cambridge University Press, 2008).

modern England? How do the plays interrogate and test, in original and powerful ways, early modern religious prejudices towards Catholics, Puritans, Jews, Muslims, and radical religious groups (e.g. Brownists)? Can these theatrical works be seen in the context of notions of toleration and intolerance in the early modern period? Do they challenge ways we think about the categories of the secular and the religious in the early modern period and the boundary critics have sometimes constructed between them? Finally, how does Shakespeare explore the relations between religious beliefs, politics, and issues of early modern English national identity and chauvinism?

The chapters in this volume likewise consider the degree to which we view Shakespeare as a religious playwright. If Shakespeare wrote "scripts that were intensely alert to the social and political realities of their times,"[8] he also wrote plays that were equally alive to the religious tensions of their times. Yet while modern criticism has produced books with such titles as *Political Shakespeare* or *Shakespeare's Political Drama*,[9] it might seem odd to entitle a study *Religious Shakespeare* or *Shakespeare's Religious Drama*. Shakespeare, after all, was not a religious playwright in the sense that John Bale or John Foxe were. Religion nonetheless permeates Shakespeare's plays: it does so in terms of their great wealth of biblical allusions,[10] in their echoes of the Book of Common Prayer and the Psalter,[11] and in their uses of religious language (sometimes for comic or parodic purposes as in the cases of characters like Bottom or the vivacious Falstaff, the latter wittily employing godly language as he banters with Prince Hal). The plays simultaneously evoke features of both Catholic and Protestant culture, and it is this richness that makes it difficult for us to pinpoint Shakespeare's own doctrinal allegiances. The plays, for example, refer to key religious concepts and places (e.g., Heaven or the fires of Hell and Purgatory); to the notion of salvation and damnation (central to understanding the non-Roman tragedies); and to religious institutions and buildings (e.g., parishes as well as chantries), financial systems (tithes), liturgical

[8] Stephen Greenblatt, *Will in the World: How Shakespeare Became Shakespeare* (New York: W. W. Norton, 2004), p. 12.

[9] Jonathan Dollimore and Alan Sinfield (eds.), *Political Shakespeare: New Essays in Cultural Materialism* (Ithaca, NY: Cornell University Press, 1985), and Alexander Leggatt, *Shakespeare's Political Drama: The History Plays and the Roman Plays* (London: Routledge, 1988).

[10] For Shakespeare's rich and various uses of biblical allusions, see now Hannibal Hamlin, *The Bible in Shakespeare* (Oxford University Press, 2013). See also Steven Marx, *Shakespeare and the Bible* (Oxford University Press, 2000), and Groves, *Texts and Traditions*, ch. 1.

[11] See Daniel Swift, *Shakespeare's Common Prayers: The Book of Common Prayer and the Elizabethan Age* (Oxford University Press, 2103).

rituals and practices, and church ales. The plays can also vividly depict the demonic imagination and demonic possession; examine both zealous and non-Protestant religious groups (e.g., Puritans, Catholics, Jews, or Muslims); and explore religious hatred and prejudices. They represent characters burdened with guilt and sinfulness, who struggle to show contrition and seek forgiveness; they dramatize spiritual resurrection, miracles, and faith;[12] and they depict individuals, notably Hamlet, who engage in anxious religious questioning and express profound uncertainty about the world beyond this one.

Yet despite the rich presence of religion in the plays, it is hard to think of Shakespeare as a religious writer in the same way that we consider Spenser or the zealous Milton as authors deeply committed to religious causes or theological doctrines.[13] Shakespeare's plays, David Kastan asserts, "assume a world in which God is immanent,"[14] and yet his most devastating tragedy and depiction of extreme human suffering, *King Lear*, arguably challenges the very idea of such immanence and the widespread religious perception in early modern England that God's hand was directly and assiduously at work in the world, constantly intervening in human affairs.[15]

It may indeed make more sense to view Shakespeare as a writer whose plays engage creatively and dramatically with various – and sometimes contradictory and dissonant – facets of religious culture in early modern England and Europe without, in the end, his being a deeply or consistently religious writer who makes clear-cut confessional choices.[16] In any case, as the chapters in this volume remind us, it is hard to think of Shakespeare as a doctrinaire religious author and even harder to think of him as a writer who identified with militant religious causes (as, say, Sidney, Spenser, and Milton did). Furthermore, as the chapters in this volume attest, it is difficult to be sure of Shakespeare's personal religious convictions, despite claims – far from certain – that his father was a Catholic,[17] in the way we can know

[12] On this topic, see Richard C. McCoy, *Faith in Shakespeare* (Oxford University Press, 2013), which examines the recovery or awakening of faith not in a narrowly religious sense but in relation to the powers of figurative language, theatrical illusion, and stagecraft. See also Chapter 11 below.

[13] See David Kastan, *A Will to Believe: Shakespeare and Religion* (Oxford University Press, 2014), p. 4. Also see Chapter 4 below for ways in which Shakespeare differs from Spenser in handling Reformation issues.

[14] Kastan, *Will to Believe*, p. 6.

[15] Walsham, *Providence in Early Modern England*, pp. 2, 6.

[16] Cf. Alison Shell, *Shakespeare and Religion*, Arden Shakespeare Critical Editions (London: Bloomsbury, 2010), who notes Shakespeare's "confessional invisibility" (p. 235).

[17] The indecisive evidence for "John Shakespeare and Catholicism" is carefully reviewed in the biographical entry for Shakespeare by Peter Holland in the *Oxford Dictionary of National Biography* (www.oxforddnb.com); moreover, as Holland notes, "there is . . . no reason to assume that the adult William shared his father's religious views," even if they were Catholic.

Jonson's with his conversion to Roman Catholicism and his re-conversion to the Church of England.[18] Despite documentary evidence concerning Shakespeare's life, we possess no personal letters, diaries, autobiography, testaments of faith, or religious tracts or treatises that might give us some insight into his religious persuasions or ecclesiastical allegiance. To be sure, the plays dramatize both Catholic and Protestant perspectives: for example, Hamlet Senior's Ghost has come from Purgatory (central to Roman Catholic teaching) and refers to Catholic liturgical practices which he has been denied (see 1.5.76–9), whereas Hamlet voices religious views that evoke the newer reformed ideas of Luther and Calvin.[19] In a larger sense, *Hamlet* imaginatively dramatizes an unresolved tension at the heart of the unfinished Elizabethan Reformation and the church: vestiges of Catholic liturgy juxtaposed with Protestant theology and a Protestant church still haunted by its Catholic past.[20] Yet this religious ambiguity or tension dramatized in *Hamlet* hardly reveals Shakespeare's own personal persuasions which, perhaps, must remain as mysterious as the cosmos Hamlet speculates about.

It may instead be more fruitful to ask why Shakespeare evokes both Catholic and Protestant dimensions in his great tragedy, and to stress *the dramatic and imaginative uses* to which he as a creative and independent-minded playwright puts these competing and dissonant religious perspectives. The Christian Hamlet is deeply influenced by a Reformation view of human nature: his corrosive and weary sense of the depravity of humankind accords with a sense that Denmark is rotten, sick, and claustrophobic, so that his world has become "a foul and pestilent congregation of vapours"

18 See Ian Donaldson, *Ben Jonson: A Life* (Oxford University Press, 2011), esp. pp. 138–44, 271–5. For Shakespeare's biography in relation to the elusive problem of his religious beliefs and the question of his father's Catholicism, see esp. Chapter 1 below; see also Kastan, *Will to Believe*, ch. 2. Cf. Jeffrey Knapp, *Shakespeare's Tribe: Church, Nation, and Theater in Renaissance England* (University of Chicago Press, 2002) for an attempt to define Shakespeare's own religious beliefs and to see English Renaissance playwrights themselves "as a kind of ministry" whose plays were intended as "contributions to the cause of true religion" (p. 9) and "godly enterprises" (p. 2), so that the theater became an alternative to the prelatical church. For a critical response to Knapp, see Chapter 11 below, p. 225.

19 For more on Catholic and Calvinist perspectives in *Hamlet*, see Chapter 1 below.

20 For this tension, see MacCulloch, *Later Reformation*, p. 5. Even the godly Elizabeth maintained the crucifix and candles in her private chapel and preferred a formal, sung liturgy over an excess of sermons: Felicity Heal, *Reformation in Britain and Ireland* (Oxford University Press, 2003), p. 361, and Chapter 3 below, p. 59. See also Chapter 2 below, p. 42. The liturgy of the Church of England was more elaborate than that of other churches in the Reformed world; it retained bishops, fully functioning cathedrals, as well as deans, canons, paid choirs and organists, and a tendency to use the English Prayer Book in a ceremonial way: Diarmaid MacCulloch, *Christianity: The First Three Thousand Years* (New York: Viking, 2009), p. 649. See as well the scholarship cited in notes 59 and 60 of Chapter 2 below.

(2.2.293).[21] That Hamlet Senior offers a Catholic perspective makes some sense in terms of the play's representation of two generations (since first-generation Protestants, after all, had Catholic parents); that his Ghost comes from Purgatory also takes on a symbolic resonance in a dark and protracted tragedy full of "foul crimes" (1.5.12) that often evokes the sense of living through a kind of Purgatory. The Christian prince whose outlook is shaped by reformed views, moreover, sees his world providentially ("There's a divinity that shapes our ends" and "a special providence in the fall of a sparrow" [5.2.10, 157–8]).[22] However, Horatio's concluding summary of the bloody revenge tragedy with its "accidental judgements" and "casual slaughters" (5.2.324–8) offers another, more skeptical interpretation of the play's events – one in tension with providential explanations. Even within *Hamlet* we get competing, contradictory, and dissonant religious perspectives. Rather than encourage easy or simple resolutions to these conflicting perspectives, Shakespeare, it seems, aims in his imaginative ways to animate, and thereby to provoke readers and spectators to think about, the deepest matters of religious belief and controversy.

Yet if Shakespeare's plays are permeated by references to early modern religious matters, they nevertheless provide little evidence of his being a committed religious writer with specific religious persuasions such as, say, Foxe, Spenser, Herbert, or Milton enunciate. In the absence of such specific allegiances, does this mean that he is ultimately a great secular writer, as many twentieth-century critics liked to emphasize? The boundary often invoked between the secular and the religious in the early modern period is too simple and unhistorical, as Brian Cummings has powerfully and persuasively reminded us.[23] One might consider Shakespeare's Falstaff, for example, as a great secular comic figure with an agile and fertile imagination; yet his clever uses of Puritan cadences – "O, thou hast damnable iteration, and art indeed able to corrupt a saint . . . God forgive thee for it" (*1 Henry IV* 1.2.80–2), he tells Hal as he wittily justifies his vocation of stealing – complicate a simple binary between the secular and the religious. Such language reminds us that Shakespeare's contemporary audiences – steeped

[21] Citations from Shakespeare in the Introduction are taken from *The Norton Shakespeare* based on the Oxford text and edited by Stephen Greenblatt, Walter Cohen, Jean E. Howard, and Katherine Eisaman Maus (New York: W. W. Norton, 1997).

[22] For Hamlet's latter providential assertion, see Matthew 10:29 and Calvin's *Institutes*, 1.xvi.1, 1.xvii.6. In the Elizabethan translation of Calvin's words, God works "by susteynyng, cherishing, & caring for, with singular prouidence euery one of those thinges that he hath created euen to the least sparrow": *The Institution of the Christian Religion*, trans. Thomas Norton (London, 1561).

[23] Brian Cummings, *Mortal Thoughts: Religion, Secularity and Identity in Shakespeare and Early Modern Culture* (Oxford University Press, 2013), esp. pp. 1–18.

in biblical culture, familiar with sermons delivered in London parishes and at Paul's Cross, and aware of the long-standing animus of zealous reformers against festivals and theater[24] – were closely attuned to such religious idioms and their biblical allusions and would have relished Falstaff's nimble, mock-sanctimonious uses of godly discourse. Even in Falstaff's inventive festive world, religious and secular issues creatively intersect. As the chapters in this volume examine Shakespeare's plays in relation to early modern religious culture, they likewise highlight the unstable and porous division between the two categories and eschew a narrative of secularization that places Shakespeare at its very center.

This volume, moreover, explores Shakespeare's imaginative and intellectual engagement with currents of early modern religious beliefs without reducing early modern religious experience to issues of power or political control.[25] Hamlet's anxious religious questing, including his ability to engage with doubts and uncertainties, for example, is symptomatic of his capacious, wide-ranging mind struggling with his profound sense of grief and acute sense of mortality; it cannot be confined to issues of power, even as he despises the sinister politics and duplicity of the Danish court. Yet, at the same time, *Shakespeare and Early Modern Religion* does at points consider ways that religious concerns in Shakespeare intersect with political ones. This point of exchange allows Shakespeare to enrich religious and political ambiguities in his plays. For instance, Shakespeare complicates and deepens the character of Claudius in *Hamlet* by portraying him as an efficient and slippery Machiavellian politician who skillfully uses regal language at the court and yet who, in private, is also burdened with a keen sense of his "rank" offense which "hath the primal eldest curse upon't"; consequently his guilty conscience cannot show genuine contrition as his soul desperately struggles "to be free": "O wretched state, O bosom black as death, / O limèd soul . . . / Help, angels! Make assay!" (3.3.36–7, 67–9).

Or consider the case of *Henry V*, which illustrates how Shakespeare dramatizes interconnected issues of religion, politics, and militant nationalism; the intertwining of these issues introduces different kinds of ethical and political ambiguities. There religious language can be exploited to

[24] For more about the antagonism between godly reformers and the stage, see Chapters 1 and 3 below.

[25] Critics identifying as New Historicist or materialist are sometimes criticized for "reducing" the complexity of the plays to a single struggle between a dominant ideology and its (real or imagined) alternatives. As with any approach, such work ranges from the very rich to the reductive. Notable examples of that work (e.g., the influential studies of Shakespeare by Stephen Greenblatt) would not be out of place in a collection like ours.

justify dubious claims to wage war in the name of national interests. When Henry V, a Catholic king whose chauvinistic national politics would have resonated in Protestant England, asks whether he has a just *casus belli* so that he can wage war against France, the Duke of Canterbury addresses the king's concern about "right and conscience," while fueling the zeal for war and national unity by invoking biblical authority (Numbers 27:8; see 1.2.96–114). In his vehement and skillful oratory, Henry V himself links vengeance and "the will of God" (1.2.189) as he justifies his nationalistic campaign against France. Even when the English Army seems enfeebled before the great battle of Agincourt, Henry asserts: "We are in God's hand" (3.6.155). And when the French suffer a spectacular defeat, Henry declares, "God, thy arm was here" (4.8.100) and calls for "all holy rites" (4.8.100, 116). Henry V's religious language is an instrument of his political and national ambitions, but is it also more than that? Shakespeare leaves the answer to this question unresolved, allowing for interpretive instabilities and ambiguities: we can see the ruthless, immoral uses of religion for militant political purposes and yet acknowledge that on some level the warlike and rhetorically skillful Henry is indeed a religious man whose chauvinistic leadership and pursuit of national unity the play enables us both to admire and question. In *Shakespeare and Early Modern Religion*, the chapters by Beatrice Groves, Peter Lake, Adrian Streete, Paul Stevens, and Michael Davies (to mention several contributions) also examine ways that religion, politics, and issues of national identity interact in other plays by Shakespeare, thereby generating ethical and political ambiguities.

## II

For several decades literary critics have approached religion as a cultural activity that shares with imaginative literature a set of common symbols, concepts, and interpretive strategies. This yoking of the domains of fiction and religion, most apparent in work on the early modern stage, was given particular impetus by New Historicist critics, who argued that symbolic activities of all kinds might be included in our notion of culture, and that purely "literary" or "theatrical" uses of language could not be restricted to imaginative writing.[26] Over the last several decades a number of critics have produced powerful interpretations of Shakespearean and early modern theatrical texts, identifying key concepts – conversion, dissimulation,

[26] The most influential articulation of this wider scope is Stephen Greenblatt's *Renaissance Self-Fashioning: From More to Shakespeare* (1980; University of Chicago Press, 2005).

dispossession, idolatry, and imitation – that place the basic operations of playing and theatrical "feigning" on the fault lines of larger sectarian debates.[27]

After the New Historicism brought an anthropological approach to thinking about religion, later approaches moved further afield into philosophy, contemporary cultural history, and the history of the book. Contributors to a notable collection of essays edited by Ken Jackson and Arthur Marotti, for example, have brought phenomenological and postmodern perspectives to the question of how religion or religious conflict is expressed in Shakespeare's plays.[28] Renewed interest in social, intellectual, and book history, as well as modern language philosophy, has introduced additional perspectives on the religious impulses and diverse religious traditions that seem to animate Shakespeare's plays.[29]

The chapters in this collection do not always represent a departure, in either direction or method, from this important body of preceding scholarly work, although our contributors tend to employ historicist rather than postmodern critical methods. Readers will, however, find a subtle shift of emphasis that is due – in part – to the context of the discussion, but also to the kinds of thinkers and critics that are part of the ongoing discussion about Shakespeare and early modern religion. We have already stressed the fact that several historians of religion contribute chapters to the volume, providing complex historical and cultural perspectives on the tensions and alignments that characterized the times in which Shakespeare lived and wrote. As a result, the texture of argument in this volume is at times more granular, more likely to recognize eddies and cross-currents in early modern

[27] See Stephen Greenblatt, "Shakespeare and the Exorcists," in *Shakespearean Negotiations* (Berkeley, CA: University of California Press, 1988), ch. 4; and *Hamlet in Purgatory* (Princeton University Press, 2002); Deborah Kuller Shuger, *Political Theologies in Shakespeare's England: The Sacred and the State in "Measure for Measure"* (Basingstoke: Palgrave Macmillan, 2001); Jeffrey Knapp, *Preachers and Players in Shakespeare's England* (Berkeley, CA: Center for Hermeneutical Studies, 1995).

[28] Ken Jackson and Arthur F. Marotti (eds.), *Shakespeare and Early Modern Religion: Early Modern and Postmodern Perspectives* (Notre Dame, IN: University of Notre Dame Press, 2011). See also Marotti and Jackson, "The Turn to Religion in Early Modern English Studies," *Criticism*, 46 (winter 2004), 167–90; Julia Reinhard Lupton, *Citizen-Saints: Shakespeare and Political Theology* (University of Chicago Press, 2005); James Knapp, *Image Ethics in Shakespeare and Spenser* (Basingstoke: Palgrave Macmillan, 2011); Julia Reinhard Lupton and Graham Hammill (eds.), *Political Theology and Early Modernity* (University of Chicago Press, 2012); Jennifer Waldron, *Reformations of the Body: Idolatry, Sacrifice and Early Modern Theater* (Basingstoke: Palgrave Macmillan, 2013); and Victoria Kahn, *The Future of Illusion: Political Theology and Early Modern Texts* (University of Chicago Press, 2014).

[29] See, e.g., Groves, *Texts and Traditions*; Shell, *Shakespeare and Religion*; Sarah Beckwith, *Shakespeare and the Grammar of Forgiveness* (Ithaca, NY: Cornell University Press, 2011); Cummings, *Mortal Thoughts*.

religious debates that cannot be captured in contrasts between "Protestant" or "Catholic" perspectives.

A more subtle shift in emphasis follows in the ways this volume explores Shakespeare's engagement with religion. The chapters herein examine not only Shakespeare's creative engagement with the diverse "religious culture" in the early modern period; they also examine Shakespeare as a kind of religious thinker, albeit one who works in the imaginative medium of drama. Many of the contributors in this collection emphasize the complexity of Shakespeare's engagement with conflicts that were debated by professional theologians during the sixteenth and early seventeenth centuries, but which also touched intimately the lives of individuals for whom confession was a defining force. That complexity – encouraged, perhaps, by an "imaginary" or provisional art form such as drama – is at odds with the more controlled nature of theological debate (focusing on concepts) or the agonism of outright sectarian conflict (in, say, controversial print literature). If Shakespeare participated in the religious culture of which he was a part, then his mode of participation may have been to compose rich and nuanced plays that provoke his audience and readers *to think* in a more open-minded way about religious issues – including religious disputes, ambiguities, and contradictions stimulated by the upheavals of the protracted Reformation – rather than nail things down. The Anglo-Saxon word "thought" sits some distance away from classical words like "concept," "idea," "theology," or even "culture." One can think about something without necessary resolving it; one can try out a perspective by "thinking" about it, even if one never fully occupies or adopts it.

This second shift in emphasis may in the end be the more important one. Contributors to this volume provide a rich picture of a playwright trying out scenarios and conflicts that in more polemical or academic circles might be called notions or beliefs. That flexibility is important, since it allows for discussion of Shakespeare's connection to early modern religious life that is not overly structured by, or aligned with, the kind of position-taking that is so common during the period. As A. D. Nuttall seems to have recognized in his book, *Shakespeare the Thinker*, there is something noticeably intransitive about thought and thinking: they do not always issue in something like action, and do not always show their effects in concrete position-taking.[30] As editors, we see the analyses in this volume unfolding in what the grammarian might call the "middle voice," a mood that suggests that Shakespeare was neither completely active, nor completely passive, in the

30 A. D. Nuttall, *Shakespeare the Thinker* (New Haven, CT: Yale University Press, 2007).

ways in which he took up and elaborated, in his own creative and independent-minded way, the religious thinking of the early modern period. While this may seem like a small point, such a deliberately dynamic sense of Shakespeare's engagement with the religious questions that almost every early modern person had to confront makes it easier to bring the insights of historians and literary critics together in a common discussion.

Plays are not themselves thoughts. But they provoke thoughts, and this thinking can be called religious – or economic, political, erotic, and so on. Shakespeare the dramatist, we suggest, was notably open-ended and flexible in his religious thinking as he worked creatively in a multifaceted Protestant culture that not only destroyed but assimilated vestiges of its Catholic past. The chapters that follow thus provide a range of perspectives on what constitutes religious thinking in this period and how it is related, on the one hand, to the sectarian and religious conflicts studied by historians and, on the other, to the imaginative achievement that Shakespeare's plays represent to literary critics and historians.

## III

We have divided the chapters into two complementary parts. Part 1, "Revisiting Religious Contexts in Shakespeare's England," provides fresh and interconnected assessments of the diversity of and tensions within religious culture in Shakespeare's England, while assessing how we might think about religious diversity in relation to Shakespeare's life and career. David Bevington reminds us of the challenges of attempting to define or circumscribe Shakespeare's own religious persuasions in the complex and changing religious culture of England in the later sixteenth and early seventeenth centuries. Yet at the same time, he illuminates Shakespeare's distinctive and independent-minded representation of contentious religious issues by reviewing evidence provided in the plays and by comparing Shakespeare to such contemporaries as Jonson, Dekker, and Middleton. From these perspectives, Shakespeare emerges as less satirically sharp in dramatizing anti-Puritan sentiment. England may have been strongly anti-Catholic during the period when Shakespeare was thriving as a playwright, but Bevington makes clear that Shakespeare does not always subscribe to predictable prejudices: *King John* does not simply demonize the Catholic Church; Shakespeare's Henry V is a Catholic king who builds chantries; *Hamlet* includes both Catholic and Protestant perspectives, despite the dramatic tensions they may create; and *Henry VIII* treats mildly Henry's first queen, the Catholic Katherine of Aragon. Shylock the Jew is treated with pity, even as *The Merchant of Venice* also exposes the savagery of Old Testament cries for revenge; but then Christians, with their often vicious treatment of Shylock (i.e., reviling him as a "misbeliever, cut-throat, dog" [1.3.107], and devil), do not always come off well, as Shakespeare's play dramatizes the contradictions between their Christian principles and their behavior. The Shakespeare portrayed by Bevington seems acutely aware of the religious divisions of his age and can address some of the strongest religious prejudices and tensions within Protestant culture itself (especially those generated by hostility to Puritans). However, his lack of predictability and the more generous perspectives he sometimes offers of different religious faiths are just some of the ways Shakespeare is distinctive in his treatment of early modern religious culture divided by faith and characterized by diversity.

Peter Marshall and Felicity Heal, historians of early modern religion, offer complementary accounts of the complexities of religious alignments in Shakespeare's England. Peter Marshall uses testimony from Warwickshire to examine the degree of debate and dispute over religion. As he shows, this impulse to discuss and debate in an animated way lay at "the heart of the religious culture of Shakespeare's age" (p. 52). Marshall gives us a complex picture of religious life in Shakespeare's England: Protestant anxieties about Catholics along with day-to-day toleration that existed among neighbors of different faiths.[31] In the midst of all this debate in an age of confessional choices, Marshall stresses Shakespeare's absence of "religious declarations." He provides plenty of evidence for the diversity, conflicts, and "kaleidoscopic elements of religious culture" (pp. 54–5) which Shakespeare was able to draw upon and reanimate imaginatively in his plays. If Marshall provides both a local (based on Warwickshire) and larger picture of complex religious alignments, Felicity Heal focuses her attention on religious culture in London during Shakespeare's years working in the metropolis. Her chapter illuminates the diverse and cacophonous world of religion in Shakespeare's London: a world characterized by a multi-faceted Protestantism, a radical Puritan underground, an underground Catholic community, and popular antipopery. In addition, London was a major center of preaching, not only at Paul's Cross, but at other venues, including Westminster Abbey;[32] as Heal observes, "Shakespeare cannot have escaped hearing, and seeing, the

[31] For more on these issues both in England and on the continent, see Kaplan, *Divided by Faith*.

[32] For major studies of this topic, see Arnold Hunt, *The Art of Hearing: English Preachers and their Audiences, 1590–1640* (Cambridge University Press, 2010); and Mary Morrissey, *Politics and the Paul's Cross Sermons, 1558–1642* (Oxford University Press, 2011).

practice of religion in the metropolis" (p. 60).[33] Together, the chapters by Marshall and Heal provide a concrete sense of the religious plurality and tensions which Shakespeare creatively drew upon in his plays, although without his engaging in a predictable, one-sided kind of Protestant propaganda (often with nationalist implications).

The chapters in Part II, "Representing Religious Beliefs and Diversity in the Plays," then explore in detail how Shakespeare's plays, written in a range of genres, engage with the religious diversity, alignments, and tensions of his age. Alison Shell's study of *A Midsummer Night's Dream* shows how Shakespeare evokes Reformation notions – notably idolatry, given the play's focus on dotage in love – and yet treats them in fresh ways that are both playful and mischievous; in effect, Shakespeare's comedy, as Shell elucidates, reworks Reformation-inflected anxieties about misdirected worship. At the same time, Shell argues for a complex and ambivalent treatment of Catholic nostalgia in the play in terms of its representations of fairies (given connections between popery and faery in the culture) since Shakespeare's fairies are specifically associated with indirection and delusion.

Shakespeare's interest in the interactions between political and religious rhetoric lies at the center of Beatrice Groves's chapter on *King John*; she illuminates how, in the first half of Shakespeare's career, he could write a history play that dramatizes both national identity and religious issues in post-Armada England. She freshly examines how Josephus' account of the fall of Jerusalem was reinterpreted in Elizabethan England (including in siege-plays) before showing how the dramatically potent Bastard in *King John* manipulates, for his own Machiavellian and independent-minded ends, the siege and fall of Jerusalem and the Elizabethan emphasis on Jewish unity. As Groves reveals, the play contains subversive elements which unsettle its patriotic rhetoric at the end; by inverting the Jerusalem trope, the play challenges contemporary uses of religious and nationalistic propaganda to reinforce the conformity of England's subjects.

Peter Lake's chapter examines the relation between politics and religion from a different perspective: by considering ways the neo-Roman or republican ideology of *Julius Caesar* is tested by Christian sensibilities. Quentin Skinner's major work on neo-Roman political thought concerning civil

[33] Hamlin, *Bible in Shakespeare*, reviews the evidence for Shakespeare's own attendance of church services, including in London (pp. 13–14). Shakespeare may well have attended "hundreds of church services throughout his life" (evidence that he was highly familiar with biblical culture and the Book of Common Prayer); however, the precise nature and intensity of his personal religious beliefs remains elusive.

liberty has given us a secular account of the early modern period by highlighting classical republicanism and downplaying religious conflict and beliefs as important political factors.[34] Yet as Lake shows, even in *Julius Caesar* secular and religious sensibilities interact, especially if interpreted from the providential perspective of Shakespeare's contemporaries. Lake begins by reading the tragedy in political terms as he explores the disastrous consequences of applying republican thought and values (e.g., about honor and political virtue) to the very different political circumstances of Caesar's Rome. However, the play, although about pagan Romans, also operates on another level that would have evoked providential culture for Shakespeare's Christian contemporaries: its numerous references to prophecies, prodigies, and portents which are misconstrued by major characters in the play. Late Elizabethans were anxious about the succession and the stability of the polity; consequently, the monarchical and Christian world of 1599 combined with providential thinking, with its emphasis on heavenly admonitions and judgments, would have shaped their responses to the play's depiction of republican conspiracy and its disastrous consequences.

Adrian Streete's contribution examines another kind of tension between early modern religion and classical culture: the tension between Lucretian and Christian ethics and between Epicurean philosophy and Protestantism as manifested in *Measure for Measure*. Streete considers, for the first time, the relation of a Protestant sensibility in the play (e.g., Angelo's stern Protestant interpretation of the law) to its creative engagement with Lucretius. As Streete emphasizes, Lucretian cosmology could seem shocking in the context of early modern Protestantism: the poet's denial of providence, his rejection of creation *ex nihilo*, and his refutation of the immortality of the soul posed a serious challenge to early modern religious culture and writers (including Calvin). The competition between Protestant and Lucretian sensibilities in *Measure for Measure* not only suggests the imperfection of the Duke and Isabella's plot in the play; it enables Shakespeare to challenge the notion of a perfect account of natural law and recapture Lucretius as "a deeply ethical thinker" in the midst of Protestant culture.

Questions of providence and early modern religious culture are likewise central to David Loewenstein's chapter on *King Lear*, which emphasizes the daring and experimental side of Shakespeare when it comes to dramatizing extreme positions with regard to religious belief. Loewenstein argues that Shakespeare's most devastating tragedy enabled him to imagine, in a culture steeped in providential thinking, a potentially agnostic perspective:

[34] See, e.g., Quentin Skinner, *Liberty Before Liberalism* (Cambridge University Press, 1998).

a pre-Christian world in which there seems to be no supernatural intervention or guidance in human affairs, and no heavenly response to protracted human calamity and misery. This tells us less about Shakespeare's own personal religious allegiances (though a zealous Protestant playwright would likely not have written such an antiprovidential play), but rather more about the freedom Shakespeare found in tragic theater to represent an extraordinary range of religious beliefs – some of them contradictory. Even *Hamlet*, as we noted above, can juxtapose a providential view of events (Hamlet's) with one (Horatio's at the end) which clashes with it. *King Lear* may be full of apocalyptic language and biblical allusions (e.g., to the Book of Job), but it subverts a providential interpretation of events and offers a particularly radical and skeptical view of any kind of religious order or way of understanding an inhospitable and stark world of violence and savagery that reduces "unaccommodated man" to "a poor, bare, forked animal" (3.4.98–100). Placed in the context of Shakespeare's other plays, the tragedy underscores the remarkable diversity of religious perspectives he represents and the freedom with which the theater enabled him to do so; these include the deeply unsettling antiprovidential point of view dramatized in *King Lear*.

Ewan Fernie's contribution considers the dark tragedy of *Macbeth* in relation to the impact of the Reformation and its notions of human sinfulness and the demonic. In particular, Fernie examines the sinfully degraded and blood-drenched Macbeth in terms of Luther's notion of demonic negativity. In the case of the demonic Macbeth, who becomes symbolic of an "abortive Protestantism," there is no possibility of redemption. Nonetheless, as Fernie shows, there are exhilarating dimensions to "sinning bravely" in *Macbeth*. He illuminates how the dense poetry of the tragedy renders distinctively – for example, by conveying creativity in destruction – the "terrible affirmation of demonic negativity that Luther seeks to admit and even magnify" (pp. 190, 182, 188).

Michael Witmore's contribution adds another dimension to this volume: a study of Shakespeare and wisdom literature that engages with early modern religious culture but is not limited to it. His account of wisdom culture likewise reveals the extent to which cultural practices that are closely aligned with religion or spirituality nevertheless reach beyond those domains. Witmore examines how Shakespeare works and thinks proverbially in his plays; this involves not only engaging with a culture in which collections of proverbs were pervasive, but also understanding how Shakespeare draws creatively and theatrically on the practices of lotteries and bibliomancy – the art of seeking advice by randomly opening a book, including the Bible. By associating wisdom culture with these practices, he offers new readings of *The Merchant of Venice* and the perverse love test in *King Lear* (which can be understood in light of the lottery in Numbers 26). Witmore further considers the implications of seeing Shakespeare's plays in terms of a kind of wisdom literature, suggesting that plays with proverbial titles (up to *Henry VIII*, with the alternative or even original title, *All Is True*) may themselves have been advertised as a kind of lottery. Throughout this analysis, Witmore argues that the plays show Shakespeare engaged with and testing the practices of early modern wisdom culture in rich and sometimes unexpected ways.

Richard McCoy's chapter turns to the romances, especially *The Winter's Tale*, to examine the deep affinities, as well as the differences, between poetic and religious faith. As he makes the case for their deep affinities, he draws upon Coleridge's insights into the parallels between religious and poetic faith and reviews Reformation interpretations of the Eucharist, including the ways English reformers understood the sacrament's semiotic efficacy. Moreover, he stresses the ways Shakespeare's theater itself cultivates some of the same responses encouraged by Reformed religion: the plays "awaken a faith that requires strenuous effort, good will, and a will to believe" (p. 225). Yet when he shifts his critical attention to *The Winter's Tale*, particularly its moving final scene, McCoy illuminates ways in which poetic faith can differ from religious belief in Shakespeare's plays so that our faith ultimately lies in the power of theatrical illusion and spectacle. As such, his chapter offers another contribution to the complex relations between the religious and the secular in Shakespeare's theater.

Paul Stevens's contribution, which includes discussions of *Hamlet* and *Henry VIII*, likewise revisits the relation between these categories, challenging critical tendencies to secularize Shakespeare's theater, and focusing instead on a "post-secular perspective" that complicates the two categories and the ways they interact. Stevens questions the critical tendency to insist on a secular interpretation of *Hamlet* (despite the play's wealth of biblical references) and deepens his argument against secularizing narratives by emphasizing how *Henry VIII*, at the end of Shakespeare's career, enables the playwright to dramatize – in its pageant-like and ceremonial accounts of tragic falls and the story of the "chosen" (5.4.48) Elizabeth's birth – the sustaining presence of God's grace in the story of England. He explores this crucial dimension of the play by analyzing its evocations of Scripture (especially Job and the Psalms) and its liturgical features (which draw upon the Book of Common Prayer). Finally, by examining Jane Austen's discerning response to the play in *Mansfield Park*, Stevens is able to expand his series of interconnected critical reflections about Shakespearean individualism, the post-secular, and the force of grace or "the grace of truth."

By looking especially at the perplexing origins of the Henrician Reformation in relation to the king's divorce, Michael Davies provides another critical perspective on the issue of historical "truth" in *Henry VIII*. Davies's in-depth discussion of the language of Henry VIII's conversion account in Act 2, scene 4 of Shakespeare's play opens out into a much broader discussion of the complex relation of history to "truth." Davies illuminates how Shakespeare gives a fresh dramatic representation to ambivalent views about Henry VIII and the question of his "conscience." He challenges the view that Shakespeare follows Catholic histories and shows instead how the Tudor *Chronicles* of Stow and Holinshed encouraged a Protestant tradition of ambivalence about Henry's conscience. Shakespeare animates this ambivalence in his historical drama. Questions about the "facts" of Henry's divorce and the beginnings of the Henrician Reformation thereby remain unresolved. Davies reveals a Shakespeare "remarkably attuned to contemporary discourses of early modern religion" (p. 279), while also provoking his audience and readers to think about the ambiguities and uncertainties of "truth" in relation to history.

The final chapter in this volume, by Matthew Dimmock, takes the reader in another direction, one already partly anticipated in David Bevington's opening chapter. How does Shakespeare represent non-Christian religions, notably Judaism and Islam, and to what degree do his plays reveal tolerance or hostility toward them? Dimmock addresses the question by situating Shakespeare in his contemporary theatrical context so that it becomes clearer how Shakespeare imitated, revised, or rejected early modern representations of non-Christian religions. Comparing Shakespeare with Marlowe, he highlights how religious divisions in *The Merchant of Venice* are less distinct, at least on the basis of faith. Nonetheless, Shakespeare's sophisticated representation of Judaism suggests that it is not a viable alternative to Christianity; nor is it simply treated satirically as Marlowe presents it in the more theologically divided world of *The Jew of Malta*, where Old and New Testament theology are sharply opposed. Given the early modern Islamic–Christian conflict, it is notable, as Dimmock goes on to argue, that Shakespeare never wrote a "Turk play," even if there are numerous references to Turks in his plays. Yet Islam and Mahomet receive little attention in his plays and Shakespeare makes no attempt to link – contemptuously and crudely in the manner of his contemporaries – Islam and Judaism. There is no deep theological engagement with Islam in his plays, suggesting that Shakespeare steers away from the theatrical bombast that often characterized contemporary depictions of non-Christian religion. This may not indicate tolerance on Shakespeare's part, but it does indicate a reluctance to promote predictable theatrical stereotypes about Islam. When it comes to the two Abrahamic non-Christian religions, then, Shakespeare provokes nuanced responses that complicate or resist stereotypes: his most famous Jew is both deeply humane and unrelentingly vengeful. However, there is no spokesperson for Islam or Mahomet in his plays, an absence that may suggest – in a different way – Shakespeare's independence of mind when it comes to the issue of non-Christian religious difference.

The range of approaches and contributions outlined here will suggest that *Shakespeare and Early Modern Religion* aims to convey the independent-minded and flexible way in which this playwright engages – throughout his career – with early modern religious culture in all its diversity and messiness. This is not to say that Shakespeare is unconstrained imaginatively by the religious conflicts, beliefs, and confessional positions he chooses to present in his plays. Rather, we hope that this collection shows just how diverse those religious currents are, and consequently, how complex and nuanced Shakespeare's representation of those currents would have to be in order to take their full measure in drama. If this emphasis provokes more critical thinking and debate about Shakespeare and religion, then this cross-disciplinary book will have achieved its principal goals.

PART I

# *Revisiting religious contexts in Shakespeare's England*

CHAPTER I

# *The debate about Shakespeare and religion*

*David Bevington*

Can one talk about Shakespeare's religious thought? He is of course a dramatist, and a great one, but drama is not for him primarily a vehicle for propounding moral, religious, and ethical values. He is seemingly content to let other writers, like Ben Jonson, pursue overtly didactic purposes. To be sure, Shakespeare is interested in the art of persuasion, but as an observer rather than as a partisan. He habitually lets his characters speak for themselves, to such an extent that we must always be careful not to ascribe to the author the views thus expressed. Shakespeare practices what John Keats, in a letter to his brother Thomas (December 17, 1817), aptly terms Shakespeare's "negative capability," a term that embraces, among other features, his ability to let contending voices argue their opposing views without prejudging the case or using the debate to prove his own point. Does he see the deposition of King Richard II as a deplorable impiety or as part of a large historical movement toward strong monarchical rule? Does he side with Hotspur, or King Henry IV, or Prince Hal, or Falstaff for that matter, in defending or critiquing honor? Does he tip his hand as to what his own religious persuasions were? Does biographical information about him provide any clues?

No issue was more controversial in Renaissance Europe and England than that of religion. It was a subject on which Shakespeare's audience at the Globe Theatre presumably had strong feelings, tending to the Protestant and at times Puritan side. The Puritans, though wary of drama generally as potentially idolatrous and profane, nevertheless were at times ready to make exceptions for plays that promoted godliness, as in the Calvinist-inspired morality plays of the mid sixteenth century and afterwards with titles like *The Longer Thou Livest the More Fool Thou Art* and *Enough Is as Good as a Feast.*[1] Drama during the Marian Catholic regime of 1553–8 had rallied to

[1] See Paul Whitfield White, *Theatre and Reformation: Protestantism, Patronage, and Playing in Tudor England* (Cambridge University Press, 1993).

the Catholic cause, simply by casting their morality-play villains as Protestants. Conversely, in Queen Elizabeth's reign, playwrights were enlisted to write for the Protestant cause. The Queen's Men, a touring company made up, on the authority of the queen, with some of the finest and best-known actors (Richard Tarlton among them) in England at the time, staged such plays as *The Famous Victories of Henry V*, *King Leir*, and *The True Tragedy of Richard III*. These plays were of course written to be entertaining, but a didactic purpose was also plentifully discernible: that of defending the Protestant Reformation and England's queen against Catholic enemies abroad and at home.

Yet the reformers grew increasingly disillusioned with the London theater in the 1590s and afterwards as it rapidly escaped official control and turned to satiric portraiture of the city and its inhabitants, many of them Puritan-leaning, like Marjorie, the wife of Simon Eyre in Thomas Dekker's *Shoemaker's Holiday* (1599). Dekker's satire is good-natured, and nominally at least the play celebrates the rise to power of the mercantile class within the city; but Dekker's delight in laughing at London foibles of every stripe is quite far from the unashamed apologetics of Thomas Heywood's *The Four Prentices of London* in the 1590s or *The Second Part of If, You Know Not Me, You Know Nobody, with the Building of the Royal Exchange, and the Famous Victory of Queen Elizabeth* (1606). The growing antagonism between reformers and stage grew more acute as the boys' companies, having been suppressed throughout most of the 1590s because of their satirical bent, were allowed to resume playing at the Blackfriars and then at other indoor theaters in 1599 and afterwards. Ben Jonson savagely satirized Puritan sanctimoniousness and hypocrisy in his Tribulation Wholesome and Ananias in *The Alchemist* (1610) and Zeal-of-the-Land Busy in *Bartholomew Fair* (1614). Dekker took up the cry. So did Thomas Middleton in his satirical comedy variously called *The Puritan Widow* or *The Puritan or The Widow of Watling Street*, staged by the Children of Paul's in 1606. The moderate Puritan William Crashaw, preaching at Paul's Cross in 1607, inveighed against this play along with other "ungodly plays and interludes" for their unfair indictment of the godly as hypocrites.

Puritan animus against theater was thus of long standing and of increasing intensity. Thomas White had preached at Paul's Cross in 1577 against theatrical performances as the ultimate cause of plague because the players' idolatrous carryings-on invited the wrath of the Almighty. Stephen Gosson's *Playes Confuted in Five Actions* (1582) inveighed against plays as "the invention of the devil, the offerings of idolatry, the pomp of worldlings, the blossoms of vanity, the root of apostasy, food of iniquity, riot, and adultery" (sig. G8r). When Christopher Marlowe died in a tavern brawl in 1593, Puritan preachers made no attempt to repress their jubilation at this manifest sign of divine retribution for a life ill spent in the theater and elsewhere. Philip Stubbes's *The Anatomy of Abuses* (1583) kept up the litany of complaints, as did William Prynne's *Histriomastix: The Players' Scourge or Actors' Tragedy* (1633). The closing of the theaters in 1642 was the predictable result of a deep-rooted animosity. The London authorities, often tending toward Puritanism and troubled too that the playhouses attracted prostitutes and other riff-raff, used outbreaks of plague as a major reason for closing down the public theaters in London as often as they could.

Where is Shakespeare in all this hubbub about Puritans and the stage? Uncharacteristically for a playwright who is so generally even-handed and unwilling to engage in polemicism, he does leave some evidence in his plays of concern about the Puritans and their presumed animus against festivals, church ales, and other forms of Carnival merrymaking, including drama. His most notable comment is in *Twelfth Night.*

When Sir Toby, Sir Andrew, and Feste have awakened a wrathful Malvolio by their carousing late into the night in the Countess Olivia's house, Malvolio and Sir Toby echo in their heated exchange the language of controversy over festive entertainment. "Do ye make an ale-house of my lady's house?" demands Malvolio, to which Sir Toby offers his superb and memorable riposte: "Dost thou think, because thou art virtuous, there shall be no more cakes and ale?" (2.3.88–115).[2] In medieval and Renaissance England, the institution known as the "church ale" was a subject of much debate. Originally a commemoration of the dedication of a church building, the church ale had become a much-loved festive gathering in parish churches, with plentiful food and wine and entertainment. Attempts by Tudor Protestant governments, beginning under Henry VIII in 1536, to regulate church ales by restricting their occurrence to a certain day or days rather than any time in the year met with determined resistance. The Puritans tended to look on church ales as part of an older pre-Protestant order of things in need of reform. Sir Toby lines up on the side of Merry Old England in its battle against the unsmiling disapproval of the reformers.

Once Malvolio has left the scene of revelry in Act 2, scene 3, Maria – whose sympathies are with the revelers even though she has done her best to quiet things down – comes up with a plan of comic revenge. She will "gull him [Malvolio] into a nayword and make him a common recreation" by

[2] Shakespeare citations are from David Bevington (ed.), *The Complete Works of Shakespeare*, 7th edn. (New York: Pearson/Longman, 2014).

devising a letter that will deceive Malvolio into thinking that he has won the heart of Olivia. Maria wishes to humiliate Malvolio, she declares, because he is "a kind of Puritan." Sir Andrew responds instantly with an outburst of revulsion: "Oh, if I thought that, I'd beat him like a dog" (2.3.139–41). Sir Andrew lamely cannot explain his reason for this, but the animus is plain enough; later in the play, Sir Andrew expostulates, "I had as lief be a Brownist as a politician" (4.3.30–1), referring contemptuously to the congregationalist followers of Robert Browne, who had been expelled to the Netherlands in 1581 for their uncompromising severity in matters of church ceremony and other vitriolic dissatisfactions with the established church. Sir Andrew may be following the popular line of conflating the Brownists with the more radical Anabaptists.[3] His testiness in Act 2, scene 3, at any rate, elicits from Maria a decidedly more moderate attempt to rephrase and qualify her objection to Malvolio:

> The devil a Puritan that he is, or anything constantly, but a time-pleaser; an affectioned ass, that cons state without book and utters it by great swaths; the best persuaded of himself, so crammed, as he thinks, with excellencies that it is his grounds of faith that all that look on him love him; and on that vice in him will my revenge find notable cause to work. (2.3.146–52)

Maria is careful not to condemn all Puritans outright by identifying them with Malvolio. After all, some Puritan-leaning citizens did attend public performances of plays in London until the atmosphere in the playhouses proved too unwelcoming. Maria's point, seemingly, is that Puritans are to be regarded as the enemy only to the extent that they behave like Malvolio, arrogating to themselves the role of moral policemen. The issue is not Puritanism as such but the behavior of certain officious killjoys.

Maria's position, then, is thoughtful and moderate, albeit on the side of innocent merrymaking. Is this Shakespeare's view also? Maria is a notably sympathetic character. Moreover, her wariness of Puritanism seems confirmed by occasional allusions elsewhere in Shakespeare's writings. The fool Lavatch in *All's Well That Ends Well* compares "young Charbon the Puritan" with "Old Paysam the papist," seeing in them a meeting of opposites that is so often the case when extremes meet; though "their hearts

[3] Peter Lake argues that Puritanism of the 1590s was not essentially radical, though it manifested a potential for both subversion and orthodoxy; see *Moderate Puritans and the Elizabethan Church* (Cambridge University Press, 1982) and *Protestantism and the National Church in Sixteenth-Century England*, ed. Peter Lake and Maria Dowling (London and New York: Routledge, 1987). See also Patrick Collinson, *Godly People: Essays on English Protestantism and Puritanism* (London: Hambledon Press, 1983), *The Elizabethan Puritan Movement* (Oxford: Clarendon Press, 1967), and *The Religion of Protestants: The Church in English Society, 1559–1625* (Oxford: Clarendon Press, 1982).

are severed in religion," he opines, "their heads are both one" (1.3.51–4). Later in the scene, Lavatch declares himself to be of the opinion that "Though honesty be no Puritan, yet it will do no hurt; it will wear the surplice of humility over the black gown of a big heart" (92–4). The Clown in *A Winter's Tale* jibes at immigrant psalm-singing Puritan weavers from the Netherlands when he observes that the "one Puritan" at the sheep-shearing festival of that play "sings psalms to hornpipes" (4.3.43–5). The Bawd in *Pericles* complains of the invincibly virtuous Marina, whom he is trying to sell into prostitution, that "she would make a Puritan of the devil if he should cheapen a kiss of her" (4.6.9–10). Falstaff mimics Puritan cadences when he mockingly protests to Prince Hal, "now am I, if a man should speak truly, little better than one of the wicked. I must give over this life, and I will give it over" (*1 Henry IV*, 1.2.92–5). These slighting allusions to Puritanism here and there in the canon are perhaps all the more telling for being so unstudied. Puritanism in Shakespeare is invariably the subject of a jest, even if Maria does go on to explain more carefully what she has meant by calling Malvolio a Puritan.

Malvolio is arguably Puritan-like in the zeal with which he can torture a text to make it yield up a meaning that will serve his purposes. "M. O. A. I.," he ponders, as he reads Maria's forged letter. "If I could make that resemble something in me! Softly! 'M. O. A. I.' –." When the letters do not seem to follow the order of his name precisely, since *O* follows *M* where he would expect *A*, Malvolio has a strategy to meet the crisis. "And yet, to crush this a little," he says, "it would bow to me, for every one of these letters are in my name." Indeed they are all there, in a word game so ingeniously devised that the first letter is followed by the last in his name, and then the second and the next to last. Malvolio triumphs in his discovery, like a reformer determined to discover all of world history in the Scriptures. "Daylight and champaign discovers not more!" he exults. "This is open" (2.5.118–57). Yet Malvolio is not a Puritan doctrinally. What Maria calls Malvolio's "grounds of faith" (2.3.150), using a favorite phrase of the Puritans, are not spiritual but an unshakable belief in his own superiority to the rank and file of humankind.

Malvolio's preference for "sad and civil" garb (3.4.5) is suggestive of Puritan insistence on plain dress. The business of tricking him into wearing cross-garters and yellow stockings is not only an appropriate satirical punishment for one who dresses severely and reproves those who do not; it is also a comic reversal of appearance and reality, madness and sanity, of which the play is so full. Malvolio is tricked into becoming the very smiling church-ale reveler that he so abhors. These inversions take visible form on stage when Malvolio is incarcerated in a dark room as a madman, while the fool Feste, in a clerical gown and false beard, disguises his voice to counterfeit Sir Topas the curate, reproving Malvolio as a "hypocritical fiend" and "dishonest Satan" for his benighted opinions about Pythagoras and such. The distraught Malvolio is driven at last to plead with Feste, "I am as well in my wits, Fool, as thou art" (4.2.29–58).

Malvolio's departure from the scene of general reconciliation in Act 5 has struck many observers as perhaps the strongest suggestion of anti-Puritan sentiment in *Twelfth Night*. Malvolio will have nothing to do with attempts to mollify his fury. "I'll be revenged on the whole pack of you!" he shouts as he storms off (5.1.378). Is this, as C. L. Barber imagines, a premonition of the Puritans' closing of the theaters in 1642?[4] Shakespeare and his company cannot have predicted that outcome, of course, nor was it historically any more inevitable than the civil war itself, but the Lord Chamberlain's Men and their spectators certainly had reason to worry, in 1600 or thereabouts, that the reformers were not through with insisting on a ban of "profane" theatrical performances.

Characteristically, Shakespeare depicts the confrontation as one that calls for calm and accommodation. "He hath been most notoriously abused," declares the Countess Olivia as Malvolio strides away, presumably never to return. She offers to chastise the perpetrators of a "revenge" that has gone too far. Shakespeare's depiction of a ridiculous figure with certain Puritan-like characteristics is far more gentle and generous than the attacks mounted by Jonson, Dekker, and Middleton, among others. It is as though Shakespeare and his company wished to alert Londoners to the threat to theater posed by the reform-minded civic leaders of the city while at the same time holding out an olive branch to the reformers. Yet the hour was already late. English drama in the next three decades was to become more and more oriented to the court and to the so-called "private" theaters, with their severely reduced capacity of audience size, while the culturally heterogeneous audiences who had jubilantly supported one of the most remarkable phases in all dramatic history dwindled into a shadow of their former selves.

Shakespeare's seeming wariness of Puritanism, then, was not doctrinal so much as it was an antipathy toward any who claimed a higher moral ground from which to censor and repress forms of social recreation like theater. Can we discern his thoughts and feelings about the bitter controversy between

4 C. L. Barber, *Shakespeare's Festive Comedy: A Study of Dramatic Form and its Relation to Social Custom* (Princeton University Press, 1959), pp. 256–7.

Catholics and Protestants? The standard view has assumed that he conformed to the state religion, whatever his own skeptical thoughts may have suggested to him. Conversely, the argument persists that he harbored Catholic sympathies. An international gathering of scholars at a conference at the University of Lancaster in the summer of 1999 examined at length the theory that Shakespeare may have spent time in 1580 or so, when he was aged 16, at Hoghton Tower in Lancashire, a country estate where, appropriately enough, the 1999 conference was held. According to Richard Wilson, the conference organizer, Shakespeare had been right there at Hoghton Tower in about 1580, in the company of the Jesuit priest Edmund Campion, at the start of what was for Shakespeare a period of some ten years in a succession of Catholic households in that part of England.[5] The idea thus provides a hypothetical scenario for the undocumented years of Shakespeare's life from his marriage in 1582 and the births of his three children in 1583–5 down to his being mentioned as a playwright in London in 1592.

John Aubrey reports anecdotally in his *Brief Lives* (written in the late seventeenth century, though not published until 1898), with the theatrical manager John Beeston as his authority, "Though, as Ben Jonson says of him [Shakespeare], that he had but little Latin and less Greek, he understood Latin pretty well, for he had been in his younger years a schoolmaster in the country."[6] Samuel Schoenbaum adds that though Shakespeare's lack of university training would have disqualified him for a mastership in a grammar school, he might have been employed in "the humbler post of usher or *abecedarius*."[7] Wilson and others propose instead that Shakespeare is to be identified with the "William Shakshafte" who is named in the will of Alexander Hoghton (or Houghton) of Lancashire and is recommended to Hoghton's half-brother Thomas, or to a friend, Thomas Hesketh, for future employment.[8] Secret Catholics often adopted aliases to hide their identity, argues Wilson, and Shakespeare had good reason to be circumspect. The school he presumably attended in Stratford-upon-Avon gave the post of schoolmaster from 1579 to 1581 to John Cottam, from Lancashire, whose younger brother Thomas, a Jesuit priest, was arrested in 1580 on a secret

5 See Richard Wilson, *Secret Shakespeare: Studies in Theatre, Religion, and Resistance* (Manchester University Press, 2004).

6 John Aubrey, *Brief Lives* (London, 1898), ed. Oliver Lawson Dick (London: Secker & Warburg, 1949; Ann Arbor: University of Michigan Press, 1962). Quoted in Samuel Schoenbaum, *William Shakespeare: A Documentary Life* (Oxford University Press, 1975), p. 88.

7 Ibid.

8 See, for example, E. A. J. Honigmann, *Shakespeare: The "Lost Years"* (Manchester University Press, 1985).

mission headed by Campion; Campion was tortured and executed in 1581, Thomas Cottam in 1592. Another schoolmaster at the Stratford school, Simon Hunt, occupying the post from 1571 (when Shakespeare was 7) to 1575, went on to become a member of the Jesuit order at Douai and then at St. Peter's in Rome, where he succeeded Robert Parsons as English penitentiary. Might Cottam have recommended to William Hoghton a bright young scholar from a clandestinely Catholic family in Stratford to serve as tutor in the Hoghton household? And are we to believe the statement of the late seventeenth-century clergyman Richard Davies that Shakespeare "died a papist"?[9]

The devotees of this theory are generally persuaded that Shakespeare's father, John Shakespeare, was a Catholic. The most notable piece of purported evidence here is the so-called Borromeo testament, a spiritual last will and testament which appears to have been an English translation of a document prepared by the Archbishop of Milan, Cardinal Carlo Borromeo, to be carried in multiple copies into the countries of western Europe by Jesuits to offer comfort to those wishing to die as faithful Catholics. The document itself, stated in formulaic terms, offered an opportunity for the beleaguered Christian "to secure himself from the temptations of the devil at the hour of death" by affixing his or her signature.[10] A document of this sort was purportedly found in the eighteenth century by a master builder, Joseph Moseley, in the rafters of a house on Henley Street owned by the Hart family, who were descended from Shakespeare's sister Joan. The will, containing fourteen articles of profession to the Catholic faith, soon came into the hands of the reliquary John Jordan, who in turn sent it to the great Shakespeare scholar Edmund Malone, who published it in 1790 but eventually recanted his endorsement, leaving Jordan to be accused of a forgery. The document itself is now lost, thus providing no opportunity now to study the authenticity of John Shakespeare's signature or mark. Still, Malone's published transcript shows that it was derived via translation from the Borromeo original.

Against this argument for John Shakespeare's purported Catholicism loom several considerations. The scenario itself, with the finding of a document in the rafters of a house in Stratford on Henley Street, has aroused suspicions of being a fabricated romantic tale. We cannot verify

9 Richard Davies, in Fulman MS xv (Corpus Christi College, Oxford, MS 309); reproduced photographically in Schoenbaum, *Documentary Life*, p. 79.

10 Carlo Borromeo, Cardinal and Archbishop of Milan, *The Testament of the Souls*. Reproduced photographically in Schoenbaum, *Documentary Life*, pp. 43–5.

now if the signature or mark was John Shakespeare's. We do know that as a civic official in Stratford, he was responsible on occasion for implementing the decrees of the Elizabethan government, including the whitewashing and defacing of a Last Judgment mural over the chancel arch in the town's Guild Chapel and another mural depicting Saint George's victory over the Dragon. In his role as chief alderman in 1571 he presumably concurred with the decision of the town council to sell off all Catholic vestments in the inventory of the Guild Chapel. His being fined in 1576 and afterwards for nonattendance at the Eucharist, once thought to be evidence of recusancy, now appears to have been a result of severe financial difficulties obliging him to stay at home for fear of process of debt. His being allowed by the Corporation to remain on as alderman even in the midst of his financial woes would seem to suggest that he was regarded as an upstanding member of the community and the official church. He and his wife Mary baptized their children in Holy Trinity in Stratford, all of whom were buried there.

Mary herself may have come from a family with Catholic connections.[11] Her father, Robert Arden, appears to have died in the faith in 1556. Possibly Mary was related also to Edward Arden of Park Hall, who seems to have provided refuge for a Catholic priest, and whose son-in-law, John Somerville, was arrested in 1583 on suspicion of having plotted against the life of Queen Elizabeth. Edward Arden was hanged, drawn, and quartered; his son-in-law was strangled in his cell in the Tower of London before a similar sentence could be carried out on him. Both their heads were displayed on London Bridge as a warning to all would-be traitors and conspirators. To be sure, the connection of Mary's family to these Ardens is uncertain, and the import of the language of her father's testament has been called into question as possibly formulaic; it reads like other wills written during the reign of the Catholic Queen Mary (1553–8). In any case, evidence is lacking for Mary's having held Catholic persuasions or having shared them with her husband in their family life in Stratford.

Stephen Greenblatt speculates that religious differences may have been a source of contention between Shakespeare and his father, with the son skeptically on his way to becoming neither Catholic nor Protestant, while the father, wishing to keep his options open in an era when the battle between Catholicism and Protestantism in England veered first one way

[11] See, among others, Germaine Greer, *Shakespeare's Wife* (London: Bloomsbury, 2007); Katherine Duncan-Jones, *Ungentle Shakespeare: Scenes from his Life*, Arden Shakespeare (London: Bloomsbury, 2001); Park Honan, *Shakespeare: A Life* (Oxford University Press, 1998); Stanley Wells, *Shakespeare for All Time* (Oxford University Press, 2003); and René Weis, *Shakespeare Revealed: A Biography* (London: John Murray, 2007).

and then the other, outwardly conformed to the new religion while worshipping in secret the faith of his ancestors.[12] This idea is fanciful, to be sure, but it does provide an intriguing interpretation of Hamlet's encounter with his father's Ghost on the battlements of Elsinore Castle. Shakespeare's father died in 1601, close to the time when Shakespeare wrote *Hamlet*; which event came first is hard to say, but the father could have been ill or near death in any case. In 1596 Shakespeare had applied for a coat of arms for his father – the same year in which Shakespeare's only son and heir, Hamnet, had unexpectedly died. Do these personal circumstances encourage an autobiographical reading of *Hamlet*? Did the son's name, Hamnet, take on for the dramatist a particular relevance when he chose to write a play named *Hamlet*?

Certainly the meeting of the father's Ghost with his son would have been laden with religious significance for London audiences in 1600–1, attuned as they were to sectarian conflict. "I am thy father's spirit," the Ghost tells his son, "Doomed for a certain term to walk the night, / And for the day confined to fast in fires, / Till the foul crimes done in my days of nature / Are burnt and purged away" (1.5.10–14). Audiences would recognize at once that the Ghost has come from Purgatory. Protestants in the sixteenth century had rejected as Catholic superstition the idea of a place or state of punishment after death where the sins of flawed but worthy Christians would need to be purged before their souls could proceed to heavenly reward, but the idea was still an essential doctrine of Roman Catholic teaching. The Ghost describes himself as being in that state of needing purgation. The "foul crimes" that he has committed during his days on earth, though imagined by some critics to be his violent warlike menacing of Polacks and Norwegians (1.1.65–7), are doubtless instead the countless sins that all proud and covetous mortals commit in their daily lives. *Hamlet* plainly invites its audience to admire Hamlet Senior's warlike bravery; conversely, that audience would understand that in broadly Christian terms we are all sinners, and that a sudden death would leave any of us with a roster of sins not yet acknowledged or forgiven.

The doctrine of Purgatory presumably was a controversial one for *Hamlet*'s original audience. Hamlet Senior has died suddenly, having been murdered in his sleep by his brother. He has had no time for confessing his sins. As the Ghost tells his son, he was "Cut off in the blossoms of my sin, / Unhousled, disappointed, unaneled, / No reck'ning made, but sent to

[12] Stephen Greenblatt, *Will in the World: How Shakespeare Became Shakespeare* (New York: W. W. Norton, 2004).

my account / With all my imperfections on my head" (1.5.76–80). The terms he uses are those of Catholic liturgical practice: to die "Unhousled, disappointed, unaneled" is to die without having received the Holy Sacrament at the last moment. No priest was by to administer to Hamlet Senior the Last Rites of contrition, confession, satisfaction, and absolution. Protestants generally, in reducing the seven sacraments to two (Baptism and the Eucharist, thus leaving out Confirmation, Penance, Holy Orders, Marriage, and Last Rites), denied the sacramental efficacy of the Catholic Church's prescribed ritual for a dying person. Contrition and confession were of course still vital to salvation, but not as a rite in which a clergyman would pronounce individual absolution. The English Church, under Archbishop Cranmer, had established instead a Prayer of General Confession, to be recited by a congregation in unison.[13] No Anglican priests heard individual confession or assigned penances for sins.

Hamlet's encounter with his father's Ghost, then, assumes a world of Catholic faith and ritual. Why should it not, in dramatizing a tale of medieval Denmark? At the same time, Shakespeare chooses to present Hamlet as one who has studied at Wittenberg, famous in Renaissance Europe for its university where Martin Luther had posted his 95 Theses in 1517 in the opening salvo of the Protestant Reformation. Hamlet refers to Horatio as his "fellow student" (1.2.177), and we gather that their conversations took up serious philosophical and religious questions. Moreover, Hamlet seems to have absorbed theological ideas that had been enunciated by Martin Luther and John Calvin. "We are arrant knaves all, believe none of us," shouts Hamlet at Ophelia; though he considers himself "indifferent honest," that is, no worse than the run of ordinary Christians, he admits to being so "proud, revengeful, ambitious" that "it were better my mother had not borne me." "What should such fellows as I do crawling between earth and heaven?" (3.1.122–30), he asks. When Polonius tells Hamlet that he will find accommodations for the visiting players "according to their desert," Hamlet fires back, "God's bodikin, man, much better. Use every man after his just desert, and who shall scape whipping?" (2.2.527–30). These are truisms affirming the fallen state of the human race, to be sure, in the teachings of St. Augustine and other church fathers, but in Renaissance Europe they were given new cogency by the reformers.

The Calvinist bifurcation of humanity into the unregenerate and the saved, according to the infinite and unknowable will of the Creator,

[13] See Ramie Targoff, *Common Prayer: The Language of Public Devotion in Early Modern England* (University of Chicago Press, 2001).

manifests itself starkly in *Hamlet* in the contrasting images of Claudius and Hamlet Senior. As Hamlet says to his mother in her private chambers, upbraiding her for her loose behavior as he shows her portraits of the two men she has married, "Look here upon this picture, and on this." The one is a "mildewed ear, / Blasting his wholesome brother" (3.4.54–66). One is a satyr; the other Hyperion. One is reprobate, unable to help himself spiritually by doing what he knows he must do if he is to seek forgiveness. Claudius knows only too well that he must transform his life altogether by giving up the worldly things for which he has committed fratricide, if he is to hope for pardon. Claudius knows that his prayers will not ascend to heaven because he is "still possessed / Of those effects for which I did the murder: / My crown, mine own ambition, and my queen" (3.3.36–71). Claudius realizes to his horror that, like Doctor Faustus, he cannot repent because he lacks the will to do so. He is one of the unregenerate.

Conversely, Queen Gertrude, though a miserable sinner in Hamlet's eyes, is, as he appraises her, recoverable to virtue. His father's Ghost seems to think so too; he has told Hamlet to "leave her [Gertrude] to heaven / And to those thorns that in her bosom lodge, / To prick and sting her" (1.5.86–8). Hamlet takes upon himself the role of stinging conscience, while promising to himself and to us that he will "speak daggers to her, but use none" (3.2.395). He accosts her so roughly that she cries out in alarm, with the result that Polonius is slain in his place of hiding, and the Ghost is so perturbed that he puts in an appearance to warn Hamlet about his "almost blunted purpose" (3.4.115), but Hamlet is in an important sense doing what his father has ordered. Exhorting his mother in the cadences of a reforming preacher, he issues his dire warnings: "Confess yourself to heaven, / Repent what's past, avoid what is to come" (156–7). Though in Hamlet's view Claudius is unregenerate, Gertrude is not. As even the drunken Cassio in *Othello* knows, "there be souls must be saved, and there be souls must not be saved" (2.3.98–9).

Roman Catholic theology and Calvinist theology stand side by side in *Hamlet*, then, along with more broadly Christian ideas about the inherent depravity of the human race. Yet the playwright seems more intent on dramatizing the differences than in promoting one side or the other. Is the play Catholic or Calvinist in its perspective? One cannot say with certainty. We can agree, though, that Hamlet is devoutly Christian, more and more so as the play works its way toward a resolution that Hamlet interprets as providential. "There's a divinity that shapes our ends," he admonishes Horatio, "Rough-hew them as we will" (5.2.10–11). In retrospect, he sees even the unfortunate death of Polonius as an integral part of Heaven's intent; Hamlet is to become, in the wake of that disaster, heaven's "scourge and minister," punished for what he has done but at the same time becoming an instrument of divine will in a way that he could not have anticipated (3.4.180–2). Similarly, he sees heaven as "ordinant" in prompting him how to outwit Rosencrantz and Guildenstern, his escorts to England, by exchanging his own letter to the English king for one by Claudius stipulating that Hamlet be executed (5.1.48–53). Hamlet exults in his newly heightened awareness of the deep necessity of things. "There is special providence in the fall of a sparrow," he insists to Horatio, when that dear friend urges him to postpone the duel if the prospect seems ominous. "If it be now, 'tis not to come; if it be not to come, it will be now; if it be not now, yet it will come. The readiness is all" (5.2.217–20). As Hamlet interprets his own story, this perception of the inevitability of things is borne out in what happens. The duel provides Hamlet with something he has not planned and could not have foreseen: an opportunity to kill the King essentially without premeditation and with a just cause, while at the same time bringing to a close his own troubled life from which he has fervently longed to be freed. Hamlet's story is, in his own view, triumphantly providential and Christian.

Yet Horatio sees this same story in entirely different terms. Having been a skeptic throughout the play, doubting the existence of the Ghost until he beholds it with his own eyes, debating with Hamlet about natural versus providential explanations of things that happen, Horatio is prepared at last to "speak to th' yet unknowing world

> Of carnal, bloody, and unnatural acts,
> Of accidental judgments, casual slaughters,
> Of deaths put on by cunning and forced cause,
> And, in this upshot, purposes mistook
> Fall'n on th'inventors' heads. (5.2.381, 383–7)

This is the secular humanist speaking, and it sorts well with the dramatic voice in *Julius Caesar*, *King Lear*, and other tragedies of the Jacobean period that explore the daunting prospect of a world that is presided over not by a benign overseeing deity who makes sure that every smallest event in our lives is ultimately meaningful, but by unforeseen accidents, "casual" violence, and profound ironies in which human beings are too often the unwitting authors of their own unhappiness.[14]

[14] For *Julius Caesar* and *King Lear*, see Chapters 6 and 8 below.

Are we to read *Hamlet* from Hamlet's own perspective, or that of Horatio, or even that of Fortinbras, who perceives in the tragic events of the play a vindication of his claim to the Danish throne? Fortinbras is given the last word, after all. What we can say is that the playwright is fascinated with philosophical and religious controversy, among other matters, and not least of all with skeptical uncertainty about the role purportedly played by divinity in human affairs. Shakespeare shows that he is well versed in details of Roman Catholic liturgy and practice. He seems no less knowledgeable about other current theologies, including Calvinism, and about skeptical philosophy. Perhaps we should care less about whether Shakespeare was Catholic or not, and pay more attention to the astuteness with which he uses theological issues of the day to construct a brilliant tragedy like *Hamlet*.

Whatever his own private beliefs, Shakespeare is more generous and forbearing in his plays than many of his fellow dramatists in his depiction of Catholics. *King John* offers a case in point.[15] It focuses not on issues of Magna Carta (virtually ignored as an idea in Shakespeare's day) but on John's wrongful occupation of the English throne and by his unsuccessful defiance of Rome. Essentially two views of King John (who reigned from 1199 to 1216) were current in the English Renaissance. To some, he was a tyrant who deprived his nephew, young Arthur, of his throne and life. To others, particularly those on the religious left, he was a precursor of those who were to defy the Roman Church some three centuries later, even if his attempt to stand up to the authority of the papacy failed. John Foxe, in his *Actes and Monuments of Martyrs* (1583 edition), known popularly as *The Book of Martyrs*, championed the latter view of John as a flawed saint. This monumental and vividly illustrated book, with copies installed in English cathedral churches,[16] saw King John as an early martyr of Catholic oppression. He had been portrayed in similar terms in the earlier play of *King Johan* by John Bale, and similarly in the anonymous *The Troublesome Reign of King John* (published 1591). Shakespeare's representation of John is demonstrably more aware of his failings and less inclined to demonize the Catholic Church. In *Troublesome Reign*, for example, an entire scene is devoted to a conversation in which an abbot offers absolution to a friar for the "meritorious" deed of poisoning King John. Shakespeare mentions, briefly and matter-of-factly, the rumor that the king has been poisoned by a monk, and leaves the matter at

[15] For a more extensive discussion of *King John*, see Chapter 5 below.

[16] Patrick Collinson, "Literature and the Church ('The Era of Elizabeth and James VI')," in David Loewenstein and Janel Mueller (eds.), *The Cambridge History of Early Modern English Literature* (Cambridge University Press, 2002), pp. 374–98.

that. Earlier, this same abbot is discovered in *Troublesome Reign* to be hiding nuns in his treasure chest. In Shakespeare, admittedly, Cardinal Pandulph is a duplicitous maneuverer in his plan to submit the English crown to Rome, but other statesmen are no less Machiavellian.

Shakespeare's *Henry VIII* (1613), written seemingly in collaboration with John Fletcher, deals mildly not only with the Catholic Church but especially with Katherine of Aragon, the daughter of Ferdinand II of Aragon and Isabella I of Castile whose marriage to Henry VIII was annulled in 1533, thereby precipitating the break with Rome and the beginning of the English Reformation. Even though Fletcher evidently wrote parts of the play, Shakespeare is generally credited with having written the scene of the trial of Queen Katherine (3.2), with its manifest sympathy for her at the expense of her devious and skirt-chasing husband, and the scene of Katherine's death (4.2), in which a heavenly vision of "spirits of peace" seems to assure her ascent into eternal bliss. Katherine is charitable and submissive to the will of the King even in her state of having been abandoned. In the final scene, written evidently by the Protestant John Fletcher but surely with Shakespeare's assent, the birth of Elizabeth holds out the promise of a happy future to which the participants in this remarkable story have contributed. The play leaves in doubt the vexed question as to whether Katherine had previously been legitimately married to Henry VIII's older brother Arthur, thereby implicitly choosing not to endorse the Protestant view that her first marriage to Arthur had in fact been consummated and that Henry was therefore free to annul his contract with Katherine. The play's depiction of Anne Bullen (or Boleyn) is studiously ambivalent; it suggests at moments that she was a pretty foxy young lady, but is nonetheless careful not to defame the mother of Queen Elizabeth. All in all, on the hot controversial issue of how the Reformation started in England, Shakespeare is circumspect and multiple in his sympathies.[17]

Elsewhere, we see that he treats some Catholic clergymen with respect and even affection. Friar Laurence in *Romeo and Juliet* is a kindly and well-meaning adviser to the young lovers, interested in their welfare and in the need for restoring peaceful relationships between the two families. He never talks of theological matters. So too with Friar Francis in *Much Ado About Nothing*; in the scene of the aborted wedding of Claudio and Hero (4.1), he is the first male to speak up for Hero as innocent of the promiscuity with

[17] For discussions of *Henry VIII* and the Reformation, see Chapters 12 and 13 below. See also Thomas Betteridge, "Writing Faithfully in a Post-Confessional World," in Andrew J. Power and Rory Loughnane (eds.), *Late Shakespeare, 1608–1613* (Cambridge University Press, 2013), pp. 236–41.

which she is charged. The Abbess in *The Comedy of Errors* turns out to be the devoted and long-lost wife of old Egeon.

Some Catholic churchmen of high station in Shakespeare are cunning and unprincipled statesmen, like the Bishop of Winchester, later Cardinal Beaufort, in *1* and *2 Henry VI*, but so are his secular counterparts, the Dukes of Suffolk, Somerset, and York. Conversely, some members of the church hierarchy in Shakespeare are principled and godly, like the Bishop of Carlisle in *Richard II*. In the *Henry IV* plays, the Archbishop of York joins the rebellion against King Henry but does so on principled grounds; his opposite number, Prince John of Lancaster, is the Machiavel who outwits the Archbishop and the rebel leaders with duplicitous promises.

Shakespeare's treatment of the religious question in *Henry V* is as skillful as it is tactful and generous. Henry is unquestionably a Catholic ruler, not simply in that he came to the throne in 1413 well before the English Reformation, but also in his professions of faith at moments of crisis. On the night before the great Battle of Agincourt, 1415, having talked incognito with some of his captains and his soldiers, Henry prays. He prays that "the fault" that his father made "in compassing the crown" may not be held against Henry himself, the son of that sin-burdened usurper. In his prayer, Henry V recites his efforts at seeking forgiveness. He has had Richard II's body reinterred with dignity and with "contrite tears." More than that, Henry has set up an endowment at his own expense whereby "Five hundred poor" are to raise up their withered hands in supplication "to pardon blood." Most impressively of all, perhaps, Henry has "built / Two chantries, where the sad and solemn priests / Sing still for Richard's soul" (4.1.287–300). Chantries were, in the eyes of Protestant reformers, an especially offensive desecration perpetrated by the Roman Church, to be defaced and torn down. Yet Henry V is one of England's greatest kings for Shakespeare, as he is traditionally in England.

Shakespeare makes no attempt to hide Henry's devout Catholic ways. At the same time, the play depicts Henry as an absolute monarch who, however, also knows how to govern by consent. Henry V is thus the precursor of English monarchism at its very best, under Queen Elizabeth, in the implicit view of this patriotic play. The fact that Henry seeks forgiveness by doing good works, such as building chantries and endowing church benefices, is not held against him in *Henry V*. To be sure, Martin Luther would no doubt have objected that one cannot buy one's way into heaven by doing good works of this kind, but King Henry is quick to agree with this Lutheran view about works versus divine grace: though he has built two chantries, he acknowledges that "all that I can do is nothing worth, / Since that my penitence comes after all, / Imploring pardon" (4.1.301–3). He is Catholic in his royalty and Protestant in his theology, just as he is an absolute monarch with the democratic touch. The play, in these terms, implicitly makes the case for an accommodating and inclusive political-religious agenda in England at the troubled moment of Elizabeth's presumably last days as monarch.

Shakespeare's representation of Jews is much like his treatment of Christians in showing a marked degree of tolerance and accommodation when we compare his writings with those of other dramatists. Marlowe's *The Jew of Malta* (*c.* 1589) depicts its central figure, Barabas, as virulent in his hatred of Christians and increasingly deadly in his cunning, even if he is given some reason for his animus and feigned eloquence in his protests against persecution. Shylock, by contrast, is a man who deserves pity and understanding, even if he is intent on obtaining his pound of flesh from the breast of Antonio. To be sure, the ideals of Christianity (however poorly practiced by some of its adherents in this play) seem to embody a higher vision of generosity and risk for friendship than the grudging wariness practiced by Shylock the moneylender and overly protective father.

Elsewhere, too, Shakespeare's more offhand references to Jews and Judaism seem to betray a substratum of ethnic bias. "If I do not love her, I am a Jew," says Benedick of Beatrice in *Much Ado About Nothing*, using "Jew" as an epithet for one who cannot love generously. When Lance, in *The Two Gentlemen of Verona*, says of his dog that "A Jew would have wept longer at our parting" (2.3.211–12), "Jew" signifies cold-heartedness. And so too when Falstaff protests that he is telling the truth by averring, "I am a Jew else, an Ebrew Jew" (*1 Henry IV* 2.4.177). The very casual nature of such utterances seems symptomatic of the anti-Semitic culture in which Shakespeare lived. He rose above the level of such insularity, but he was part of it still.

In this sense, his treatment of Judaism may seem somewhat less sophisticated and self-aware than his mediating negotiations of Catholic and Puritan. Judaism comes across in his plays as something alien, strange, and ultimately beyond the range of his vast powers of sympathy and understanding. So too with his occasional references to Tartars, Turks, Scythians, Saracens, Indians, Moors, Cathayans, and the like.[18] Shakespeare speaks from the vantage point, and to audiences who share that perspective, of belonging (despite internal differences that can be bitter) to a Christian culture.

[18] See David Bevington, "Imagining the East: Shakespeare's Asia," in Douglas A. Brooks, with Lingui Yang and Ashley Brinkman (eds.), *Shakespeare and Asia*, Shakespeare Yearbook 17 (Lewiston, ME: Edwin Mellen Press, 2010), pp. 29–44; and Nabil Matar, *Turks, Moors, and Englishmen in the Age of Discovery* (New York: Columbia University Press, 1999). On the question of Shakespeare's representation of religious and ethnic others, see Chapter 14 below.

CHAPTER 2

# *Choosing sides and talking religion in Shakespeare's England*

*Peter Marshall*

In January 1584, when William Shakespeare was 19 years old and most likely living in the county, a letter about a Catholic trouble-maker made its way from one Warwickshire Justice of the Peace to another. Job Throckmorton wrote to Ralph Warcupp that he had arrested William Skinner, and searched his house at Rowington, some nine miles north of Stratford as the crow flies. Enclosed with the letter were the examinations of nine witnesses, including the minister of Rowington, the parish clerk, the church court summoner, and various yeomen and husbandmen, one with the pleasingly Shakespearean name of Sly. The depositions show that Skinner had been harboring within his house a seminary priest, called Baker or Bird, disguised as a schoolmaster, and also that he held some pretty rebarbative opinions about politics and religion. Thomas Sly recalled Skinner saying to him "that the protestants doctors of theire owne syde did defende that a woman coulde not be supreme heade"; this, a proposition that Skinner confidently ascribed to Calvin. Equally seriously, he had heard Skinner "defende the Queene of Scots tytle and saye that she is next heyre apparante to the crowne" – the truth that dare not speak its name in Elizabethan England, and the eventuality that committed Protestants, from William Cecil downwards, were desperate to avoid.

The fullest testimony came from the parish clerk, John Fairfax. He too, about four or five years ago, he thought, had had the conversation with Skinner about the royal supremacy, and listened to the argument that Protestants themselves denied the queen's status as Supreme Head, calling her only "supreme governes." Skinner had added that St. Peter was pope of Rome "and thence, sayde he, comethe the trewe succession." Warming to his theme, Skinner demanded of Fairfax what he thought of the bishops of new making. Fairfax scrupulously replied (or so he now claimed) that "they are lawfully made by the prynce as supreme heade." "Why, thow fool," scoffed Skinner, "yf one make thee a lease under a bushe, is that a good lease? No more . . . are our Byshops lawfull Byshops." A couple of years after this, Fairfax and Skinner had "had other talke." Skinner was now "in good hope that religion wold turne," or at least that the government was shortly to decree a liberty of religion, that "every man shoold live as he lyke." If such a decree were to be made, he rhetorically demanded of Fairfax, "how many thinckeste thow . . . wolde come to churche?" Skinner had his own answer ready to hand: "not passinge x of our parishe, I warrante thee." Fairfax, whether solemnly or jocularly, remarked that such a decree would be a recipe for endless discord, it "wolde goo neare to bringe us all to gether by the eares." But his companion was in no mood for levity: "no, sayd Mr Skynner, ye will never be able to stand wth us, we shalbe v: to one against you." And just in case Fairfax was still in any doubt about how things stood, Skinner added: "Thow art a foole . . . dooeste thow thinke, that this religion is the trewthe? In my conscience I thinke it is not."[1]

Readers can relax: no new biographical revelations about the young Shakespeare, and no claims of direct textual resonances in his work, are connected to this incident.[2] And yet we seem to start here in very familiar territory: the world of "hot" Warwickshire Catholicism, which Shakespeare of course knew, and which, according to some commentators at least, substantially nurtured and shaped him. Less than six months after the arrest and interrogation of Skinner, Francis Throckmorton, scion of a Warwickshire Catholic house (and first cousin of Skinner's interrogator, Job) was executed for his part in the plot against Elizabeth that bears his name.[3] And less than a year before that, another Warwickshire squire, John Somerville, kin-in-law to Shakespeare's Arden relatives, died mysteriously in the Tower on the eve of his execution for devising a madcap scheme to assassinate the queen with a pistol.[4] An ideologically straight line (and some only slightly twisted familial and genealogical ones) runs from the Somerville and Throckmorton plots to the Gunpowder conspiracy of 1605, which, as everyone knows, was substantially hatched in Shakespeare's county.[5] Foreshadowing this, several of the characteristic notes of the

[1] National Archives, State Papers 12/167, fos. 54r–61r (hereafter SP followed by the series number).

[2] The closest connection that can be made is that John Shakespeare of Rowington, a distant kinsman, was in litigation with William Skinner in the 1570s: C. C. Stopes, *Shakespeare's Family* (Gloucester: Dodo Press, 2009), p. 118. See also Edgar I. Fripp, *Shakespeare's Haunts near Stratford* (Oxford University Press, 1929), pp. 65–82.

[3] John Bossy, *Under the Molehill: An Elizabethan Spy Story* (New Haven, CT: Yale University Press, 2001).

[4] Ian Wilson, *Shakespeare: The Evidence* (London: Headline, 1993), pp. 52–3.

[5] For the connections of 1605 conspirators to the Throckmorton family, see table in Antonia Fraser, *The Gunpowder Plot* (London: Weidenfeld & Nicolson, 1996), p. xiii.

English Counter-reformation are struck in the Skinner testimony of 1584. It speaks of militancy, separatism, and the articulation of sharp ideological binaries. Here we have protection of a valid, sacrament-delivering priest, against the compromised lackeys of the state church; recognition of true bishops in despite of Protestant pseudo-bishops; an assertion of the rightful Petrine succession against a royal supremacy which was such an evident charade that even Calvin could see it.[6]

Shakespeare was born in the mid 1560s into a world of (relatively) benign confusion in religious affairs. The English Reformation was already a generation old – his father, John Shakespeare, was likely born just as Henry VIII's divorce campaign was reaching a crescendo – and deep divisions had certainly emerged across society, particularly after the bloodletting of Mary I's reign. Yet in Elizabeth's first years, the lines might still seem fuzzy and permeable, a pattern encouraged by a monarch who was herself a specialist in sending out ambiguous signals. This was a Protestant queen who retained cross and candlesticks in her chapel royal and displayed a pronounced disdain for clerical marriage. Out of a mixture of optimistic delusion and Spanish diplomatic pressure (Philip II was much more concerned about the threat from France), the papacy held back from excommunicating Elizabeth and offered little guidance to Catholics in England about how they should respond to the new realities. At the start of the reign, a group of leading Catholic laymen petitioned the Council of Trent, asking what "men of true piety and learning think they ought to do" with regard to the legal requirement (under the 1559 Act of Uniformity) to attend church services. Forwarding the petition, the Spanish ambassador made clear his view that it was not a question of such very great moment: the "Common Prayers" of the Church of England, he judged, "contain no false doctrine whatever nor anything impious. It is all Scripture or prayers taken from the Catholic Church." Catholics might thus attend them with only slightly compromised consciences.[7]

As virtually all historians now agree, Catholics – or at least religious conservatives – constituted a clear majority of the nation in Elizabeth's first years. Moreover, they also supplied a substantial proportion of the "political nation," that small minority of the populace whose views counted for something. A survey of justices of the peace, commissioned from the

[6] Calvin's dislike of Henry VIII's royal supremacy was a staple of Catholic propaganda in this period: Peter Marshall, "John Calvin and the English Catholics, *c.* 1565–1640," *Historical Journal*, 53 (2010), 864–5.

[7] Ginerva Crosignani, Thomas M. McCoog, and Michael Questier (eds.), *Recusancy and Conformity in Early Modern England* (Toronto: Pontifical Institute of Medieval Studies, 2010), pp. 3, 7.

bishops by the Privy Council in the year of Shakespeare's birth, revealed that only a third of magistrates were judged to be "favorable" to the religious settlement, while another third were positively "unfavorable." In Warwickshire, Job Throckmorton's father Clement was among the "favourers of true religion," but his uncle Robert was one of its "adversaries."[8] Yet, despite his avowed Catholicism, Robert was able to remain a justice of the peace until 1570, when the authorities began more systematically to impose the oath of supremacy on office-holders.[9] In urban and borough government too, Catholic sympathizers (John Shakespeare of Stratford most probably among them) continued to exercise authority and influence through the opening years of the reign.

A succession of events at the end of the 1560s changed the ground rules and the mood music: the establishment in 1568 at Douai in the Spanish Netherlands of a seminary for training missionary priests; the flight into England the same year of the deposed Mary Queen of Scots; the 1569 rebellion of the northern earls, designed to free Mary from captivity; the hard-line papal excommunication (and deposition) of Elizabeth in a bull of 1570. Divisions hardened, legislative pressure on Catholics increased, and efforts to Protestantize the nation as a whole took on a new impetus. As Patrick Collinson once remarked, it makes sense to think of the Reformation, the real Reformation, as "something which happened in the reigns of Elizabeth and James"[10] – or, as Collinson implied elsewhere, something which happened during the life span of William Shakespeare.[11] By the time Shakespeare reached adulthood, a decade on from the traumatizing events of 1568–70, the divisions had deepened and the middle ground had been squeezed still further in the wake of a succession of Catholic plots and the furore caused by the start of the Jesuit mission. The soul and inspiration of that mission, Edmund Campion, was executed at Tyburn in 1581, an event which, as several scholars have argued, may have been deeply traumatic for the Catholic community in Shakespeare's Warwickshire.[12] On the scaffold, Campion was urged by the attending Protestant preacher

[8] Mary Bateson (ed.), "A Collection of Original Letters from the Bishops to the Privy Council, 1564," in *Camden Miscellany*, vol. IX, Camden Society n.s. 53 (London, 1895), pp. 7–8.

[9] Peter Marshall, *Faith and Identity in a Warwickshire Family: The Throckmortons and the Reformation*, Dugdale Society Occasional Paper 49 (Stratford-upon-Avon: Dugdale Society, 2010), p. 13.

[10] Patrick Collinson, *The Birthpangs of Protestant England: Religious and Cultural Change in the Sixteenth and Seventeenth Centuries* (New York: St. Martin's Press, 1988), p. ix.

[11] Patrick Collinson, "William Shakespeare's Religious Inheritance and Environment," in his *Elizabethan Essays* (London: Hambledon Press, 1994), pp. 219–52.

[12] Richard Wilson, *Secret Shakespeare: Studies in Theatre, Religion, and Resistance* (Manchester University Press, 2004), esp. ch. 2; Peter Milward, "Shakespeare's Jesuit Schoolmasters," in

to pray with him and make the conventional gestures of end-of-life penitence. Yet Campion refused to do so: "you and I, we are not of one religion."[13]

This, then, was an era of choosing sides, of – to employ a favored historians' term-of-art – "confessionalization."[14] It was a decade or two into Elizabeth's reign that the categorical nomenclature of "Catholic" and "Protestant" became stabilized into something like its modern form, supplemented by new terms of divisive distinction, notably "Puritan."[15] The shapers of religious opinion expected people to stand up and be counted. A tacit understanding of the imperatives which might lead to dissimulation under persecution, characteristic of the early Reformation period, gave way to a growing barrage of "anti-Nicodemite" rhetoric in the second half of the sixteenth century.[16] Clerical writers, like the Jesuits Robert Persons and Henry Garnet, usually insisted that a stance of strict recusancy (refusal to attend any Church of England services) was the only acceptable one for Catholics, while Protestant moralists, strengthened by the example of the Marian martyrs, demanded doctrinal purity and moral earnestness, and an end to mere "carnal gospelling." The distillation of clearer confessional identities was facilitated by preaching and catechesis, and by the martyrologies and copious religious polemic produced on all sides. It was underwritten by the processes of generational change, as England transformed itself, over the course of Shakespeare's lifetime, from a nation reformed in name and law, to one that had become deeply culturally Protestant, or at least viscerally anti-Catholic.[17]

The undoubted "confessionalization" of late sixteenth- and early seventeenth-century England was not, however, solely a matter of the progressive social and theological divergence of self-identifying groupings,

Richard Dutton, Alison Findlay, and Richard Wilson (eds.), *Theatre and Religion: Lancastrian Shakespeare* (Manchester University Press, 2003), pp. 58–70; Michael Wood, *In Search of Shakespeare* (London: BBC Books, 2003), pp. 73–80.

13 Henry Ellis (ed.), *Holinshed's Chronicles*, 6 vols. (London, 1807–8), vol. IV, p. 459.

14 See Ute Lotz-Heuman, "Confessionalization," in David M. Whitford (ed.), *Reformation and Early Modern Europe: A Guide to Research* (Kirksville, MO: Truman State University Press, 2008), pp. 136–57.

15 Peter Marshall, "The Naming of Protestant England," *Past & Present*, 214 (2012), 87–128.

16 The derogatory term *Nicodemite*, popularised by Calvin, referred to the Pharisee Nicodemus (John 3:1–2; 7:50–1; 19:39), who came to Jesus by night. For earlier dissimulation strategies, see Susan Wabuda, "Equivocation and Recantation during the English Reformation: The 'Subtle Shadows' of Dr. Edward Crome," *Journal of Ecclesiastical History*, 44 (1993), 224–42.

17 On generational issues, see Norman Jones, *The English Reformation: Religion and Cultural Adaptation* (Oxford: Blackwell, 2002); Alexandra Walsham, "The Reformation of the Generations: Youth, Age and Religious Change in England, *c.* 1500–1700," *Transactions of the Royal Historical Society*, 6th series, 21 (2011), 93–121.

or a zero-sum game of Protestant advance and Catholic retrenchment and retreat. Recognizing this may not be any kind of hermeneutic key to unlocking Shakespeare's meanings, but it is arguably vital to an understanding of the world in which he was formed and performed. Already at the start of his adult life (inverting the conditions of a generation before) England had become a nation with a dominant Protestant culture and a repressed Catholic subculture. But we should not imagine that the former was confidently unshakeable, or the latter self-evidently shrinking and introspectively sectarian; that Shakespeare must by definition have been a poet and playwright of a "post-Reformation" established order, within which Catholicism carried at most a nostalgic or unsettlingly atavistic charge. Contemporaries certainly did not see matters this way.

Let us return to the Rowington testimony of 1584 and take note of some features of it that may not have immediately impressed themselves upon our attention. One is that the evidence of dispute and debate to which the document so evidently attests took place within a context of social, and indeed sociable, interactions between the papist Skinner and his Protestant, or at least conformist, neighbors. Skinner, it would appear, was ready to talk theology and politics with almost anyone who would listen. Thomas Sly, John Fairfax, and the summoner, Richard Richardson, were able to testify that Skinner was harboring a priest because they had all been guests in his house and at his table and had seen there a schoolmaster who didn't seem quite like a schoolmaster.[18]

Another related characteristic of the Rowington vignette is that it does not present a picture of Warwickshire Catholicism as an inverted, isolated sect. Skinner affected to believe, and perhaps really believed, that a large majority of his churchgoing neighbors were Catholics at heart: not more than ten in the parish were Protestants by choice and conviction.[19] Indeed, it is not at all clear that Skinner himself was at this time a recusant in the full technical sense. A couple of the witnesses noted that he had kept his son Anthony and daughter Martha from attending church, but none of them said that he himself was a persistent nonattender. He does not appear on a *circa* 1580 list of "obstinate recusants" in the diocese of Worcester (which included Thomas Otwell of Rowington), and it is notable that he and his

[18] SP 12/167, fos. 57r, 58r, 60r.

[19] Rowington was certainly a remarkably Catholic place: in 1605–6 there seem to have been at least sixty recusants in the parish: V. T. J. Arkell, "An Enquiry into the Frequency of the Parochial Registration of Catholics in a Seventeenth-Century Warwickshire Parish," *Local Population Studies*, 9 (1972), 24–5; in 1628 the number had dropped somewhat to a still impressive thirty-two: Ann Hughes, *Politics, Society and Civil War in Warwickshire, 1620–1660* (Cambridge University Press, 1987), p. 63n.

family conformed during the antirecusant crackdown of 1592, the occasion which produced John Shakespeare's famous, and much disputed, explanation of absence from church by reason of debt.[20] Nor were Skinner's attitudes those of a fatalistic nonconformist, resigned to the prospect of political and social marginalization. His buoyant hopes for a decree of toleration were almost certainly linked to his reading of the final round of marriage negotiations between Elizabeth and the Catholic Duke of Anjou, coming to their inconclusive conclusion only in 1582.[21] And for Skinner, toleration was not so much a life raft of conscience as a springboard to recovered dominance: "we shalbe v: to one against you."

These glimpses of what was happening in Rowington can serve as pointers to some dynamic patterns of religious life in Shakespeare's Warwickshire and in the nation more broadly. William Skinner's militantly ideological Catholicism, paradoxically combined with his pragmatic willingness to attend church, and his views on the outward conformity of his Catholic neighbors and tenants, confirms what scholars have been saying for some time about the phenomenon of "church papistry" in Elizabethan and Jacobean England. Namely, that far from being a moribund symptom of the decaying half-life of medieval England, the willingness of those who thought of themselves as Catholics intermittently to attend the services of the Protestant Church of England was a flexible and effective survival strategy, and one which was very widely practiced, despite what the clerical purists wanted to say about the matter.[22]

One result of this is that contemporaries did not have any real idea, any more than modern historians, of just how many "Catholics" there were across the nation as a whole. Protestant anxieties were thus kept in a permanently heightened state. Semicyclical movements of Catholics out of conformity and into recusancy could provoke apprehensive claims about

[20] SP 12/167, fos. 56r, 60r; Lambeth Palace Library, CM IV/183; Fripp, *Shakespeare's Haunts*, p. 75. For a recent discussion of the 1592 campaign, arguing that John's explanation should be accepted at face value, see Glyn Parry, "The Context of John Shakespeare's 'Recusancy' Re-examined," in Douglas A. Brookes (ed.), *The Shakespeare Apocrypha* (Lampeter: Edwin Mellen Press, 2007), pp. 1–31.

[21] Susan Doran, *Monarchy and Matrimony: The Courtships of Elizabeth I* (London: Routledge, 1996), pp. 154–94.

[22] The key discussion is Alexandra Walsham, *Church Papists: Catholicism, Conformity and Confessional Polemic in Early Modern England* (Woodbridge: Boydell & Brewer, 1993). See also Crosignani et al., *Recusancy and Conformity*; W. J. Sheils, "Household, Age, and Gender among Jacobean Yorkshire Recusants," in Marie Rowlands (ed.), *English Catholics of Parish and Town 1558–1778* (London: Catholic Record Society, 1999), pp. 131–52; Peter Lake and Michael Questier, *The Trials of Margaret Clitherow: Persecution, Martyrdom and the Politics of Sanctity in Elizabethan England* (London: Continuum, 2011), ch. 4.

great and daily "increase" in the number of papists.[23] Conversely, the outward conformity of Catholics might stoke fears about the enemy within, as with the (false) report circulating in Westmorland in 1589 that the pope had granted pardons for all papists to attend services when ordered to, "alwaies provided that they doe not gyve any creditt to any thinge done in the churche."[24]

Fear and suspicion were not, however, the only outcomes of the relative integration of Catholics into their local communities. One of the paradoxes of the period is that ferocious antipopery sat alongside a fair degree of day-to-day practical toleration, and many instances of social and sociable interactions between neighbors of different faiths.[25] Meanwhile, there were persistent complaints that authorities at every level were not rigorous or severe enough in enacting the laws against recusants. In 1573, for example, Richard Cook, curate of Stone in Staffordshire, was in trouble with his bishop, the sternly Protestant Thomas Bentham, for "tomoch familiaritie and baryng with them in Stone which are iudged to be papists."[26] In Staffordshire in early 1588 the county magistracy and the clergy blamed each other for sluggishness in prosecuting Catholic dissidents, and not properly certifying their names; in Herefordshire, sheriffs, justices of the peace and juries alike were said "to wincke at the offenders," drawn away from their duty by claims of "kindred and friendship."[27] William Chadderton, bishop of Lincoln, complained in 1605 about the difficulty of getting local people to report recusants: "there is no man will become an accuser of his neighbors unless he be very malicious or be charged upon his oath by authority."[28] Religious divisions rubbed against the bonds of

[23] For example, *Calendar of State Papers Domestic: Elizabeth*, vol. CLV, 42: Earl of Leicester to Walsyngham (Sept. 1582); vol. CCLXII, 25: Dean of Durham to Sec. Cecil (Feb. 1597). (Hereafter *CSPD* followed by volume number.)

[24] SP 12/22, fo. 43r. Cf. Michael Questier's perceptive conclusion that "papistry was regarded as a threat precisely because of its malleability, its capacity to adapt and its readiness to integrate": "The Politics of Religious Conformity and the Accession of James I," *Historical Research*, 71 (1998), 30.

[25] Anthony Milton, "A Qualified Intolerance: The Limits and Ambiguities of Early Stuart Anti-Catholicism," in Arthur Marotti (ed.), *Catholicism and Anti-Catholicism in Early Modern English Texts* (Basingstoke: Macmillan, 1999), pp. 85–115; William Sheils, "'Getting on' and 'Getting along' in Parish and Town: Catholics and their Neighbours in England," in Benjamin Kaplan, Bob Moore, Henk van Nierop, and Judith Pollman (eds.), *Catholic Communities in Protestant States: Britain and the Netherlands c. 1570–1720* (Manchester University Press, 2009), pp. 67–83; Christopher Haigh, *The Plain Man's Pathways to Heaven: Kinds of Christianity in Post-Reformation England* (Oxford University Press, 2007), pp. 197–8.

[26] Folger Shakespeare Library, L.a.65; Clergy of the Church of England Database: Person ID 25512 (www.theclergydatabase.org.uk).

[27] Folger Shakespeare Library, L.a.3; L.a.72; SP 12/195, fo. 88r; J. S. Cockburn, *A History of English Assizes 1558–1714* (Cambridge University Press, 1972), p. 211.

[28] Haigh, *Plain Man's Pathways*, p. 197.

community life; they also competed with the claims of blood. It would scarcely be an exaggeration to say that every family in Elizabethan England was a religiously divided one, at least in the minimal sense that all first- and second-generation Protestants must have had Catholic parents and grandparents. But vertical divisions within families were common too. One contemporary "database" of autobiographical information, the questionnaires completed by young seminarians entering the Catholic colleges at Rome and Valladolid around the turn of the seventeenth century, shows that a strikingly high number came from families with members who were either "schismatics" or "heretics."[29] As we have already seen, the Warwickshire Throckmorton family was (deeply) religiously divided, but its members were not irrevocably estranged from each other across confessional lines, and in that at least it must have been typical. Several times in the 1580s Arthur Throckmorton, the firmly Protestant son of Elizabeth I's minister Nicholas Throckmorton, went hunting in the Midlands with his solidly Catholic (and persistently recusant) uncle, Anthony. The party habitually overnighted both with their Catholic cousins at Coughton Court and Weston Underwood and with the Puritan one (Job) at Haseley.[30] Was religion a diplomatically taboo subject on these occasions or an irresistible magnet of discussion and argument?

There is in fact considerable evidence that, as at Rowington, the people of Elizabethan and Jacobean England did not always politely steer clear of religious controversy in the course of their everyday social interactions. We see this very clearly in a (frustratingly undated and unlocated) report of an encounter taking place in a coastal inn or lodging house during the second half of Elizabeth's reign. One of the customers, Owen Griffeth, announced to a large company that "he had ben at masse & would againe be att masse." When he was reproved for saying this, he retorted that "the papists do in their masse serve god better or aswell as . . . the protestants do," and also that executed seminary priests and Jesuits were martyrs who "suffer for religion & not for treason." Protestants in the company protested that papists were traitors for upholding the supremacy of the pope, but Griffeth contended that they were as good or better subjects than Protestants were. He further defended the veneration of images, as serving to put their devotees in remembrance of God, thus prompting the writer of the complaint, William

[29] Michael C. Questier, "Clerical Recruitment, Conversion and Rome *c.* 1580–1625," in Claire Cross (ed.), *Patronage and Recruitment in the Tudor and Early Stuart Church* (York: Borthwick Institute, 1996), pp. 76–94; Lucy Underwood, "Youth, Religious Identity, and Autobiography at the English Colleges in Rome and Valladolid, 1592–1685," *Historical Journal*, 55 (2012), 349–74.

[30] Marshall, *Faith and Identity*, pp. 16–19.

Hoelman, to allege Psalm 105 and 1 Corinthians 10 as proof that "in theire masse & Idolles they served not god but the devil." But Griffith was nonetheless confident that "if he might have private conference with me, then I wold be of his minde." The landlord meanwhile reproved Hoelman and Thomas Feak for contending with his guest over "a masse of mustard," declaring "that he would medle with no such matters but do as he shalbe taught by the churche," and "that he must be for all companies & all mens money."[31]

Whether the landlord was himself a closet papist, or just a canny businessman, his intervention suggests that the clienteles in inns (as also in theaters?) were known to be religiously mixed, and also that discussion of religious matters may have been commonplace but was not expected to get too heated or out of hand. That discussion of religion may have been an instinct among all classes of people in the late Elizabethan period is suggested by the fact that the instructions for the fleet drawn up by the Earl of Essex and Lord Admiral Howard in 1596 sought to ban it, laying down that "noe man, souldier or other marriner doe dispute of matters of religion, unles it bee to bee resolved of some doubts, and in such case that hee converseth with the minister of the Armie, for it is not fitt that unlearned men should openlie argue of high and mysticall matters."[32] Nonetheless, they clearly did, though almost by definition we learn about such arguments only when they pathologized their way into the record of discipline and denunciation.

Alehouse talk turned to religion in late 1595 at Wisbech in Cambridgeshire, the town where captured missionary priests were interned in the local castle. William Wagg, butcher, wanted to know "what bablynge and great noyse the papistes mad at dinner times, the which he had often hard as he passed that waye." But another drinker, Edward Hall, countered that "it was a foolishe speatche to call it bablinge, for it was but readinge of certaine chapiters of the bibell in Latin and we have it in Englishe . . . as good matter as we have eyther redd or tought or preatched unto us."[33] Gentry dinner tables might also be places of vigorous religious exchange. The execution of the recusants John Bodey and John Slade at Andover in Hampshire in November 1583 led a couple of weeks later to passionate debate at the house of Eustace Moon in Farnham, Surrey. One of the guests, Peter Hampden, recounted what he had heard of the conference

[31] Folger Shakespeare Library, L.d.980, a document from the Bacon-Townsend collection, suggesting a Norfolk provenance. The allusion to execution of Jesuits securely dates it after 1581.

[32] SP 12/257, fo. 65r. [33] SP 12/255, fos. 17r, 18r.

held at Winchester between the condemned men and the Dean of Winchester, Lawrence Humphrey, and the Warden of Winchester College. This centered on whether the Emperor Constantine or the pope had the requisite authority to summon the first Council of Nicea in 325, Bodey resting his case on a reading of Eusebius. When John Hardy defended Bodey's position to the company as "good & lawful," another of the guests, the preacher Peter German, went off to fetch his own copy of Eusebius, and the two men argued furiously over the translation of key passages to the possible bemusement of other diners.[34] At table in 1586, the Catholic servants of the Berkshire recusant Francis Parkyns spoke freely, too freely as it turned out, about local preachers, "knaves all & one," trusting that "their tyme is but shorte." A local tailor who was present, Roger Plumpton, denounced them to the justices of the peace.[35]

Yet despite the risk of condemnation, the relative openness with which provocative religious opinions might be expressed is often striking. Herefordshire Catholics were reported in late 1586 to be "woonderfull bould & sticke not to geeve evell speeches."[36] In November 1589 it was said of the recusant Robert Goldesborowe that "in his publique and private speaches hee maynteyneth the popish religion and seeketh to confute the religion established."[37] William Forest, an Essex thatcher, landed up in the Marshalsea after telling Robert Debney that he thought that "Campyon was a good man and that there was none but turkes and cobblers that were putt in truste with godes worde."[38] John Easton, a Devon recusant, went so far in 1587 as to propose toasts to King Philip while visiting his neighbors' houses. Easton was, as they say, not unknown to the authorities. The rector of his parish of Morchard Episcopi testified that he had had "secrete conference with hime tochinge matters of fayth and Religion," but that he had found Easton "vearie obstinate, and altogeather addicted to superstition & erronyous doctrine."[39] Scarcely less provocative were two butlers of the Inner Temple, Thomas Martin and Edward Mellers, who bluntly contradicted people speaking sympathetically of the plight of "hir highness afflicted poore neighbors in Flanders" (i.e., the Dutch rebels against Philip II). They asked whether if Elizabeth herself faced rebels, and a foreign prince

[34] SP 12/167, fos. 28r–31v. For Bodey's own articles, see SP 12/162, fo. 13. Hardy was also reported to have made speeches in defence of Bodey and Slade "in a publique place": Folger Shakespeare Library, L.b.198. German was ordained in 1574 and instituted as vicar of Farnham in 1592: Clergy of the Church of England Database, Person ID: 69585. (Hereafter CCED.)

[35] SP 12/193, fo. 28r. [36] SP 12/195, fo. 88r.

[37] SP 12/228, fo. 103r. His denunciation may also have something to do with his reportedly defacing an English Bible with a knife.

[38] SP 12/173/1, fo. 48r. [39] SP 12/198, fos. 76r–77r.

"shold mainteyne them, whether this were well doen yea or no"? Reportedly, they praised the King of Spain and rejoiced at news of setbacks for the English expeditionary force in the Netherlands. And for good measure they denounced the *Actes and Monuments* of John Foxe as "a legend of lyes" and argued for the legitimacy of Prince Arthur's marriage to Catherine of Aragon, the question at *fons et origo* of the Reformation in England.[40]

In all these examples the forwarding of reports to the authorities seems to have been unpremeditated, *post facto* impulses of religious and political loyalism. But in an unusual case from Henley, Oxfordshire, in 1585, Evan Arden (no relation?), a servant of the solidly Protestant treasurer of the household of Sir Francis Knollys, took it upon himself to incriminate Gregory Gunnes, alias Stone, whom he had met at the Bell Inn and took to be a "lewd fellow" by his speech. Gunnes was in fact an old Marian priest who had served in the Elizabethan Church but then given up his benefice of Yelford some seven years earlier "for his conscience." Arden lured the priest into a lane where he had caused "two honest men to be behind a pale where they myght heere their conference." These testified that Gunnes had spoken in praise of Campion and that he trusted one day to see a religious house erected in recompense on the spot where the Jesuit had suffered. Interestingly, rather than pretending to be a sympathizer (the classic tactic of the agent provocateur), Arden freely engaged Gunnes in debate about the authority of Scripture and papal supremacy, leaving the priest in no doubt that "yoe are of Luthers opynyon." One wonders if Gunnes, who admitted that since giving up his benefice he had been "vagrant heere and there," was in the habit of arguing religion with people he met in pubs.[41]

It would be wrong to suppose that people habitually spoke whatever was on their mind in matters of religion, in whatever the company they found themselves. Naturally, they were aware that there might be times to mind their words and guard their tongues. Once he was in full flow, Gunnes seems to have realized he had gone too far, telling Arden "nowe I am in yor handes to accuse mee yf you will." A conversation on the road in Hampshire in September 1594 turned quickly from conventional asking after news to dangerous opinionizing about it. Two Catholics, Thomas Dymock and Tristam Cotterill, bemoaned to their travel companion the recent fate of

40 SP 12/203, fo. 97r. For other instances of people speaking in favor of the King of Spain, see SP 12/226, fo. 115r; David Cressy, *Dangerous Talk: Scandalous, Seditious, and Treasonable Speech in Pre-Modern England* (Oxford University Press, 2010), pp. 80, 86, 88–9.

41 SP 12/179, fos. 9r–13r. For Gunnes's rectorship of Yelford, given up in 1576: CCED Person ID: 16421.

Dr. Lopez, with Cotterill reportedly asserting the papal supremacy and observing that in Spain the queen was commonly termed "the whore of babilon." Belatedly, Dymock thought to say to their fellow traveller, "I doupt not but you wilbe silent touching anything here spoken." This was not to be. It was only eighteen months after, imprisoned in the Fleet for debt and desperate to curry favor, that the third man, Richard Vennar (later a patriotic writer and famously unsuccessful theater impresario), decided to spill the beans.[42]

We cannot, of course, know how many "seditious words" went unreported; how many religious discussions were quietly folded away to memory and reflection. But there were surely many. In 1595 the London silk weaver Richard Garret only gave evidence against his tenant Anne Dryland concerning her treasonously pro-Spanish views after they had come to the mayor's attention by another route, claiming that he had simply been "ignorant of the law" in these matters.[43] Pressed as to why it had taken him so long to report the treason of dinner-table controversialist and Eusebian exegete, John Hardy, the Farnham preacher Peter German rather limply explained "that he shortlie fell lame . . . for the space of a whole quarter of the year."[44]

The impulse to discussion and debate was, in fact, at the heart of the religious culture of Shakespeare's age. Works of religious polemic and persuasion, as well as of pastoral encouragement, habitually utilized the dialogue form, in which representative characters of divergent viewpoints, meeting at inns or on highways, argue freely with each other and are often given, within the overweening didactic purposes of the author, a more or less fair hearing.[45] The Protestant clergy regularly sought to encourage the faithful and persuade the recalcitrant through the habit of "conference," that is, private discussion – something which was not infrequently made a condition of acceptance of recusants back into conformity with the Church of England.[46] Catholics for their part might express enthusiasm for the ideal, which, formally at least, granted a kind of parity to their beliefs and opinions. The Jesuit Henry Walpole, in prison in 1594, claimed to have found fewer differences than expected when he conferred with the learned

[42] SP 12/256, fos. 134r, 135r. See Herbert Berry, "Vennar, Richard (*bap.* 1564, *d.* 1615)," *Oxford Dictionary of National Biography* (www.oxforddnb.com).

[43] SP 12/252, fo. 177r. [44] SP 12/167, fo. 30v.

[45] See Antoinina Bevan Zlatar, *Reformation Fictions: Polemical Protestant Dialogues in Elizabethan England* (Oxford University Press, 2011).

[46] Michael Questier, *Conversion, Politics and Religion in England, 1580–1625* (Cambridge University Press, 1996), ch. 6, esp. pp. 154–5.

Protestant clergy in York, and he argued that a "free assembly of learned men of all sorts of opinions" might procure unity and secure the safety of the realm.[47] Thomas Throckmorton of Coughton, cited for recusancy by the churchwardens of St. Pancras in the Fields in 1605, explained to the ecclesiastical commissioner that he had no objection to "conference" and would in fact happily attend services if the king would convene a meeting of learned divines from both sides, their deliberations satisfying him "that it is noe synne for him to come to the church."[48] This kind of conference on terms of equality was precisely what Edmund Campion had sought, and been denied, in 1580–1; a lay supporter in Hampshire thought it invidious that souls should hang in jeopardy because "learned and godly personnes, which offered disputations, weare refused to be hearde."[49]

The intended end of conference was, of course, not the achievement of mutual respect and understanding but the success of persuasion, conversion. That made it – from the authorities' point of view – a risky and unstable exercise if the conditions were not tightly controlled, as they were for Campion's debates in the Tower in 1581.[50] By contrast, in 1599 Archbishop Matthew Hutton of York was decidedly unhappy about the activities of the former Jesuit, Thomas Wright, who had returned to England and placed himself under Essex's protection, "by reason of his often disputing with the ministers of Yorke, and talking with others of Religion."[51] Not always, but often enough, religious discussion was initiated with the clear intention of converting the other party to the side of true religion; this was the *raison d'être* of the Jesuit missioner and the Puritan preacher alike, though laypeople too sometimes took it upon themselves to cajole or argue an acquaintance into changing their allegiances.[52]

Part of the calculus of conversion, of choosing sides, was not just the question of who was in the right, but that of who was going to win – issues not unconnected with each other in the thought patterns of a deeply providential age. It is important to reiterate here that Catholics did not know they were the defeated party, destined for permanent minority and subcultural status in a Protestant and imperial nation. Like William Skinner

47 *CSPD: Elizabeth*, vol. CCXLIX, 44. 48 Warwickshire Record Office, CR 1998/Box 62/33.
49 SP 12/147, fo. 127r.
50 James Holleran (ed.), *A Jesuit Challenge: Edmond Campion's Debates at the Tower of London in 1581* (New York: Fordham University Press, 1999).
51 SP 12/271, fo. 57r. Wright was a consistent advocate of engagement with religious adversaries, disagreeing with Robert Persons over the legitimacy of occasional conformity, and particularly about the permissibility of Catholics attending Protestant sermons: Crosignani et al., *Recusancy and Conformity*, pp. 352–400.
52 For example, SP 12/222, fo. 18r; 12/155, fo. 12r; 12/193, fos. 17r, 30r–v, 32r–v.

of Rowington, they might be decidedly upbeat about prospects for the future. The papists "looke for a golden day," warned a report from Norfolk in 1584, and boast how "they have as much favoure in ye courtt as the protestantes have."[53] Skinner was not alone in Warwickshire in the early 1580s in thinking that an imminent royal marriage to the Duke of Anjou might totally transform the religiopolitical scene. One of the curates of the vicar of Wooton (serving either Henley or Ullenhall) was shamed (though sadly not named) in the Puritan survey of the ministry in 1586: "upon rumour of a change in religion in Monsieur's days [he] did shave his beard."[54] The beard was the identifying mark of the Protestant minister; the clean cheek that of the celibate Catholic priest. Despite the failure of the Anjou match and of successive Spanish invasion schemes, Catholic political aspirations were far from receding in the final years of Elizabeth's reign. Hopes that the likeliest successor, James VI of Scotland, might offer toleration in return for Catholic support, or that he himself – son of a sainted martyr – might declare himself for the Catholic cause, were rife in some Catholic circles through the 1590s and beyond. Protestants meanwhile might be worried. It was reported in 1597 that "the King of Scots talks carelessly about religion," saying that purgatory and the real presence of Christ in the sacrament were matters on which there need not be dispute between Protestants and Catholics.[55] In the event, Catholic disappointment with the new regime was palpable, and an important contributory factor to the debacle of the Gunpowder Plot. But thereafter, James's commitment to a "pacific" foreign policy, and to the pursuit of a Catholic match for his heir, combined with the discreet presence of a Catholic queen at the court, continued to supply grounds for optimism about the prospects for the faith through the first decades of the seventeenth century.

I have been arguing that the religious atmosphere of later Elizabethan and Jacobean England, in the Midlands and elsewhere, was articulate, animated, and contested; that the religious future of the country was frequently seen as uncertain, and its current state widely regarded as contingent and unsettled; that discussion and debate involving sensitive religious matters was by no means unusual among people at a variety of social levels, and in a variety of private and semipublic settings. The kaleidoscopic elements of religious

[53] SP 12/169, fos. 30v–31r.

[54] Albert Peel (ed.), *The Seconde Parte of a Register*, 2 vols. (Cambridge, 1915), vol. II, p. 166.

[55] *CSPD: Elizabeth*, vol. CCLXII, 125 [3]. For Catholic schemes and hopes regarding the succession, see Peter Lake, "The King (the Queen) and the Jesuit: James Stuart's *True Law of Free Monarchies* in Context/s," *Transactions of the Royal Historical Society*, 6th series, 14 (2004), 243–60; Thomas M. McCoog, *The Society of Jesus in Ireland, Scotland, and England, 1589–1597* (Farnham: Ashgate, 2012).

culture were most evident in the capital, as Felicity Heal confirms elsewhere in this volume.[56] But they were far from absent in a rural county such as Warwickshire.

What, then, should we make of the absence of overt religious declarations in the life and works of William Shakespeare, of his apparent quiet determination, in an age of confessional choices, to choose to refuse to choose?[57] Is this a pointer to the inwardness of Shakespeare's own social and spiritual predilections, an indicator of the priorities and functions of theater in this period, or a suggestive clue that very many people may simply have wished quietly to get on with life amidst the sound and fury of the zealous doctrinalism highlighted in this chapter? I pose the questions without assuming any of the responsibility for answering them. But I will take occasion to note here that Shakespeare scholarship has for some decades now been in fruitful communication with the evolving historical interpretations of the Reformation and the religious culture of his age. The "revisionist" turn of scholarship on the Reformation in the 1980s and 90s, drawing attention to the theme of resistance, and to the hitherto relatively neglected Catholic "other," was undoubtedly influential in the revival of "Catholic Shakespeare" theories which had lain semidormant in the bloodstream of Shakespeare biography for a century and more.[58] Yet shadowing and eventually subsuming revisionism has been a "postrevisionist" version of England's Reformation experience, one which, rather than returning to progressivist and triumphalist narratives of Protestant advance, has emphasized both continuities and confusions, a Reformation which succeeded precisely because in many ways it represented less of a clear, clean, and complete break with pre-Reformation habits of thought than we were accustomed to think.[59] This too has made its mark on Shakespeare studies of the last few years: in careful analysis of Shakespeare's putatively "hybrid

[56] For more on the religious diversity and debate in the capital city specifically, see Chapter 3 below.

[57] Perhaps the most persuasive recent delineation and explication of Shakespeare's "confessional invisibility" is Alison Shell, *Shakespeare and Religion* (London: Methuen, 2010), quote at p. 235.

[58] Significant works here include Wilson, *Secret Shakespeare*; Dutton et al., *Theatre and Religion*; David N. Beauregard, *Catholic Theology in Shakespeare's Plays* (Newark, DE: University of Delaware Press, 2008). Influence on more populist treatments is evident in Wilson, *Shakespeare: The Evidence*, and Wood, *In Search of Shakespeare*. Seminal revisionist accounts of the Reformation are Christopher Haigh, *English Reformations: Religion, Politics, and Society under the Tudors* (Oxford University Press, 1993) and Eamon Duffy, *The Stripping of the Altars: Traditional Religion in England 1400–1580* (New Haven, CT: Yale University Press, 1992). Duffy has made his own foray into the ring: "Was Shakespeare a Catholic?," *The Tablet*, April 27, 1996, 536–8.

[59] For example, Tessa Watt, *Cheap Print and Popular Piety, 1550–1640* (Cambridge University Press, 1991); Ronald Hutton, "The English Reformation and the Evidence of Folklore," *Past & Present*, 148 (1995), 89–116; Alexandra Walsham, *Providence in Early Modern England* (Oxford University Press,

faith," in attention to the "elegiac nostalgia in many of Shakespeare's plays which interacts with the residual Catholicism present in Elizabethan England as a whole," and in the notion of a playwright wrestling, almost literally, with the ghosts of the nation's Catholic past.[60]

But as contemporaries were all too well aware, Catholicism belonged not just to England's past but to its present and (perhaps) its future. Reformation (the definitive article may be a distraction here) was an unfinished process, and exposure to it, and to its proponents and opponents, was a condition of life in late sixteenth- and early seventeenth-century England. The idea that an observer of society as astute as Shakespeare could have been oblivious to or uninterested in the highly topical religious (and therefore political) questions of the day stretches credulity.[61] If we cannot observe him making distinct religious choices (like a Jonson or Donne) and cannot readily identify confessional statements or stances in his writings, we can at least be certain of one thing: that this was not because he inhabited a milieu where the questions simply did not present themselves.

1999) and *The Reformation of the Landscape: Religion, Identity, and Memory in Early Modern Britain and Ireland* (Oxford University Press, 2011); Peter Marshall, *Beliefs and the Dead in Reformation England* (Oxford University Press, 2002).

60 Jean-Christophe Mayer, *Shakespeare's Hybrid Faith: History, Religion, and the Stage* (Basingstoke: Palgrave Macmillan, 2006); Beatrice Groves, *Texts and Traditions: Religion in Shakespeare 1592–1604* (Oxford University Press, 2007), quote at p. 32; Stephen Greenblatt, *Hamlet in Purgatory* (Princeton University Press, 2001). Arthur F. Marotti also displays a distinctly post-revisionist sensibility in assigning Shakespeare to "the great muddled middle in English Christianity": "Shakespeare and Catholicism," in Dutton et al., *Theatre and Religion*, p. 219.

61 A point well made by Brian Cummings in his British Academy Shakespeare Lecture, "Shakespeare and the Reformation," delivered on May 1, 2012.

CHAPTER 3

# *Experiencing religion in London: diversity and choice in Shakespeare's metropolis*

*Felicity Heal*

A few years ago the parish of St. Andrew by the Wardrobe, adjacent to Blackfriars, erected two wooden wall plaques. Both show gentlemen kneeling in prayer. One is to the musician John Downame, buried in St. Ann, Blackfriars, but a parishioner of St. Andrew. The other reads "William Shakespeare: Poet; Playwright; Parishioner," adding mention of his part ownership of the Blackfriars Theatre and his purchase of a property in Ireland Lane. It is indicative of our assumptions about the opacity of Shakespeare's religious views, and of his "lack of rootedness" in the metropolis, that a parish's claim upon his allegiance has some power to shock.[1] We are aware that his colleagues in the theater certainly played a role in parochial life: Henry Condell and John Heminges, of First Folio fame, were both churchwardens of St. Mary Aldermanbury, while Richard Burbage and Edward Alleyn were select vestrymen at St. Saviour, Southwark.[2] The little we know of Shakespeare's London lodgings, however, suggests that he moved from St. Helen, Bishopsgate, to St. Saviour, and thence to St. Olave, Silver Street, and finally to St. Andrew, without making any visible mark on parish life.[3] Was a quiet, bourgeois playwright therefore regularly to be found in the pew along with his fellows (at least after the theaters were forcibly silenced on Sundays from 1603)? Or should

1 The phrase is Ian Archer's, from his chapter "Shakespeare's London" in David Scott Kastan (ed.), *A Companion to Shakespeare* (Oxford: Blackwell, 1999), p. 55.

2 Mary Edmond, "Condell, Henry (*bap.* 1576?, *d.* 1627)," *Oxford Dictionary of National Biography* (www.oxforddnb.com) (hereafter *ODNB*). S. P. Cerasano, "Alleyn, Edward (1566–1626)," *ODNB.*

3 Park Honan, *Shakespeare: A Life* (Oxford University Press, 1998), pp. 322–5, 379. St. Olave's records do not survive for this period: there are churchwardens' accounts for St. Helen's and St. Andrew, and an excellent range of sources for St. Saviour's. The fact that Shakespeare does not appear among those receiving communion tokens for St. Saviour's has been regarded as significant, but Jeremy Boulton points out that only heads of household were so recorded. London Metropolitan Archives, MSS P69/HEL/06876, P69/AND1/02088, P92/SAV/450, 787–98. Beatrice Groves, *Texts and Traditions: Religion in Shakespeare, 1592–1604* (Oxford University Press, 2007), p. 31. Alison Shell, *Shakespeare and Religion*, Arden Shakespeare Critical Editions (London: Bloomsbury, 2010), p. 82, n. 8.

we assume that a nominal identity to the parish that was mandatory for all Londoners was merely the factitious consequence of a place of lodging, telling us nothing of the playwright's religious or, indeed, other concerns? Certainly, what Shell calls Shakespeare's "confessional invisibility" ensures that we can do no more than speculate on his experience of the pews of Protestant London.[4]

The expansion of London in the later sixteenth century made it increasingly difficult to ensure that the bonds of parochial identity were preserved. London historians' estimates for church attendance, even those that optimistically assess Easter Communion as involving the vast majority of residents, underline that association between residence and parochial engagement was far from universal.[5] Discipline might be maintained more effectively in the city than in the burgeoning suburbs, yet even central parishes were not immune to high levels of delinquency. Apart from active nonconformity there were many, like the playwright, who were Londoners neither by birth, nor exclusive residence, nor citizenship. They might, like the diarist and sermon-goer John Manningham, be students at the Inns of Court, experiencing the capital for a few years, or gentry visitors in London for the season only.[6] But for an example of a long-term migrant like Shakespeare we can turn to Richard Stonley, diarist and Teller of the Exchequer. Stonley was an established resident of St. Botolph's, Aldersgate, and a man whose devout adherence to the Protestant Settlement is consistently revealed in the diaries he kept in the early 1580s and 1590s. They record a steady diet of prayer and religious reading, his book purchases including much current religious controversy. Stonley also had a rural estate at Doddinghurst, Essex, and lived there as often as his official duties permitted. We might anticipate that his commitment to both his parishes was strong, and indeed in the country he was punctilious in attending church, commenting on sermons and entertaining the clergy. In town, however, though he paid his dues to St. Botolph, he seems to have been a very intermittent Sunday attender. Otherwise he divided his Sabbath

4 Shell, *Shakespeare and Religion*, p. 235.

5 The most optimistic assessment is given by Jeremy Boulton in his study of Easter communion in Southwark, in which he estimates from the issue of tokens that between 80 percent and 98 percent of parishioners took the Eucharist in the 1620s: "The Limits of Formal Religion: The Administration of Holy Communion in Late Elizabethan and Early Stuart London," *London Journal*, 10 (1984), 135–54. On the other hand, Ian Archer's figures for two city parishes show percentages no higher than 75 percent in the later Elizabethan period: *The Pursuit of Stability: Social Relations in Elizabethan London* (Cambridge University Press, 1991), pp. 90–1.

6 Robert P. Sorlien (ed.), *The Diary of John Manningham of the Middle Temple, 1602–1603* (Hanover, NH: University Press of New England, 1976), pp. 260–8.

energies between visits to the great open-air pulpit at Paul's Cross and Bible reading at home, the latter being his commonest mode.[7] His considerable knowledge of the religious world around him seems to have derived, in descending order of significance, from reading, discussion with his London friends and kin, and sermon-gadding. Stonley's outlook is that of a conformist Protestant: it is not clear that this translated into parochial loyalty in the capital.

Richard Stonley's diaries offer an insight into the diverse ways in which the religious environment of the capital could be experienced, one which does not automatically privilege the obvious routines of the established church. The London of the 1590s to the 1620s offered a range of religious experience. There was a multifaceted official Protestantism, with its ideological roots in Calvinist theology; a culture of the godly for whom intense preaching had become the focus of experimental faith; formal liturgical ritual maintained in cathedral and court; and the beginning of a new form of religious identity that was to become English Arminianism by the 1630s. These public expressions of faith were paralleled by a radical puritan and sectarian underground and by a vigorous Catholicism, both forms of recusancy seeking to intervene in open debate through print and manuscript. The Jesuit Robert Persons in his *A Brief Discours* (1580) thus represented this diversity to the queen: "There are in this your Maiesties Realme fower knowen religions, and the professors thereof, distinct both in name, spirit and doctrine, that is to say the Catholickes, the Protestants, the Puritanes, and the howsholders of love [Familists]. Besids al other petye sects, newly borne and yet grovelinge on the ground."[8] Persons was not offering a neutral description: his agenda sought to demonstrate the priority of Catholics, the divisions between Protestants and Puritans and the troubling growth of radical minorities. But he was an astute observer, playing on the fears of an establishment already spooked by divisions within Protestantism, recently alerted to the activities of the Family of Love and perturbed by the possibility of the Anjou match and toleration for Catholics.

A decade after Persons's challenge it might, however, have appeared that in London two of the "fower knowen religions" had buried many of their visible differences and secured overwhelming influence over the public

[7] Three of the Stonley diaries survive, for 1581–3, 1593–4, and 1596–8, though the last covers a period during which Stonley was imprisoned in the Fleet for indebtedness to the crown and therefore was unable to engage with his parish: Folger Shakespeare Library, V.a. 459–61.

[8] Robert Persons, *A Brief Discours Containyng Certayne Reasons why Catholiques Refuse to Goe to Church* (false imprint Douai, actually Greenstreet House Press, 1580), sig. ≠iiir.

practice of religion.[9] Puritan leaders, never *pace* Persons of different religion to the conformist clergy, had emerged from the conflicts over church government of the 1570s and 1580s bruised but accepting that they must perforce live within one ecclesiastical structure.[10] By the mid 1590s the energies of moderate Puritans were forcibly canalized towards the preaching of sound doctrine and the maintenance of parochial discipline, while awaiting another day for the Presbyterian nirvana, or even the abolition of residual popish remnants within the existing church. London had developed a formidable reputation as the heart of reformed religion and the cockpit of its preaching ministry. Anthony Maxey, preaching at court in 1606, described a city full of "painfull preaching frequented with infinite congregations, and mightie assemblies."[11] Seaver calculated that approximately one hundred sermons were being preached each week by lecturers in 1600, and by the end of the Jacobean era few city parishes can have been without regular Sunday provision.[12] The author of *The Prentises Practice in Godlinesse* (1608) expressed thanks that individuals could go to some lecture after evening prayers in their parish, "as there be divers (blessed bee God) in divers parts of the City."[13] In addition to parochial provision there was the regular Sunday sermon at Paul's Cross, and the specialized pulpit of the Temple Church for the lawyers, while at Westminster there was the Abbey and above all preaching at court when the monarch was in residence. Arnold Hunt's study of preaching in late Elizabethan and early Stuart England is appropriately called *The Art of Hearing*, and Shakespeare cannot have escaped hearing, and seeing, the practice of religion in the metropolis.[14] As Hunt says, "it was impossible to avoid exposure to the Protestant preaching ministry, even if, for some, it was merely part of the background hum of urban life."[15]

For many of the godly this abundant provision led to an almost frenetic gadding from parish to parish to hear the latest minister of the Word.

9 In what follows I have endeavored to use the term London to include the separate jurisdictions of Westminster and the near suburbs, while specifically identifying the City when appropriate.

10 The 1592 trials of Thomas Cartwright and the nine ministers represented at least a major caesura in the struggle for a Presbyterian style of settlement: Patrick Collinson, *The Elizabethan Puritan Movement* (London: Jonathan Cape, 1967), pp. 417–32.

11 Anthony Maxey, *The Churches Sleepe, Expressed in a Sermon Preached at the Court* (London, 1606), sig. C4v.

12 Paul S. Seaver, *The Puritan Lecturerships: The Politics of Religious Dissent, 1560–1640* (Stanford University Press, 1970), pp. 125–7.

13 B. P., *The Prentises Practise in Godlinesse* (London, 1608), sig. G8r.

14 Arnold Hunt, *The Art of Hearing: English Preachers and their Audiences, 1590–1640* (Cambridge University Press, 2010).

15 Ibid., 205.

Fashionable preachers like Stephen Egerton at St. Ann, Blackfriars, or Edward Philips at St. Saviour, Southwark, both, interestingly, Puritan parishes with which Shakespeare would have had personal acquaintance, attracted large congregations, including many visitors to the metropolis. Sermon notebooks like those of John Manningham, William Platte, or later Simonds D'Ewes reveal eclectic patterns of attendance at parish, Temple and Paul's Cross.[16] The riches of the spoken Word were reinforced by published sermons: Mary Morrissey's figures for Paul's Cross sermons show the numbers printed rose from 15 in the 1590s to 62 in the 1610s, and these are merely the tip of a large iceberg of preaching translated into print.[17] While all of this might be thought to demonstrate the commitment of Londoners to the reformed faith, there were inevitably preachers who remained dissatisfied. Mobility in attending sermons led John Whalley to complain that there were too many individuals who might run up and down to hear the Word with Bibles under their arms, but their spirits remained "vast rooms unswept, with many dark corners" filled with disobedience and sin.[18] One of the most familiar sermon structures of the period developed the theme of a failure of godliness: the favored jeremiad theme, sometimes known as "England's warning by Israel," castigated the sins of the city, denounced the particular vices of the age (including of course gadding to playhouses) and threatened divine judgment on those to whom God had thus far been merciful.[19] Stephen Egerton was a master of this mode: he told his Sunday congregation that if they, as parishioners and fellow Londoners, did not repent then "the most wicked and prophane Cittyes in the world . . . shall rise in iudgement against you."[20]

The specific form of the jeremiad was only one of many alternatives open to the urban preacher, who had to tune the pulpit to occasion and auditors. The range of possibility, from the political defense of secular and

16 See, for example, Lady Margaret Hoby and Sir Richard Paulet, both of whom attended a stream of godly sermons when in town: Pauline Croft, "Capital Life: Members of Parliament Outside the House," in Thomas Cogswell, Richard Cust, and Peter Lake (eds.), *Politics, Religion and Popularity in Early Stuart Britain: Essays in Honour of Conrad Russell* (Cambridge University Press, 2002), pp. 72–81.

17 Mary Morrissey, *Politics and the Paul's Cross Sermons, 1558–1642* (Oxford University Press, 2011), p. 42. For a comparative figure, see Peter McCullough's calculation that 141 Jacobean court sermons were published, as against only 28 from Elizabeth's reign: *Sermons at Court: Politics and Religion in Elizabethan and Jacobean Preaching* (Cambridge University Press, 1998), p. 8.

18 John Whalley, *Gods Plenty, Feeding True Pietie* (London, 1616), pp. 16–17.

19 Alexandra Walsham, *Providence in Early Modern England* (Oxford University Press, 1999), pp. 281–325.

20 Egerton's comment here was noted by George Frevile, an assiduous sermon note-taker: British Library, Egerton MS 2877, fo. 29v.

ecclesiastical authority, through the anti-Catholic disquisition, to the exposition of demanding predestinarian doctrine, might indicate that preachers were led to underline ideological division through their choice of homiletic subject. But the emphasis was most often upon unity, both of theme and method. In part a commonalty of preaching method assisted the preacher. His purpose was the proper exposition and application of a passage of Scripture: the choice of a short text, followed by its dissection and explication, was then expanded into lessons appropriate to the congregation. This method of dissecting and expounding Scripture offered rich opportunity for promoting mainstream Protestant doctrine. It was here that the views of most London clergy could legitimately be described as articulating a "Calvinist consensus." By the turn of the sixteenth century most had been educated at university in an environment that valued above all Calvin's scriptural commentaries, and debated interminably the nuances of a predestinarian view of grace and election.[21]

While the fundamentals of reformed theology might be agreed, London ministers had to ask how far "difficult" doctrine was appropriate to the pastoral context of the pulpit.[22] There were differences of emphasis on this, as on a number of other aspects of biblical interpretation among the London clergy, but no general hesitation in speaking or writing of the "comfortable doctrine" of assurance, or even the essential topic of reprobation. Edward Philips's lectures at St. Saviour's, Southwark, printed from the notes taken by Henry Yelverton, gave considerable attention to the practical implications of the idea of election, urging his auditors to get "as many testimonies as we can to prove that this election pertaineth to us," though Hunt observes that he kept his most rigorous interpretations to the weekday lectures on Romans 8.[23] Stephen Egerton, on the other hand, was more prone to address predestinarian issues in his Sunday sermons than in his more moralistic addresses to his weekday congregations.[24] Even court preaching might address predestinarianism with an explicit boldness, at least under James. Anthony Maxey handled it deploying the language of the great Puritan William Perkins in his 1606 sermon *The Golden Chaine of*

[21] Patrick Collinson, *The Religion of Protestants: The Church in English Society 1559–1625* (Oxford: Clarendon Press, 1982), pp. 177–88.

[22] J. F. Merritt, "The Pastoral Tightrope: A Puritan Pedagogue in Jacobean London," in Cogswell et al., *Politics, Religion and Popularity*, pp. 143–61.

[23] Edward Philips, *Certaine Godly and Learned Sermons, as They Were Delivered by him in Saint Saviors in Southwarke* (London, 1605), pp. 192–4. Hunt, *Art of Hearing*, pp. 354–6.

[24] Hunt, *Art of Hearing*, pp. 222–3.

*Mans Salvation.*[25] More cautious clerics, for example those at Paul's Cross, often cast their predestinarianism in a broader providential frame. Thus John Pelling, having talked of the "immutable decree" of election and reprobation, used Psalm 104 to hymn divine providence: "God . . . in wisdom . . . made, maintained, governed and ordained . . . the heavens spred like a curtaine, and light to decke all as with a glorious garment."[26] The pastoral message constantly repeated by the London preachers was that the divine decree was inescapable, but that men's actions were nevertheless to display moral autonomy: their upright actions being the proper fruits of their faith.

The agreed-upon political message resounding from the London pulpits in these years was that of antipopery. Paul's Cross sermons from the 1580s onwards included an antipapal diatribe as at least an obligatory sub-theme of their message.[27] Many-faceted as hostility to Catholicism could be, in the following decades it had hardened into a series of well-rehearsed themes that had apparently won wide acceptance from their auditors. Providential deliverances from the great forces of Spain and the papacy – the queen's preservation; the execution of Mary, Queen of Scots; the Armada's defeat; and later James's preservation from the Gunpowder Plot – all confirmed the need for "thankfull remembrance" amid denunciation of the Antichrist.[28] John Manningham solemnly described antipapal and anti-Catholic diatribes of this kind as a staple fare of his sermon-going.[29] This was a topic upon which the godly could venture without much fear of contradiction, touching as it did both popular fears and the continuing uncertainties of the political nation. It identified the absent "other" mired in sin and error, and provided, in Alex Walsham's words, a "kind of cultural cement" for the congregation.[30] Special preaching, especially after the Gunpowder Plot, kept alive the established rhetoric of anti-Catholicism, weaving it into the other themes of the jeremiad favored by the godly.[31] This ensured an

25 Anthony Maxey, *The Golden Chaine of Mans Salvation, and the Fearefull Point of Hardening, Opened and Set Downe in Severall Sermons preached before the King* (London, 1606).

26 John Pelling, *A Sermon of the Providence of God* (London, 1607), p. 5.

27 Morrissey, *Politics and Paul's Cross*, pp. 181–2.

28 For a good example of the two themes run together, see John Dove, *A Sermon Preached at Pauls Crosse the 3 of November 1594* (London, 1594).

29 Sorlien, *Diary of John Manningham*, pp. 92, 100, 111, 143.

30 Peter Lake, "Anti-Popery: The Structure of a Prejudice," in Richard Cust and Ann Hughes (eds.), *Conflict in Early Stuart England: Studies in Religion and Politics, 1603–1642* (London: Longman, 1989), pp. 72–106. Walsham, *Providence*, p. 248.

31 See, for example, Martin Fotherby, *The Third Sermon Preached at Paules Crosse, November 5 anno 1607* (London, 1608).

integrated approach to the nation and its spiritual needs, which only began visibly to fray in the second decade of James's reign.[32]

However, no one who observed the state of public religion in London would for long have been persuaded that the Calvinist consensus of the preachers, or even the relative unanimity of hostility to Rome, meant that harmony prevailed among Protestant brethren. Presbyterian visions might have been suppressed, but the church establishment continued to fear conspiracy. Most attempts at discipline were undertaken through the church courts, though Richard Bancroft's 1589 sermon at Paul's Cross, rightly described by Patrick Collinson as a "diatribe" against Puritanism, took the challenge into the heart of the London godly community.[33] Public confutation was not something, in Bancroft's view, to be directed only against Catholics or sectaries; rather, it had to be addressed, too, to the enemy within, to those "false prophets" who were the "precise" brethren. In the wake of the Marprelate pamphlets, Bancroft was determined to treat "the godly" as no longer members of the English religious commonwealth but as another, and seditious, church. Two years later the prophet "Frantik Hacket" was proclaimed in Cheapside by his besotted followers as a savior of the true church of the presbyters, and Bancroft and his ministers seized the opportunity again to denounce the Presbyterian ministers in a pamphleteering war.[34] From time to time in the early years of James there was a return to this public assault: in 1607, for example, Bancroft's chaplain Samuel Collins preached at the Cross a generalized critique of the godly clergy who "bite the lip and hang the head, at Supremacie of princes, in each kinde of causes, mentioned in prayers, as if that were but flatterie, being cast upon kings, and the truer right thereof in Ecclesiasticall ménages belongd to the Presbiters."[35]

It is perhaps surprising that Londoners heard only a limited number of sermons of confrontation with the godly preachers. For the public face of moderate Puritanism was always in danger of being undermined by various forms of radicalism within and without the church. Most visibly, there was that sanctioned form of Calvinist church order, the Stranger congregations of the Dutch and French Reformed. Curiously, the French Stranger

32 Anthony Milton, *Catholic and Reformed: The Roman and Protestant Churches in English Protestant Thought, 1600–1640* (Cambridge University Press, 1995), pp. 35–42.

33 Richard Bancroft, *A Sermon Preached at Pauls Crosse, the 9 of February, being the First Sunday in the Parleament Anno 1588* (London, 1589). Collinson, *Elizabethan Puritan Movement*, p. 397.

34 Alexandra Walsham, "'Frantik Hacket': Prophecy, Sorcery, Insanity and the Elizabethan Presbyterian Movement," *Historical Journal*, 41 (1998), 27–66.

35 Samuel Collins, *A sermon Preached at Paules-Crosse upon the 1 of November, being All-Saints Day, anno 1607* (London, 1607), p. 26.

Church is the one congregation with which we can be reasonably confident Shakespeare was familiar. In 1612 he was witness in a dispute over a dowry involving Christopher Mont and his family, with whom the playwright had lodged between 1602 and 1604. Mont was a French Huguenot refugee and a member of the French Stranger Church, though scarcely a godly one, since he was later excommunicated for his dissolute life.[36] By the 1590s the Dutch and French congregations had long been settled respectively in Austin Friars and St. Anthony, Threadneedle Street. Acute fears that the English would be infected by the doctrinal radicalism of their guests were largely past, though sensitivities remained about their relationship to order in the English Church. In the 1580s London clergy were still petitioning that citizens visited the Stranger churches illegally in order to benefit from their pure Calvinist worship, but by the end of the century at least part of the flow was in the other direction, as settled Strangers often turned to English parish worship. Tensions with the Strangers were more frequently about their economic role at a time of general crisis than about their challenge to church order.[37] However, the two churches continued in key respects to represent an institutional vision at odds with that of their hosts. They adhered, of course, to the ministerial structure of Geneva, with its pastors, elders, and deacons, each church being served by three pastors, none of whom should "assert priority or dominion over the other." The elders had autonomy in managing their congregational affairs and discipline that many a London churchwarden must have envied. And they followed all the "best reformed" in not celebrating holy days or festivals – no Christmas, and not even Easter Communion until 1616.[38] Small wonder, then, that their freedom later attracted the hostility of Archbishop Laud: denounced as "nurseries of ill-minded persons to the Church of England," they were made subject to his Injunctions, which were designed to integrate them into their own English parishes. It is indicative of the cohesion of the Strangers that they managed first politically, and then by passive resistance, to survive such pressures and to emerge in 1641 to charge the archbishop with having assaulted their privileges.[39]

[36] Honan, *Shakespeare*, pp. 323–5.

[37] Andrew Pettegree, *Foreign Protestant Communities in Sixteenth-Century London* (Oxford University Press, 1986), pp. 276–305.

[38] Ole Peter Grell, *Calvinist Exiles in Tudor and Stuart England* (Farnham: Ashgate, 1996), pp. 34–42; quotation from reprint of "Ecclesiastical Discipline of the French Churches in England, 1641, Des Pasteurs," *Huguenot Society of London*, 54 (1984), 103.

[39] *Calendar of State Papers Domestic: Charles I, 1633–4*, vol. CCLXV, 81. Grell, *Calvinist Exiles*, pp. 46–8.

The French and Dutch Strangers were fortunate in usually having a measure of public protection. Others who wished to live by congregational discipline, including many of those led by the godly London preachers, could but envy their relative security. But most, even of the most zealous Puritan ministers, would not countenance the formal separation that this would have demanded. The opponents of the godly preachers – Bancroft or Harsnett – alleged, of course, that separatism was the inevitable result of nonconformity, and the stage made such zeal into the parodic representation of extreme Puritanism like Jonson's *Bartholemew Fair* and *Alchemist* characters Zeal-of-the-Land-Busy and Deacon Ananias from Amsterdam.[40] In practice, Bancroft knew that most zealous behavior, and most "voluntary religion," to use Collinson's language, did not issue in separation from the national church: Puritans might like to call one another brethren, and praise the virtues of the saints, as did Jonson's characters, but most still accepted some form of tarrying for the magistrate.[41] However, voluntary religion, with its emphasis on the shared society of the godly, and the pursuit of edification by a community of the faithful, led readily towards a radicalism which in practice barely stopped short of separation. Lake and Como are surely right to stress that for many Londoners the parish church was far less significant than this underground network. Laymen sometimes misunderstood the limits on voluntarism imposed by the radical preachers: Edward Philips, Stephen Egerton, and Giles Wigginton were singled out by members of gathered congregations as having in their sermons pointed the way to withdrawal from the national church.[42]

For separation there was, and Londoners would have been made aware of it in the early 1590s through the trials and executions of Henry Barrow, John Greenwood, and John Penry. Henry Barrow was unequivocal that the national church was a false church, its worship, ministry, government, and national identity all irrevocably tainted by worldly corruption.[43] Salvation was to be sought in separation, "to reduce all things to the true and ancient and primitive pattern of God's word," established through an

40 For Jonson's assault on the godly, see Peter Lake with Michael Questier, *The Anti-Christ's Lewd Hat: Protestants, Papists and Players in Post-Reformation England* (New Haven, CT: Yale University Press, 2002), pp. 583–610.

41 Collinson, *Religion of Protestants*, pp. 242–83.

42 Wigginton, though no separatist, was one of the few ministers willing to go as far as supporting Hacket: Walsham, "'Frantik Hacket,'" 35. For the underground network, see David R. Como, *Blown by the Spirit: Puritanism and the Emergence of an Antinomian Underground in Pre-Civil War England* (Stanford University Press, 2004); Peter Lake, *The Boxmaker's Revenge: "Orthodoxy," "Heterodoxy" and the Politics of the Parish in Early Stuart London* (Manchester University Press, 2001).

43 Henry Barrow, *A Brief Discoverie of the False Church* (?Dort, 1590).

act of covenant by the congregation.[44] Barrow and Greenwood spent six years in the Fleet prison after their arrest, and there, in the usual lax security conditions of an Elizabethan jail, they were able to have some impact on others, as well as write in defense of their distinctive religious vision. In 1592 Greenwood was released long enough to be chosen as pastor of a London congregation. Even after his second arrest significant meetings were uncovered, like that at which fifty-six people were arrested in the woods near Islington in 1593. The removal of the Barrowists to Amsterdam broke some of the immediate challenge to the establishment, though a steady flow of printed materials were then able to be distributed through London networks. Francis Johnson, Barrow's successor in leading the congregation, was optimistic that regime change in 1603 would facilitate their return, and he endeavored to gain personal access to James I with a petition for toleration in the form allowed to the Dutch and French Stranger churches.[45]

Others in the radical underground also saw the beginning of the new reign as a moment of possible liberation. The Familists, adherents of the Netherlands visionary and perfectionist Hendrick Niclaes, seized this opportunity to emerge from the shadows for the first time since the 1580s to address a petition for protection to a deeply unsympathetic king.[46] Since the Familists were Nicodemites and prepared to assimilate to the worship of the established church, it is pointless to try to demonstrate sectlike survival in London. But the ideas of Familism do seem to have survived, sometimes making curious accord with radical Puritanism in the quest for religious purity. They became part of what David Como, in a vivid phrase, calls the "cacophonous religious scene of the capital" in the mid-Jacobean years.[47] The anti-Trinitarian Bartholomew Legate became the last person burned for heresy at Smithfield in 1612; forms of Anabaptist belief were represented by the followers of the self-baptized "Se-baptist," John Smyth, who returned to London after 1612; and by 1616 Henry Jacob had established his semi-separatist congregation in Southwark.[48] This is the world that has been most closely observed in Peter Lake's study of the conflict between the "orthodox" preacher Stephen Denison and the box-maker John Etherington.[49] Although their conflict involved much complexity and the

44 Barrington Raymond White, *The English Separatist Tradition from the Marian Martyrs to the Pilgrim Fathers* (Oxford University Press, 1971), pp. 73–6.

45 Ibid., pp. 111–12.

46 See Christopher W. Marsh, *The Family of Love in English Society, 1550–1630* (Cambridge University Press, 1994), esp. pp. 198–205. James had assailed both Anabaptists and Familists in his *Basilicon Doron.*

47 Como, *Blown by the Spirit*, p. 146.

48 David R. Como, "Legate, Bartholomew (*d.* 1612)," *ODNB*.

49 Lake, *The Boxmaker's Revenge.*

type of polemical grandstanding by Denison that only obfuscates the narrative, Etherington in his own account seems to have followed a trajectory from sympathy with Familism in the 1590s (indeed perhaps to as late as 1610) to a species of Calvinist orthodoxy by the 1620s. En route to his affirmation of predestinarian belief in *A discovery of the Errors of the English Anabaptists* (published under the *nom de plume* of Edmund Jessup), he encountered various radical beliefs, including those of the unidentified T. L., whose prophetic and eschatological writings were laced with enough Calvinist language to escape censorship.[50] Etherington also acknowledged that in these questing years he had known Anabaptists and separatists, giving details of the activities of the group around the Legate brothers, while firmly denying that he had himself ever been a practicing separatist. By the 1620s he apparently sat dutifully in the parish pew, satisfying himself, though not Denison, of his return to orthodoxy. This pulse in and out of radical dissent is more visible in the career of the preacher Henoch Clapham, whose "maverick" career took him from Presbyterianism, via Brownist views, flight to the separatists in Amsterdam, conversion to orthodox Calvinism, some successful years as a London preacher, conflict with the ecclesiastical authorities, and final promotion to a living in Kent. Indeed, Clapham's popularity as a London preacher helped to alert a wide audience to the cacophony of dissent.[51]

When Persons identified his four kinds of English Christians in 1580, he had little justification for seeing Protestants and Puritans as holding different ideologies. But by the late 1590s an enthusiastic Londoner could have sermon-gadded to a kind of preaching different from the standard Paul's Cross fare, one which quickly opened a genuine division. Lancelot Andrewes was appointed to St. Giles, Cripplegate in 1588, and in the 1590s preached parochial sermons that sought to restore the liturgical significance of the sacraments and to instill in his auditors an understanding that the Eucharistic elements themselves could remit sins.[52] Other manifestations of what we usually call "avant garde conformity" were to be found in the ritual life of

[50] Ibid., pp. 120–47. T. L., *An Exposition to the XI, XII, XIII Chapters of the Revelations* (1623), but first printed in 1589, and especially *Babylon is Fallen* (London, 1597), which was dedicated to the Earl of Essex.

[51] Clapham both preached and wrote on the multiplicity of religious errors of his time, concluding in favor of the Church of England (at least in his printed works): *Errour on the Right Hand, Through a Preposterous Zeale* (London, 1608) and *Errour on the Left Hand, Through a Frozen Securitie* (London, 1608). Alexandra Walsham, "Clapham, Henoch (*fl.* 1585–1614)," *ODNB*.

[52] Kenneth Fincham and Nicholas Tyacke, *Altars Restored: The Changing Face of English Religious Worship 1547–c. 1700* (Oxford University Press, 2007), pp. 85–6. Peter McCullough (ed.), *Lancelot Andrewes: Selected Sermons and Lectures* (Oxford University Press, 2005), pp. xix, 141–2. We should note that St. Giles was the parish adjacent to St. Olave, Silver Street, one of Shakespeare's parishes.

Westminster Abbey and St. Paul's. Westminster under the conservative, and anti-Calvinist, Dean Goodman had long maintained a very formal view of ceremony, and had apparently endeavored to keep men of Puritan attitude out of the pulpit. Copes and vestments for the clergy were retained, as was a strong musical tradition, and when Goodman finally died and was succeeded first by Andrewes and then by Richard Neile, it was relatively easy to move from Elizabethan continuities to the beginnings of the new concern for the "beauty of holiness."[53] Attendance at occasions of public ceremonial at the Abbey would have offered a markedly different view of the Protestant Church from that of most London churches. The case of St. Paul's was less obvious: there the equally long tenure of Dean Nowell meant that the cathedral was more in accord with the Puritan ethos of the city, while the canons seem to have felt under siege from the tide of humanity that used the nave as a social exchange.[54] But at the turn of the century, and especially after the arrival of Dean Overall in 1602, ceremonialism increased, and music became significant again. One account in praising the music described the singers and preachers with white surplices "making use of many popish ceremonies, all kneeling down on entering the church and otherwise keeping good order."[55]

When the royal court was at Whitehall it offered another site for the articulation of beliefs that might challenge mainstream consensus. Though the chapel royal was a relatively closed environment designed for the private devotions of the sovereign and the royal entourage, the outdoor preaching place was the focus of the Lent sermon cycle and attracted crowds which Peter McCullough has compared to those attending the Easter theater season at Bankside.[56] Court sermons, both delivered and printed, gave, of course, greater access to commentary on the duties of kings than those delivered in the city; but under James they also allowed pleas for a ceremonialist view of religious behavior. Calvinist preachers remained in favor for the Lenten seasons and godly Protestant prelates such as John King and James Montagu were heard regularly. However, they were balanced from early in the reign by proto-Arminians such as Richard Neile, John Buckeridge, and, of course, Lancelot Andrewes.[57] At court, Andrewes

[53] J. F. Merritt, "The Cradle of Laudianism? Westminster Abbey, 1558–1630," *Journal of Ecclesiastical History*, 52.4 (2001), 625–3; Fincham and Tyacke, *Altars Restored*, pp. 82–3.

[54] David J. Crankshaw, "Community, City and Nation, 1540–1714," in Derek Keene, Arthur Burns, and Andrew Saint (eds.), *St. Paul's: The Cathedral Church of London, 604–2004* (New Haven, CT: Yale University Press, 2004), pp. 52–5.

[55] Ibid., p. 55. [56] McCullough, *Sermons at Court*, p. 134.

[57] Peter Lake, "Lancelot Andrewes, John Buckeridge, and Avant-Garde Conformity at the Court of James I," in Linda Levy Peck (ed.), *The Mental World of the Jacobean Court* (Cambridge University Press, 1991), pp. 113–33.

could use the favor shown him by the monarch along with his general popularity to laud ceremonialism from the pulpit while also assailing Puritans' sermon-centered piety. The bishop swept king and subjects together in his criticism that the present generation of Protestants were "carried away with the common error, that *Sermon-hearing* is the *Consummatum est* of all *Christianitie*."[58]

Though Andrewes and his circle remained the only fully sanctioned voices challenging the Calvinist mainstream during Shakespeare's London years, there were sufficient indicators of an alternative vision for the church to raise the anxieties of the godly and generate cries against these "innovators." As early as 1595 the Court of High Commission had supported a group of parishioners of Christ Church, Newgate, who sought to maintain a choir of singing men, despite the protests of the civic authorities that the parishioners were "infected with some supersticion [and] preferred singing before the preaching of the word of God."[59] The following years saw extensive rebuilding of city churches, a process that cannot automatically be identified with anti-Calvinism, but which took parishes in directions that might challenge rigorous Puritan perceptions of worship.[60] The parishioners of Christ Church repaired their existing stained glass in 1605, and by 1613 the parishioners of St. Stephen, Walbrook had paid for new stained-glass windows, which contained images; and gifts of church plate and such furnishings as Communion tablecloths increased in number. Edmund Howes, the continuator of Stow's *Annals of England*, clearly thought the St. Stephen's example admirable, if somewhat unusual, since he remarked on the fact that the glass had been "made only for that purpose."[61] But the hunt for Laudian antecedents is, as Merritt has argued, surely less significant than the sheer scale of refurbishment. Wainscoting, pewing, pulpit, and gallery building is more likely to represent an affirmation of greater security in the current ecclesiastical climate, an acceptance that London under King James had a confident Protestant identity.

That identity was still challenged most fully by the presence of Catholics, which must have been well known to ordinary citizens: London preachers manifest anxiety about the threat within as well as grand papal conspiracy.

58 Lancelot Andrewes, *XCVI Sermons*, ed. William Laud and John Buckeridge (London, 1629), p. 142.

59 Quoted in Fincham and Tyacke, *Altars Restored*, p. 97.

60 J. F. Merritt, "Puritans, Laudians and the Phenomenon of Church-Building in Jacobean London," *Historical Journal*, 41.4 (1998), 935–60. Fincham and Tyacke, *Altars Restored*, pp. 98–106.

61 Fincham and Tyacke, *Altars Restored*, pp. 102, 105–6. John Stow, *The Annales or Generall Chronicle of England* (London, 1615), p. 892. Anthony Munday's continuation of Stow's *Survey of London* also includes information on churches "repaired and beautified," much of it specifically relevant to the Jacobean period: *The Survey of London ... begunne first by ... John Stow* (London, 1633), pp. 819–86.

Until the 1580s Catholics in the city, as elsewhere, had oscillated between the desire for integration into the parish on their own terms and the demands of separation. The patchy evidence suggests that in a few parishes, like St. John, Clerkenwell, or St. Andrew, Holborn, there was a degree of participation by known Catholics until the mid-Elizabethan years.[62] An aristocrat like the First Viscount Montague, whose London residence was in the Southwark parish of St. Saviour, was minimally conformist until his death in 1592, though it is likely that the synod of 1580, in which the Jesuits first debated with some of the established English Catholic clergy, was held in his residence.[63] But such behavior was becoming wholly problematic in the face of the pressures of the post-Armada years and of the determination of the missioners to challenge the compromises involved in occasional obedience to the state. In these late Elizabethan years the committed recusant community in London depended on occasional meetings with the mission priests, who managed, with difficulty, to provide mass for groups of the faithful. Safe houses were established for these priests, who, even in these adverse circumstances, found it better to operate from the capital than elsewhere. The Jesuit John Gerard's vivid autobiography of his life in London and beyond in the 1590s gives a powerful sense of the struggles involved. He was able to rent or purchase a variety of properties, which were then adapted with concealed hides and secured with the support of devout laymen. Once established he could sometimes, as in the house he shared with the Heywoods, "set up quite a large and well-equipped chapel" and say Mass for significant numbers of the faithful.[64]

Lisa McClain argues that despite the underground nature of London Catholicism, it possessed a flexibility and diversity unparalleled by the faith elsewhere in the kingdom.[65] This is questionable for the 1590s, but more convincing for the Jacobean period. Although the oscillating pattern of persecution by James's regime provided little security for London recusants, there was hope in the changed international environment and in the king's

62 W. J. Sheils, "'Getting On' and 'Getting Along' in Parish and Town: Catholics and their Neighbours in England," in Benjamin Kaplan et al. (eds.), *Catholic Communities in Protestant States: Britain and the Netherlands c. 1570–1720* (Manchester University Press, 2009), pp. 74–5. On the concentration of Catholics in these parishes, with St. Dunstan in the west, St. Giles in the Field, and St. Giles Cripplegate, see John J. LaRocca, *Jacobean Recusant Rolls for Middlesex, Catholic Record Society*, 76 (1997), vii.

63 Michael C. Questier, *Catholicism and Community in Early Modern England: Politics, Aristocratic Patronage and Religion, c. 1550–1640* (Cambridge University Press, 2006), pp. 161–5.

64 *John Gerard: The Autobiography of an Elizabethan*, trans. Philip Caraman (London: Longman, 1951), pp. 140–4, quotation at p. 142.

65 Lisa McClain, *Lest we be damned: Practical Innovation and Lived Experience Among Catholics in Protestant England, 1559–1642* (London: Routledge, 2004), pp. 142ff.

desire to avoid creating martyrs without necessary cause. An important consequence for ordinary Catholics was a greater ability to access a key resource for worship – the foreign embassies. Of course no English citizens were supposed to attend Mass at the Spanish, French, or Venetian embassies, but the fact that some did had been a source of tension since the early 1560s and had become a recurrent conflict between ambassadors and the Privy Council in the years following peace with Spain. Successive Spanish ambassadors refused to close their doors to coreligionists, and those Catholics wishing to hear Mass, especially at the great festivals, became progressively bolder. By 1614 the Easter feast at the embassy was celebrated with processions – "as if I were in Seville" says Gondomar – and the attendance of a large number of Englishmen.[66] That same year the pursuivants seized a number who attended the Palm Sunday Masses, and who had carried off boughs/palms which, in some cases, they passed on to other Londoners.[67] In these same years we have the remarkable mission career of Luisa de Carvajal, who lived as a nun with her companions ministering to English Catholics under the partial protection of the Spanish embassy. At her funeral, a few months before the Palm Sunday arrests, the Spanish accounts talk of English Catholics being publicly in attendance, something which had not been seen for many years.[68] The culmination of this invisible visibility of Catholics came in 1623: at "the fatall vesper" three hundred crammed into the makeshift chapel of the French ambassador's residence in Blackfriars suffered disaster as the floor collapsed and over ninety were killed.[69]

While lay Catholics struggled to maintain identity in a London dominated by Protestant antipopery, the mission clergy saw persecution as opportunity, and used the means at hand to articulate their faith. The most sustained possibility for intervention in a public environment came, as it did for proscribed Protestant radicals, from books and other circulated literature. A flood of devotional writing, most printed abroad, some on the clandestine presses at home, some of it widely circulated in manuscript,

[66] Albert J. Loomie (ed.), *Spain and the Jacobean Catholics*, Record series 64 and 66 (Catholic Record Society, 1973 and 1976), vol. II, pp. 32–3. For other complaints to the Spanish, see vol. I, pp. 150, 172–3, 180, 187.

[67] "Proceedings Against Catholics for Attending Mass at the Spanish Embassy on Palm Sunday, 1613–14," in *Catholic Record Society, Miscellanea VII*, 60 (London, 1911), pp. 122–6.

[68] Glyn Redworth, *The She-Apostle. The Extraordinary Life and Death of Luisa de Carvajal* (Oxford University Press, 2008). The funeral, as described by Spanish sources, is detailed at pp. 223–5.

[69] The vesper generated a large contemporary literature. See Alexandra Walsham, "'The fatall vesper': Providentialism and Anti-Popery in Late Jacobean London," *Past & Present*, 144 (1994), 36–87.

characterized the whole period.[70] Londoners participated in their distribution: in 1617 a cache was discovered in a printer's house in St. Paul's churchyard and duly burned. Illicit presses had to be highly mobile, but several were located around London, taking advantage of the weaker jurisdictional control outside the city.[71] These "domme preachers" allowed ideas, to quote John Wilson in 1616, to "penetrate where the priests and religious cannot enter."[72] Popular works like the poetry of Robert Southwell and Persons's *First Booke of the Christian Exercise* clearly reached wide audiences, conformist as well as recusant. From Campion's brag challenging Protestants to disputation, through Persons's sensational *Conference about the next Succession*, to the polemics against the Jacobean Oath of Allegiance, the Catholic presses were used publicly to intervene in the religious politics of the realm.[73] But the priests did not rely solely on the battle of the books: the stream of executions of the late Elizabethan years, and the slower, still significant, persecution under James, offered powerful possibilities for representing Catholic faith via the gallows, especially in London, the nation's main theater of execution. Lake and Questier have shown how much significance was attached to last dying words, and the ability of the condemned of all conditions to utter them. Central to Catholic performance in these cases was the constant affirmation that the martyrs died only for their faith, though they frequently sought to disrupt the drama of state punishment by deliberate movement from meek acceptance of political claims upon them to active defiance on religion. The crowd had rich opportunity to witness these critical events, though it was difficult to sway this theater in favor of Catholic belief given the strength of popular London antipopery. And always, whether at the gallows or in the literary rehearsal of constancy and suffering, there was the electric possibility of conversion. Even Joseph Hall, acting as Protestant propagandist, could not deny the bravery with which Henry Garnet met his end after the Gunpowder Plot, despite the falseness of the latter's cause.[74]

70 Anthony F. Allison and D. M. Rogers (eds.), *The Contemporary Printed Literature of the English Counter-Reformation between 1558 and 1640*, 2 vols. (Aldershot: Scolar Press, 1989 and 1994). On manuscript and oral circulation, see Alison Shell, *Oral Culture and Catholicism in Early Modern England* (Cambridge University Press, 2007).

71 McClain, *Lest we be damned*, pp. 158–9. Hackney and Islington were particularly useful centers of activity for both Catholics and Separatists: Sheils, "'Getting On,'" pp. 75–6.

72 Alexandra Walsham, "'Domme Preachers'? Post-Reformation English Catholicism and the Culture of Print," *Past & Present*, 168 (2000), 72–123. *Calendar of State Papers and Manuscripts in the Archives and Collections of Milan: 1385–1618* (London: H.M. Stationery Office, 1912), p. 654.

73 Peter Lake and Michael Questier, "Puritans, Papists and the 'Public Sphere' in Early Modern England: The Edmund Campion Affair in Context," *Journal of Modern History*, 72 (2000), 587–627. Campion's brag was printed as *Rationes decem* (1581) from a secret press at Stonor.

74 Lake and Questier, *Anti-Christ's Lewd Hat*, pp. 243–7.

Though books and gallows witness offered the most significant public face of Catholicism in Protestant London, contemporaries and historians have often been tempted to stress a third environment. This chapter began with the parish and the pew, thus it is fitting it should end with the prison. London's jails offered one of the few opportunities for dissenters of all types to gather a congregation in the heart of the city, rather than flee to the suburbs or the protection of the private household. There is some danger of over-crediting the statements of contemporaries, especially the priests, that prisons were successful venues for clandestine Masses: for Persons they were "excellent communication centres," for some even the site of true Catholicism.[75] "Captivity," wrote Southwell, "is our principal freedom," using of course a martyrological trope.[76] Historians are wise to preface accounts of London jails with a reminder that there was extreme suffering and restriction for many prisoners. But there is plenty of evidence from hostile pursuivants and Privy Council material as well as Catholic sources that Masses were being held, missions planned, and responses to opponents debated from apparently strict confinement. Garnet boasted that he was able to say Mass for all the Catholic prisoners in the Clink in the 1590s, and in February 1600 John Chamberlain reported a crowd of "three or four score" who were seized at the Marshalsea listening to a Capuchin preach. Luisa de Carvajal actually gained access to Newgate to visit two condemned priests on the night before their execution.[77] By the mid Jacobean years a hostile witness complained that Newgate seemed "rather a chapel for superstitious service than a prison."[78] And London's other underground faiths had some of the same flexibility. Brownists and Barrowists were able to comfort their followers from prison, and, when a messenger was sent to Newgate to fetch the radical Bartholemew Legate to audience with King James, he was missing having been allowed to wander freely into the London streets![79] Prisons continued to function, as they had done since the earliest days of the Reformation, as theaters for challenge, debate, and attempts at conversion. Both Catholic missionaries and Puritan clergy

[75] For example, McClain, *Lest we be damned*, pp. 65, 144–5, tends to take a very optimistic view of the strength of Catholic life within the prisons. Lake and Questier are also positive about the possibilities of the prisons as "ideological nerve centres," but they are more properly critical about the nature of the sources: *Anti-Christ's Lewd Hat*, pp. 188–207.

[76] Robert Southwell, *An Epistle of Comfort* (Paris, 1587–8), pp. 129, 126, 128.

[77] *Gerard: Autobiography*, pp. 78–9; Redworth, *She-Apostle*, pp. 194–5.

[78] This was a comment made during proceedings against the keeper of Newgate in Star Chamber, cited in E. D. Pendry, *Elizabethan Prisons and Prison Scenes*, 2 vols. (Institut für Englische Sprache und Literatur: University of Salzburg, 1974), vol. 1, p. 129.

[79] Pendry, *Elizabethan Prisons*, vol. 1, p. 128.

strove to counsel notorious felons, the former rejoicing particularly when a last-minute convert declared his Catholic faith on the scaffold.[80]

By now we have moved a considerable distance away from the vision of London as a city largely dominated by godly preachers, who watched over an essentially conformist laity in a well-organized parochial structure. Robert Persons's four religions, and more, could all be apprehended by listening, reading, and responding to the cacophony of the city. However, we should not always be persuaded by the voices of criticism and opposition, or by the laments of the preachers over the backsliding, atheism, and heresy of Londoners. Conformity could indeed be found there, even in the environment of the prison. Garnet had to rattle his chains in the Clink to drown out Geneva psalms.[81] And Richard Stonley, imprisoned in the Fleet in 1597 for debts to the crown, there became a more assiduous follower of sermons than he had ever been back in his home parish, carefully noting the preacher in chapel almost every Sunday. On one occasion, he reported that a "Mr Hutchinson" (most likely William Hutchinson) had been unjustly forbidden to preach by the prison warden, merely "For blamying vice," that stock-in-trade jeremiad of the London preacher.[82] Stonley was appalled at the warden's attempt to silence such a necessary and healthful castigation of sinfulness, and in a prison of all places; Shakespeare, for his part, would surely have been amused.

The loss of Stonley's diaries for much of the early 1590s means that we cannot be certain if he himself was ever a playgoer, but many men of his kind must have witnessed performances on the public stage. The citizens and artisans who, Andrew Gurr argues, were "the silent majority" in audiences, came from the parishes of London and from a regular diet of sermons both there and at Paul's Cross.[83] They were equipped to respond to the latest religious propaganda: the attacks on the authors of the Marprelate Tracts in the early 1590s, for example, or the "Elect Nation" plays of Rowley, Dekker, Webster, and Heywood staged by Henslowe in the first years of James's reign.[84] If the London preachers were even partially successful, an audience would have contained many who could

80 Michael C. Questier, *Conversion, Politics and Religion in England, 1580–1625* (Cambridge University Press, 1996), pp. 193–8.

81 *Gerard: Autobiography*, p. 77.

82 William Hutchinson was a prebendary of St. Paul's and one of those who took an active part in the conferences in the Fleet with Greenwood and Barrow in 1590. Folger Shakespeare Library, V.a.461: Hutchinson entry at fo. 62v.

83 Andrew Gurr, *Playgoing in Shakespeare's London* (Cambridge University Press, 1987), pp. 60–4.

84 Ibid., p. 142; J. D. Spikes, "The Jacobean History Play and the Myth of the Elect Nation," *Renaissance Drama*, n.s. 8 (1977), 117–49.

comprehend the main elements in Protestant ideology. Even for the less zealous, reared as they had been in the culture of the Elizabethan Settlement, the Bible and the Psalter were highly familiar territory. Congregations were constant auditors of the Protestant liturgy through the Prayer Book services. And finally, diversity of religious belief and practice, overt or clandestine, was, as we have seen, the subject of common knowledge in London.

Shakespeare refused to stage those forms of Protestant propaganda to which his fellow Londoners were routinely exposed.[85] The idea of God's providential judgment on the elect nation influenced his writing only when it was an integral part of the historical narrative. In *King John*, for instance, at the first appearance of the Legate Pandolph, John conjures the full rhetoric of Henrician authority – "we, under God, are supreme head" – while denouncing the Pope as "this meddling priest," with a reference to the sale of indulgences thrown in for good measure (3.1.81, 89, 90–3).[86] In *Henry VIII*, Archbishop Cranmer prophesies the triumph of Elizabeth and ultimately of James; yet it is a triumph cast as much in terms of secular as spiritual providentialism. The baby brought to Cranmer for baptism shall be "A pattern to all princes living with her"; his "honour and the greatness of his name / Shall be, and make new nations" (5.4.22, 51–2). Anti-Puritan propaganda was another matter, though Shakespeare's seems more concerned with the godly's hostility to the theater than with making a deeper ideological attack per se. Puritans were mocked in this way in *Twelfth Night*, where incidentally Shakespeare expected his audience to know who the radical sectaries were – Andrew Aguecheek in *Twelfth Night* claims he would "as leif be a Brownist as a politician" (3.2.26).[87]

But the limited appearance in his plays of representations of current religious politics in no sense indicates that Shakespeare's work was disengaged from the language of belief. On the contrary, his plays are steeped in biblical references, from both the Geneva and Bishops' Bibles.[88] For example, in the preparation for the duel at the end of *Hamlet*, Horatio comments to his friend that "I knew you must be edified by the margin ere you had

85 On Shakespeare's unusual reluctance to take a firm religious stand in his plays in an age of widespread "confessionalization," see Chapter 2 above.

86 All citations from Shakespeare's plays are to *The Norton Shakespeare*, 2nd edn., ed. Stephen Greenblatt et al. (New York: W. W. Norton, 2008). Line numbers are cited in the text.

87 For more on Shakespeare's particular style of anti-Puritan critique in plays like *Twelfth Night*, see Chapter 1 above.

88 Naseeb Shaheen, *Biblical References in Shakespeare's Plays* (Newark, DE: University of Delaware Press, 1999). Shaheen concludes that Shakespeare must have had access to both texts, and not simply heard the scriptural passages read as part of the liturgy, given the breadth of his referencing (pp. 54–8).

done" (5.2.114.1–2), a clear reference to the Geneva Bible's claim that readers must be edified by the marginal commentaries on the text. *Measure for Measure*, *Henry IV*, and *Hamlet* are all rich in explicit biblical allusion, which would have helped intensify a contemporary audience's appreciation for the spiritual struggles of Hamlet as well as the hypocrisy of characters like Angelo and Falstaff. In a work like *Hamlet*, moreover, Shakespeare's intertextual use of Scripture goes beyond mere individual allusions and actually tries to make serious demands on the doctrinal understanding of its audience. *Hamlet* confronts the old Catholic world, represented by the Ghost who claims to be in Purgatory, with a prince trained in Wittenberg, where he apparently absorbed the Protestant theology of both Luther and Calvin. In Hamlet's eyes, therefore, men are inherently depraved, the elect saved only by God's decree. His famous reference to the "special providence in the fall of a sparrow" (5.2.157–8) echoes closely a passage from Calvin's *Institutes*.[89] Hamlet's paralysis of will in the face of the demands of his dead father can be read as Protestant uncertainty about the existence of Purgatory, and his later self-destruction as the consequence of his familial conflicts. The later confirmation of the Ghost's truth-telling, especially the fact that he had died "unhouseled," or denied his last rites, can also be read as a way of justifying the staging of Catholic belief in the cockpit of Protestant England. As David Bevington stresses in Chapter 1 above, *Hamlet*'s audience is offered alternative interpretations of the Prince's fall: on the one hand, that of the protagonist himself, who by Act 5 comes to view his own drama and that of the world around him largely in terms of Protestant providentialism; on the other, that of Horatio, whose perspective remains essentially secular, political, and humanist.[90]

A different way of looking at the tragedy of Hamlet's madness is to locate the play, as Stephen Greenblatt does, in a world of "maimed rites."[91] The unhouseled Ghost cannot be properly buried; Ophelia is brought to the ground without ceremony; Hamlet jokes blasphemously about the eating of Polonius's corpse. The common experience of the liturgy, especially its patterning of the rites of passage, was meant to provide a form of spiritual stability to Elizabeth's subjects. Shakespeare shows how this might be so in

89 Based originally on Matthew 10:29, Calvin's passage reads: "by susteynyng, cherishing & caring for, with singular providence every one of those thinges that he hath created even to ye least sparow." *The institution of Christian religion*, trans. Thomas Norton (London, 1561), 1.xvi.1.

90 See Chapter 1 above.

91 Stephen Greenblatt, *Will in the World: How Shakespeare Became Shakespeare* (New York: W. W. Norton, 2004), pp. 320–1. The phrase is David Bevington's, from *Action is Eloquence: Shakespeare's Language of Gesture* (Cambridge, MA: Harvard University Press, 1984), p. 174.

several of his comedies, where ceremony, though frequently the subject of witty mockery, is just as frequently affirmed and valorized. In *As You Like It*, for instance, the rite of marriage is first entered into playfully with Rosalind's binding of Orlando, then affirmed more seriously with the fulfilled promises at the end of the play. Similarly, in *Romeo and Juliet*, Friar Laurence presides over a rite of marriage that the Book of Common Prayer insisted upon as the essential part of true union.[92] Yet the regular enforced hearing of Cranmer's words did not necessarily breed widespread religious harmony in late sixteenth-century London: to the godly, the Book of Common Prayer was "the Mass book full of abominations," while to others it was an uncertain and sometimes inconsistent guide to forms of Christian living and dying.[93] Many might have wished to reject it, but few could avoid assimilating its rhetorical structures. Shakespeare surely took from the pew both Cranmer's words and their uncertain ideological shape, using them to fashion superb drama of human alienation and redemption.

[92] Daniel Swift, *Shakespeare's Common Prayers: The Book of Common Prayer and the Elizabethan Age* (Oxford University Press, 2012), pp. 67–96.

[93] Walter Howard Frere and Charles Edward Douglas (eds.), *Puritan Manifestoes: A Study of the Origin of the Puritan Revolt* (London: SPCK, 1954), p. 21. It is not clear how far the Prayer Book served the spiritual needs of conformists in the late sixteenth century. Two interesting attempts to do so are Judith D. Maltby, *Prayer Book and People in Elizabethan and Early Stuart England* (Cambridge University Press, 1998), and Ramie Targoff, *Common Prayer: The Language of Public Devotion in Early Modern England* (University of Chicago Press, 2001).

PART II

# *Representing religious beliefs and diversity in the plays*

CHAPTER 4

# *Delusion in* A Midsummer Night's Dream

*Alison Shell*

Endings are never completely happy in Shakespeare's comedies. Even *A Midsummer Night's Dream*, Shakespeare's sweetest confection, is soured by the fact that one of the lovers, Demetrius, remains under a spell at the close of the play.[1] Demetrius, whose desertion of Helena for Hermia precipitates the play's misadventures, has his former love magically restored when Oberon anoints his eyes with flower-juice, a spell which, unlike the similar one cast on Lysander, is never reversed. Explaining to Theseus how the case is altered, Demetrius declares:

> But, my good lord, I wot not by what power
> (But by some power it is) my love to Hermia,
> Melted as the snow, seems to me now
> As the remembrance of an idle gaud
> Which in my childhood I did dote upon;
> And all the faith, the virtue of my heart,
> The object and the pleasure of mine eye,
> Is only Helena. To her, my lord,
> Was I betrothed ere I saw Hermia;
> But like a sickness did I loathe this food.
> But, as in health come to my natural taste,
> Now I do wish it, love it, long for it,
> And will for evermore be true to it. (4.1.161–73)[2]

The fairies mean well by their intervention, and no one is happier than Demetrius at the result, yet given that what he sees as his "natural taste" is

I would like to thank Arnold Hunt, Chris Laoutaris, and Kate Maltby for their help with this chapter, and the audiences at University College London and the Shakespeare Institute, Stratford-upon-Avon, where a preliminary version of it was delivered.

[1] Cf. David Bevington, "'But we are spirits of another sort': The Dark Side of Love and Magic in *A Midsummer Night's Dream*," in Richard Dutton (ed.), *A Midsummer Night's Dream* (New York: St. Martin's Press, 1996), pp. 24–35.

[2] From R. A. Foakes (ed.), *A Midsummer Night's Dream*, rev. edn. (Cambridge University Press, 2003). All quotations are from this edition unless otherwise stated.

the result of enchantment, his remarks are also disturbingly ironic. The question of why Shakespeare chose to end the play in such a troubling manner has often been posed. To answer it more fully than hitherto, this chapter discusses a legend associated with Helena's namesake, Helen of Troy, and the ancient Greek lyric poet Stesichorus. Woven into the web of classical allusion within *A Midsummer Night's Dream*, this story also has a direct relevance to contemporary religious concerns about idolatrous perception, and echoes the play's wider, Reformation-inflected anxieties about misdirection and delusion.

## Hermia, Helena, and Stesichorus

The names of the female lovers in *A Midsummer Night's Dream* have received a good deal of critical attention. Commentators have particularly remarked upon the fact that Shakespeare picked the name "Helena" for a female character who is defined in large part by her seeming *un*desirability: after all, inside and outside Renaissance drama, the name more naturally suggests Helen of Troy's irresistible charisma.[3] Reasons for the pairing of "Hermia" and "Helena" have also been sought, one suggestion being that the name "Hermia" is a variation of "Hermione," the name of Helen of Troy's daughter. Peter Holland, for instance, points to a line from Ovid's *Ars Amatoria*, "scilicet Hermionen Helenae praeponere posses" ("Would you be able to prefer Hermione to Helena?" [2.699]) and suggests that Lysander's line, "Not Hermia, but Helena I love" (2.2.119), can be read as an answer to it.[4] While this reading is an attractive one, it has limitations taken on its own, particularly given the fact that mother–daughter relationships have no part in Shakespeare's play.[5]

A supplementary explanation for the names being paired, which also helps us to understand why a character called Helena should be portrayed as undesirable, can be found in the contemporary footnotes to Edmund Spenser's series of pastoral poems, *The Shepheardes Calender*, one of which tells the story of Stesichorus, a poet operating in Greece around the sixth century BC, and his supposed preference for one "Himera" over Helen of Troy. The two shepherds speaking the eclogue for the month of April refer to a third shepherd, Colin, and his praise of the fair Rosalind.

[3] Peter Holland remarks in his edition of the play (Oxford University Press, 1994) that Helena's name "suggests most strongly Helen of Troy, whose beauty this Helena does not have" (p. 143).

[4] Ibid., p. 61.

[5] Shakespeare was to use the name "Hermione" later in his career in *The Winter's Tale*, again with no apparent reference to Helen's daughter.

Commenting on this praise, "E. K.," the author of the footnotes, remarks that Rosalind deserves it

> no less than . . . Himera, the worthy poet Stesichorus his idol, upon whom he is said so much to have doted that, in regard of her excellency, he scorned and wrote against the beauty of Helena. For which his presumptuous and unheedy hardiness [audacity] he is said by vengeance of the gods (thereat being offended) to have lost both his eyes.

The sequel to this episode, which E. K.'s footnote does not relate, is that Stesichorus composed a poetic apology to Helen and subsequently had his sight restored by the gods.[6]

The idea that Stesichorus was in love with another woman named Himera is a mistake, one that may have originated with the notoriously unreliable E. K. himself.[7] In truth, Himera is not a woman but a town in Sicily, which, on account of being Stesichorus's birthplace, was often mentioned in connection with him.[8] The town's name can also be read as a pun on the Greek word *ἵμερος* meaning "desire" or "yearning."[9] E. K.'s mistake may show outside interference from another common classical exemplar: it is a short step from "Himera" to "Hermia," and "Hermia" was thought in the Renaissance to be the name of a prostitute whom Aristotle loved. Though now known to be a ghost character arising from a misreading of the classical sources, Aristotle's Hermia was quite real for early modern commentators and would have made a plausible counterpart to Helena, not least because both women had the reputation of being unchaste.[10] A distant memory of this story might well have led E. K. to metamorphose the town of "Himera" into Stesichorus's female "idol." While Shakespeare could have followed the same train of thought

[6] All quotations of *The Shepheardes Calender* are from Douglas Brooks-Davies (ed.), *Edmund Spenser: Selected Shorter Poems* (London: Longman, 1995). For the story of Stesichorus' restored eyesight, see Norman Austin, *Helen of Troy and her Shameless Phantom* (Ithaca, NY: Cornell University Press, 2008), ch. 4.

[7] See Brooks-Davies, *Spenser*, p. 73.

[8] E.g., Aristotle's *Art of Rhetoric*, ed. John Henry Freese (Cambridge, MA: Harvard University Press, 1926; reprinted 2000), 2.20.5, which describes Stesichorus' address to the people of Himera.

[9] Plato calls Stesichorus' birthplace "The Town of Desire" in *Phaedrus*. See Henry George Liddell and Robert Scott, *A Greek–English Lexicon* (Oxford: Clarendon Press, 1966), s.v. "ἵμερος."

[10] See Robert Greene, *Gwydonius* (London, 1584), sig. 78r, and Thomas Nashe, who refers to "Aristotle that sacrificed to his harlot Hermia" in *Have With You to Saffron-Walden*, in Ronald B. McKerrow (ed.), *The Works of Thomas Nashe*, 5 vols. (Oxford: Blackwell, 1958), vol. III, p. 111; see also vol. IV, p. 357 for the possible origin of this "mythical meretrix." Though the mistake has an ironic appropriateness to the topic of this chapter, there is probably no reason to suppose that it was intentional on Shakespeare's part. J. J. M. Tobin has argued that the heroines' names in *AMND* are ironic references to famous prostitutes: "The Irony of 'Hermia,'" *American Notes & Queries*, 17 (1989), 154.

independently, it has been argued before that *The Shepheardes Calender* is an important source for *A Midsummer Night's Dream*; and if Shakespeare read E. K.'s footnote, it could have led him firstly to connect the heroines' two names, and then link these names with the tale of Stesichorus.[11]

The fact that Stesichorus first criticized Helen but then came round to her gives us a classical precedent for what happens to Demetrius in the course of Shakespeare's drama: first speaking against Helena, he ends up becoming her advocate once his perceptions have been magically altered. This is all the more appropriate since, because of Stesichorus's poetic apology to Helen, he is best known in literary history as the originator of the palinode, a literary genre signifying conversion and repentance.[12] For instance, the *Proverbs* of Macarius (*c.* 300–91) state that "Stesichorus sings a palinode: used of those who change their minds for the better."[13] Plato's dialogue *Phaedrus* gives perhaps the most authoritative commentary on the legend, purporting to preserve Stesichorus's actual palinode, which reads, as if to Helen: "This tale I told is false. There is no doubt: / You made no journey in the well-decked ships / Nor voyaged to the citadel of Troy."[14] In the accounts with which the twenty-first-century reader is most familiar, Helen is well known as the begetter of the Trojan War; but the apology recorded by Plato taps into an alternative mythological tradition in which she never went to Troy, instead remaining in Egypt while a phantom or *eidolon* in the shape of Helen journeyed on to Troy.[15] In some accounts this was an illusion created by Zeus, in others by the shape-changing sea-god Proteus, in others still by Hera. Among ancient writers, Euripides developed this alternative version of the story in his tragedy *Helen*.[16] And it was also a

[11] On the play's links with *The Shepheardes Calender*, see Harold F. Brooks (ed.), *A Midsummer Night's Dream*, Arden Shakespeare, 2nd series (London: Routledge, 1988), p. lxxvi. Some of Brooks's arguments are more compelling than others, but his footnote to 3.2.388 does identify a striking parallel between the two texts.

[12] See Patricia Phillippy, *Love's Remedies: Recantation and Renaissance Lyric Poetry* (Lewisburg, PN: Bucknell University Press, 1995); and my chapter "William Alabaster and the Palinode," in Lowell Gallagher (ed.), *Redrawing the Map of Early Modern English Catholicism* (University of Toronto Press, 2012). On the relationship between conversion and formalist concerns, see Molly Murray, *The Poetics of Conversion in Early Modern English Literature* (Cambridge University Press, 2009).

[13] Macarius, *Proverbs*, 2.210, quoted in J. M. Edmonds (ed.), *Lyra Graeca*, vol. II, Loeb Classical Library (London: William Heinemann, 1924), pp. 30–1.

[14] Plato, *Phaedrus*, ed. Christopher Rowe (Harmondsworth: Penguin, 2005), p. 22.

[15] On the related notion of the automaton, see Wendy Beth Hyman (ed.), *The Automaton in English Renaissance Literature* (Farnham: Ashgate, 2011).

[16] *Helen*, lines 31–48, in Euripides, *Helen. Phoenician Women. Orestes*, trans. and ed. David Kovacs (Cambridge, MA: Harvard University Press, 2002). In this version, Hera creates an eidolon of Helen for Paris, out of jealousy at not having been judged more beautiful than her, while Hermes and Zeus

familiar anecdote in Shakespeare's England.[17] George Puttenham, for instance, writing about the loss of reputation as an appropriate subject for poetic lament, describes how "if it [reputation] be unjustly taken away, as by untrue and famous libels, the offender's recantation may suffice for his amends: so did the poet Stesichorus, as it is written of him, in his *Palinode* upon the dispraise of Helen, and recovered his eyesight."[18]

As this suggests, the term "palinode" was common within Renaissance literary theory; but it is less familiar nowadays, and where it is used it tends to refer to poetry rather than plays. So how helpful is it to import this term into the discussion of an early modern play? Turns of circumstance are basic to plots of all kinds; drama would not exist without the idea of *peripeteia*, or reversal. And even if something more is needed for a palinode – an element of repentance, of changing one's mind, of unsaying – that still leaves the field unhelpfully wide: most of Shakespeare's plays yield elements that might fall into this category. Nevertheless, Shakespeare's use of names in *A Midsummer Night's Dream* does suggest that he intended to make a sharp, specific use of Stesichorus's story and the commentary it generated; and this decision would have been an appropriate one for a play so clearly engaged with the issue of perception. The play's comic misadventures are precipitated when Oberon takes offense at Demetrius's failure to appreciate Helena properly and orders Puck to apply love-juice to the young man's eyes. When this happens, Demetrius is blinded in the sense that he loses touch with his former perceptions; yet in another sense the love-juice causes his sight to be restored, in that he regains his initial desire for Helena.[19]

transport the real Helen to the palace of the King of Egypt, near Proteus' tomb. For a recent partial demolition of the story, see Matthew Wright, *Euripides' Escape-Tragedies: A Story of Helen, Andromeda and Iphigenia among the Taurians* (Oxford University Press, 2002), pp. 87–109.

17 Among the numerous references to the story on Early English Books Online (EEBO), see Robert Abbott's *Wits Theater of the Little World* (1599), p. 76, a work that dates from near the time of Shakespeare's play.

18 George Puttenham, *The Art of English Poesy*, ed. Frank Whigham and Wayne A. Rebhorn (Ithaca, NY: Cornell University Press, 2007), p. 136. A typical early modern definition of the palinode can be found in Thomas Blount's *Glossographia* (1661): "a recantation, a contrary song, an unsaying that one hath spoken or written, the sound of the retreat" (sig. Ff2r). The word was also used to mean "repetition" or "refrain": see *OED*'s etymology for "palinode, n.," and also Richard Leighton Greene (ed.), *The Early English Carols* (Oxford: Clarendon Press, 1977), p. xxxii. See also the definitions of *palinodia* in Charlton T. Lewis and Charles Short, *A Latin Dictionary* (Oxford: Clarendon Press, 1879), and of πᾰλῐνῳδέω and πᾰλῐνῳδία in Liddell and Scott, *Greek–English Lexicon*.

19 See Laurie Maguire, *Studying Shakespeare* (Oxford: Blackwell, 2004), p. 63: "Demetrius vows to love Helena not because of an external event (the application of juice from the pansy) but because of an internal event: the reordering of his vision, a change in perception, *pensée*."

Demetrius's retraction, which this chapter began by quoting, is a full-scale palinodic reversal and, in the opinion of the other characters listening to it, comes across as almost incredible. The exchange between Hermia and Helena is particularly suggestive. Hermia says in wonder, "Methinks I see these things with parted eye, / Where everything seems double," to which Helena replies, "So methinks; / And I have found Demetrius, like a jewel, / Mine own, and not mine own" (4.1.186–9). It is the last thing Helena says in the play, leaving us with the impression not only that she cannot believe her good luck, but that she fears being dispossessed of her beloved at any moment. One can detect a note of unhappiness in this provisionality: another way of reminding us that Demetrius is still under the enchantment of the flower-juice.

## Eidola and the conversion experience

Unlike Stesichorus, Demetrius both does and does not regain his former perceptions after having had his sight supernaturally tampered with. This leads to the question of whether, in an exaggeration of Stesichorus's tale, Demetrius actually ends up loving an eidolon, an imaginative phantom going under the name of Helen.[20] If so, the event would not be without precedent in Renaissance drama. The most famous example, of course, is the phantom Helen of Troy in Marlowe's *Dr. Faustus*, to whom Faustus addresses the famous rhetorical question: "Was this the face that launched a thousand ships / And burnt the topless towers of Ilium?"[21] The answer is both yes and no: Faustus is indeed looking at the *face* that launched a thousand ships, but – for better-informed audience members at least – it would have been open to question whether that face was Helen's own or that of a phantom look-alike. In any case, to complicate the matter further, Faustus does not experience the actual Helen here, but rather a diabolically induced illusion. While no one's soul is under threat in *A Midsummer Night's Dream*, the notion of Helen as eidolon is still hauntingly present: not because Helena herself is unreal, but because Demetrius's perception of her has been magically altered.[22] Hence, as this chapter began by remarking, his

[20] In *Helen of Troy: From Homer to Hollywood* (Oxford: Blackwell, 2009), Laurie Maguire discusses how Helen's beauty is defined by its effect on others.

[21] Christopher Marlowe, *Doctor Faustus*, 5.1.90–1 (A-Text), quoted from David Bevington and Eric Rasmussen (eds.), *Doctor Faustus and Other Plays* (Oxford University Press, 1995).

[22] On doubling in the play, see David Marshall, "Exchanging Visions: Reading *A Midsummer Night's Dream*," *ELH*, 49 (1982), 543–75.

union with Helena begs troubling questions – even though he publicly recants his former cruelty to her in an orthodox palinodic vein, and even though the public consequences of the match are everything one could hope for in a comedy.

Meditating the change from one love-object to another in tones of quasi-religious portentousness is a staple of love poetry and comic drama. We see it in *A Midsummer Night's Dream*, for instance, when Lysander wakes up after Puck's attentions, sees Helena, falls instantly in love with her, and cruelly repudiates his former beloved, Hermia:

> For, as a surfeit of the sweetest things
> The deepest loathing to the stomach brings,
> Or as the heresies that men do leave
> Are hated most of those they did deceive,
> So thou, my surfeit and my heresy,
> Of all be hated, but the most of me! (2.2.143–8)

Many Renaissance poems, poetic sequences, and poetic careers chart a movement away from love and towards religion, another source of the common imaginative slippage between the two. All this made the notion of conversion both a comic and a gravely serious matter in early modern England, while the notion of the palinode, of turning and apologizing for previous detractions, has considerable relevance to religious conversion at any date. Nothing is more important within the Christian agenda than the conversion from unregeneracy to repentance, and in the years of the Reformation no subject was more high-profile than that of conversion between religious denominations. So within the context both of amorous and of religious discourse, the idea of changing an object of desire by anointing someone's eyes with flower-juice is bound to suggest a facetiously deterministic notion of conversion. After all, at the time Shakespeare was writing his comedy, the English Church's prevailing Calvinist theology held that divine grace was entirely within God's gift and that humans were powerless to do anything to warrant it or seek it out. *A Midsummer Night's Dream* could, then, possibly be read as parodying this view if one were to interpret Oberon as God – an indictment, perhaps, of the switch-backs of the Tudor regime, or a commentary on the debate between advocates of predestination and free will – but there are several problems with reading the play as this kind of systematic, coded commentary on the English Reformation.

To illustrate why, it will be helpful to glance again at the poetry of Spenser, not *The Shepheardes Calender* this time but *The Faerie Queene*, a work chronologically close to Shakespeare's play.[23] Both the epic and the comedy ask questions about being and seeming; both use the faery world as a crucible in which perceptions can be tested and problematized. But in Spenser's work, false perception is insistently related back to the deceptions of popery. When, for instance, readers are introduced to Archimago in his religious guise, they are told: "Sober he seemde, and very sagely sad, / . . . / Simple in shew, and voide of malice bad, / . . . / And often knockt his brest, as one that did repent" (I.i.29, ll. 5–9).[24] Nudgingly conditional – "seemde," "in shew," "as one that did" – these lines are a famous Spenserian caveat, cautioning against first impressions. Archimago, as a director of spirits, is in some ways analogous to Oberon, and references to Catholic practice cluster round both: of Archimago, Spenser relates that "He told of Saintes and Popes, and euermore / He strowd an *Aue-Mary* after and before" (I.i.35, ll. 8–9), and Oberon's order to asperge the bridal chambers, discussed later in this chapter, also contains strong Catholic overtones. But Archimago, unlike Oberon, is malevolent, and his characterization leaves one in no doubt that magic, delusion, hypocrisy, and Catholicism are all closely and negatively interrelated in Spenser's world.[25] This Spenserian example allows us to see what Shakespeare is *not* doing in *A Midsummer Night's Dream*: not only does he not flourish his Reformation credentials, but his designs on the reader are not those of an allegorist, even one as subtle as Spenser. *A Midsummer Night's Dream* is more plausibly read as an ironic comment on the comic consequences of thinking one has changed one's mind oneself, when in fact it has been changed *for* one: an attitude that displays Shakespeare's prevailing skepticism and could be applied to a wide variety of cases, religious and secular.[26]

However, the notion of eidola remains wide open to religio-polemical application. In the context of the English Reformation, the term is bound to recall both the accusations of idolatry that the first reformers leveled at Catholics, as well as the broader way in which fears of idolatry could give a

[23] Edmund Spenser, *The Faerie Queene*, ed. A. C. Hamilton, 2nd edn. (London: Longman, 2007). Books I–III were first published in 1590, books IV–VI in 1596. *A Midsummer Night's Dream* has generally been dated to 1595–6: see Foakes, p. 4. A. Kent Hieatt believes there is good evidence that Shakespeare read books I–III of *FQ*: see his essay on Shakespeare in *The Spenser Encyclopedia*, gen. ed. A. C. Hamilton (University of Toronto Press, 1997), p. 641.

[24] All quotations are taken from *The Faerie Queene*, ed. Hamilton.

[25] On Spenser's anti-Catholicism, see especially Anthea Hume, *Edmund Spenser: Protestant Poet* (Cambridge University Press, 1984), and John N. King, *Spenser's Poetry and the Reformation Tradition* (Princeton University Press, 1990).

[26] On Shakespeare and skepticism, see John D. Cox, *Seeming Knowledge: Shakespeare and Skeptical Faith* (Waco, TX: Baylor University Press, 2007).

polemical charge to all instances of misdirected adoration.[27] It was common enough, for instance, to compare the excesses of sexual desire to idolatry, as we see from Lysander's description of Helena's lovesickness at the beginning of *A Midsummer Night's Dream*:

> Demetrius, I'll avouch it to his head,
> Made love to Nedar's daughter, Helena,
> And won her soul; and she, sweet lady, dotes,
> Devoutly dotes, dotes in idolatry,
> Upon this spotted and inconstant man. (1.1.106–10)

If Demetrius ends the play in love with a magically induced perception of Helen, an eidolon instead of the real thing, this could be seen as little different from Helen's extravagant, but unaided, devotion. Both invite accusations of misdirected worship that have a moral and religious inflection as well as an amatory one.

Helena herself, earlier in the play, shows she is well aware that her love of Demetrius goes to sinful extremes: "And as he errs, doting on Hermia's eyes, / So I, admiring of his qualities. / Things base and vile, holding no quantity, / Love can transpose to form and dignity" (1.1.230–3). Preachers and moralists of the time did indeed counsel against lovers making idols out of one another: Thomas Adams, for instance, wrote that "Some make their wife a goddesse, dote upon her with the extremest Idolatry: a faire coloured peece of clay hath more worship then the Lord of heauen."[28] In an age so acutely aware of misdirected worship and its perils, the play's stress on the relativity of desire, the notion that an idol can be anything one makes it, is a deeply unsettling one. Looked at in this way, Helena is confirmed in sin by the happy ending, while Demetrius is plunged into idolatry by the action of the spell: one recalls his exclamation on first seeing Helena after having his sight altered, "O Helen, goddess, nymph, perfect, divine!" (3.2.137). The doubt about whether he loves an eidolon of Helen or the real Helen confuses matters still further. Thus, although this is plainly a drama whose plot depends on Demetrius's turning back to Helena and

[27] On Reformation notions of idolatry and iconoclasm, see esp. Margaret Aston, *England's Iconoclasts*, vol. I, *Laws Against Images* (Oxford University Press, 1988); Michael O'Connell, *The Idolatrous Eye: Iconoclasm and Theater in Early-Modern England* (Oxford University Press, 2000); Ann Kibbey, *The Interpretation of Material Shapes in Puritanism* (Cambridge University Press, 1986). On Catholic lexis in late Elizabethan love poetry, see Helen Hackett, *Virgin Mother, Maiden Queen* (Basingstoke: Palgrave Macmillan, 1995), p. 151, and her "The Art of Blasphemy? Interfusions of the Erotic and the Sacred in the Poetry of Donne, Barnes and Constable," *Renaissance and Reformation*, 28 (2004), 27–51, esp. 42.

[28] Thomas Adams, *The Happines of the Church* (London, 1619), p. 30.

apologizing, Shakespeare is doing a good deal more with the palinode than that, deploying the notion of eidola in a way that teasingly alludes to contemporary Protestant concerns about misdirected worship.[29]

## Faery delusions

Palinodes often crop up in the context of religious conversion and apostasy. At the time Shakespeare was writing, it was a technical term for texts associated with recantation or disavowal.[30] The word could denote apology, but also describe the kind of retrograde step that, so far from denoting repentance, might seem to deserve it. This explains how it came to be associated with backward glances towards old religious custom, and Spenser's *Shepheardes Calender* is, again, a helpful source. The shepherd-priest "Palinode," one of the speakers in the "May" section of the poem, is characterized as possessing pro-Catholic nostalgia; he is suspicious of the reformers' energetic ways and tolerant of folk beliefs and practices to the extent that, as Spenser would have seen it, he promotes superstition within his flock.[31] Within *A Midsummer Night's Dream*, the fairies glance backwards to the old religion on the occasion when Oberon orders them to bless Theseus's palace with holy water, a ceremony which recalls the Catholic practice of asperging, and would have seemed as superstitious as faery beliefs themselves to many members of Shakespeare's post-Reformation audience:

> Now until the break of day
> Through this house each fairy stray.
> . . .
> With this field-dew consecrate,
> Every fairy take his gait,
> And each several chamber bless
> Through this palace with sweet peace. (5.1.379–80, 393–6)

Like other religious allusions in the play, this has received much critical attention recently.[32] Sometimes seen as evidence of Shakespeare's own

[29] Cf. Regina Buccola's comment: "Were anyone to take issue with the play's mischievous dance with Catholicism, the ready response available is anachronism. *A Midsummer Night's Dream* is ostensibly set in pre-Christian Athens." *Fairies, Fractious Women, and the Old Faith: Fairy Lore in Early Modern British Drama and Culture* (Selinsgrove, PA: Susquehanna University Press, 2006), p. 27.

[30] See Shell, "William Alabaster and the Palinode," in Gallagher (ed.), *Redrawing the Map of Early Modern English Catholicism*, p. 116.

[31] See *Shorter Poems*, ed. Brooks-Davies, p. 80.

[32] For a summary of recent work, see Buccola, *Fairies*, pp. 79–80. On fairies in the imaginative literature of the era, see Marjorie Swann, "The Politics of Fairylore in Early Modern English Literature," *Renaisance Quarterly*, 53 (2000), 449–73; and Diane Purkiss, *Troublesome Things: A History of Fairies*

Catholic nostalgia, it does, at the very least, indicate his willingness to evoke feelings of that kind. Either way, one must acknowledge that the imaginative association of fairies with Catholic nostalgia is itself a double-edged concept. In Shakespeare's time, and thereafter, it testified to the residual pagan element in early modern folk belief, the fact that the reformers were only too happy to represent Catholics as pagans, and the syncretism between the old and the older religions that sometimes occurred when Catholic religious practice was, like pagan ritual, disapproved of officially and driven underground.[33] As Robert Herrick was to write, somewhat later than Shakespeare, "Now this the Fairies wo'd have known, / Theirs is a mixt religion. / And some have heard the Elves it call / Part Pagan, part Papisticall."[34] Herrick's archly nostalgic faery poems may draw on Shakespeare's scene, and they certainly provide a useful analogue to it; their author's conformism reminds us, with some relevance to recent debates about Shakespeare's own sympathies, that any writer who wanted to endorse the old religion through imaginative writing would have been wary of associating it with fairies.[35] Certainly, the ambivalence in the fairies' blessing is striking. It is intended to bring about marital happiness and prevent birth defects in the married couples' offspring – the reverse, in fact, of what was normally ascribed to faery intervention – but the word "stray" is jarringly pejorative, showing that Shakespeare does not treat Catholic nostalgia in an unequivocally positive manner.[36] As one of the play's most direct commentaries on religious practice, this passage gives us a means of contextualizing Demetrius's deluded devotion to the eidolon of Helena – though, as with this instance of the faery blessing, a clear party line is absent.

*and Fairy Stories* (London: Allen Lane, 2000), chs. 3–5. For the association of Catholics and fairies, see Peter Marshall, "Protestants and Fairies in Early-Modern England," in C. Scott Dixon, Dagmar Freist, and Mark Greengrass (eds.), *Living with Religious Diversity in Early Modern Europe* (Farnham: Ashgate, 2009), ch. 2, Buccola, *Fairies*, esp. pp. 55–7 and ch. 2; and Alison Shell, *Oral Culture and Catholicism in Early Modern England* (Cambridge University Press, 2007), ch. 2. On this scene, see Wendy Wall, "Why Does Puck Sweep? Fairylore, Merry Wives, and Social Struggle," *Shakespeare Quarterly*, 52 (2001), 67–106.

33 Ronald Hutton, "The English Reformation and the Evidence of Folklore," *Past & Present*, 148 (1995), 89–116.

34 "The Fairie Temple," lines 22–5, quoted from Robert Herrick, *Poetical Works*, ed. L. C. Martin (Oxford: Clarendon Press, 1956).

35 See my own discussion of the Ghost in *Hamlet* in *Shakespeare and Religion*, Arden Shakespeare (London: Bloomsbury, 2010), ch. 2.

36 On the association of fairies and birth defects, see Swann, "Politics of Fairylore," 452; and Buccola, *Fairies*, p. 36. On the dark side of fairies, see Bevington, "'But we are spirits,'" and Buccola, *Fairies*, pp. 62–3. Contemporary meanings of the word *stray* – "scatter" (*OED* v.[1]), "roam about free from control" (v.[2] 2.a), and "err" (4.a) – confirm the double entendre. On swerving and veering in literary texts, see Nicholas Royle, *Veering: A Theory of Literature* (Edinburgh University Press, 2011).

More generally, though, and returning to the double meaning of "stray," the association of fairies with losing one's way broadens the theme of delusion and begs comparison with anti-Catholic polemic. One of the fairies describes Puck as "[misleading] night wanderers, laughing at their harm" (2.1.39), and when Oberon orders Puck to "lead these testy rivals so astray / As one come not within another's way" (3.2.358–9), Puck displays both an aptitude for misdirection and a delight in it. When he chants, "Up and down, up and down, / I will lead them up and down; / I am feared in field and town. / Goblin, lead them up and down" (3.2.396–9), Puck echoes an earlier speech that he delivers after giving Bottom an ass's head and putting the other Rude Mechanicals to flight:

> I'll follow you: I'll lead you about a round,
> Through bog, through bush, through brake, through briar;
> Sometime a horse I'll be, sometime a hound,
> A hog, a headless bear, sometime a fire,
> And neigh, and bark, and grunt, and roar, and burn,
> Like horse, hound, hog, bear, fire at every turn. (3.1.88–93)

Demetrius's comment, early in the play, that he is "wood [i.e. mad] within this wood" (2.1.192), introduces the idea of the forest engendering mental confusion. Shakespeare may be pointing here to the notion of "panic," originally understood as fear brought on by a forest;[37] and Puck could certainly be interpreted as having some of the attributes of Pan. But the folkloric notion of being pixy-led has even more relevance to Puck's particular agency and would have been closer at hand for Shakespeare's audience.[38] Being pixy-led could simply refer to losing one's way and wandering in circles, but it was also invoked in relation to the phenomenon of *ignes fatui*: methane gases, especially common in marshy areas, which had a misleading resemblance to lanterns. Under this and other names – Will-o'-the-Wisp, Jack O'Lantern – they were a real danger for the early modern traveler.[39]

[37] Contemporary instances of the term "panic" in the *OED* confirm its strong association with Pan at this date (see adj. 1); the first use of the word in a looser sense (adj. 2.a) is dated 1603.

[38] On the overlap between Will-o'the-Wisps and legends of Puck, see Jennifer Westwood and Jacqueline Simpson, *The Lore of the Land: A Guide to England's Legends* (Harmondsworth: Penguin, 2005), p. 492; cf. pp. 318, 502. See also Mary Ellen Lamb, "Taken by the Fairies: Fairy Practices and the Production of Popular Culture in *A Midsummer Night's Dream*," *Shakespeare Quarterly*, 51 (2000), 277–312. Richard Corbett's mid-seventeenth-century poem "The Fairies' Farewell" was inspired by an occasion on which Corbett and his party lost their way, and his manservant, William Chourne, claimed they had been pixy-led: *Poems*, ed. J. A. W. Bennett and H. R. Trevor-Roper (Oxford: Clarendon Press, 1955), pp. xxi (intro.), 49–52 (poem), and 128–30 (notes).

[39] For a recent scientific exploration of the phenomenon, see A. A. Mills, "Will-o'-the-Wisp Revisited," *Weather*, 55.7 (Royal Meteorological Society, 2000), 20–6.

Like being pixy-led, *ignes fatui* became a common metaphor for false guidance, almost too easy to integrate into allegorizations of faery lore and the supernatural, and were also much invoked in a nonfictional context by religious polemicists of all stamps.[40] However, the common association of popery and popular superstition made them particularly irresistible to anti-Catholic writers: Alexander Roberts, for instance, referred to the "imagined fire" of purgatory, and Daniel Price, in a sermon condemning popish learning, described knowledge not employed to the glory of God as "a Meteor, a Cloud, an Ignis Fatuus."[41] Even in the context of natural history rather than religion, it was used to demonstrate how natural phenomena could become diabolically charged. Writing specifically of *ignes fatui* that appeared in churchyards, William Fulke commented: "oftentimes ar such lightes seen, which ignorant & superstitious fooles, have thought to be soules torme[n]ted in the fyre of purgatorie. In dede [th]e devill hath used these lightes (although they be naturally caused) as strong delusions to captive the myndes of men, w[i]t[h] feare of the Popes purgatorie."[42]

In the manuscript verse of one university poet, the idea of being pixy-led is used autobiographically to convey pain brought about by a friend's Catholicism. Nicholas Oldisworth's "Recollection of Certaine Scattered Poems," written between 1629 and 1634 and transcribed in 1644, includes a number of verses written to, or about, Oldisworth's close friend Richard Bacon, who had converted to Catholicism around the time the verses were written, and traveled overseas to the English College at Douai. They range from the epistolary to the reproachful, even the passionate, and among them is one with the title "On my loosing my way":

> Have you seene fairies dance the Ring? or clowns
> Besiege a May-pole in your country-townes?
> Have you seene Badgers fetch a circling race
> Or giddy Seas the wanton Iles embrace?
> So doe I wheele; and compassing the ground
> Of three miles long, I make nine hundred round.[43]

[40] Richard Carpenter, for instance, uses the topos against Anabaptists in *The Anabaptist Washt and Washt* (London, 1653), quoted from William Hunt's edition, p. 378.

[41] Alexander Roberts, *A Sacred Septenarie* (London, 1614), p. 150 (side-noted '*Ignis fatuus Purgatorij*'); Daniel Price, *David his Oath of Allegeance to Jerusalem* (Oxford, 1613), p. 34.

[42] *A Goodly Gallerye with a Most Pleasant Prospect, Into the Garden of Naturall Contemplation* (London, 1563), sig. 12r. In his account of Ireland in *Britannia* (1610 edn.), Camden gives a translation of a Latin verse describing the site known as "Sir Brendans Purgatory": "If common fame say true, a place of Brendan taking name, / There is: and often times cleere lights doe shine within the same. / The soules have licence here to passe through Purgatory fire, / That worthily before that Judge, they may at length appeere" (p. 116).

[43] Quoted from Bod. MS Don.c.24, fo. 25.

The seemingly arbitrary linkage of fairies, rustic maypole dancers, badgers, and waves is, in fact, quite intentional. All move in circles, but all, too, are associated with Bacon's defection: fairies because of their euphemistic association with Catholics; maypole dancers because of the polemically induced associations between Maytime revels, popery, and paganism;[44] badgers because, like fairies and Catholics, their activity takes place in the dark; and waves because – as Oldisworth laments elsewhere – Bacon is overseas. Their circular careers trace the erroneous path of Catholicism, into which Oldisworth is reluctantly drawn through his love for Bacon. Wishing for Bacon's reconversion but attracted to whatever path Bacon is following, Oldisworth uses the idea of being pixy-led as a metaphor for his spiritual confusion without ever explicitly mentioning it:

Could I but have his Comming home, & enter
My port with him, as well as I can venture,
Did I not (like the Sun) transgresse my line,
I would scorne Drake; but now, though I decline
And rise againe, though upp & downe I bend
I draw noe nearer to my journey's ende:
I runne a bootlesse Maze; and whirling so
I stand-still faster than most men doe goe.

As this illustrates, the experiences of being pixy-led and of the *ignis fatuus* are among those elements in faery lore that went beyond mere topoi and could provide a theme for literary compositions. In *A Midsummer Night's Dream* they even supply a structure, since the idea of faery misdirection drives the plot more than any other. Both comic and frightening, Puck's false turns have taken us some way away from the liturgical nostalgia with which this section began, but are another sign of how Shakespeare deployed ideas of delusion in the referential field where popery and faery interconnected.

## Conclusion

Eidola and *ignes fatui* both lend themselves to the broader idea that acting itself is deceptive, a critique commonly invoked by Tudor and Stuart antitheatricalists.[45] It was not always given a pejorative slant, though, and its more playful metatheatrical implications are often exploited by

[44] On Catholics and festivity, see Phebe Jensen, *Religion and Revelry in Shakespeare's Festive World* (Cambridge University Press, 2008).

[45] See Shell, *Shakespeare and Religion*, ch. 1; Jonas Barish, *The Antitheatrical Prejudice* (Berkeley, CA: University of California Press, 1981); and the contributors to the antitheatrical debate collected in Tanya Pollard (ed.), *Shakespeare's Theater: A Sourcebook* (Oxford: Blackwell, 2004).

Shakespeare in *A Midsummer Night's Dream* and elsewhere. One example can be seen in the play's final deployment of the palinodic mode, the well-known epilogue that Puck speaks to the audience:

> If we shadows have offended,
> Think but this, and all is mended:
> That you have but slumbered here
> While these visions did appear;
> And this weak and idle theme,
> No more yielding but a dream,
> Gentles, do not reprehend;
> If you pardon, we will mend.
> And, as I am an honest Puck,
> If we have unearned luck
> Now to 'scape the serpent's tongue
> We will make amends ere long,
> Else the Puck a liar call.
> So, good night unto you all.
> Give me your hands, if we be friends,
> And Robin shall restore amends. (5.1.401–16)

A preemptive apology for wasting the audience's time on trivial matter is utterly conventional in terms of contemporary stage practice. But here as elsewhere one must ask how apologetic such epilogues are really meant to be; for Puck's speech, like Stesichorus's original palinode, is only apologizing up to a point. Just as Stesichorus retracted his criticism of Helen by saying that he was only speaking against her phantom look-alike, Puck is deflecting opprobrious comment by saying that the audience have only witnessed the behavior of phantoms; he apologizes on those phantoms' behalf, but also says that, after all, nothing else can be expected of them. One should remember firstly that this is a play, and secondly, that it is a play couched as a dream: both dreams and drama produce eidola, meaning that players can, like dream-figures and indeed like fairies themselves, be described as "shadows."[46] Puck, like the rest, can be called an eidolon, which could work against taking him seriously. Nevertheless, it is through him that Shakespeare gives a mischievous pinch to contemporary prejudices against idolatry, superstition, and the theater via the palinode, the apology that is sometimes not really an apology; while at the same time the courtship of Demetrius and Helena, inflected as it is by the story of the first palinode, complicates the relationship between being and seeming in a way that would have exacerbated Reformation sensitivities still further.

[46] On fairies as actors, see Buccola, *Fairies*, pp. 40, 48, 94.

CHAPTER 5

# *The siege of Jerusalem and subversive rhetoric in* King John

*Beatrice Groves*

The famously patriotic ending of *King John* is a warning about the danger of internecine strife at a time of national danger: "This England never did, nor never shall, / Lie at the proud foot of a conqueror / But when it first did help to wound itself."[1] The phrase recalls – *inter alia* – the history of Jerusalem. Jerusalem's destruction by Rome was attributed to the self-wounding religious factionalism of its inhabitants, and its fate had been explicitly connected with the rebellion against King John in *The Homily against Disobedience and Wilful Rebellion* (1571). In this homily the English rebellion (incited by "Romish wolues") is drawn as a parallel to Jerusalem's fall to Rome as an example of the calamitous results of disobedience springing from "ignorance in GODS word."[2] The connection is likewise made in Shakespeare's main source, *The Troublesome Raigne of King John* (1591), a strongly anti-Catholic play which ends with a final, rousing vision of England's glorious future as a new, Protestant Sion.[3] In *Troublesome Raigne*, as King John prepares to relinquish his power to Rome, the portents of Jerusalem's fall hang in the English sky.[4] The message of these "Ensignes" is clear: the new Jerusalem (England) must unite against the Roman Church or be destroyed just as the old Jerusalem had been by the Roman Army.

1 William Shakespeare, *King John*, ed. E. A. J. Honigmann, Arden Shakespeare 2nd series (London: Bloomsbury, 2000), 5.7.112. All subsequent references are to this edition.

2 Mary Ellen and Thomas B. Stroup Rickey (eds.), *Certaine Sermons or Homilies: Appointed to Be Read in Churches: In the Time of Queen Elizabeth I (1547–1571): Facsimile Reproduction of the Edition of 1623* (Gainesville, FL: Scholars' Facsimiles & Reprints, 1968), pp. 316, 317; see also pp. 315–18. See also Knapp, who likewise relates the fall of Jerusalem to the subject of schism in *King John*: Jeffrey Knapp, *Shakespeare's Tribe: Church, Nation, and Theater in Renaissance England* (University of Chicago Press, 2002), pp. 95–102.

3 For the relationship between Shakespeare's play and *Troublesome Raigne*, see Beatrice Groves, "Memory, Composition, and the Relationship of *King John* to *The Troublesome Raigne of King John*," *Comparative Drama*, 38 (2004), 277–90.

4 "Before the ruin of *Jerusalem*, / Such Meteors were the Ensignes of his wrath / That hastened to destroy the faultfull Towne." *The Troublesome Raigne of John, King of England*, ed. J. W. Sider (New York: Garland, 1979), 8.147–9.

The patriotic closing lines of Shakespeare's *King John* (which represent Shakespeare's most sustained borrowing from his more jingoistic predecessor)[5] are central to the traditional reading of *King John* as a "mirror" of Tudor policy.[6] More recently, however, critics have begun to argue that instead of projecting John as a proto-Protestant martyr (as most Tudor texts do) Shakespeare's play appears to question the ideas such as "royal supremacy, the legitimacy bestowed by patrilineal inheritance, and the validity of religious authority" which were embedded in the sixteenth-century image of John.[7] Rather than championing the Protestant cause, *King John* is a play in which "sectarian rhetoric ... points at once to its origins and to its contradictions."[8] In this reading, the ending suppresses but does not silence the subversive elements of the play, and the abrupt, messy denouement indicates the problematic nature of the claim that England once more stands united under a legitimate king. Like Mayer, my own chapter argues for the "disconcerting ambivalence" of the play's anatomization of the sectarian discourse of the post-Armada period, but it argues further that the play actively critiques the bombast of nationalistic propaganda in the figure of the Bastard.[9] The Bastard dramatizes the radical idea that those who rebelled against conformity could yet be passionate in their fidelity to the English crown.

Henry III's succession is secured in the final lines of the play as the Bastard unites the barons in submission to the young prince. But even as the Bastard invokes the dominant discourse which equates conformity with safety, he is violating the traditional hierarchy: a bastard secures the succession of a king, and a subject (rather than the new monarch) speaks the final ringing couplet of the play: "Nought shall make us rue / If England to itself

5 Virginia M. Vaughan, "*King John*: A Study in Subversion and Containment," in Deborah T. Cullen-Aquino (ed.), *King John: New Perspectives* (Newark, DE: University of Delaware Press, 1989), p. 73.

6 For the classic statement of this position, see Lily B. Campbell, *Shakespeare's Histories: Mirrors of Elizabethan Policy* (San Marino, CA: Huntington Library, 1947), pp. 126–67.

7 Vaughan, "*King John*," p. 65. See also Marsha Robinson, "The Historiographic Methodology of *King John*," in Cullen-Aquino, *King John*, pp. 29–40; Phyllis Rackin, *Stages of History: Shakespeare's English Chronicles* (Ithaca, NY: Cornell University Press, 1990), pp. 146–200; Deanne Williams, *The French Fetish from Chaucer to Shakespeare* (Cambridge University Press, 2004), pp. 206–7. One long-running approach that complements the reading of *King John* as subversive of Tudor ideology has been an attempt to read it as a pro-Catholic play: David Bevington, *Tudor Drama and Politics: A Critical Approach to Topical Meaning* (Cambridge, MA: Harvard University Press, 1968), pp. 197–8; Lukas Erne, "'Popish Tricks' and 'A Ruinous Monastery': *Titus Andronicus* and the Question of Shakespeare's Catholicism," in Lukas Erne and Guillemette Bolens (eds.), *The Limits of Textuality*, 13 (Tübingen: Gunter Narr, 2000), p. 142.

8 Jean-Christophe Mayer, *Shakespeare's Hybrid Faith: History, Religion and the Stage* (Basingstoke: Palgrave Macmillan, 2006), p. 85.

9 Ibid., p. 90.

do rest but true!" (5.7.117–18). When in the folio version of *King Lear* the two final couplets – spoken by Albany in the quarto version – are taken by Edgar, it is a sign that he has accepted the crown that Albany has offered. Prior to this point in *King John*, the Bastard has exerted pressure on precisely this issue of the necessity of conformity through the reversal of one its central tropes. As this chapter will illustrate, when the Bastard makes the Machiavellian suggestion that the besieging forces at Angiers should "Do like the mutines of Jerusalem, / Be friends awhile and both conjointly bend / Your sharpest deeds of malice on this town" (2.1.377–9), he is inverting a popular exemplum of contemporary homilies. The Bastard's "iconoclastic idiom" is one of the joys of *King John*, but it is also crucial to the play's subversive stance on political and religious questions of its time.[10] The Bastard's critique of the rhetoric of unity is part of his unique characterization, but it is also part of the play's own independent vision. Independence of mind in *King John* is not a sign of dangerously heretical opinions but evidence that Englishmen can maintain their identity and liberty while remaining loyal subjects. Preachers who threatened England with the direful example of religious factionalism at the siege of Jerusalem were inveighing against those (Catholic or Puritan) who rejected the Elizabethan religious settlement. The history of Jerusalem's fall was used to suggest that independent spiritual choices would result in England being invaded by its enemies. The Bastard's inversion of this trope implicitly questions such a conclusion. The truest, most loyal Englishman in *King John* is also the one who keeps his independence and his integrity.[11]

In the 1580s and nineties the preoccupations of an island nation laboring under the fear of Spanish invasion can be read in the performance of endless besieged castles, women, and cities on the early modern stage.[12] The pervasive habit of mind which caused early modern Englishmen to cast

[10] Rackin, *Stages of History*, p. 185.

[11] This positive interpretation of the Bastard is by no means universal, but it is becoming the dominant reading: Tim Spiekerman, *Shakespeare's Political Realism: The English History Plays* (Albany: State University of New York Press, 2001), p. 52; Robert C. Jones, *These Valiant Dead: Renewing the Past in Shakespeare's Histories* (University of Iowa Press, 1991), pp. 46–68.

[12] Such plays include: Thomas Legge's *Solymitana Clades* (*c.* 1580); *Siege of London* (*c.* 1580–94); the Coventry *Destruction of Jerusalem* (1584); Lodge's *Wounds of Civil War* (1586–91); *Wars of Cyrus* (1587–94); Peele's *Battle of Alcazar* (1588–9); *Guy Earl of Warwick* (*c.* 1590–1615); *Edmund Ironside* (1590–1600); Marlowe's *Jew of Malta*; *Jerusalem* (1592); *Titus and Vespasian* (1592); *Edward III* (1592–3); *Huon of Bordeaux* (1593–4); Heywood's *The Foure Prentises of London* (1594); *Godfrey of Bulloigne* (1594); *Troy* (1596); Munday's *The Downfall of Robert, Earl of Huntington* (*c.* 1598); Heywood's *First Part of Edward IV* (1599); Chettle and Dekker, *Troilus and Cressida* (1599); Shakespeare's *Henry V* (1599).

the fate of their nation in Israelite terms[13] made it inevitable that comparisons would be drawn between an isolated and threatened England and the Jews besieged within Jerusalem's walls.[14] The fashion for dramatizations of siege at this time (the siege of Jerusalem was a particularly popular topic) has a clear parallel in the political reality of England's position. The trope of Britain as an island (a "precious stone set in the silver sea," as Gaunt famously puts it) might seem a simple geographical description, but it is in fact very much an early modern phenomenon: in *King John* England is part of the Angevin Empire with lands on both sides of the Channel. The final French possessions were lost under Mary Tudor, which meant the Elizabethans were the first generation of Englishmen without any claims on mainland Europe. England's conversion to Protestantism heightened her separation in a predominantly Catholic Europe, but it also coincided with the time when Britain became geographically isolated.

The defeat of the Armada illustrates the extent to which England's "separateness" was read as evidence for her destiny as the new Israel. England's escape from Spanish invasion was seen as her equivalent of the Israelite escape from Egypt, and English propagandists exploited to the full the coincidence that it was an east wind which had decimated the Spanish fleet, just as it was a strong east wind that had blown all night to part the Red Sea (Exodus 14:21).[15] The official *Psalme and Collect of Thankesgiuing* (1588), for example, proclaimed: "The Lorde scattered them with his windes . . . the helpe that is done by sea and by land, is his."[16] Preachers likewise exultingly proclaimed that God had enlisted the elements in England's defense as he had for his first chosen people: "*the Lord strong in battell was our refuge, the God of Iaakob was our defence* . . . The winds fought against them, and against their shippes, as they did against the shippes of *Ahasia*. The sea fought against them and against their host, as it did against the power and

[13] For an excellent discussion of this mode of scriptural comparison, see Achsah Guibbory, *Christian Identity: Jews & Israel in Seventeenth-Century England* (Oxford University Press, 2010).

[14] The comparison is an old one: at the siege of Jerusalem, Titus taunted the Jews for daring to take arms against Rome, and wondered on what they were relying: "On the solidity of your walls? But what wall could be a greater obstacle than the ocean, encompassed by which the Britons yet do homage to the Roman arms?": *Josephus: The Jewish War*, trans. H. St. J. Thackeray, 3 vols. (Cambridge, MA: Putnam, 2006), vol. III, p. 331. All subsequent references to *The Jewish War* are to this edition, unless otherwise stated.

[15] Oliver Pigge, *Meditations Concerning Praiers to Almighty God, for the Safety of England, When the Spaniards Were Come into the Narrow Seas, August 1588* (London, 1589), sigs. C2v, E2v; John Vicars, *Englands Hallelu-Jah* (London, 1631), sigs. B3r, F4r, F4v; Paul Knell, *Israel and England Paralelled . . .* (London, 1648), sigs. Cv, Bv.

[16] *A Psalme and Collect of Thankesgiuing, Not Vnmeet for This Present Time: To Be Said or Sung in Churches* (London, 1588), sig. A3r.

host of Pharao."[17] *King John* participates in the dominant discourse of England as a nation protected by God through its encircling seas, a "water-walled bulwark, still secure / And confident from foreign purposes" (2.1.27–8); indeed, it might seem that Shakespeare is directly participating in Armada propaganda when he dramatizes an invading Catholic "armado" destroyed by a Channel storm: "So, by a roaring tempest on the flood, / A whole armado of convicted sail / Is scatter'd and disjoin'd from fellowship" (3.3.1–3). *King John*'s sources state that this loss was due to English action, but Shakespeare (like the preachers above) imputes the destruction of the invading ships to the providential intervention of the wind and sea.[18] The parallel with pious homilies, however, is invoked only to be undermined. The victory at the end of *King John* is full of reversals, and directly after the audience hear of the loss of Lewis's reinforcements at sea, they are told that the Bastard's soldiers have likewise been "devoured" by the tides (5.5.13; 5.6.39–40). The dramatization of war reminds the audience that such seemingly "providential" reversals in battle can occur to both sides.

For many, however, the victory of the Armada was proof that Englishmen were justified in thinking of themselves as the new Israel. The victory was read as nothing less than a covenant between God and his new Israel, a promise that God would protect English Protestantism as he had protected his people in the Old Testament.[19] The unifying force of conceiving of England as God's "little Mount Sion"[20] was exploited to the full:

> That yeere of *Eighty-Eight*, ô neuer spare it,
> To blaze the praise of *That yeere*, all thy yeeres:
> Let English Isre'll, sing and say allwayes,
> *Not unto us, but to the Lord be prayse.*[21]

These apparently triumphalist parallels were, however, drawn because of a perception of England's weakness as much as of her strength. Those who preached the unity of Sion were implicitly inveighing against the religious factionalism they believed to be rife in their lands. According to the English

17 Martin Fotherby, *Foure Sermons, Lately Preached, by Martin Fotherby Doctor in Divinity, and Chaplain Vnto the Kings Maiestie* (London, 1608), p. 82.

18 "Holinshed, Foxe, M. Paris etc. say that the French navy was defeated by an English force. Only Coggeshall also mentions the storm." Honigmann, *King John*, p. 166.

19 David Cressy, *Bonfires and Bells: National Memory and the Protestant Calendar in Elizabethan and Stuart England* (Berkeley: University of California Press, 1989), p. 122; also pp. 110–29.

20 The phrase is from a letter from Sir Edward Barton to Walsingham on September 13, 1588: William Douglas Hamilton (ed.), *Calendar of State Papers, Domestic, Charles I. 1639*, vol. CDXX (London, 1873), p. 200.

21 Vicars, *Englands Hallelu-Jah*, sig. B3v.

Psalter, "Jerusalem is built as a city that is at unity in itself" (Psalm 122:3), and it was a unity that England – under the fracturing pressure of a Protestant faith which "pressed inexorably toward variety in the expression of the religious impulse"[22] – yearned to emulate. Patrick Collinson has noted how the Psalter ameliorates the claustrophobic force of the original Hebrew of this phrase.[23] The Geneva Bible likewise, although it has a more accurate translation ("Ierusalem is builded as a citie, that is compact together in it selfe"), nonetheless glosses the word "compact" positively: "By the artificiall ioyning and beautie of the houses, he meaneth the concord, and loue that was betweene the citizens." Collinson argues that Protestantism's clarion call to unity carried an implicit recognition that it had fractured English identity "by dividing along lines of formal religious division communities which were previously at least nominally at one."[24] The highly regarded preacher John King (who went on to become Bishop of London) ended his 1594 sermon series on Nineveh with the wish that the "division [which] had well-nigh broken of late the heart-strings of religion amongst vs" should be overcome and followed by "the peace of our Ierusalem."[25] Fifty years later the radical William Sedgwick desired that London might be truly "*the new Jerusalem* . . . a City at unity in it self; there shall not be the least sound of discord in thee."[26] The longing to embody the New Jerusalem, embraced by both King and Sedgwick, is always a longing for unity, the desire that a factious country should become one, should be unified as "the house of the chosen Israelites."[27]

Josephus wrote that internal dissension was the principal reason for the Jewish defeat, asserting in the preface to *The Jewish War* that "my country . . . owed its ruin to civil strife" (1.4). His stress on Jewish faction may be read as providing a distraction from the disunity of Rome herself in the year of the four emperors. As suggested in Dylan Sailor's brilliant analysis of Tacitus, Flavian propaganda presented Rome as ending Judea's civil war while (in fact) using the Judean victory to end the Roman civil war.[28] Josephus's reasons for stressing the factious

22 Charles H. George and Katherine George, *The Protestant Mind of the English Reformation 1570–1640* (Princeton University Press, 1961), p. 375.

23 Patrick Collinson, *The Birthpangs of Protestant England: Religious and Cultural Change in the Sixteenth and Seventeenth Centuries* (New York: St. Martin's Press, 1988), p. 28.

24 Ibid., p. 31.

25 John King, *Lectvres Vpon Ionas, Delivered at Yorke in the Yeare of Our Lorde 1594* (Oxford, 1599), p. 660.

26 William Sedgewick, *The Spirituall Madman* . . . ([London], 1648), p. 6.

27 *The Complete Works of Thomas Lodge*, 4 vols. (New York, 1963), vol. 1, p. 48.

28 Dylan Sailor, *Writing and Empire in Tacitus* (Cambridge University Press, 2008), p. 240.

war leaders in Jerusalem are – in this reading – strikingly close to the reasons why early modern preachers were so drawn to his history. They, like the Flavians, were holding up the fall of Jerusalem as an exemplum for accepting the status quo at home: endlessly reiterating that the "*English-Israelites*," like the first-century Jews, were rendered vulnerable by "factious *Parts* within" to the "fierce *Force*" of Rome.[29] The bishop of Salisbury, John Jewel (who insisted on strict conformity to the church's discipline despite his own desires for further reformation), used the fall of Jerusalem as a warning against sedition. Preaching on Luke 11:5 ("Every kingdom that is divided in itself shall be brought to desolation"), he reminded his auditors that "when Vespasian the emperor and his sone Titus came with an army against Hierusalem, the whole nation of the Jews was divided into three factions, each of them ready to undo the other. Then followed the overthrow of the kingdom."[30] Josephus's history was used to admonish all who deviated from the established religion: both Puritans and recusants were constantly reminded that "*Ierusalem* had not so soone beene wonne by *Vespatians* sonne, had it not beene for ciuill discord within the Citie; and nothing more to bee feared for the ruine of our Nation, then ciuill dissention, domesticall foes."[31] In the anti-Martin Marprelate tracts those who might be tempted by Puritan arguments for rebellion against Episcopal authority were threatened with Josephus's direful history: "though the Iewes at the siege of Ierusalem were pressed by theyr enemies without the walles, and punished wyth such a mortalitie within, that the carkases of the dead did dunge the grounde, yet they neuer went to the wall, till they grew to be factious, & fell to taking one another by the throate."[32] Religious factionalism was presented as having the most serious consequences, and such texts declared that conformity was a matter of national safety rather than individual conscience.

The Bastard in *King John*, however, uses Josephus's account of the fall of Jerusalem rather differently. As he stands outside the besieged city of

[29] Vicars, *Englands Hallelu-Jah*, sigs. Bv, B3r.

[30] *The Works of John Jewel*, ed. John Ayre (Cambridge, 1847), vol. II, p. 1028. It is noticeable how popular this trope was among bishops: see also Edwin Sandys, *Sermons Made by the Most Reuerende Father in God, Edwin, Archbishop of Yorke, Primate of England and Metropolitane* (London, 1585), p. 86; Gilbert Burnet, *A Sermon Preached at Bow-Church, before the Court of Aldermen, on March 12. 1689/90* (London, 1690), pp. 14–15, 24; William Laud, *Seven Sermons Preached Upon severall occasions* (London, 1651), p. 103.

[31] William Hampton, *A Proclamation of Warre from the Lord of Hosts* (London, 1627), p. 21.

[32] *The Returne of the renowned Caualiero Pasquill* (1589) in *The Works of Thomas Nashe*, ed. Ronald B. McKerrow and F. P. Wilson, 5 vols. (Oxford: A. H. Bullen, 1958), vol. I, p. 76.

Angiers, that account becomes, not a request for cohesion for the sake of defense, but a call to arms:

> Do like the mutines of Jerusalem,
> Be friends awhile and both conjointly bend
> Your sharpest deeds of malice on this town. (2.1.377–9)

The Bastard's allusion is to the alliance among the Jews caused by a Roman attack. In the year's respite from hostilities that resulted from the death of Nero in the summer of 68 AD (because that led to an automatic cessation of Vespasian's command) Jerusalem split into three factions.[33] The city was divided between the followers of John of Gischala, Eleazar, son of Simon, and Simon, son of Gioras. Josephus gives a graphic account of the bloodshed and suffering caused by their in-fighting, as well as the way this internecine strife led inevitably to the fall of the city to the foreign power. However, in the spring of 70 AD Titus assembled his army near Jerusalem, and his approach temporarily united the warring factions: "And now for the first time the mutual dissension of the factions within the town, hitherto incessantly at strife, was checked by the war from without."[34] The factions joined forces for a surprise attack on the tenth legion while the Romans were occupied with fortifying their camp, a sortie that proved a minor success.[35] The factions renewed their accord – "the parties, consigning their hatred and private quarrels to oblivion, thus became one body" (5.279) – and more military success followed: John's men undermined the Roman siege-works threatening Antonia and two days later Simon's men likewise disabled some of the siege-engines at the western end of the north wall (5.466–90). This presentation of a united front forced Titus into ending his direct attacks, and he starved the inhabitants into surrender instead (5.491ff.).

Josephus repeatedly reiterates that it is only the fear of Roman invasion that enables the violent partisans to unite – suggesting a fractious force with no ultimate chance of success. Recent historians have stressed (in contradistinction to the view promulgated by Flavian propaganda) that the archaeological evidence points to cohesion and confidence among the Jews who revolted against Roman rule.[36] The early modern affinity with the besieged Jews meant that they too had a stronger belief in the power and

[33] This paragraph draws on E. Mary Smallwood, *The Jews under Roman Rule: From Pompey to Diocletian* (Leiden: Brill, 1976), pp. 298ff.

[34] Josephus, *Jewish War*, 5.71. [35] Ibid., 5.71–84.

[36] Martin Goodman, "Coinage and Identity: The Jewish Evidence," in Christopher Howgego, Volker Heuchert, and Andrew Burnett (eds.), *Coinage and Identity in the Roman Provinces* (Oxford University Press, 2005), pp. 163–6; Smallwood, *Jews under Roman Rule*, p. 300.

reality of unity among the Jews than Josephus did. The Elizabethans were much attached to a work that had more faith than *The Jewish War* in the potential of this cooperation: a tenth-century Hebrew adaptation of *The Jewish War* (the *Josippon*) which was believed to have been written by Josephus for a Jewish audience.[37] The English translation of the *Josippon* (which pre-dated that of the *Jewish War* by forty-five years) was phenomenally successful; it was reprinted fourteen times between 1558 and 1615. In the *Josippon* a lasting league is formed (in which "the seditious now earnestly [began] to thinke of unitie & concorde amongst themselues") and factionalism is transformed into competitive comradeship: "these exhortyng one another to play the menne, dyd ualiauntly resyst the Romanes."[38] While for Josephus the makeshift unity never compels belief – it is "a sorry alliance" (*Jewish War*, 5.72) – the author of the *Josippon* has confidence in the Jewish ability, when united, to defeat their invaders. When they fight together the Jews achieve striking military success – "Thus the Jewes put the Romanes to flyght thryse uppon one day" – and miraculous victories, such as 500 Jewish soldiers engaging the Roman Army of 40,000 and killing 8,000 of them without sustaining a single casualty.[39]

The popularity among English readers of the story of uniting factions is illustrated by George Sandys's annotations to his translation of Grotius's *Christus Patiens* (1608): while Grotius writes only that faction hastened Jerusalem's fall, Sandys adds, "but upon every Assault of the *Romans*, setting their private Hatred aside, united themselves, as if of one Mind, and with admirable Courage repulsed the Enemy; but, upon the least Cessation, renewed their bloody Discord."[40] Writers who hoped that England's factions would emulate the Jewish accord sometimes gave it an implicitly Protestant colouring: Thomas Gainsford, for example, wrote that when the Jewish factions were joined "with one truth, and promise," then "the *Romaines* back with losse were driuen."[41] The preacher Nathaniel Cannon explicitly desired that zealous English Puritans, like the Jewish "Zealots," might join with their countrymen in repulsing the Roman threat:

[37] Joseph ben Gorion, A *Compendious and Most Marueilous Historie of the Latter Tymes of the Iewes Common Weale* . . ., trans. Peter Morwen (London, 1579), sigs. Av–A2v; *The Famous and Memorable Workes of Josephus*, trans. Thomas Lodge (London, 1609), sig. Ggg2r.

[38] *Compendious*, sig. Y2r. [39] *Compendious*, sigs. Xr, Bb6r.

[40] George Sandys, *Christ's Passion, a Tragedy; with Annotations*, 2nd edn. (London, 1687), p. 95. See also John Taylor, *Taylors Urania* . . . (London, 1615), sig. E6v.

[41] Thomas Gainsford, *The Vision and Discourse of Henry the Seuenth. Concerning the Unitie of Great Brittaine* (London, 1610), p. 51.

> I will turne my face vnto the wall and weepe, when I shall remember, that wee should haue lesse care in preseruing Gods Church, then the seditious had in preseruing their City. *Iosephus* in his *Bello Iudaico*, tels us of *Simeon*, *Iehochanan*, and *Eliazor*, though they raised many mutinies in Ierusalem, and shead much bloud in their seditious skirmishes, yet when the Romans came against their City, they would presently vnite their forces and ioyne against the common enemy: if wee had bent our forces ioyntly together against Rome, then those of the separation would haue had no leisure to thinke vpon these trifles.[42]

The Jewish pact is held up as a model for England's sectaries to emulate, given as evidence that the "unity of the besieged"[43] could bring safety where dissension had threatened destruction.[44]

The Bastard's version of the trope, however, is aggressive rather than defensive: the league will destroy, not protect, the city of Angiers, leaving it in "unfenced desolation" (2.1.386). A historical example traditionally used to promote national and religious cohesion is transformed into a cloak for an excessive use of force. The Bastard's Machiavellian misapplication of the Josephan trope is made clear as he comments: "Smacks it not something of *the* policy?" (2.1.396, italics mine). By wrenching his historical example out of context – inverting the moral it carried in both Josephus and early modern homiletics about concord in adversity – the Bastard alerts his listeners not only to his own "policy" but also to the way that history can be (and was) twisted by those who used it to justify their actions. The acceptability of such "wild counsel" (2.1.395) is shown by the fact that King John not only accedes to the Bastard's idea, but accepts his rhetorical identification of Angiers and Jerusalem. John coolly asks: "France, shall we knit our powers / And lay this Angiers even with the ground; / Then after fight who shall be king of it?" (2.1.398). John's phrase "even with the ground" likewise figures Angiers as the besieged Jerusalem, for it evokes Jesus's prophecy of the Roman siege: "For the days shall come vpon thee, that thine enemies shall cast a trench about thee, and compasse thee round, and keepe thee in on euery side, And shall make thee euen with ye ground" (Luke 19:43–4, Geneva Bible).[45] The King accepts and

[42] Nathaniel Cannon, *The Cryer* (London, 1613), p. 24.

[43] For the idea that siege unifies those who undergo it, see Malcolm Hebron, *The Medieval Siege: Theme and Image in Middle English Romance* (Oxford: Clarendon Press, 1997), p. 90; also pp. 71, 119.

[44] A number of the chapters in this volume consider the issue of early modern reading practices of ancient and modern history and the habit of applying historical *exempla* to contemporary religious and political issues. See, for instance, Chapters 6 and 13 below.

[45] The phrase "even with the ground" is also used by the Bishops' Bible (the Geneva and Bishops' Bible are those to which Shakespeare alludes most consistently: Naseeb Shaheen, *Biblical References in Shakespeare's Plays* (Newark: University of Delaware Press, 1999), pp. 17–50). This is a newly identified

reinforces the Bastard's image, a tacit acknowledgment that there is nothing unusual in the self-interested identification of Jerusalem-parallels by those in power.

The aggressive nature of the Bastard's trope is to some extent explained by the equivocal status of the sacking of Jerusalem on the early modern stage. The siege of the Holy City was dramatized in two types of early modern siege-play: plays about the Roman destruction of the city – such as the Coventry *Destruction of Jerusalem* (1584), Thomas Legge's *Solymitana Clades* (*c.* 1580), and the spectacularly successful *Titus and Vespasian* (1592)[46] – and crusading plays such as *Huon of Bordeaux* (1593–4), Thomas Heywood's *The Foure Prentises of London* (1594), and the two parts of *Godfrey of Bulloigne* (1592–4). In the crusading plays, Christians are retaking Jerusalem from the "infidel" and sympathy is rarely elicited for the city's inhabitants. In the plays about the fall of Jerusalem to Titus, however, the action plays out among the Jews rather than in the camp of the besieging forces, and the horrors of the siege seem intended to elicit a natural sympathy with suffering vulnerability – such as is likewise inspired for the besieged Londoners in Heywood's *First Part of Edward IV* (1599) or the citizens of Antwerp in *A Larum for London* (1602). The Bastard has taken a trope about Jerusalem's fall to Titus and reimagined it in a crusading context where victory is portrayed as triumph, not tragedy.

The Bastard is a character whose theatrical heritage links him with besiegers both of London and in the Holy Land. He shares his name with the "bastard of *Fauconbridge*," whose 1471 siege of London had been dramatized in the *Siege of London* (*c.* 1580–94) and in Heywood's *First Part of Edward IV*.[47] Falconbridge shares the name of one besieger and is the bastard son of another: "Richard, that robb'd the lion of his heart / And fought the holy wars in Palestine" (2.1.4–5). The Bastard (who is rechristened Richard in his father's honor [1.1.162]) is closely allied to the crusader king: he has "a trick of Cœur de lion's face" (1.1.85), shares his military

allusion (Shaheen's definitive work does not note it). Jesus' famous prophecy meant that for a long time (despite contrary evidence in Josephus and the Holy Land) Christians continued to argue that Jerusalem: "twas beat quite flat and plain to the Ground; exactly according to our Saviour, *They shall lay thee even with the Ground, and thy Children within thee.*" Samuel Wesley, *The Life of our blessed Lord & Saviour* (London, 1693), p. 254.

46 *Titus and Vespasian*'s run at the Rose earned almost double Henslowe's average takings at this time: E. K. Chambers, *The Elizabethan Stage*, 2nd edn., 4 vols. (Oxford: Clarendon Press, 1951), vol. II, pp. 122–3.

47 For a narrative of this siege, see John Stow, *A Survey of London by John Stow: Reprinted from the Text of 1603*, ed. Charles Lethbridge Kingsford, 2 vols. (Oxford, 1908), vol. II, p. 203; Raphael Holinshed, *Holinshed's Chronicles of England, Scotland, and Ireland*, 6 vols. (London, 1807–8), vol. III, pp. 221–4.

prowess, and is identified with his arms.[48] He is even described as the issue of Richard's mastery of the arts of siege-craft: Falconbridge's mother recalls forceful wooing "so strongly urg'd past my defence" (1.1.258). Richard I "wan diuerse townes and castels out of the enimies hands" on the third crusade,[49] and the Bastard's rhetoric at Angiers is designed to draw attention to his connection with this famous besieger. Richard's greatest military triumph was the siege of Acre (1191), and it is this siege that the central action of *King John* most closely resembles. At Acre, the besieging parties (as at Angiers) included the English King, Philip of France, and the Duke of Austria. At Acre (as at Angiers) these parties united to attack the city. At Acre Richard (as his son does at Angiers) called Austria a coward and humiliated him.[50]

The Bastard creates an identity for himself by associating himself with Richard's myth; but he also burnishes the tarnished aspects of that myth. When the Bastard takes back the famous lion-skin from Limoges, Duke of Austria, he erases the memory (perpetuated by that trophy) of Richard's ignominious and unnecessary death at Limoges's hands.[51] Richard I, despite his military prowess, was (and remains) a somewhat equivocal figure. Samuel Daniel concluded that "hee exacted, and consumed more of this Kingdome, then all his predecessors from the Norman had done before him, and yet lesse deserued then any, hauing neither liued here, neither left behind him monument of Pietie, or of any other publique work, or euer shewed loue or care to this Common-wealth, but onely to get what hee could from it."[52] Even if Richard is judged on military success alone, the third crusade is

48 The lion which was established as the coat of arms of English royalty by Richard I is associated not with the King (as might be expected) but with the Bastard: C. W. Scott-Giles, *Shakespeare's Heraldry* (London: J. M. Dent, 1950), pp. 46–7.

49 Holinshed, *Chronicles*, vol. II, p. 232.

50 Ibid., vol. II, pp. 230, 235. The event became part of Richard's myth: "thus did *Richard* take / The coward *Austrias* colours in his hand, / And thus he cast them under *Acon* walles, / And thus he trod them underneath his feete." Anthony Munday, *The Downfall of Robert Earl of Huntingdon (1601)* (Oxford: Malone Society, 1964), ll. 1926–9; John Gillingham, *Richard I* (New Haven, CT: Yale University Press, 1999), pp. 224–6. Honigmann notes that Falconbridge's insults against Austria have exactly the same tone as Richard's (as they are rendered in the romance *Kynge Rycharde Cuer du Lyon*) "Home shrewed cowarde and go slepe." *King John*, p. xxii.

51 Shakespeare has combined the Duke of Austria (whom Richard humiliated at Acre, and who later imprisoned him) with the Viscount of Limoges. Samuel Daniel considered Richard's death, which occurred while he was besieging Limoges's castle, as the result of his blood-lust and greed. Samuel Daniel, *The Collection of the History of England* (London, 1621), p. 107. See also Gillingham, *Richard I*, pp. 323–4.

52 Daniel, *Collection*, p. 107. Daniel writes that Richard "sacked" England no less than the holy land: "From hence passes this famous king to the Holy Land, with the spoyles and treasure of three noble rich Islands, *England, Sicile*, and *Cyprus* . . . and there consumes that huge collected masse, euen as violently as it was gotten." *Collection*, p. 98. Gillingham, *Richard I*, pp. 1–14.

notable for its failure to recapture Jerusalem which, as Holinshed notes, must have been considered the crusade's primary aim.[53] The Bastard's skilful manipulation of myth and memory is visible as he recreates at Angiers the circumstances of his father's most successful exploit, the taking of Acre, and recasts it as a taking of Jerusalem, his father's greatest military failure.

In *King John* both national and personal identities are being forged in the siege of Angiers.[54] The fundamental blankness at the heart of a siege – the "enclosed space which is assailed and defended" – has made it embody many ideas throughout literature: "national solidarity and personal heroism, and the strength of religious faith in the crusading romance; or it may symbolize female beauty and sexuality, enclosing the pure spirit and the heart of the beloved in allegorical writing" (Hebron, *Medieval Siege*, p. 2). At this siege King John tries to prove his right to the English throne, and England's right to its European possessions, while the Bastard tries out his new identity as Richard I's son. At Angiers the Bastard – by recalling (and improving on) the myth of his father's glorious victories in the Holy Land – is performing his self-chosen identity as Cœur-de-Lion's son. The aggressive misapplication of Josephus's history is part of the Bastard's rhetorical creation of himself as the son of a master of siege warfare.

The Bastard's unique interpretation of the Josephan trope is typical of the independence of the stage bastard who, as Michael Neill notes, "repeatedly insists on his own self-begotten sufficiency."[55] It is a trait that reaches its zenith in Falconbridge, who has willed his own bastardy and chosen a liminal status when he might have chosen to remain legally (and landedly) legitimate. At Angiers he "persistently subverts the shaping authority of official language" just as his subversive asides – and repeated verbal taunts of Austria – consistently disrupt the form and syntax of "the authorized language of chivalric heroism."[56] Edward Gisekes, who explores the

[53] Holinshed, *Chronicles*, vol. II, pp. 232–3. The idea that the third Crusade was a failure because it did not result in the retaking of Jerusalem was voiced at the time: Gillingham, *Richard I*, p. 4.

[54] As John Watkins persuasively argues, the play presents the loss of John's Angevin possessions as the birth of an independent and "culturally, linguistically, and politically coherent England": "it turns what might look like a national disaster – the loss of England's French territories – into what might look like a national triumph." "Losing France and Becoming England: Shakespeare's *King John* and the Emergence of State-Based Diplomacy," in Curtis Perry and John Watkins (eds.), *Shakespeare and the Middle Ages* (Oxford University Press, 2009), p. 83.

[55] Michael Neill, "'In everything illegitimate': Imagining the Bastard in Renaissance Drama," *Yearbook of English Studies*, 23 (1993), 284.

[56] Ibid., 288. For more on the Bastard's language as evidence for Shakespeare's resistance to the dominant acceptance of martial methods of settling disputes, see Alan Shepard, *Marlowe's Soldiers: Rhetorics of Masculinity in the Age of the Armada* (Farnham: Ashgate, 2002), p. 3 *et passim*.

Bastard's incarnation of the idea of a "chosen" conception of identity, sees the excesses of the Bastard's battlefield rhetoric as a sign of his need to outdo the nobles in linguistic prowess in order to effectively assimilate himself into his newfound status.[57] The Angiers policy suggested "half in earnest, half in jest" is both "typical of the ridiculous stratagems of governments and kings" and a critique of such Machiavellian policies.[58] The Bastard's inversion of the Jerusalem trope encourages skepticism about the opportunism with which classical exempla were invoked in the political and religious rhetoric of the period.[59] What were presented as self-evident lessons from the inarguable precedent of history might in reality be self-serving and partial applications of the past. Fifty years ago Emrys Jones argued that in his famous "commodity" soliloquy Falconbridge is playing with the terms of early modern homiletics and suggested that he could be seen as a mouthpiece for the questioning of dominant discourse: "through the character of the Bastard we seem to overhear some of the ways Tudor Englishmen privately thought about the public events of their time."[60] The current critical consensus is that the Bastard's independent vision belongs to a more general subversion of Tudor ideology in *King John*.[61]

David Womersley is convincing in his analysis of *King John* as a play which espouses orthodoxy in a heterodox way: the Bastard's loyalty to the crown (like his parentage) is not accepted as an absolute but presented as a willed decision. The orthodoxy of his patriotism is a cloak for the heterodox suggestion that loyalty to king and country is something to which each individual needs to make their own intellectual assent (rather than accept without question).[62] The inversion of the Jerusalem trope is likewise a

[57] Edward Gieskes, "'He is but a bastard to the time': Status and Service in *the Troublesome Raigne* and Shakespeare's *King John*," *English Literary History*, 65 (1998), 794.

[58] Julia C. Van de Water, "The Bastard in King John," *Shakespeare Quarterly*, 11 (1960), 140.

[59] On this topic see the early modern use of Augustine's influential argument that as the Israelites had used Egyptian gold, so Christian exegetes could mine pagan texts: Noam Reisner, "The Preacher and Profane Learning," in Peter McCullough, Hugh Adlington, and Emma Rhatigan (eds.), *The Oxford Handbook of The Early Modern Sermon* (Oxford University Press, 2012), pp. 74–9.

[60] Emrys Jones, *The Origins of Shakespeare* (Oxford: Clarendon Press, 1977), pp. 242, 262. Some critics believe the commodity speech is self-interested and hence think that there is an irreconcilable break between the Bastard's early character and the patriot of the end of the play: see, for instance, Van de Water, "Bastard in King John," 137–46; also Watkins, "Losing France and Becoming England," p. 82. Jones, however (in my view, correctly), sees in this speech a self-directed irony (*Origins of Shakespeare*, p. 252).

[61] For example, see Rackin's argument that the play "subjects the masculine voices of patriarchal authority to skeptical feminine interrogation" and that the Bastard is linked to these subversive female voices: *Stages of History*, pp. 179, 185. See also Mayer, *Shakespeare's Hybrid Faith*, p. 98; Timothy Rosendale, *Liturgy and the Literature in the Making of Protestant England* (Cambridge University Press, 2007), p. 152.

[62] David Womersley, *Divinity and State* (Oxford University Press, 2010), pp. 280–1.

heterodox espousal of orthodoxy. The Bastard's sly inversion of a well-worn moral message supports his own aggressive military endeavor, but it may also point to the play's skepticism about conformity. The Josephan story of uniting factions was used to prove that strength was only to be found in religious conformity. In the Bastard's autonomy we hear the possibility of subjects rejecting the message they were meant to imbibe. The stage bastard, with his self-begotten sufficiency, is an embodiment – and in many ways a celebration – of those who chose to follow their own path. But while most stage bastards compound this independence with dubious morality, Shakespeare's Bastard is not only a figure of dramatic power and political acuity but also of moral rectitude.[63] His exposure outside Angiers of the self-serving nature of the authoritarian imposition of unity is a counterweight to the post-Armada rhetoric he endorses at the end of the play. In the Bastard Shakespeare has created a character who embodies a challenge to the idea that conformity is the ultimate test of loyalty, a character who combines rigorous independence of mind with an absolute fidelity to his king and country. Independence of outlook might have been thought of as subversive by those who enforced Elizabethan religious conformity, but in *King John* it is the independent thinker who is the greatest patriot.

The orthodox end of *King John* resolves, but does not ultimately suppress, the play's argument for the freedom of those who chose to ignore the endlessly reiterated message that England's safety necessitated the conformity of her subjects. *King John*'s anatomization of sectarian discourse (including this inversion of a ubiquitous homiletic trope) challenges the dominant rhetoric of its time. The actions, as well as the words, of the Bastard dramatize the oppositional idea that those who rebelled against conformity need not be feared as enemies to the public good who might support invading armies rather than defend their country. As Womersley writes, "drama's potential to be tentative, exploratory, and hypothetical had allowed Shakespeare to stage forms of political action latent with heterodox implication, and the consequences had been liberating in respect of both theatrical art and political vision."[64] In the Bastard Shakespeare created a character of great dramatic potency (his role – central yet choric, comic, and independent – was to be developed by Shakespeare into both Falstaff and Hamlet), but which also has wider political ramifications. Shakespeare's play subtly endorses an idea which ran counter to the prevailing discourse of the age: that independence of mind and practice could coexist with a passionate fidelity to England.

[63] Neill, "'In everything illegitimate,'" 270–92.

[64] Womersley, *Divinity and State*, p. 268.

CHAPTER 6

# *Shakespeare's* Julius Caesar *and the search for a usable (Christian?) past*

*Peter Lake*

One of the most significant recent developments in the intellectual and political history of post-Reformation England has been the recuperation of a "classical republican" or, in Quentin Skinner's terminology, "neo-Roman" strand of political thought and feeling, which its discoverers want to place somewhere near the heart of the political culture of the period. This strand of thought is classical in its origins and, in its early modern resonances, almost entirely secular.[1] It offers itself as a central explanatory tool for the explication of the political arguments of the period in direct rivalry with accounts centered on religious conflict as the motor for all the really serious political disagreements of the period. In this chapter I want to argue that in *Julius Caesar*[2] Shakespeare both reanimates and stages this neo-Roman, republican ideology and then tests it to breaking point by subjecting it not merely to a secular historical and political critique, but also to a religious, indeed, a Christian critique. I will first examine the play's Roman and secular view of politics and honor, and then, in the later stages of the chapter, suggest some ways in which the play might be thought to bring the Christian sensibilities or impulses of its first audiences into critical engagement with those views.

## I

In recovering the play's version of the neo-Roman view of politics, let us begin with the scene in which Cassius attempts to broach the subject of Caesar's murder to Brutus. Brutus asks,

[1] Quentin Skinner, *Liberty Before Liberalism* (Cambridge University Press, 1998). Also see Markku Peltonen, *Classical Humanism and Republicanism in English Political Thought, 1570–1640* (Cambridge University Press, 1995). For a discussion of republicanism and Shakespeare, see Andrew Hadfield, *Shakespeare and Republicanism* (Cambridge University Press, 2005).

[2] References are taken from William Shakespeare, *Julius Caesar*, ed. David Daniell, Arden Shakespeare 3rd series (London: Bloomsbury, 2002).

What is it that you would impart to me?
If it be aught toward the general good,
Set honor in one eye, and death i'th' other,
And I will look on both indifferently.
For let the gods so speed me as I love
The name of honor more than I fear death. (1.2.84–9)

A number of the central features of what emerges in the play as Roman republican honor can be found in this speech. To begin with, Brutus equates "honor" with service of "the general good" and locates the essence of the honorable man in his capacity to risk his life in that service, and, if necessary, to choose death rather than dishonor. Cassius immediately takes his cue from these remarks and produces his own disquisition on "honor":

I know that virtue to be in you, Brutus,
As well as I do know your outward favor.
Well, honor is the subject of my story.
I cannot tell what you and other men
Think of this life; but for my single self
I had as lief not be as live to be
In awe of such a thing as I myself.
I was born free as Caesar, so were you. (1.2.90–7)

Here, then, "honor" is further associated with "virtue" and "freedom" and again with the honorable man's willingness to choose death rather than dishonor. "Freedom" here appears to mean not being "in awe" of any other mortal. To be reduced to such a state of dependent subordination, willingly or no, is for Cassius *the* great shame to which, for the honorable man, death is always preferrable. Later soliloquizing on Brutus's character, and on the ways in which his traits might allow Cassius to bend him to his purposes, Cassius adds a third crucial term to the list: "Well, Brutus, thou art noble: yet I see / Thy honorable mettle may be wrought / From that it is disposed" (1.2.307–9). Here, then, we have "honor" and "nobility" being associated together and linked with the service of the "general good" and with "freedom" to form a nexus of interrelated terms.

At another point in their dialogue, Cassius explains to Brutus that despite the fact that Caesar is a mere mortal, as subject to the weaknesses of the flesh as any other man, he "is now become a God"; indeed, having got "the start of the majestic world," he now "bears the palm alone" and his countrymen must always "mark him, and write his speeches in their books." So great has Caesar's preponderance grown that "Cassius is / A wretched creature, and must bend his body / If Caesar carelessly but nod on him" (1.2.116–18, 126, 130–1). As he later tells Casca, despite the fact that Caesar is "a man no mightier than thyself, or me, / In personal action," he is now "prodigious grown / And fearful." Like the preternaturally violent storm then raging above their heads, Caesar "thunders, lightens, opens graves and roars / As doth the lion in the Capitol." His arrogation of so much power has, in effect, rendered Rome "a monstrous state" and reduced to the status of "a willing bondman" all those Romans who are prepared passively to acquiesce in his dominance (1.3.71–8, 113). Caesar's greatness – the fact that he "doth bestride the narrow world / Like a colossus" – has reduced his countrymen to mere "petty men," walking "under his huge legs" "to find ourselves dishonorable graves" (1.2.134–7). In Cassius's view, therefore, Caesar's dominance has reduced the Romans to "bondage," the polar opposite of "freedom." Acceptance of that condition is the ultimate source of dishonor. On this view, Rome is already a tyranny and freedom has already been lost. Moreover, on Cassius's account, the graves of those Romans who have submitted passively to this new dispensation will be dishonorable not merely because their subjection to Caesar has rendered them servile, but also because, by allowing one man such power, they have connived at, indeed, acquiesced in, the loss of their own freedom – and nothing could be more dishonorable than that.

Thus for Cassius the blame for the loss of their freedom rests primarily not on Caesar's but on the Romans' own heads. For Cassius, it is not Caesar's preponderant virtue that has won him preponderant power in the state but rather the Romans' lack of virtue, indeed their corruption, that has ceded such a wholly unnatural preponderance to him. As he tells Casca,

> And why should Caesar be a tyrant then?
> Poor man, I know he would not be a wolf
> But that he sees the Romans are but sheep.
> He were no lion, were not the Romans hinds.
> . . .
> What trash is Rome?
> What rubbish, and what offal? When it serves
> For the base matter to illuminate
> So vile a thing as Caesar? (1.3.103–11)

Earlier Cassius had taken a similar tack to Brutus:

> The fault, dear Brutus, is not in our stars
> But in ourselves, that we are underlings.
> . . .
> Upon what meat doth this our Caesar feed
> That he is grown so great? Age, thou art ashamed!
> Rome, thou has lost the breed of noble bloods!

When went there by an age, since the great flood,
But it was famed with more than with one man?
When could they say, till now, that talked of Rome,
That her wide walks encompassed but one man?
Now is it Rome indeed, and room enough,
When there is in it but one only man.
O, you and I have heard our fathers say
There was a Brutus once that would have brooked
Th'eternal devil to keep his state in Rome
As easily as a king. (1.2.139–60)

In his later exchange with Casca, Cassius makes the same point, only in gendered terms: "Romans now / Have thews and limbs like to their ancestors: / But woe the while, our fathers' minds are dead, / And we are governed with our mothers' spirits: / Our yoke and sufferance show us womanish" (1.3.80–4). On this account, then, it was lost virtue that led to lost liberty, and the loss of liberty that is now leading to a further loss of honor and virtue. Rome has entered a cycle of decline from which, both Cassius and Brutus believe, it can only be rescued by the death of Caesar. From the manly Roman virtue and active service of the common good displayed by their ancestors the current Romans have declined to a "womanish" subservience and passivity.

Honor and nobility are thus a function of freedom and virtue; that is to say, true nobility is displayed and honor acquired through the exercise of virtue in the defense or prosecution of the general or public good, in a state that is not dominated by the power or authority of any one man. "Freedom" consists in the absence of such domination and in the free competition for honor between a variety of autonomously noble and virtuous servants of the general good. The resulting honor system is intensely emulous and competitive, but the result is not a "zero-sum" game. It is the combination of competition and collaboration, of mutual respect and self-regard, that defines this honor code and community as republican. Men compete for honor, but however great the achievements and virtues of any given individual, permanent dominance, still less institutionalized power, is never to be ceded to any. The competition for honor must remain free, and in recognizing the genuine honor of – and indeed in ceding moral primacy and even a form of political authority to – another bearer of true *Romanitas*, the true man of honor does not deplete his own store of honor but rather displays and thus augments it. Under this system of rule, no one is ever more than *primus inter pares* and the competition between actual or wannabe honor-bearing individuals to vindicate their honor and nobility through service to the state operates to keep everyone honest.[3] It is the preservation of this system of government that is connoted by the phrase "liberty" or "freedom," precisely the slogans which the conspirators rush to the marketplace to proclaim immediately after they have killed Caesar: "Tyranny is dead" (3.1.78–9) or, with Brutus, "Peace, Freedom and Liberty" (3.1.109–10).

## II

Thus far, in Shakespeare's account we have been dealing with an entirely civic ideology concerned with service to the common good, the vindication of one's honor, and the achievement of "fame" through the esteem of one's peers and the plaudits and electoral support of the people. But Shakespeare does not leave it there. Crucial to Roman honor, as he describes it, is an acceptance – indeed, in the right circumstances, an embrace – of death, up to and including the point of suicide. Confronted by the virtual certainty that, as Casca explains, "the senators tomorrow / Mean to establish Caesar as a king, / And he shall wear his crown by sea and land / In every place save here in Italy," Cassius takes this as a sign of the certain arrival of tyranny and servitude to the Roman state. But this, he claims, is a form of "bondage" that cannot contain the likes of Cassius:

> I know where I will wear this dagger then:
> Cassius from bondage will deliver Cassius.
> Therein, ye gods, you tyrants do defeat.
> Nor stony tower, nor walls of beaten brass,
> No airless dungeon, nor strong links of iron,
> Can be retentive to the strength of spirit:
> But life being weary of these worldly bars
> Never lacks power to dismiss himself.
> If I know this, know all the world besides,
> That part of tyranny that I do bear
> I can shake off at pleasure.

[3] For early modern English notions of honor see, amongst a large literature, Mervyn James, *Society, Politics, Culture* (Cambridge University Press, 1986), esp. chs. 8 and 9; Richard Cust, "Honor and Politics in Early Stuart England: The Case of Beaumont v. Hastings," *Past & Present*, 149 (1995), 57–94. The best overview of a complex subject is Keith Thomas, *The Ends of Life* (Oxford University Press, 2009), ch. 5. While resonating with a range of contemporary Elizabethan attitudes, the play goes out of its way to construct a recognizably Roman, republican, and as we shall see below, pagan honor code.

To which Casca replies:

> So can I.
> So every bondman in his own hand bears
> The power to cancel his captivity. (1.3.85–102)

Here, then, is an acceptance of death's inevitability and of the immutability of fate reaching its apogee, its logical end point, in the willingness of the genuinely free man to cheat the tyrant by ending a life that had, through the loss of freedom, become the utterly dishonorable lot of a bondman and a subject, rather than that of a free Roman.

Cassius's sentiments prefigure those of Brutus expressed later in the play when, in another exchange with Cassius about the appropriateness of suicide as a response to final defeat and disgrace, he censures Cato "for the death / Which he did give himself – I know not how." For, Brutus explains, "I do find it cowardly and vile, / For fear of what might fall, so to prevent the time of life." Until all else fails, it is incumbent on the man of honor to "arm himself" with "patience" and "to stay the providence of some high powers / That govern us below." But that condemnation of the cowardice of a suicide undertaken prematurely, as a sign of "fear of what might fall," itself comes in a speech in which Brutus declares his intention to die by his own hand if he is defeated by Antony and Octavian. Moreover, he justifies that decision as having been informed "by the rule of that philosophy by which I did blame Cato" for his suicide. "Think not, thou noble Roman, / That ever Brutus will go bound to Rome. / He bears too great a mind. But this same day / Must end that work the Ides of March begun" (5.1.100–13). In all this, Caesar, Cassius, and Brutus are repeating and claiming as their own what Miles calls "orthodox stoic wisdom." For Seneca, suicide "is the last defense of the sapiens against fortune." The wise man knows that "life itself is an 'indifferent' thing" and is thus able, "if it comes to a choice between life and virtue," to choose virtue, honor and, it is to be hoped, an immortal Cato-like fame by taking his own life.[4]

Thus, while the capacity to contemplate one's own death with equanimity, up to the point of being prepared to end it oneself, is indeed a central characteristic of the man of honor, such readiness to die should, in the truly honorable, be neither a cause nor a sign of an unmanly passivity before events. For an enervating fatalism, a womanish "fear of what might fall" was the polar opposite of the active virtue that characterized the Roman man of honor. As the tragic fate of Portia shows, premature suicide was the

[4] Geoffrey Miles, *Shakespeare and the Constant Romans* (Oxford University Press, 1996), p. 54.

woman's part. Genuine equanimity before the inevitability of death and the immutability of fate should enable the honorable man to risk all for the general good and, only in extremity, prompt him to choose death rather than dishonor: an option that should be taken only after all other available avenues for the exercise of an active virtue, up to and including desperately dangerous expedients – like those that start on the Ides of March and culminate at Philippi – have been exhausted. Only then, when confronted by inevitable defeat and dishonor – represented here by the prospect of being "led in triumph / Through the streets of Rome" (5.1.108–9) – can the "noble Roman" of genuinely "great mind" contemplate ending his own life.

## III

Having recuperated with extraordinary economy and precision in *Julius Caesar* almost the exact lineaments of the ideology identified by Skinner as neo-Roman, Shakespeare then juxtaposes it against a pseudo-monarchical, indeed a proto-tyrannical, version of the same ideology, epitomized in the political milieu around Caesar and openly expressed by Caesar's megalomaniacal claims to a superhuman version of Roman constancy, honor, and virtue. While this might seem to tilt the moral balance in favor of the republican position, Shakespeare then proceeds to test to the breaking point the claims of republican ideology that it provides the basis, within the moral and political circumstances delineated by the play, for effective political action or rule. I say in the precise circumstances outlined in the play because Shakespeare is very careful to locate the action in a political society in the throes of change: ceasing to be a republic, Rome has yet to become a monarchy. If Rome is still a republic, then Caesar's semiregal power in the state, compounded by what Brutus calls his "ambition" to become king, renders him not a legitimate prince at all but at best a usurper, at worst a traitor to the state, bent on undermining the very principles of government that determine legitimacy in Rome. But if Caesar's rise to power has already changed Rome so that it is no longer really a republic but in fact some kind of incipient monarchy, then Calpurnia's calling Caesar a prince is a simple statement of fact and the third and fourth plebeians' proposals, made immediately after Caesar's murder, to "let Brutus be Caesar" and to "crown" Brutus (3.2.51–2) are not as ludicrous as they might at first seem. Certainly, in that case, Caesar would be a legitimate ruler, and killing him would be an act of treason.[5]

[5] See Robert Miola, "Julius Caesar and the Tyrannicide Debate," *Renaissance Quarterly*, 38 (1985), 271–89.

This constitutional liminality is reflected in the very different estimations of the current condition of Caesar and of Rome to be found amongst the leading characters of the play. For Cassius, king or not, Caesar is already a tyrant, a man whose de facto dominance of the political system has made him "the only man in Rome" and thus reduced the rest of his erstwhile fellow citizens to a state of servitude. Cassius tries very hard to persuade Brutus of this view of the matter, and in the famous soliloquy in the orchard Brutus tries very hard to persuade himself that Caesar is already a very bad man, rendered a tyrant both by his current position in the state and by the corruption of his own character, and therefore someone who thoroughly deserves to die. But Brutus (let alone Cassius) entirely fails to persuade himself of any of this. For him Caesar remains the noblest of all the Romans, a man whose current preeminence is a just reward for his supervening virtue and service to the state. It is just that that current preeminence must not be given permanent institutional form in an offer of kingship. It is thus not what Caesar is but what he will become, or, more precisely, what his becoming king would do to Rome, that is the problem; it is thus his "ambition" to become a king that threatens to destroy the republic and the cause of Roman liberty for good and all, and it is for that reason that he must die.[6] Having toyed with more viscerally personal reasons to kill Caesar, it is to that purely ideological, coherently republican, rationale that Brutus reverts when he makes his pitch to the Roman people after the assassination. Thus if Antony, even as he conflates the bleeding corpse of Caesar with Rome itself, is clear that what has just happened is "treason," so the conspirators are just as certain that it is a state-saving act of purgation that has preserved "liberty" and averted "tyranny." The ease with which the Roman people are convinced, in rapid succession, of both views of the matter might be taken as an index not merely of the fickle volatility of the mob, but also of the extraordinarily volatile condition of the polity itself, caught in a limbo of betwixt and between, neither one thing nor the other.

The play thus presents us with a society in the midst of the most profound political, moral, and ideological change. It also shows us a group of malcontent nobles working themselves up to take action by resurrecting from the Roman past ideals of political virtue and liberty, nobility, and honor. When Cassius is ranting about the honor of the current

[6] The binary choice between slavery and freedom, and the equivalence between those states and a Rome with Caesar alive and one with him dead, can be characterized, in Schanzer's phrase, as "quite unreal," or in Chernaik's as "fallacious," only if these basic republican premises are ignored. Ernest Schanzer, *The Problem Plays of Shakespeare* (New York: Schocken Books, 1965), p. 48; Warren L. Chernaik, *The Myth of Rome in Shakespeare and his Contemporaries* (Cambridge University Press, 2011), p. 83.

generation's forebears, he is doing so not to emphasize issues of hereditary right or the prerogatives of noble lineage, but rather to recall to mind the masculine Romanness and constancy of their ancestors in general and of Brutus's king-killing forebears in particular. In other words, he exhorts his contemporaries to emulate the zeal of those ancient Romans who had risked their lives defending Rome from the tyranny of monarchy, and, in expelling the Tarquins, founded the Roman republican state. In these exchanges, Cassius uses examples from the Roman past in precisely the way that Elizabethan readers and commentators were trained to do: that is to say, extracting certain exempla of moral or political virtue, certain political and moral insights and apothegms, certain rules to live (and die) by, not merely for the moral instruction or improvement but for the active emulation of contemporaries.

As Wayne Rebhorn and Coppélia Kahn have both emphasized, emulation was central to the process whereby Roman virtue is produced in the play.[7] It involves the use of models of right behavior, of virtuous dedication to the commonweal, culled both from the Roman past – *vide* Cassius's citation of Brutus's glorious forebear – and from the present. These models are then held up for imitation. The process is inherently competitive, the aim being not merely to copy or reproduce but to exceed the virtue displayed by the original. The same notion was equally central to humanist education in sixteenth-century England; as Kahn observes, "emulation as the imitation of approved Latin authors was integral to Renaissance pedagogy and poetics." Again the process was inherently competitive, imitative or emulous rivalry with the original "creating a competitive model of appreciative emulation focused on outdoing the original text or precedent." Emulation was "intended to teach judgment and analysis and was meant to create excellence of character as well of speech." It transcended the realm of rhetoric and became a social and a moral process. Vernon Dickson quotes George Abbot to the effect that "it is not in rhetoric only that imitation holdeth, but in all the course of life."[8] The play thus shows us the ancient Romans doing to one another, and with the Roman past, what English gentlemen were taught to do with the moral and literary examples of the ancient Romans. It is just that in the play Cassius is using such modes of argument and exhortation to persuade his fellow conspirators to an act of

[7] Wayne Rebhorn, "The Crisis of the Aristocracy in *Julius Caesar*," *Renaissance Quarterly*, 43 (1990), 78–109; Coppélia Kahn, *Roman Shakespeare* (New York: Routledge, 1997), pp. 16–17.

[8] Vernon Guy Dickson, "'A pattern, precedent and lively warrant': Emulation, Rhetoric and Cruel Propriety in *Titus Andronicus*," *Renaissance Quarterly*, 62 (2009), 376–409 (385–6).

annihilating political violence. He succeeds in doing that, and the play then reveals the consequences of that success to be disastrous.[9]

They are disastrous because Cassius and not Brutus is right about the current moral and political state of Rome. Caesar's dominance has stripped both the Roman people and the political elite of their republican virtue. Rhetorical appeals couched in terms of the key words of republican *Romanitas* ("liberty," "tyranny," "slavery," and "Rome") used as a synonym for the free state, service to which was the cynosure of all true nobility and honor, can no longer constrain the actions or compel the allegiance of either the Roman people or key members of the elite, like Mark Antony. It is Brutus's tragedy that throughout he frames all his political actions and calculations on the assumption that the actions and reactions of his contemporaries would and could be so constrained. As Joseph Simmons observes, he even assumes that "when Caesar is rooted out, so localized is the state's corruption that even Antony will either be regenerated or die."[10] It is as though once Caesar and the prospect of kingship have been removed from the scene all the organizing assumptions and constraints of the republic will snap back into place and the rule of men of the greatest honor and nobility – amongst whom, of course, Brutus assumes himself to be preeminent – will be assured.

It is this assumption that prompts all Brutus's fatal political mistakes: his decision not to include Antony on the original hit list; his belief that, after the murder of Caesar, even Antony can be co-opted and morally coerced into collaboration with the restored republican clique; his assumption that his own sternly republican pitch to the Roman people will work so definitively that thereafter Antony can be safely entrusted with the funeral oration. Not only that, but it is the cult of Roman republican honor, operating within and between the conspirators, that ensures that, at all the really crucial moments, it is always Brutus's (politically mistaken) view of the matter that prevails, and the greater political sagacity and military skill of the palpably less honorable Cassius that loses out. In the confrontation at Sardis, Brutus's brutal performance of his superior virtue reduces Cassius to the position of moral inferiority from which he feels compelled to let Brutus have his way over how and where to engage the enemy, with disastrous consequences for the republican cause. It is as though the more perfectly the

9 For more on the widespread use of imitative reading practices in Shakespeare's day, and especially the application of *exempla* from classical history to contemporary problems, see Chapter 5 above, on *King John*.

10 Joseph Larry Simmons, *Shakespeare's Pagan World: The Roman Tragedies* (Charlottesville: University Press of Virginia, 1973), p. 99.

conspirators manage to recuperate and perform republican *Romanitas* and honor, the more mistakes they make.

As a number of commentators, perhaps most notably Sigurd Burckhardt, have observed, what seems to be at stake here is a question of timing.[11] In a crucial line, Cassius reassures Brutus that "men at some time are masters of their fates" (1.2.138). The basic political questions the play poses are, firstly, is this true? And, secondly, even if it is true, how can we best tell the time? By what criteria might men decide whether and when the time, their time, is ripe? Certainly what the play shows us is a group of men of no inconsiderable virtue – the audience is surely meant at least partially to share Mark Antony's judgment, delivered over Brutus's corpse, that "this was the noblest Roman of them all" – who have decisively got their timing wrong. By applying a carefully reconstructed and exquisitely performed version of antique Roman virtue and republican honor to a set of circumstances in which such virtues are no longer salient, the conspirators not only fail to realize their objectives, they ruin the very state they have been trying to save. Far from being saved from tyranny, Rome is pitched into a violent civil war, the result of which (as any contemporary audience would have known) would be the emergence of an imperial polity far more monarchical, and arguably far more tyrannical, than anything Julius Caesar would have been likely to visit on the vestigial remains of the republican polity that had produced him. The play operates, then, as a dreadful warning about the misapplication of a set of historical lessons drawn from a classical Roman republican past to a set of political circumstances to which they are wholly inappropriate.

## IV

We have here an entirely secular, this-worldly account of the failure of republican ideology to work in the circumstances delineated by the play. Given the pagan classical sources for the play and the ideology it is depicting with such close attention, and the relentlessly secular account of the early modern period produced by scholars of political thought who have put such time and effort into reconstructing the neo-Roman view of the world, that is precisely what we might expect. But Shakespeare does not just leave it there. For *Julius Caesar* is a play notoriously suffused with the supernatural. A plethora of prodigies and prophecies, of omens and curses, recur throughout the action. Perhaps the most overtly prophetic of the prophecies is the

[11] Sigurd Burckhardt, *Shakespearean Meanings* (Princeton University Press, 1968), pp. 5–9.

pronouncement of the soothsayer about the Ides of March. Not far behind comes Calpurnia's dream foretelling the death of Caesar. This, of course, is seconded by the results of the augurers' sacrifice. Antony's vision of a Roman world torn asunder by the devastations of civil war is part prognostication, part curse, and part prophesy. Artemidorus's warning to Caesar (2.3.1–6) is not so much a prophesy as a tip-off, but even here Artemidorus makes the outcome of his efforts to forewarn Caesar a test of the role of the fates in deciding the course of human affairs: "If thou read'st this, O Caesar, thou mayst live; / If not, the Fates with traitors do contrive" (2.3.14–15).

As for portents and prodigies, the play has no end of them. Chief of these, of course, is the prodigious storm that rages the night before Caesar is assassinated. A range of different characters attests to the extremity of this event and to the extraordinary prodigies and portents with which it is attended. Casca reports a series of wonders to Cicero, reports which are confirmed by Calpurnia's account of the same or similar events to Caesar (1.3.5–28). Later in the play, Brutus is visited by Caesar's ghost, "a monstrous apparition" that "mak'st my blood cold, and my hair to stare" (4.3.275–8). Immediately before the battle of Philippi, on his birthday, Cassius reports what he now takes to be an omen to his intimate Messala:

> Coming from Sardis, on our former ensign
> Two mighty eagles fell and there they perched,
> Gorging and feeding from our soldiers' hands,
> Who to Philippi here consorted us:
> This morning are they fled away and gone,
> And in their steads do ravens, crows and kites
> Fly o'er our heads and downward look on us
> As we were sickly prey. (5.1.79–86)

While most of the characters in the play are convinced that these portents and wonders must mean something, they are entirely incapable of deciding just what that might be. Thus Casca exclaims that "when these prodigies / Do so conjointly meet, let not men say, / 'These are their reasons, they are natural': / For I believe they are portentous things / Unto the climate that they point upon" (1.3.28–32). But his awestruck claim that "it is the part of men to fear and tremble / When the most mighty gods by tokens send / Such dreadful heralds to astonish us" (1.3.54–6) is met by Cicero's somewhat downbeat reply, "But men may construe things after their fashion / Clean from the purpose of the things themselves" (1.3.34–5).

Significantly, it is the play's most consistent and rigorous bearers of republican honor who are least impressed, or indeed intrigued, by such seemingly supernatural pyrotechnics. Awe-inspiring portents to Casca, such prodigies provide Cassius with another occasion to display his constancy of mind, a crucial aspect of which is a decided absence of awe:

> For my part, I have walked about the streets,
> Submitting me unto the perilous night,
> And thus unbracèd, Casca, as you see,
> Have bared my bosom to the thunder-stone:
> And when the cross blue lightning seemed to open
> The breast of heaven, I did present myself
> Even in the aim and very flash of it. (1.3.46–52)

Asked by Casca, "But wherefore do you so much tempt the heavens?" (1.3.53), Cassius uses the question as the starting point for another rant about the way the unnatural preponderance of Caesar has turned Rome into a veritably "monstrous state" (1.3.62–71). For Cassius, then, the prodigies of the storm are not fit objects for wonder or fear; they do not presage horrors to come, so much as prompt present action – the very action, in fact, which he is already bound and determined to take.

Brutus is even less alarmed than Cassius by the "exhalations whizzing in the air" (2.1.44). Trapped between what he later calls "the acting of a dreadful thing / And the first motion" (2.1.63–4), deep in reverie about what must be done about Caesar, Brutus remains entirely unconcerned about the meaning of these prodigies. Instead of pondering the storm as a possible sign regarding his, Caesar's, or Rome's fate, he merely uses the light shed by the lightning to read the anonymous missives sent to deceive him by Cassius and his accomplices.

Indeed, until the very end, Brutus and Cassius sustain a position of settled indifference to such concerns. Before Philippi, even as Cassius takes the "ravens, crows and kites flying o'er our heads" to be some sort of omen – "a canopy most fatal, under which / Our army lies, ready to give up the ghost" – he also tells Messala that "I believe it but partly, / For I am fresh of spirit and resolved / To meet all perils constantly" (5.1.89–91). Even as Brutus is confronted by the specter of Caesar's ghost, while he sweats in fear and his hair stands on end, he maintains an exemplary constancy of mind in the face of the "monstrous apparition." Unsure of what it is – his question, "Art thou some god, some angel, or some devil?" remains, for now, unanswered – its claim that it is "Thy evil spirit, Brutus" and that "thou shalt see me at Philippi" elicits only the response, "Why, I will see thee at Philippi then" (4.3.275–84). Indeed, the attitude expressed by Brutus to Cassius on the eve of battle represents something like the quintessence of

Roman honor as delineated by the play. Brutus starts out wistfully: "O that a man might know / The end of this day's business ere it come." But that, he knows, is a fond wish. "But it sufficeth that the day will end, / And then the end is known" (5.1.122–5). Facing an unknowable fate, the man of constant mind, knowing that death is certain, must be ready to embrace and face down any eventuality. The worst that can happen is death, and death is inevitable. Learning of Portia's suicide, Brutus observes that "We must die, Messala: / With meditating that she must die once / I have the patience to endure it now," a remark which draws from Cassius the entirely admiring, even awestruck, comment that "I have as much of this in art as you, / But yet my nature could not bear it so" (4.3.188–93).

The play, then, presents us with a variety of pagan Romans, all of whom have been taught by the demands of Roman virtue and the dictates of "philosophy" to regard any concern with prodigies, portents, or prophecies as "superstition." They have also been taught to regard fate as unknowable and the best way to meet it an acceptance of the inevitability of death; an acceptance that, by fortifying one against fear of the unknown and the tergiversations of fortune, leads not to fatalistic passivity but rather to an active pursuit of virtue and honor, safe in the knowledge that, if all else fails, one can choose death rather than dishonor or servitude and, by dying by one's own hand, cheat both tyranny and fate. That certainly is the view taken throughout by Brutus, Cassius, and Caesar and in the end is acted upon by both Brutus and Cassius. There is, then, a sense in which suicide – the capacity and willingness, in the face of a malign and unknowable fate, to choose death rather than dishonor – represents the coping stone in the arch of the pagan philosophy and Roman honor politics attributed by the play to all its central characters.

On this view, attention paid to the sorts of prodigies and prophecies which suffuse the play amounts to what Cassius contemptuously describes as "superstition." That claim occurs in a speech in which Caesar is said to have grown superstitious only "of late." Clearly, Caesar's attitudes to such things are changing, and in this he is not alone. Calpurnia enters claiming that "I never stood on ceremonies, / Yet now they fright me" (2.2.13–14). Cassius, too, by the end can be found telling Messala that he has changed his mind on the subject of portents and prophecies: "You know that I held Epicurus strong / And his opinion: now I change my mind / And partly credit things that do presage" (5.1.76–8). Of all the central figures in the play, it is the virtuous Brutus who is the last to come to such a change of heart. Only at the very end, when all is lost, does he admit that his end has been foretold: "The ghost of Caesar hath appeared to me / Two several times by night: at Sardis once, / And this last night, here in Philippi fields: / I know my hour is come" (5.5.16–19). Earlier, coming upon Cassius, slain by his own hand, Brutus had exclaimed, "O Julius Caesar, thou art mighty yet. / Thy spirit walks abroad and turns our swords / In our own proper entrails" (5.3.94–6). With his dying breath, Brutus again acknowledges the hand of fate in his own end: "Caesar, now be still. / I killed not thee with half so good a will" (5.5.51–2). Brutus's dying words pick up those of Cassius, who immediately before he dies cries, "Caesar, thou art revenged / Even with the sword that killed thee" (5.3.45–6).

Thus the play also shows us each of the central characters unlearning the lessons of (pagan) philosophy, Roman virtue, and republican honor – coming, in fact, to believe in what Calpurnia calls "ceremonies" and what Cassius calls "things that do presage" and "superstition." And it shows us that they are quite right to do so. After all, all the prophecies with which the play is studded come true. Caesar should have been wary of the ides of March; he does die under the daggers of his countrymen, as Calpurnia has foreseen; he should have looked out for Brutus, Cassius and the rest; subsequent to his death the Roman world is plunged into a bloody civil war, as Antony prophesies. The portents, too, prove the true harbingers of a variety of the disasters that at least some of the characters take them to be; the prodigies of the night before Caesar's assassination have indeed "blazed forth the death" of a prince; the crows and kites flocking above the republican army at Philippi and the visitation of Caesar's ghost as Brutus's "evil spirit" do indeed mean that the conspirators' number is up. Having set out to slay "the spirit of Caesar" (2.1.166), Brutus and Cassius succumb to the revengeful attentions of that very spirit, killing themselves with the same swords with which they had cut Caesar down.

What, to the philosophy espoused by Brutus and Cassius, looks like superstition, is thus presented by the play as something indeed that any Elizabethan audience, inured to the structuring assumptions of innumerable tracts, sermons, and indeed plays, would have identified as the operation of providence, to whose (both admonitory and punitive) interventions into events, it was anything but "superstitious" to attend.[12] As has been argued above, the depiction in history plays and tragedies of the operations of providence, in particular through the framing presence of prophecies, prodigies, and portents, allows the audience access

[12] The seminal account of early modern English attitudes to providence is to be found in Alexandra Walsham, *Providence in Early Modern England* (Oxford University Press, 1999). On prodigies and prophecies, see esp. ch. 4.

to what the play presents as the patterning of events by providence that is far more complete and panoptical than anything available to any of the characters. Ceded, through the operation of such providences, something like a God's-eye view of the action, the audience can indulge in processes of judgment – moral, theological, political – that constitute, inside their own heads, what we might take to be the meta-argument of the play. Certainly they can see as "providential" things that are ignored or misunderstood by the characters on stage. One thinks of the repeated pattern whereby, disagreeing about what to do next, Brutus always wins the argument and always with disastrous results. Armed with the providential framework provided to them by the play's insistent pattern of portents and prophecies, the audience might well see this not only as a commentary on the contradictions between, say, the politics of honor and faction, or even between the characters and moral qualities of Brutus and Cassius, but as an expression of a providential patterning of events, which uses the dominant characteristics (in Christian terms, the defining "sins") of the central figures to frustrate their own (sinful) purposes, bringing the conspirators to judgment and death at Philippi, even as the sins of Caesar and Rome have been punished in their turn by the conspirators' resort to political violence and all its dreadful consequences. Built into such a providential reading of the play would be the extraordinary blindness of the leading characters in the face of the signs and prophecies provided to them, which, if heeded, would have saved them from the fates visited upon them by the play's end. Such failures to see things literally thrust in their faces by providence could themselves be seen as "providential." For here was providence using the sins and weaknesses of these men to bring them to punishments that their sins had deserved and that, however clear the warnings that they had been vouchsafed by heaven, their own (fallen) capacities had been entirely unable to perceive, let alone avert. Having been warned, and having ignored the warning, they were thus doubly culpable.

Such a reading of the play's action would, of course, be an intensely Christian one, predicated on the existence of an omnipotent and immutably just and merciful God whose both mysterious and beneficent purposes could be seen working their way through the events of human history, in ways that not merely conferred meaning and coherence on those events but sent messages of admonition and exhortation about that meaning and coherence to all those with eyes to see. But the play, of course, is not about Christians, but Roman pagans, exponents of an entirely pagan philosophy. It is true that that philosophy, as the play stages it, has somewhere near its heart notions of "liberty" and "justice," of "nobility" and "honor" entirely recognizable to a Christian audience as moral goods. It also prominently features a concern with the nature of the good death and of the need to square the purposes of humanity with the dictates and outcomes of a fate that no human can penetrate that parallel quite closely the central concerns of many sixteenth-century Christians. But still it has no place for the omnipotent Christian God and no place, therefore, for providence as Christians constructed and applied it to their lives and times; no place, either, for the immortal Christian soul, nor for any concept of an afterlife in which salvation and damnation depend on some combination of the operations of divine grace and the conduct of the individual in this life.

None of the characters show the slightest regard for their fate in the next life. Insofar as it means anything to them, immortality is a function of immortal fame, something to be won by honorable service to the republic and the public performance of true honor and nobility, even in the face of death. Immediately after the murder of Caesar, Brutus and Cassius imagine their deed winning them fame down the centuries as it is played out in "sport" upon the public stage: "So oft as that shall / So often shall the knot of us be called / The men who gave their country liberty," crows Cassius (3.1.114–19). It is, of course, one of the many ironies in which the play abounds that this very play is itself contributing to the process whereby such an immortal fame is conferred upon Caesar's killers. But, as the play shows, they have become famous not for having "given their country liberty," which, after all, is something that they signally fail to do, but rather for giving their all in the service of what they take to be the general good and then meeting honorable deaths, when all is lost, at Philippi.

These of course were not positions or opinions open to the Elizabethan Christians that made up the play's first audiences, whom the play constructs as Christians by enabling, even inducing, them to place the (inherently Christian) providential frame, afforded them by the prophecies, prodigies, and structural symmetries of the plot, around the (decidedly un-Christian) doings of the Roman, pagan, and republican protagonist of the play. Put crudely, the audience could see more than the characters not merely because, given the fame of the play's subjects, they already knew the outcome, nor because, as the audience, they were situated outside the action, and thus able to see the overarching structures of the plot in ways that the characters simply could not – but also because they were Christians. Thus the audience's application of their own (at least residually) Christian hermeneutic impulses to the providential signs that structure and comment upon so much of the play would have served as a constant reminder of the cultural gap that separated the pagan and republican Rome being staged in the play from the Christian and monarchical world in which the play was being staged.[13]

If we take the providential view upon which the play virtually insists, we might ask, if the play's outcome represents a series of judgments, upon what sins precisely have those judgments been visited? A conventional answer would be the violent resistance, regicide, and rebellion of the conspirators. But as we have seen the play is carefully structured to render such a pat response unavailable. We are left with the conclusion that the providential judgments staged in the play are being visited not on the perpetrators of "resistance" but rather on the perpetrators of a certain sort of political mistake, a mistake predicated on a disastrously anachronistic and over-literal reading of classical republican notions of honor, liberty, and political virtue onto a political context in which they no longer fit.

## V

And, of course, what applies to the republican faction in the world of the play would have applied in spades to any contemporary Elizabethan political actors, who, stimulated by their readings from the classical past, were thinking about applying insights and principles gleaned therefrom too directly to contemporary problems and conjunctures. And that in 1599 was a decidedly threatening possibility. With the prospect of the queen's death without a settled successor looming, and the question of peace with Spain an open and vigorously debated question, both at court and in the public sphere described by circulating manuscripts, Elizabethan England appeared to many contemporaries to be a polity in flux.[14] With the Earl of Essex known to be chafing under the rebukes of the queen, and standing on his honor as a nobleman and servant of the commonweal as he did so;[15] with his Irish expedition crashing and burning and with wild rumors about events there in circulation and speculation about his intentions

[13] A number of chapters in this volume consider the role of providence in Shakespeare's plays, e.g. Chapter 1 on *Hamlet*, Chapter 8 on *Lear*, and both Chapters 12 and 13 on *Henry VIII*.

[14] Alexandra Gajda, "Debating War and Peace in Late Elizabethan England," *Historical Journal*, 52 (2000), 851–78. Essex's *Apology*, a manuscript outlining the reasons for his opposition to the peace, was in circulation at precisely this period.

[15] This was well known because of the circulation in manuscript in 1598 of an exchange of letters between Essex and Egerton. This had been occasioned by an extraordinary scene between Essex and the queen in the course of which she had boxed his ears and he had turned towards her with his hand on the pommel of his sword, before storming out of the room. Egerton responded with a letter counseling caution and accommodation, Essex with a shrill self-justification, which proceeded to do the rounds as some sort of manifesto for his honor and independence. The letters are reprinted in G. B. Harrison, *The Life and Death of Robert Devereux, Earl of Essex* (London: Cassell, 1937), pp. 196–201.

rife at court,[16] there was every reason for contemporaries to be concerned both about what might be happening now and what might be about to happen next, over the summer and autumn of 1599.

Moreover, the circle around Essex was characterized by a particular enthusiasm for certain styles of politic history, in and through which moral principles and prudential axioms were to be extracted from ancient histories, particularly those by Tacitus, for application to current conditions and predicaments.[17] The dangerous potentials lurking within such interests had recently been highlighted by the scandal over Dr. John Hayward's heavily Tacitean and recently called in, indeed publicly burnt, *Life of Henry IV*, which, in its dedication to Essex, hailed the earl, with a quite stunning lack of tact, as "our Bolingbroke."[18] In this context a warning about the dire consequences of getting the reading of the Roman past wrong and, in particular, about applying values and expectations culled from a republican and pagan Roman past too directly to a monarchical and Christian present were entirely apposite.

There remains, of course, one final paradox. If the play does operate as a warning against the dangers of an overly literal exercise in politick history and emulation, it does so through its own application of classical, Roman republican history to current concerns. It serves, therefore, not so much as a warning against the use of history as a source of moral and political insight into current political realities, but rather as a warning against doing it badly; and it does so by presenting its audience with an extended example of how to do it well.[19] And it was to be done well not by simply recuperating past values and examples and applying them to the present, but rather by

[16] Robert Lacey, *Robert, Earl of Essex, Elizabethan Icarus* (London: Weidenfeld & Nicolson, 1971), p. 234. Also Harrison, *Life and Death*, pp. 246–7. On the general air of crisis and unease at this point, see James Shapiro, *1599: One Year in the Life of William Shakespeare* (London: Faber, 2005), ch. 13.

[17] Malcolm Smuts, "Court-Centred Politics and the Uses of Roman Historians, *c.*1590–1630," in Kevin Sharpe and Peter Lake (eds.), *Culture and Politics in Early Stuart England* (Stanford University Press, 1993), pp. 21–43; and Alexandra Gajda, "Scholars and Martialists: The Politics of History and Scholarship," in *The Earl of Essex and Late Elizabethan Political Culture* (Oxford University Press, 2012), pp. 216–54, and "*The State of Christendom*: History, Political Thought and the Essex Circle," *Historical Research*, 81 (August 2008), 423–46. Paulina Kewes, "Henry Savile's Tacitus and the Politics of Roman History in Late Elizabethan England," *Huntington Library Quarterly*, 74.4 (2011), 515–51.

[18] Cyndia Susan Clegg, *Press Censorship in Elizabethan London* (Cambridge University Press, 1997), pp. 202–7; Richard Dutton, "Buggeswords: The Case of Sir John Hayword's *Life of Henry IV*," in *Licensing, Censorship and Authorship in Early Modern England* (Basingstoke: Palgrave Macmillan, 2000).

[19] We might add that history was a newly tender, not to say controversial topic, subsequent to the bishop's ban of May/June 1599, which, amongst other things, ordered that "no English histories be printed, except they be allowed by her majesty's Privy Council." Shakespeare's decision to write what

accurately analyzing the nature of the times and by carefully establishing, both in the past and the present, the contours of the political conjuncture within which the events being studied were taking place and the persons and values to be emulated were operating. This was to use the study of the past not only as a source of ideals and principles to emulate but also of practical prudential political wisdom with which to navigate the particular political circumstances with which one was confronted. This was to put a heightened sense of what was indeed politick back into the exercise of politick history.

But this was not a matter merely of "history" but also of "religion." For, on the current reading, the play puts at the very center of its account the difference between a pagan value system or world view and Christianity. Under the former dispensation, immortality might well be a function of fame achieved, or indeed, as the fates of Brutus and Cassius show, even of glorious failure suffered, in the service of the common good, and suicide might well provide a perfectly acceptable, even meritorious, response to failure. But for Christians none of that could be true; their aims could not be centered solely on the values and contingencies of this world. Theirs must be a more than civic vision. And thus, if they wanted to succeed where Brutus and Cassius had failed, contemporary political actors would have not only to get their history right, but also attend to the warnings, admonitions, and judgments of divine providence. In short, they would have to remember that they were Christians.

was, on the current reading, a staged disquisition of the right, as well as the wrong, way to use history to think about politics, using not, as had hitherto been his custom, English, but Roman history, might have had some relation to the ban.

CHAPTER 7

# *Lucretius, Calvin, and natural law in* Measure for Measure

*Adrian Streete*

## I

While the intellectual significance of Lucretius's great work *De Rerum Natura* (*c.* 50 BC) during the latter part of the seventeenth century has long been recognized, a number of scholars have argued that the poem's literary influence can in fact be traced much earlier in the period.[1] Stephen Greenblatt's *The Swerve: How the Renaissance Began* (2011) has given a new impetus to the question of Lucretius's "influence" in the medieval and early modern periods. In particular, a number of medievalists have criticized Greenblatt for a caricatured view of the medieval period, one that reinforces outdated notions of periodization that many scholars, medieval and early modern alike, have done much to question in recent years.[2] Occasionally these criticisms can sound shrill – following one line of argument commonly used to critique Greenblatt to its logical consequence, it sometimes seems as if the very fact of writing scholarship focused on the early modern period must invariably collude in an implicitly disrespectful oppression of the medieval period and its scholarship. However, this chapter tries to build positively on these debates by examining a confluence of themes not usually studied together, namely the relationship between Epicurean

[1] For important earlier accounts of Lucretius in the early modern period, see L. C. Martin, "Shakespeare, Lucretius and the Commonplaces," *Review of English Studies*, 83 (1945), 174–82, and William G. Elton, *King Lear and the Gods* (San Marino, CA: Huntington Library, 1966), esp. pp. 46–57. See also Reid Barbour, *English Epicures and Stoics: Ancient Legacies in Early Stuart Culture* (Amherst: University of Massachusetts Press, 1998); Jonathan Gil Harris, "Atomic Shakespeare," *Shakespeare Studies*, 30 (2002), 47–51; William Hamlin, *Tragedy and Scepticism in Shakespeare's England* (Basingstoke: Palgrave Macmillan, 2005); Eric Langley, *Narcissism and Suicide in Shakespeare and his Contemporaries* (Oxford University Press, 2009); Jonathan Goldberg, *The Seeds of Things: Theorizing Sexuality and Materiality in Renaissance Representations* (New York: Fordham University Press, 2009); R. Allen Shoaf, "'If imagination amend them': Lucretius, Marlowe, Shakespeare," in David Schalkwyk (ed.), *The Shakespearean International Yearbook* (Farnham: Ashgate, 2010), pp. 257–80; and Stephen Greenblatt, *The Swerve: How the Renaissance Began* (New York: W. W. Norton, 2011).

[2] See, for example, Jim Hinch, "Why Stephen Greenblatt is Wrong – and Why it Matters," *Los Angeles Review of Books*, December 1, 2012.

philosophy, Protestantism, and the work of William Shakespeare. Lucretius's high poetic reputation amongst a variety of medieval and humanist commentators recommended him to early modern poets like Spenser, Donne, Greville, as well as to a range of dramatists including Jonson, Marston, Tourneur, and Chapman. Developing upon a seminal article written by L. C. Martin in 1945 which focused mainly on *Measure for Measure* and *King Lear*, a small number of scholars have argued that the influence of *De Rerum Natura* can also be found in other works by Shakespeare, including *Troilus and Cressida*, *Venus and Adonis*, and *A Midsummer Night's Dream.*[3] In what follows, I want to develop this argument further.

Lucretius's poem is, of course, deeply rooted in Epicurean philosophy. But it is also a distinct philosophical document in its own right, one that offered a number of potent challenges to certain aspects of early modern intellectual culture. This is particularly the case in relation to the dominant religion of early modern England, Protestantism. In what follows, therefore, I want to examine more fully the relationship between Lucretian philosophy and the Calvinist theology that predominated in England from the mid sixteenth to the early seventeenth century.[4] In particular, I want to use this interface as a way of thinking about *Measure for Measure*. Of course, this text has been frequently discussed in relation to early modern theology, especially Calvinism.[5] Yet, so far, no one has examined the play's theological language in relation to its equally extensive engagement with Lucretius. Martin showed that much of the Duke's famous Act 3 speech on death is drawn from book III of Lucretius.[6] But the play's Lucretian engagements go well beyond this one speech. Given the Roman poet's well-known antipathy towards institutional religion, the connection is worth pursuing. I want to suggest that throughout the play, Shakespeare pits the claims of Lucretian

[3] Langley, *Narcissism*, pp. 74–5; Shoaf, "'If imagination,'" *passim*.

[4] On the centrality of Calvinism in early modern England, see e.g. Alan Sinfield, *Literature in Protestant England 1560–1660* (London: Croom Helm, 1983); Nicholas Tyacke, *Anti-Calvinists: The Rise of English Arminianism c. 1590–1640* (Oxford University Press, 1987); Brian Cummings, *The Literary Culture of the Reformation* (Oxford University Press, 2002); and Adrian Streete, *Protestantism and Drama in Early Modern England* (Cambridge University Press, 2009).

[5] The *locus classicus* of such approaches is G. Wilson Knight, *The Wheel of Fire: Interpretations of Shakespearean Tragedy with Three New Essays* (London: Methuen, 1954), ch. 4. See also Darryl J. Gless, *Measure for Measure, the Law and the Convent* (Princeton University Press, 1979); Louise Schleiner, "Providential Improvisation in *Measure for Measure*," *PMLA*, 97 (1982), 227–36; Steven Marx, *Shakespeare and the Bible* (Oxford University Press, 2000), pp. 79–102; and Debora Kuller Shuger, *Political Theologies in Shakespeare's England: The Sacred and the State in Measure for Measure* (Basingstoke: Palgrave Macmillan, 2001).

[6] Martin, "Shakespeare, Lucretius," 176–80.

and Protestant philosophies against each other, using this opposition as a source of dramatic, ideological, and philosophical contention. The play's Lucretianism throws an often unflattering light on the dominant Protestantism of early modern England. Indeed, I will argue that, in its discussion of natural law, religion, and sex, *Measure for Measure* dramatizes a Calvinistic world becoming Lucretian.[7]

## II

The reception of Lucretius in early modern England is varied and complex, and writers commonly draw on medieval discussions of the poet's work and reputation.[8] The term "Epicurean" and its cognates are commonly used in the sixteenth and seventeenth centuries as catch-all terms to refer to any kind of skeptical philosophy, including that of Lucretius. "Epicurean" is also frequently used as a general term of approbation and abuse in early modern writing. But it is also clear that writers understood Lucretius's poem as a separate and important offshoot of Epicureanism, one with its own distinct and problematic philosophy. Parts of the text of *De Rerum Natura* were known to medieval scholars, and he is often referred to in philosophical and literary works from the ninth century onwards. A full copy of the text was rediscovered in 1417 and printed in a number of Latin editions. Early Renaissance Italian humanists like Marsilio Ficino and Lorenzo Valla, while expressing admiration for Lucretius as a literary stylist and acknowledging the persuasiveness of some of his ideas, nonetheless struggled to reconcile his version of Epicurean philosophy within a Christian framework. As Jill Kraye notes, a particular difficulty was presented by the idea that human pleasure was the supreme good.[9] This struggle can be observed in a number of early modern English texts.

A great deal of the hostility towards Lucretius arose from a misunderstanding, sometimes willful, sometimes not, of his Epicurean doctrine of *ataraxia* (calmness or tranquillity). While some commentators recognized the essentially philosophical nature of this commitment, many more took this doctrine to imply devotion to sensuous pleasures, luxury, and vice. In

[7] For a different reading of a Shakespeare play that appears to be pitting a recovered classical belief system against the tenets of early modern English Protestantism, see Chapter 6 above, on *Julius Caesar*.

[8] For Lucretius' reception in the early modern period, see Jill Kraye, "Moral Philosophy," in Charles Schmitt et al. (eds.), *The Cambridge History of Renaissance Philosophy* (Cambridge University Press, 1988), esp. pp. 374–86; and Stuart Gillespie, "Lucretius in the English Renaissance," in Stuart Gillespie and Philip Hardie (eds.), *The Cambridge Companion to Lucretius* (Cambridge University Press, 2007), pp. 242–53.

[9] Kraye, "Moral Philosophy," p. 377.

some quarters, Lucretius became a byword for unrestrained sexuality. Writing in 1592, Abraham Fraunce invokes Lucretius on human desire:

> *Lucretius* hereby vnderstandeth our vnthankfull mindes and vnsatiable desires, who still hauing, desire still to haue: so that nature powreth her infinite blessings into vs, as into broken vessels, which are euer empty and ready for more. It may signifie the whole estate of mans life, neuer setled, neuer satisfied, euer dooing and vndooing, and dooing almost all, to no purpose at al.[10]

In this reading, fairly typical of the anti-Lucretian argument, Fraunce represents the Lucretian subject as one in thrall to drives that cannot be tamed or regulated. The fact that these drives lead to a conception of life as having "no purpose at al" seems especially concerning: is there a place for providence in such a system? Another example is found in a 1606 tract written by Joseph Hall called *Heauen vpon earth, or Of true peace, and tranquillitie of minde*. As his title suggests, Hall's Christian defense of tranquillity reveals the extent to which the intellectual fascination with Lucretian *ataraxia* was seen by many Protestants as profoundly dangerous. Contrary to Lucretius's claim that death should inspire no terror, Hall says that "Neither prophane *Lucretius*, with all his Epicurean rules of confidence, nor drunken *Anacreon*, with all his wanton Odes, can shift of the importunate, and violent horror of this aduersarie."[11] Here Lucretius is seen as a foolish dilettante whose philosophy of tranquillity induces false hope in humans; when it comes to confronting mortality, the "violent horror" of Christian eschatology is to be preferred. For some early modern Protestants, then, such views confirmed the commonly held view that all Epicurean thought is damnable and atheistic.

Writers and thinkers were alternately fascinated and appalled by Lucretian cosmology, not least because it challenged the predominantly Aristotelian basis of the physics taught in the universities and that underpinned so much Christian theology. In addition to stating that there are infinite numbers of worlds, Lucretius denies providence, rejects creation *ex nihilo*, and refutes the immortality of the soul. Yet while attitudes towards Lucretius were generally wary, they were also not universally negative. William Hamlin has demonstrated the various ways in which "scepticism enters the lexicon of English poets and intellectuals" in the late sixteenth

10 Abraham Fraunce, *The third part of the Countesse of Pembrokes Yuychurch Entituled, Amintas dale.* (London: Thomas Woodcock, 1592), p. 31v.

11 Joseph Hall, *Heauen vpon earth, or Of true peace, and tranquillitie of minde* (London: Iohn Windet for Samuel Macham and Matthew Cooke, 1606), pp. 100–1.

and early seventeenth centuries.[12] A good example is John Dove's 1605 treatise *A Confutation of Atheisme*,[13] which approvingly quotes book v of Lucretius in support of his argument that "the worlde shall haue an end."[14] Despite the ritual condemnation of Lucretius in early modern England, this reveals an important strain within continental humanism, one not completely overwritten by Protestantism. Beginning with Petrarch, a number of humanists argued that if they could not exactly reconcile Epicurean and Christian ethics, then they might at least bring them into conversation with one another.[15] Most of these writers were much less inclined than English Protestants to use Christian doctrine as a stick with which to beat Epicurean thinkers like Lucretius. Although this approach did not achieve its full expression until the work of men like Pierre Gassendi in the middle of the seventeenth century, it can be seen in embryo in a small number of earlier writers such as Michel de Montaigne.[16]

Commonly scholars see Montaigne as one of the foremost conduits through which skepticism enters the mainstream of early modern intellectual culture.[17] And, of course, Shakespeare's interest in and use of Montaigne's work is well known. Less often noted is his extensive engagement with *De Rerum Natura* throughout his essays and especially in his *Apologie of Raymond Sebond.* Shakespeare could have picked up a decent working knowledge of Lucretius from John Florio's 1603 translation of Montaigne's works, published a year before *Measure for Measure.*[18] Indeed, it is worth noting that while there is no surviving early modern English translation of *De Rerum Natura* until Lucy Hutchinson's in the mid seventeenth century, Florio's Montaigne offers a serviceable "edited highlights" of the poem for interested readers. And it is interesting that as a French Catholic, Montaigne quotes a number of passages which, in an English Protestant context, would have been used to condemn the poet, coopting Lucretius in defense of Montaigne's own skeptical reading of natural theology. For example, he quotes the poem on man's tendency to

[12] Hamlin, *Tragedy and Scepticism*, p. 56.

[13] See John Dove, *A confutation of atheisme . . .* (London: Edward Allde, 1605), p. 2 and p. 27.

[14] Ibid., p. 94. The section quoted is from book v, lines 95–7 of *De Rerum.* All references are to Lucretius, *On the Nature of the Universe*, trans. Ronald Melville (Oxford University Press, 1999). I have also consulted and cross-referenced with the Latin original: Titi Lucreti Cari, *De Rerum Natura, Libri Sex*, ed. Cyril Bailey (Oxford: Clarendon Press, 1947).

[15] For texts by Petrarch and others dealing with Epicurean and Christian ethics, see Jill Kraye (ed.), *Cambridge Translations of Renaissance Philosophical Texts,* vol. 1, *Moral Philosophy* (Cambridge University Press, 1997), pp. 229–66.

[16] See ibid., pp. 385–6. [17] See Hamlin, *Tragedy and Scepticism*, pp. 61–9.

[18] See Martin, "Shakespeare, Lucretius," 178. Harris points out that Latin editions of the text were also available, of which Shakespeare's friend Ben Jonson owned a copy ("Atomic Shakespeare," 48).

anthropomorphize God: "Who with termes of mortality / Note things of immortality."[19] Like Lucretius, Montaigne abhors the evil that humans can do in the name of God and is not afraid to condemn the improper uses of religion, attacking those rulers who "replenish their religion and stuffe it with divers bad effects." He follows this with a quotation from book 1 of *De Rerum Natura*: "Religion hath oft times in former times / Bred execrable facts, ungodly crimes." Unlike Lucretius, however, Montaigne's intention is not to condemn doctrine outright, no matter how much he deplores religious strife. If Montaigne *is* attracted to Lucretian skepticism concerning religion, then it is surely in the broader context of developing his claim that because our perceptual faculties are invariably "full of weaknes and falsehood" – to use a phrase of John Calvin's – and since humanity is incapable of reaching the divine, the political abuse of religion is misplaced and tragically futile.[20] True Christian knowledge is revealed knowledge.

Even though they stood on either side of the major early modern theological divide, Montaigne and Calvin would have both agreed that all human knowledge is revealed yet imperfect. Where the two thinkers depart from each other is first in their approach to natural law – Calvin is by far the more systematic thinker – and secondly in the conclusions that Calvin argues follow from his account of natural law, specifically in its consequences for humanity. Calvin's is a resolutely unspeculative, even skeptical, theology. As he says, those who ask "What is God?" are "merely toying with idle speculations." Knowledge of the divine cannot be founded upon speculative reasoning. When it comes to comprehending God it is first necessary to reframe our terms of reference:

> It is more important for us to know of what sort he is and what is consistent with his nature. What good is it to profess with Epicurus some sort of God who has cast aside the care of the world only to amuse himself in idleness? What help is it, in short, to know a God with whom we have nothing to do?

The possibility of knowing the divine is refashioned here as a philosophical proposition, one rooted in an epistemology where what humans know of God does not equate ontologically to what he actually is. "God" is a being whose existence is refracted in certain worldly, observable phenomena and human perceptions. If humans do know God then it is not in himself but analogously, through those mimetic secondary things that are "consistent

[19] Michel de Montaigne, *An Apologie of Raymond Sebond*, in *The Essayes of Michael Lord of Montaigne Translated by John Florio*, ed. Henry Morley (London: George Routledge & Sons, 1886), p. 252.

[20] Ibid., p. 306.

with his nature."[21] Yet the secondary nature of these phenomena is not to be dismissed lightly. They are signs of God's providential control over his creation, and the fact of their existence helps to refute the Epicurean charge that the divine is indifferent to human affairs. For Calvin, natural law is synonymous with, and emblematic of, God's will.[22] This connection would not be possible unless "men's minds had not already been imbued with a firm conviction about God, from which the inclination towards religion springs as from a seed."[23]

Nevertheless, the problem is that humans are all too apt to mistake these secondary mimetic reflections, whether in nature or in their own perceptual faculties, for God himself, and to falsely assume that the law governing earth and heaven is essentially contiguous. Humans have been given laws to live by, as codified in the Commandments, because "man is so shrouded in the darkness of errors that he hardly begins to grasp through this natural law what worship is acceptable to God ... the Lord has provided us with a written law to give us a clearer witness of what was too obscure in the natural law."[24] Natural law is operative in humans, but it is dangerous to over-emphasize its efficacy in a postlapsarian world. Indeed, Calvin goes so far as to argue, in one of his very few positive presentations of the issue, that "idolatry is ample proof of this conception." As he notes, humans would prefer "to worship wood and stone rather than to be thought of as having no God."[25] The very fact that such an implacable opponent of idolatry should co-opt a practice prohibited by the Decalogue in order to argue that religion is the *sine qua non* of all human existence demonstrates the extent to which Calvin's articulation of natural law is essentially a defensive, skeptical one.[26] Although knowledge of God is possible, the corruption of humanity after the Fall is so severe that very few have access to that knowledge. This is the point at which Calvin's Protestantism and Montaigne's Catholicism part company.[27] Idolatry proves for Calvin that laws are necessary in order to

[21] John Calvin, *Institutes of the Christian Religion*, ed. John T. McNeill, trans. Ford Lewis Battles (London: SCM Press, 1961), I.ii.2 (p. 41).

[22] In my discussion of Calvin on natural law, I have found the following studies helpful: François Wendel, *Calvin* (London: Collins, 1973), pp. 150–65; R. S. White, *Natural Law in English Renaissance Literature* (Cambridge University Press, 1996), esp. pp. 36–43; J. B. Schneewind, *The Invention of Autonomy: A History of Modern Moral Philosophy* (Cambridge University Press, 1998), pp. 32–6; and David Van Drunnen, *Natural Law and the Two Kingdoms: A Study in the Development of Reformed Social Thought* (Grand Rapids, MI: William Eerdmans, 2010), pp. 67–115.

[23] Calvin, *Institutes*, I.iii.2 (p. 45). [24] Ibid., II.viii.1 (p. 368). [25] Ibid., I.iii.1 (p. 44).

[26] R. S. White is certainly correct that Calvin "did not deny at least the potential for reason and conscience within people" when encountering natural law. But his conclusion that "the more positive aspects of his theology show that he believed depravity could be overcome" is too optimistic a reading of Calvin's thought (*Natural Law*, p. 40).

[27] Too often, critics allow Montaigne's commitment to philosophical skepticism to obscure the equally important fact of his Catholicism.

structure human society and to tame the wilder instincts of humanity. The difficulty, as J. B. Schneewind succinctly puts it, is that in the fallen world "We know what we ought to do but we do not do it."[28] Obeying the civil law is necessary, and humans might accomplish this to some degree, but invariably most will fall short. This is why the law should be rigorously enforced. Strict civil laws reflect the transcendent nature of divine law. Because humans have deteriorated so far from their original glory, only a very few will have true knowledge of God's law. Crucially *this* knowledge is revealed by Scripture and through the gift of grace, which is bestowed gratuitously upon those whom God has saved: the elect. Only through revealed knowledge can the kingdoms of man and God, natural and civil law, human and divine knowledge, be reconciled. And proper, unadulterated knowledge of God can only be attained after death and judgment: here we find most of the central theological threads that are later emphasized in early modern Puritanism and that are associated with Angelo in *Measure for Measure.*

In making this point, Calvin returns to a suggestive metaphor that we have already encountered: "As experience shows, God has *sown a seed of religion* in all men. But scarcely one man in a hundred is met with who fosters it, once received, in his heart, and none in whom it ripens – much less shows fruit in season . . . all degenerate from the true knowledge of him."[29] The idea of religion as a seed is, of course, biblically derived, and Calvin most likely has this source in mind. It is commonly used by Christ in the Gospels, most notably when he rebukes his disciples for their lack of belief and likens faith to "a graine of mustard seede" (Matthew 17:20).[30] But the metaphor is also central to discussions of physics in classical philosophy, as, for example, in Lucretius's *De Rerum Natura.*

Despite his popular reputation to the contrary in the early modern period, Lucretius is not an atheist: he simply argues that the gods have nothing to do with creation, are indifferent to human concerns, and do not providentially interfere in human affairs. Lucretius departs from the skepticism of the more radical Pyrrhonists in generally valuing sense perception: "whatever at any time / Has seemed to the sense to be true, is true" (IV.498–9). But he also notes that the senses can deceive and that "nothing is more difficult than to distinguish / And separate plain things from

[28] Schneewind, *Invention*, p. 34. [29] Calvin, *Institutes*, I.iv.I (p. 47, my emphasis).

[30] All references to the Geneva Bible. *The Bible, That Is, The Holy Scriptures* (London: Christopher Barker, 1599). The passage also draws on Psalm 1:3. The most well-known early modern exposition of the idea is found in William Perkins's treatise *A graine of musterd-seed* (London, 1597).

doubtful things" (IV.468). This view is close to what Hamlin has termed academic skepticism: although "epistemological certainty is impossible to attain," humans should still "develop forms of probable knowledge based on a scrupulous study of appearances."[31] To reject the false "images" co-opted in the name of religion is to achieve what Florio's translation calls "Ataraxie": "the condition of a quiet and settled life, exempted from the agitations which we receive by the impression of the opinion and knowledge we imagine to have of things."[32] This is partly due to Lucretius's atomistic conception of existence and partly because of his ethical desire to release humans from what he calls the "terror of the priests" (I.103). For Lucretius, creation *ex nihilo* is impossible since "each thing is created / From fixed specific seeds." These seeds are themselves made up of the "primal atoms" that constitute all matter in the universe (I.167–70).[33] In fact, the only things that exist in the universe are atoms and the void within which they move, or rather swerve. As Lucretius explains, although atoms move downwards through the void, at certain times "they swerve slightly from their course" (II.219). This "swerve" is what causes things to be created and is also "the origin of this free will / Possessed by living creatures" (II.256–7). God does not enable free will: the random motion of atoms does, a "swerve" that has no predetermined ethical purpose. The linear or teleological conception of time, found in Aristotle's *Physics* and later taken up by Christian theologians, is challenged by Lucretius's poem.

Lucretius is attacked with such vehemence by Calvin – and, as we have seen, by many of Calvin's English followers – because his providentially ordered, predestinarian world finds its dialectical counterpart in *De Rerum Natura*. For Calvin, any kind of motion, whether expressed as free will, perception, or knowledge, is only valid because it points to a revealed truth *beyond* this world. For Lucretius, any kind of motion, initiated in the atomic "swerve" and expressed as free will, is simply a fact of material existence, one that has no providential meaning. No matter how vigorously Calvin tries to oppose this view, it continues to haunt his understanding of natural law. As Shakespeare shows in *Measure for Measure*, the Christian "graine of mustard seede" is always potentially in danger of morphing into the Lucretian atomistic seed.

[31] Hamlin, *Tragedy and Scepticism*, p. 3.

[32] Montaigne, *Apologie*, pp. 254–5. Montaigne frequently raises this possibility in his quotations from Lucretius, even if he stops short of personally endorsing it.

[33] All references are to Melville's translation.

## III

The opening scene of the play stages a central ethical question: is the law something that is known or revealed? Shakespeare explores the issue through a complex interrelation of religious and political language. In his first speech, the Duke interestingly declines to outline the "properties" of "government." Unlike King James, only too happy to expound his political theology at length, Vincentio simply declares that in Escalus's case "science / Exceeds, in that, the lists of all advice / My strength can give you" (I.I.I–7).[34] If the Duke represents the civil law, then it is a rational system based on knowledge ("science") whose precepts have already been acquired and internalized. He is content that the "nature of our people" is known to Escalus in his "sufficiency" (I.I.8). Nevertheless, having handed over his "commission" he also tells Escalus that it is an injunction "From which we would not have you warp" (I.I.I4). From the opening scene, then, two conceptions of the law are at play. The first sees the law as something which is inherent to all and rationally known, and the second sees the law as something which is prescribed and immutable. The former relates to our epistemic access to the law, and the latter to the law's nature and constitution. Ultimately, these two conceptions may well be compatible, but the play is striking for the way in which it explores how this compatibility might be attained. Whatever else he does, the Duke is wary of *his* commission warping or swerving: man may know the law but it still needs to be enforced. He says of the puritanical Angelo that he has "Elected him our absence to supply; / Lent him our terror, drest him with our love, / And given his deputation all the organs / Of our own power" (I.I.I8–2I). Undoubtedly the primary meaning of "elected" here is political. Yet in early modern English the word invariably also carries overtones of religious election, the state of being one of the saved or elect.[35] The Duke's use of the term is wryly ironic and plays on this dual meaning: a secular ruler can mimetically elect a deputy in his stead, but only God may "elect."

The fact that Angelo's election, and the "terror" that it lends him, is temporary is crucial. One of the hottest topics within early modern Calvinism was whether or not it was possible to know the state of one's election. In his discussions of this issue, William Perkins argues that assurance is extended not only to the elect but also to the reprobate, who enjoy what he calls temporary faith, an extremely powerful force that makes

[34] All references are to William Shakespeare, *Measure for Measure*, ed. J. W. Lever (London: Routledge, 1994).

[35] See Gless, *Law and the Convent*, pp. 22–40.

them "dreame that they are Kings, when they are very beggars."[36] Perkins likens faith to the imprint of a seal on wax. He writes that "we may beholde in our selues some sure representations of all these imprinted, and euen stamped in vs by the worde," and a little later that "by the similitude of the forme of a seale fashioned in waxe, we do easily vnderstand what is the very forme and fashion of the seale." In this "the manner of god by the effects of his election and predestination [is] imprinted in vs."[37] The difficulty lies in verifying the sufficiency of the seal on the wax. How can anyone tell the difference between justifying and temporary faith?

Significantly, the opening scene of *Measure for Measure* also utilizes the metaphor of the seal. Before Angelo appears, the Duke asks Escalus "What figure of us, think you, he will bear?," a question that draws upon the metaphor of the "ducal stamp on the seal of the commission."[38] It also implies that in mimetic terms Angelo may fashion himself in any number of guises before the Duke's authority. From the start, Angelo is wary of the commission, perhaps revealing a puritanical ambivalence towards the substitutory nature of the authority that he is taking on. His political election as mimetic substitute does not necessarily imply his divine election by God. He must "enforce or qualify the laws / As to your soul seems good" (1.1.65–6). Angelo is represented as a simulacrum, a seal upon the wax, a man whose virtue might be "good" but which may just as easily prove to be counterfeit. His position as "elected" substitute implies that the divine law is always opaque, impartially known, even to its adherents: all we have are "figures" that imperfectly reflect that law. It also suggests that the one who propagates the law may also be condemned by it.

Once Angelo assumes control, it quickly becomes apparent that his rule is governed by a strict Protestant interpretation of the law, one that promulgates "a harshly penal enforcement of virtue."[39] When Mistress Overdone realizes that "all our houses of resort in the suburbs be pulled down," she comments, "Why, here's a change indeed in the commonwealth!" (1.2.93–6). Pleasure, especially sexual pleasure, is to be rigorously policed in Angelo's reformed state. But hypocrisy, greed, and class enmity are at work here too. While all the brothels in the suburbs are condemned, those inside the city walls, says Pompey, "shall stand for seed: they had

[36] William Perkins, *A Case of Conscience, the greatest that euer was* . . . (London: John Legat, 1595), sig. D4v. Perkins was no Puritan, however, and the sheer popularity of his work coupled with his sincere efforts to conciliate between Protestant and Catholic meant that he was widely read across the spectrum of theological opinion in early modern England and beyond.

[37] Ibid., sigs. E1v, E2v. [38] Shakespeare, *Measure for Measure*, p. 4.

[39] Shuger, *Political Theologies*, p. 118.

gone down too, but that a wise burger put in for them" (1.1.91–2). The vocabulary here is comically ironic. As Lucretius notes, nature "never reduces anything to nothing . . . since all things are composed / Of everlasting seeds" (1.217–22). Just like the forces of nature, then, sexuality can never be completely tamed. Hypocrisy and greed may determine sexual ethics: but neither of these forces is as powerful as sexual desire.

The religious underpinnings of Angelo's new dispensation are wryly alluded to in Lucio's banter with the First Gentleman: "Grace is grace, despite all controversy; as for example, thou thyself art a wicked villain, despite of all grace" (1.2.24–6).[40] Given Lucio's subversive choric role throughout the play, we need hardly assume that this is what *he* thinks about grace. But it is notable that his construction of the doctrine is informed by Romans 11:6 and by the logic of predestinarian Calvinism: just as temporary faith is not the same as justification, so no amount of grace can save the reprobate villain who has already been condemned by God. A similar argument is drawn upon by Claudio when he explains his arraignment to Lucio:

> Thus can the demi-god, Authority,
> Make us pay down for our offence by weight.
> The words of heaven; on whom it will, it will;
> On whom it will not, so; yet still 'tis just. (1.2.112–15)

The law under which Claudio is being punished is analogous to the Calvinist doctrine of justification: it is staggeringly arbitrary yet incomprehensibly just. But, as the scene also suggests, human sexuality threatens to exceed the limits of the law, even to destruction: "Our natures do pursue, / Like rats that ravin down their proper bane, / A thirsty evil; and when we drink, we die" (1.2.120–2). A more positive, Lucretian gloss is given by Lucio. Telling Isabella of her brother's predicament, he says that "from the seedness the bare fallow brings / To teeming foison, even so her plenteous womb / Expresseth his full tilth and husbandry" (1.4.42–4). Justification exceeds the law because of God's arbitrary and incomprehensible decree. According to the logic of Angelo's laws, sexuality is similarly arbitrary, incomprehensible, and accidental. But can a strict law prohibiting sexual excess properly function in a world determined by the atomistic seed, one that expresses itself with such "teeming foison"? If his sexual drives position

40 See Romans 11:6: "And if *it be* of grace, it is no more of workes: or els were grace no more grace: but if it be of works, it is no more grace: or els were worke no more worke."

Claudio as analogous to a reprobate then, by extension, the rest of humanity must be similarly condemned.

This scene points up a key ethical contradiction that operates in Angelo's state. In the case of the wise burgher, sex affords him a chance to turn a profit: in Claudio's case, sex positions him as a reprobate whose drives and appetites need to be curbed. Lucio says that Angelo represses his natural instincts in favour of "mind, study and fast." He claims he is "one who never feels / The wanton stings and motions of the sense" (1.4.58–61). Yet as Lucretius points out, in an atomic universe, motion and sense are, like "wanton" sex, inescapable facts of material existence: atoms are "tossed perpetually / In endless motion through the mighty void," producing matter (2.122–3). Similar to Shakespeare in this play, Lucretius sees humanity's inability to order their sexual impulses as inherently comic. The suburbs of Vienna are populated by people whose "hollow" (1.2.52) bones stand, like the Lucretian void, as a bodily comment on their swerving/swiving. Claudio and Lucio may be right that the deputy's attempt to regulate sexuality is a form of "tyranny" (1.2.152) and "fear" (1.4.62), but at this stage in the drama, those on the wrong side of the city walls do not have the luxury of contesting the ethical standards by which they are to be judged.[41]

In Act 2 Shakespeare continues his exploration of natural law in the extraordinary scenes between Angelo and Isabella. Throughout their sparring, the relationship between the law and sexuality as opposing forces is particularly acute. Isabella asks Angelo to punish her brother's crime, not her brother. Angelo's central principle throughout is based on an implacably puritanical predestinarian logic: "Condemn the fault, and not the actor of it? / Why, every fault's condemned ere it be done" (2.2.38). He maintains that his will is merely the conduit through which the law operates, arguing that "It is the law, not I, condemn your brother" (2.2.80). Isabella calls this a "just but severe law" (2.2.41) and is only persuaded to pursue her suit by Lucio's exhortations.

Interestingly, most of Lucio's interjections in this scene pertain to motion. He frequently accuses Isabella of being too cold, that is to say not active or masculine enough, and tells her to "touch" Angelo, to speak further, to say more and to go "to him": after one of her pleas he says that

[41] It is worth noting that this scene, and some others in the play, may well have been written by Thomas Middleton. See the introduction to John Jowett's edition of *Measure for Measure* in *Thomas Middleton: The Collected Works*, ed. Gary Taylor and John Lavignino (Oxford: Clarendon Press, 2007), pp. 1542–6. Middleton's writings are generally more sympathetic to Calvinism than are Shakespeare's.

Angelo is "coming," a word with clear sexual overtones (2.2.126). Just as Lucretius says that "Touch is the body's sense" (2.435), so Lucio is the Lucretian *malin genie*, one whose tactile interjections provoke the motion that enables Isabella to challenge Angelo's teleological, deterministic logic.[42] She asks that he extend "mercy," which "will breathe within your lips, / Like man new made" (2.2.78–9). This is an image of Pauline *renovatio* where the "old man" of sin is destroyed in Christ, where grace is made possible, and where "death hath no more dominion" (Romans 6:6). She also asks, "Who is it that hath died for this offence? / There's many that have committed it" (2.2.89–90), an argument that we saw advanced in Act 1, and that Lucio predictably approves of. But Angelo is unmoved and emphasizes death as a literal, Mosaic sanction:

> The law hath not been dead, though it hath slept:
> Those many had not dar'd to do that evil
> If the first that did th'edict infringe
> Had answer'd for his deed. Now 'tis awake,
> Takes note of what is done, and like a prophet
> Looks in a glass that shows what future evils,
> Either new, or by remissness new conceiv'd,
> And so in progress to be hatch'd and born,
> Are now to have no successive degrees,
> But ere they live, to end. (2.2.91–100)

The text invoked here is chapter 7 of Romans where Paul writes of the shift from the Old Mosaic Law to the New Law of Christ: "ye also are become dead to the law by the body of Christ . . . now we are delivered from the law, that being dead wherein we were held; that we should serve in newness of spirit, and not *in* the oldness of the letter" (Romans 7:4–6). With his absolute adherence to death as the punishment for fornication, Angelo reinscribes a literal, Mosaic reading of the law that denies mercy and grace. In his commentary on this passage, Calvin warns explicitly against doing just this: "Paul shows by contrast still more clearly how wrong the zealots of the law are to keep believers under its power. As long as the literal teaching of the law rules and is in force without connexion with the Spirit of Christ, the lust of the flesh is not restrained but rather

[42] Lucio's name is often read by critics as recalling "Lucifer, the fallen angel of light and mocking father of lies" (Marx, *Shakespeare and the Bible*, p. 79). But does the name perhaps have other overtones? Throughout *De Rerum Natura*, religion is presented as irredeemably dark: freedom from its tyranny is likened to shining a "clear light" (1.144). Might this not help contextualise Lucio's subversive, choric role throughout the play?

increases."[43] For a biblically minded audience, this speech would have figured Angelo as a mistaken, perhaps even willfully hypocritical misinterpreter of Scripture. Significantly, though, it is Angelo's "sense" (2.2.169) that is touched throughout the scene. His literal interpretation of the law opens the way to Pauline "lust of the flesh," just as his denial of desire gradually exposes him to the snares of Lucretian sensuality.

When Isabella enters in Act 2, scene 4, she says to Angelo that she is "come to know your pleasure." He replies, "That you might know it, would much better please me, / Than to demand what 'tis" (2.4.31–3), a comment that ironically juxtaposes a philosophically minded "knowing" and "pleasure" with their more fleshly counterparts. In Angelo's opening soliloquy, he describes the change that Isabella has engendered in him through various metaphors of sexual motion and arousal. Contrasting them with his inability to engage with "Heaven," he speaks of "the strong and swelling evil / Of my conception" (2.4.6–7) and of the "blood" mustering round his "heart" (2.4.20). It is the involuntary nature of these movements that seems to perturb Angelo the most. In *De Rerum Natura*, Lucretius speaks of sexual desire in terms that contextualize the deputy's predicament. The poet uses the metaphor of racehorses leaving their traps in order to explain that "heart begins the motion / Then mind and will join in and drive it on / Until it reaches all the body and limbs" (II.268–70). Desire begins in the heart, is intellectualized by the mind and then manifested in the body. There is no religious sanction for sexual desire. As Angelo complains, "Heaven hath my empty words" (2.4.2). Lucretius then explains that sexual desire makes the genitals "swell with the seed, then comes desire / To eject it where the dire craving pulls / And the body seeks that which has wounded the mind with love" (IV.1045–7). This conception of desire is different from the patriarchal Aristotelian model that predominated in the early modern period. For Lucretius, sexual union can involve male *and* female pleasure: both partners are "liquefied in rapture."[44] I will return to this point shortly.

Here again, then, as in their previous encounter, sexual ethics are refracted through theologically inflected debate. In the play's opening scene the image of the seal on wax is used to denote the difficulty of distinguishing the righteous from the unrighteous. Throughout Angelo and Isabella's second scene, the problem of similitude is similarly invoked

[43] John Calvin, *Calvin's Commentaries: Romans and Thessalonians*, trans. Ross Mackenzie (Grand Rapids, MI: William Eerdmans, 1995), p. 140.

[44] Thomas Laqueur, *Making Sex: Body and Gender from the Greeks to Freud* (Cambridge, MA: Harvard University Press, 1992), p. 47.

to explore the ethics of Angelo's sexual proposition to Isabella. For example, he asks:

> Which had you rather, that the most just law
> Now took your brother's life; or, to redeem him,
> Give up your body to such sweet uncleanness
> As she that he hath stain'd? (2.4.52–5)

Again Angelo takes a key biblical text, in this case Romans 1:21–7, and manipulates it to his own ends. For Paul, the law and the lusts of the flesh are utterly antithetical. Isabella agrees: "I had rather give my body than my soul" (2.4.56). Paul writes of those who ignore or corrupt the law and "turn the glorie of the incorruptible God to the similitude of the image of a corruptible man." As punishment, "God gaue them vp to their hearts lusts, vnto vncleanesse, to defile their owne bodies betweene themselues . . . the men left the naturall vse of the women, and burned in their lust one toward another . . . God deliuered them vp vnto a reprobate minde." In his false alignment of the law and sex, Angelo evokes this Pauline nightmare of reprobate, mimetic sexual "uncleanness."

Isabella attempts to reclaim a sense of Pauline rectitude: "lawful mercy / Is nothing kin to foul redemption" (2.4.112–13). Angelo responds by constructing her refusal as a kind of false mimesis. He says that her "sense pursues not mine" and claims that "either you are ignorant, / Or seem so, crafty" (2.2.74–5). Isabella rejects this mimetic slur, stating that women are "credulous to false prints" (2.4.129) and that Angelo's honor and purpose are in fact nothing more than "Seeming, seeming!" (2.4.149). The problem, already outlined in Perkins's discussion of justification, is in distinguishing "seeming" from truth. As Calvin notes in his commentary on Romans 1, "Ungodliness is a hidden evil," or as Angelo puts it to Isabella, "my false o'erweighs your true" (2.4.169).[45] Moreover, as Lucretius explains, desire operates in an analogous, mimetic fashion: "from a pretty face or rosy cheeks / Nothing comes into the body to enjoy / But images, thin images . . . / So in love *Venus mocks lovers with images*" (IV.1095–101, my emphasis). When it comes to sexual desire, humans are impelled into a world of mimetic signs: in such a world, pleasure and pain are never far from each other. In a sense, the Pauline reprobate and the Lucretian subject are similarly figured as in thrall to drives that are accidental and irresistible: the former sees this as tragic, the latter as inherently comic, a fact that may in part account for the bittersweet generic makeup of this play. The difficult

[45] Calvin, *Commentaries*, p. 34.

question raised by Shakespeare in these scenes is whether or not such sexual drives can coexist with a religiously determined requirement to behave in an ethically acceptable manner.

Angelo states that "now I give my sensual race the rein" (2.4.159), a line that also draws upon equine imagery. It may also have reminded some in the audience of James 3:1–10. Interestingly, whereas Lucretius uses equine imagery to explain the movement of desire, James uses similar imagery to suggest that desire should be curtailed. The text speaks about the man who does not sin as one "able to bridle all the body . . . Behold, wee put bittes into the horses mouthes, that they should obey vs," and notes just how difficult it is for man to "bridle" his appetites (James 3:2–3). Counterfeiting himself as a godly, disinterested arbiter of the law who proclaims, like God in Genesis, that sexual malefactors shall "die the death" (2.4.164; Genesis 2:17), Angelo in 2.4 continues to emerge as a Lucretian sensualist in thrall to his sexual desires.[46] In fact, the scene turns on the keen tension between a Christian and a materialist understanding of sex.

Angelo's command that Isabella "Lay by all nicety and prolixious blushes / That banish what they sue for" (2.4.161–2) is based on a patriarchally conceived Christian misogyny. Lucretius writes in an analogous vein about the "glances," the "snares of love" (IV.1139; 1146), and the "pains" that women take for "those they wish to hold in chains of love" (I.1187). The crucial difference is that, unlike Angelo's Christian-inspired rhetoric, Lucretius also recognizes the potential for equality in sexual relations: "Not always is a woman feigning love / When she sighs and clings to a man in close embrace." Indeed, when it comes to sex "the pleasure is mutual" (4.1191–2; 1207). It is significant that Claudio describes his sexual relationship with Juliet as "our most mutual entertainment" (1.2.143). The term is also used in the scene between the Duke and Juliet where she agrees that their "offenceful act" was "mutually committed" (2.3.27). Whether or not mutuality offers an adequate basis for sexual ethics is a moot point. But whereas the Duke enjoins repentance for this sexual mutuality (2.3.30), Angelo offers sexual coercion and death. He wants pleasure for himself at the same time as he denies the broader social and ethical utility of pleasure. His hypocrisy is explored by Isabella in her closing soliloquy:

O perilous mouths,
That bear in them one and the self-same tongue
Either of condemnation or approof,

[46] The note to this verse in the Geneva Bible says that this moment represents "the separation of man from God."

> Bidding the law make curtsey to their will,
> Hooking both right and wrong to th'appetite,
> To follow as it draws! (2.4.171–6)

The language here is redolent of the Bible and of Lucretian atomism. Again, James 3 is the biblical source text. By way of explaining just how difficult it is for man to curb his desires, James develops the metaphor of the tongue as something that "can no man tame. *It is* an vnrully euill, full of deadly poison." We should "blesse God" and "curse men" because the latter are "made in the similitude of God. Out of one mouth proceedeth blessing and cursing; my brethren, these things ought not so to be" (James 2:8–10). The point is clear: Angelo is a hypocritical "similitude" whose law condemns others as it approves his own "perilous" sexual will.[47]

But even more fascinating than this is Isabella's conceit that Angelo's actions are "Hooking both right and wrong to th'appetite, / To follow as it draws!" This is the only place in his writings that Shakespeare uses the verb "hooking." Obviously it draws upon the metaphor of fishing. However, in book II of *De Rerum Natura*, Lucretius offers an atomistic explanation as to why things are different shapes and how this affects our sense perceptions of them:

> So you can easily see that smooth round atoms
> Make up things which give pleasure to our senses,
> But, by contrast, things that seem harsh and bitter
> Are more composed of atoms that are hooked [*hamatis*],
> Which therefore tear their way into our senses,
> And entering break the surface of our bodies. (II.402–7)

Angelo's will is like the hooked Lucretian atom, breaking its way into Isabella's "soft" (2.4.128) body. In this way, his command – "Fit thy consent to my sharp appetite" (2.4.160) – can also be seen as an attempt to force his "harsh" (from the Latin *asper*) "appetite" on to an opponent whose only defense is Christian "chastity" (2.4.184).

Isabella notes that her brother has similarly fallen "by prompture of the blood," but that he has

> such a mind of honour,
> That had he twenty heads to tender down
> Or twenty bloody blocks, he'd yield them up
> Before his sister should her body stoop
> To such abhorr'd pollution. (2.4.177–82)

[47] The *OED* quotes this line from the play in its second definition of "aproof" as "sanction, approval, approbation."

This section of Isabella's speech makes the shocking connection between execution and sex, both of which involve a stooping or bending over. In stating that her brother would sooner bend to the block than allow her to "stoop" to Angelo, I think that this passage may well draw indirectly on what was, in the early modern period, the most controversial passage in Lucretius's poem. Describing the best way for a woman to conceive, and in keeping with his view that sex involves mutual pleasure, Lucretius writes:

> What matters most of all is the position
> In which the soothing pleasure itself is taken;
> For in the manner of four-footed beasts,
> It is generally thought that women best conceive,
> Breast down and loins uplifted, so the seeds
> Can take more easily their proper places.

However, he goes on to note:

> Wives have no need at all of wanton movements.
> For a woman avoids conception and fights against it,
> If in delight she holds his penis close
> Between her buttocks, and all her body limp,
> Flows with the waves and sways with every tide.
> She turns the furrow from its rightful course
> Under the ploughshare, makes the seed fall wide.
> Whores do this for their private purposes
> Lest they be filled too often and lie pregnant,
> And to make their loves more pleasing to their men. (IV.1262–76)

As Isabella says in act 3, her "bending down" (3.1.143) for Angelo would be bad enough. But if she were to avoid becoming pregnant then she would need to behave as Lucretius says prostitutes do in order to expel the "abhord'd pollution" of Angelo's seed. Claudio's death is therefore preferable to the sexual death that Isabella's Christian vows demand she forswears. Via the clash of Lucretian and Christian imagery and language in these scenes, Shakespeare shows how the potential ethical utility of Lucretian pleasure and mutuality is compromised on the one hand by Angelo's puritanical hypocrisy and on the other by Isabella's Catholic disavowal of human sexuality. He doesn't seek to excuse Angelo's actions nor Isabella's willingness to condemn her brother. Rather, it is the perversion or repression of "simple pleasures" (II.22) which causes personal and political strife.

As I noted earlier, Lucio is the most Lucretian figure in the play. He claims that Angelo is incapable of sex, calling him in language redolent with

Lucretian materialism, a "motion ungenerative" (3.2.108) and an "ungenitured agent" who will "unpeople the province with continency" (3.2.167–9). Significantly, he also says that the Duke is well known in Vienna for his sexual activity. The Duke denies this, saying he "was not much detected for women; he was not inclined that way" (3.2.118–19). While this may be a metatheatrical dig at James I's own sexual preferences, it surely also goes to the heart of the Duke's dilemma: in order to reclaim sexuality from the condemnation of the hypocritical Puritan, he needs to restate his own sexual virility in the public sphere. Lucio inadvertently brings this issue to the fore; and while in most respects he stands as the complete antithesis to Angelo, what does unite them is their shared sexual hypocrisy. Lucio has made a woman pregnant but has denied it in order to avoid marrying her. In admitting this to the Duke he concludes by saying, "I am a kind of burr, I shall stick" (4.3.177). The metaphor is well chosen: similar to a hooked atom, a burr hooks on to a host in order to disseminate its seed as widely as possible. The burr is also an accidental parasite, dependent upon a host who is unaware of its presence. But it is perhaps the Duke who gives the game away best in Act 4. When Claudio's look-alike, the pirate Ragozine, dies, the Duke has no compunction in commanding his head to be sent to Angelo, commenting on the substitution: "O, 'tis an accident that heaven provides" (4.3.76). In this claim, resourcefulness and hypocrisy sit side by side: in a world where the civil law is contingent upon the divine, the Duke cannot be seen to valorize the accidental simply on its own terms. If he is to return to Vienna, he will need to reclaim in some way the political utility of accidentals within a religious framework.

The Duke's phrase therefore nicely crystallizes the central political dilemma of the play. Whether in the relationship between the hypocritical Angelo and the absolute Isabella, in the comedic subplot, or in a Duke whose sexual interests may be unconventional, no amount of religious morality will stop humans from spilling their seed, sexually or volitionally, in places they shouldn't. Viewed as a drive over which humans have a limited amount of control, sex can be seen as the ultimate expression of an atomic universe. As the witty Lucio suggests, a Lucretian universe where sexual pleasure and mutuality are valued is largely preferable to one that tries to control or deny human sexuality. However, the image of Lucio as a "burr" and of Angelo's hooked will also points up the potential for parasites and hypocrites to flourish in such a society, one that decouples the claims of sexual pleasure from the equally important claims of ethical responsibility. To see sex as an uncontrollable drive is, as the play notes in various places, a rapist's charter. So can a materialistic understanding of sexuality as accident coexist with a more deterministic religious ethics that seeks to regulate and protect humans from the worst excesses of that sexual imperative?

Lots of critics of *Measure for Measure* get somewhat over-excited by the Pauline turn that the play takes, especially in the last act, claiming for example that the Duke and Isabella are Christ-like figures. In the universe of *Measure for Measure*, where Calvin and Lucretius strive for precedence, I think this is an interpretative step too far. The point is surely the imperfect, mimetic, and *fleshly* nature of the Duke's and Isabella's plot: it turns on a comical redaction of Pauline and Lucretian mimesis where accidentals are manipulated in order to refashion the law. As Lucretius points out in book 1, "nature works by means of hidden bodies" (1.329), a statement that could stand as epigraph for the machinations of *Measure for Measure*. Such a reading is not necessarily incompatible with Christian ethics either. As the Pauline epistles insistently point out, the fleshly types of this world offer an eschatological prefiguration of the world to come. This is what Giorgio Agamben, following Walter Benjamin, has called "messianic time." This period represents not a future time of perfection but rather instantiates a "summary recapitulation of the past" which saturates or fulfils the "time of the now" in "*anticipation* of eschatological fulfilment."[48] The key word here is "anticipation." Both Pauline "Messianic time" and Lucretian "fluid time"[49] do not offer us the thing itself: under each dispensation, the figure and the image is all. Paradoxically, the promise of this time to come may also offer a useful basis for law.

The final act of the play begins with the sound of trumpets as the Duke enters the gates of the city in triumph. Mariana and the Duke are unveiled, literally brought face to face (5.1.170–1; 204; 352) with their nemeses in a manner that recalls the Pauline promise of 1 Corinthians 13:12. The play then concludes with a series of marriages. All of this may recall, as numerous critics have argued, the patterning of the eschatological promise laid out in the New Testament, especially the Pauline epistles, and the book of Revelation which ends with the divine comedy of Christ's mystical marriage to the church. Modern critics are more likely than an earlier generation of commentators to treat such theological patterns with skepticism, and a number have pointed out the resolutely "fleshly" aspects of the last act as a way of critiquing the play's engagement with these patterns. In Robert Watson's words, "The Duke's performance of a Last Judgement at the gates of his city, rather than the gates of heaven, is a culminating instance of the

[48] Giorgio Agamben, *The Time That Remains: A Commentary on the Letter to the Romans*, trans. Patricia Dailey (Stanford University Press, 2005), pp. 61, 76.

[49] Jonathan Gil Harris, *Untimely Matter in the Time of Shakespeare* (Philadelphia: University of Pennsylvania Press, 2009), p. 172.

way *Measure for Measure* parodies pious archetypes in asserting the priority of earthly order and human survival."[50] Certainly Isabella's attempts to invoke eschatology ("truth is truth / To th'end of reck'ning"; "make the truth appear where it seems hid" [5.1.48–9; 69]) fall on deaf ears. But my difficulty with such readings is that they replicate Isabella's credulity by assuming that there is parody at work here.

Just because the close of the play is unable to invest the *present* time with any final eschatological significance, it doesn't follow that Act 5 is parodying this discourse. This may sound like an overly literal point, but it is one that is central to early modern political theology. The Duke's return does not inculcate a superior "spiritual" truth in the present, one that transcends the flesh and invests the earthly ruler with divine political sanction. Vincentio is, like Angelo, also a fleshly substitute. He too is subject to the radically antidualistic trajectory of Protestant typology. The final act may imply the end time, might signal its importance through figures and similitudes. But it cannot instantiate the end.

The unease that critics have often felt with the marriages that conclude Act 5 is understandable. Perhaps they stand as a wry comic reflection on *Measure for Measure*'s Pauline ethics. "It is better to marrie then to burne" (1 Corinthians 7:9) is hardly a ringing endorsement of wedded bliss. Nor, according to a conventional Christian interpretation, is the end of Act 5. But such a reading only works if it ignores the Lucretian thread that I've been following throughout the play. The mocking, bawdy presence of Lucio in the act is crucial here. When Mariana decorously and figuratively says that she stood in Isabella's "imagin'd person" in the garden, Lucio immediately stresses the carnal basis of this meeting (5.1.212–13). And it is Lucio's constant jibes against the Duke's sexual probity that rattle him more than anything else. Undoubtedly the Duke invokes the religious harshness of the Old Law in his condemnation of his deputy:

> The very mercy of the law cries out
> Most audible, even from his proper tongue,
> 'An Angelo for Claudio, death for death!'
> Haste still pays haste, and leisure answers leisure;
> Like doth quit like, and Measure for Measure. (5.1.405–9)

And in sentencing Angelo to "the very block / Where Claudio stoop'd to death" (5.1.412–13), his words recall Isabella's in Act 2 and seek to offer them

[50] Robert N. Watson, "False Immortality in *Measure for Measure*: Comic Means, Tragic Ends," *Shakespeare Quarterly*, 41 (1990), 430–1. See the similar argument in Beatrice Groves, *Texts and Traditions: Religion in Shakespeare, 1592–1604* (Oxford: Clarendon Press, 2007), pp. 181–2.

legal quittance. However, as is soon revealed, Claudio did not in fact "stoop," and so the pattern of substitutions upon which the Duke's threatened justice is based is happily shown to be false.

Moreover, the Duke's final speech signals an aptly imperfect assimilation of Lucretian and Christian ethics. Lucio is sent off to be whipped at the Duke's "pleasure" (5.1.519) and ordered to marry a prostitute. If a workable political order and hierarchy is to be restored, then the anarchic Lucretian "fluid time" channelled by Lucio is now redirected by the Duke in the service of the conventional sacrament of marriage. But this is convention with a twist. First, sexual mutuality and pleasure is stressed: "She, Claudio, that you wrong'd, look you restore. / Joy to you, Mariana; love her, Angelo" (5.1.522–3). If we react to this, especially in the case of Angelo, by thinking "as if," then that is, really, the whole point. In an early modern culture that caricatures Lucretius as a pagan sensualist, Shakespeare offers an alternative view of sexuality based not upon these cultural clichés, but upon asking what society might look like if its sexual ethics were based upon the principle of imperfect mutuality. Consider too the Duke's concluding words to Isabella:

Dear Isabel,
I have a motion much imports your good;
Whereunto if you'll a willing ear incline,
What's mine is yours, and what is yours is mine.
So bring us to our palace, where we'll show
What's yet behind that's meet you should all know. (5.1.531–6)

The Duke certainly stresses the mutuality implicit in the wedding vows. Notice the very last word of the play, implying that there is a more perfect knowledge to be gleaned "behind," off stage. If the final act is informed by the discourses of Christian eschatology, then this sentiment has a certain logic. The Duke's new dispensation may be based on a "semblance" which papers over a fundamental lawlessness: in a society where Christianity forms the basis of the law, that is, perhaps, inevitable. However, we might also notice that word "motion," a term which combines sexual activity with Lucretian atomism. Notice too that the Duke invites Isabella to "incline" her ear to this motion: as its etymology and early modern usage show, "incline" means to bend forward or downwards. Certainly, this is a different kind of "stooping" to the one proposed by Angelo. Yet it also takes place "behind," a knowing that is "meet" or, as Lucretius says, proper (IV.1267).

So the play doesn't end with a Calvinistic world turned *completely* Lucretian. Religious law, with its mimetic and eschatological promise, cannot be completely disavowed: it is a useful if imperfect tool for managing human "motion." Nevertheless, the Lucretian thread in the play insists that a political theology rooted in a patriarchal condemnation of human sexuality is always likely to fail. If "messianic time" is necessary for the political and ethical regulation of subjects, then Lucretian "fluid time" tempers the more punitive manifestations of the former through its skeptical emphasis on mutual pleasure. Shakespeare does not formulate an unproblematic or perfect account of natural law in *Measure for Measure*. But perhaps the play's most radical challenge is to reclaim Lucretius as a deeply ethical thinker, one whose philosophy offers a potent challenge to a dominant Calvinistic conception of natural law, and who celebrates, rather than condemns, human sexuality.

CHAPTER 8

# *Agnostic Shakespeare?: the godless world of* King Lear

*David Loewenstein*

Just how daring was Shakespeare in imagining – and testing – the limits of religious belief, order, faith, and divine powers in the widespread providential culture of early modern England? In particular, what does a dark experimental tragedy like *King Lear*, set in a pre-Christian world, tell us about the later Shakespeare's willingness to examine a brutal world in which neither a Christian God nor "the kind gods" (to borrow Gloucester's words, 3.7.35) respond to human savagery and suffering and offer any hope of consolation?[1] What does this tragedy about extreme old age, the devastating loss of a king's political authority, the fragility of human life, and the shattering of the moral order tell us about Shakespeare's exploration of a world in which there indeed seems to be no ultimate role for "providence" in human affairs? To what degree did tragic drama itself enable Shakespeare to speculate in exceptionally daring, radical, and skeptical ways about religious assurances and beliefs in relation to catastrophic events? This chapter attempts to address these questions and to do something more: to argue that Shakespeare was capable of taking great risks when it came to dramatizing religious beliefs (or their absence) and daring enough to write a drama that imagines a dark, pitiless world without God or gods in an age in which providential thinking dominated religious culture.

Determining Shakespeare's personal religious beliefs remains elusive.[2] We can discern much more about Shakespeare's major rival, Ben Jonson, in

[1] Citations from Shakespeare's plays are taken from *The Norton Shakespeare* based on the Oxford text and edited by Stephen Greenblatt, Walter Cohen, Jean E. Howard, and Katherine Eisaman Maus (New York: W. W. Norton 1997); for *King Lear* I cite from the conflated text. I have also consulted the excellent Arden edition of the play prepared by R. A. Foakes (Walton-on-Thames: Nelson & Sons, 1997).

[2] See David Bevington's chapter in this volume (Chapter 1 above) for a concise account of the debates about Shakespeare and his religion. For the elusiveness of Shakespeare's personal religious beliefs, see David Kastan, *A Will to Believe: Shakespeare and Religion* (Oxford University Press, 2014), ch. 2, as well as the Introduction to this volume. Cf. Stephen Greenblatt, *Will in the World: How Shakespeare Became Shakespeare* (New York: W. W. Norton, 2004), for speculations about Shakespeare in relation

terms of his personal religious allegiances (including his Catholicism and reconversion to the Church of England) than we can about Shakespeare's.[3] Nonetheless, Shakespeare's plays allowed him to dramatize a range of diverse and contradictory religious beliefs (whatever his own may have been) in an age when the orthodox view about religion's role in a commonwealth and human life was "that without religion the life of man would be filled with all foolishnes, madnesse and mischiefe."[4] *King Lear* dramatizes in a distinctive and intensely tragic way a world where religious beliefs, expressed by means of appeals to the heavens or to the gods, remain uncertain as we watch "all foolishness, madnesse and mischief" profoundly disrupt a kingdom and human life. As I argue here, one of the most daring positions Shakespeare attempted to imagine is close to what we would consider agnosticism: his tragedy depicts a meaningless and hostile universe where neither God nor gods answer multiple human appeals to supernatural powers, whether these appeals be for protection, divine justice, or vengeance in a world in which suffering can "top extremity" (5.3.206).[5] This is a radical position to dramatize in a providential culture in which God was usually believed to be acting directly in human affairs and in which we find religious writers expressing anxieties that "men [who] would make a dout of Gods providence" and "escape the iudgement of God" were threatening to subvert the religious, social, and political order.[6] And the play's radicalism regarding the question of providentialism is likewise apparent when we keep in mind that James I believed that kings are "justly called Gods" who intervene actively in human affairs with the power to "make and unmake" their subjects.[7] I am not claiming, however, that the author of *King Lear* was

to the old religion, including his imaginative grappling with Catholic practices and beliefs; Greenblatt also concisely summarizes debates about the religion of Shakespeare on pp. 396–8. Jeffrey Knapp, *Shakespeare's Tribe: Church, Nation, and Theater in Renaissance England* (University of Chicago Press, 2002), seems more confident that we can identify Shakespeare's religious beliefs and suggests that we understand his playwriting "as a kind of ministry" (p. 9).

3 See Ian Donaldson, *Ben Jonson: A Life* (Oxford University Press, 2011), esp. pp. 138–44, 255–9, and 271–5 on Jonson's religious beliefs and allegiances.

4 [Sir John Hayward,] *A Reporte of a Discourse Concerning Supreme Power in Affaires of Religion* (London, 1606), p. 6.

5 Some points I make below about Shakespeare's skeptical attitude towards providence in relation to human affairs are partly anticipated in William R. Elton, *"King Lear" and the Gods* (San Marino, CA: Huntington Library, 1966), esp. pp. 9–62, where Elton challenges "the relevance" of the play to "the popular modern theory of Christian optimism" (p. 8); however, I emphasize more strongly Shakespeare's daring capacity *to imagine*, in dramatic tragedy, an agnostic world in the midst of a deeply providential culture in early modern England and thus to dramatize in his plays competing and contradictory religious viewpoints.

6 See, e.g., John Dove, *A Confutation of Atheisme* (London, 1605); quotations from pp. 13, 95. See also Henry Smith, *Gods Arrow against Atheists* (London, 1604).

7 *The Workes of the Most High and Mighty Prince, James* (London, 1616), p. 529.

any kind of atheist since we have no firm evidence for Shakespeare's own religious beliefs; nonetheless, he could write an experimental tragedy about an unsettled and cruel world which seems devoid of God's presence and any providential or supernatural order – quite unlike, as we will see at the end of this chapter, one of Shakespeare's main sources, *The True Chronicle History of King Leir.*

*King Lear* is a tragedy in which its characters, in the midst of expressing rage or great suffering, regularly appeal to a range of supernatural powers – the gods, the heavens, the stars, Fortune, the torments of hell and devils, apocalyptic forces – and their capacities to intervene in or explain human affairs and cruelty or to offer punishments to the wicked, as well as evidence of supernatural judgments. And yet the play also portrays a brutal and violent world without any kind of religious assurances. For all his remarkable capacity for metaphysical speculation about the mysterious cosmos and for all his efforts to negotiate the treacherous Machiavellian world of Denmark's Elsinore, Shakespeare's Hamlet remains, at the end, a Christian prince who believes that "there's a divinity that shapes our ends, / Rough-hew them how we will" (5.2.10–11) and, echoing Matthew 10:29 (in the Geneva Bible), that "there's a special providence in the fall of a sparrow" (5.2.157–8).[8] Yet *King Lear* is a play that seems to go to the other extreme: there Shakespeare imagines a pitiless and ruthless world without any providential meaning or supernatural forces or religious institutions that (despite being invoked by its characters) shape human life, actions, and events, or help to explain inhospitable conditions such as the terrifying, titanic storm Lear endures, or offer consolation in response to the harsh realities of human misery. Moreover, in early modern England providence and vengeance upon the wicked were often linked; yet in the dark, chaotic, and unsettled world dramatized in *King Lear* they seem to have little connection at all.

## Providence, vengeance, and judgment in an inhospitable world

Despite the fractious religious culture of post-Reformation England, belief in "providence," as its leading scholar emphasizes, was a widespread and

[8] On providence exemplified in the sparrow, see John Calvin, *Institutes* I.xvi.1, I.xvii.6; Arthur Dent, *A Platforme, Made for the Proofe of Gods providence* (London, 1608), p. 16; and Alexandra Walsham, *Providence in Early Modern England* (Oxford University Press, 1999), p. 10. On *Hamlet* and the doctrine of providence, see Brian Cummings, *Mortal Thoughts: Religion, Secularity and Identity in Shakespeare and Early Modern Culture* (Oxford University Press, 2013), pp. 212–14. Hamlet's providential vision, however, is qualified by the account of "accidental judgements" and "casual slaughters" (5.2.326) in Horatio's account, at the end, of the revenge play. On the difference between Hamlet's and Horatio's views, see Chapter 1 above.

deeply ingrained "response to chaos and crisis, a practical source of consolation in a hazardous and inhospitable environment, and an idea which exercised practical, emotional, and imaginative influence upon those who subscribed to it."[9] In Shakespeare's England, Thomas Beard's providentialist *Theatre of God's Judgements*, published in 1597 and then in a second edition in 1612, was a particularly well-known and substantial anthology of stories of heavenly anger and severe vengeance justly executed against brazen malefactors from Hebrew times to the present and "Collected out of Sacred, Ecclesiasticall, and prophane Histories." In this work, compiled by a Church of England clergyman and popular with the late Tudor and Stuart laity, one could view the dramatic acts of an all-powerful and terrifying God intervening in the spectacle of human affairs; and it promised especially to represent to readers "the admirable justice of God against all notorious sinners, both great and small" whose "power breaketh through the barres of humane justice."[10] Witnessing "the tempest of Gods wrath" in human affairs and upon "the mightie ones of the world" – especially "the most wicked, dissolute, and disordered sinners, that with loose reines runne fiercely after their lust" – offered reassurance that human beings ultimately lived in a moral cosmos; patterns of divine justice and providence could be discerned in this world, however treacherous, and wisdom could be derived from observing them, including the lesson that "everie man" should "turne from evill, and … follow that which is good."[11] All sinister or wicked persons who took "sport in cruelties and evill deeds," Beard assured his readers, would be "drawne to their finall destruction" as vengeance "pursueth malefactors to their shame and confusion in this life, and to their destruction in the world to come."[12] To be sure, the Calvinist-minded Beard insisted on "the huge corruption and perversitie of mankind" with all its unnatural savagery and wickedness; yet he also insisted that, however baffling His earthly dealings might appear, "there is a God above that guideth the sterne of the world, and that taketh care of humane matters, and that is just in punishing the unjust and malicious."[13] Classical authors, notably Seneca, could be harnessed to confirm this early modern view of providence, including reasons explaining why God afflicts good men; for instance, the pagan personification of divine vengeance, Nemesis, who

[9] Walsham, *Providence*, p. 3.

[10] Thomas Beard, *The Theatre of Gods Judgements* (London, 1612), title page. For detailed discussion of Beard's work and providential punishments, see Walsham, *Providence*, ch. 2; for his work's popularity, see p. 67.

[11] *Theatre of Gods Judgements*, sigs. A4v, A6r. [12] Ibid., sigs. A6v, A3r. [13] Ibid., sig. A7r.

embodied the principle of retribution for wickedness and vice, might be fused with the righteous and wrathful Jehovah of the Old Testament.[14]

Even Samuel Harsnett, whose anti-Catholic tract *A Declaration of Egregious Popish Impostures* (1603) conjures up a world of "Popish Impostures" and theatrical rituals of religious exorcism, offers a providential interpretation of treacherous demonic powers and spiritual fraud. It has long been recognized that Shakespeare drew upon Harsnett's vivid vocabulary and turn of phrase as he was writing *King Lear*, especially in his depiction in Act 3 of Poor Tom, the feigning madman possessed by dark demonic spirits (with such occult names as "the foul fiend Flibbertigibbet," Smulkin, Modo, Mahu, and Frateretto)[15] in an infernal, inhospitable Bosch-like landscape and rough countryside battered by violent weather; Stephen Greenblatt especially has challenged the tendency to treat Harsnett's richly suggestive text as no more than a background source for the play.[16] My point, however, is to emphasize that there is also a difference between Shakespeare and Harsnett when it comes to the matter of providence and vengeance: for all his emphasis on a sinister theatrical world created by cunning popish exorcists and their "treasonable machinations" and "diabolical incantations," the latter writer also envisions a providential cosmos in which "He that sits in the heavens, Almighty God, with his Angels, and Saints, do laugh these mishapen monsters to scorne." Harsnett, who treats exorcism as a spiritual fraud, believes that ultimately "Gods revengefull arme doth uncase [theatrical excorcists] to the view of the world." But Shakespeare's tragedy, while it also envisions exorcism as a spiritual fraud, offers no certainty that "Gods revengefull arme" can be detected anywhere in human affairs, including in a dark world of theatrical machinations and "impious dissimulation."[17] As a mad, fearful beggar vexed by invisible fiends, Poor Tom may be the catalyst that triggers some of the banished Lear's most seering insights about "unaccommodated man" (3.4.98–9) in an unnatural environment stripped of any human comforts and disguises whatsoever. Yet the shocking appearance and

[14] *The Workes of Lucius Anneaus Seneca, both morall and naturall*, trans. Thomas Lodge (London, 1614), pp. 497–509. See Samuel Gardiner, *Doomes-Day Booke* (London, 1606), pp. 4–6, for another example of a contemporary work that links classical writers (Ovid, Plato, Seneca, and other classical authorities) with Scripture to reinforce the notion that the world shall be destroyed. On the pagan notion of nemesis or divine vengeance in relation to providence, see Walsham, *Providence*, p. 8.

[15] Samuel Harsnett, *A Declaration of Egregious Popish Impostures* (London, 1603), pp. 46, 48–9.

[16] Stephen Greenblatt, *Shakespearean Negotations* (Berkeley: University of California Press, 1988), ch. 4. See also F. W. Brownlow, *Shakespeare, Harsnett, and the Devils of Denham* (Newark, DE: University of Delaware Press, 1993). Cf. Foakes, *King Lear*, pp. 102–3, who takes issue with Greenblatt's reading of Harsnett in relation to *King Lear*.

[17] Harsnett, *A Declaration*, sigs. A3r–v, A4r.

behavior of the naked, destitute, and fiend-possessed Tom in the midst of the violent storm does not trigger any kind of divine retribution or intervention, nor any kind of response from the heavens to "this extremity of the skies" and the tyranny of the night (3.4.95).

Invoking the torments of Hell might likewise seem to suggest the potential for some kind of heavenly vengeance and retributive justice. The fantasy trial envisioned by the mad Lear in Act 3, scene 6, for example, is preceded by Lear imagining Goneril and Regan suffering hellish torments: "To have a thousand with red burning spits / Come hissing in upon 'em" (3.6.13–14). Later the mad, raging, and suffering Lear will invoke the destructive fires of hell, with overtones of an apocalyptic end of the world, as he expresses hysterical disgust at monstrous female sexuality: "Beneath is all the fiends'; there's hell, there's darkness, / There's the sulphurous pit, burning, scalding, / Stench, consumption! Fie, fie, fie! pah! pah!" (4.6.124–6). Harsnett has plenty of images of hell-fire,[18] yet in Shakespeare's play there is no evidence at all that such terrifying torments, or Hell itself, exist to punish wicked behavior and effect retribution.

Shakespeare's experimental tragedy *King Lear*, then, offers a very different and more unsettling perspective than those contemporary texts like Harsnett's that suggest providential forces or agents of vengeance are at work in the world, responding with divine indignation to the sinful, obstinate, and rebellious nature of humankind. If providence could be invoked to explain terrifying natural destruction and calamities linked to human behavior, it could also be invoked to explain the abatement of such extreme suffering.[19] Yet *King Lear* offers no sense of any kind of providential order to explain its harsh dramatization of human suffering. Set in pre-Christian times, it dramatizes no assurance of providential judgments and interventions against wicked men and women and no sense of consolation in an inhospitable world with its "strange mutations" (4.1.11), to quote Edgar when he first sees his eye-less father cruelly cast out into the open country. At the height of his powers as a tragic dramatist, Shakespeare wrote a radical play flaunting the very idea of providentialism and the belief in an interventionist deity who responds to human misery, chaos, injustice, and savagery.

In order to illuminate issues of human savagery and suffering in relation to the providential religious culture of early modern England, one can

[18] See chapter 12 of *A Declaration* in Brownlow, *Shakespeare, Harsnett*, pp. 255–7, where hell-fire is associated with "the coales of Gods wrath and fearful indignation" (p. 257).

[19] See, e.g., *The last terrible Tempestious windes and weather* (London, 1613), or *Gods warning to his people of England* (London, 1607).

Figure 1. Woodcut depicting the persecution of early Christians, John Foxe, *Actes and Monuments* (1570), sig. NN1r.

compare John Foxe and Shakespeare, since both writers, in their own ways, depict extremes of violence in order to examine and test issues of providential order and divine justice. Foxe the martyrologist, himself a religious dramatist, was fascinated and horrified by extreme human violence in early Christian history, as well as in Reformation Britain and Europe. Like Shakespeare, Foxe shows us in the evolving *Actes and Monuments* or "Book of Martyrs" (1563–83), first published in English the year before Shakespeare's birth and a major influence on Beard, the "violence of mens affections" in their most terrifying forms. Thus the first illustration following Foxe's account of the Primitive Church in the expanded 1570 edition of the *Actes* presents a disturbing image of the persecution of Christians – especially "good Byshops," ministers, and "teachers of the flocke" – by the powers of heathen emperors of Rome during the days of the early church when small communities of Christians struggled to survive. Foxe emphasizes the barbarism and vicious aggressiveness of worldly powers in a world of religious fear, "dreadfull dangers, & sorrowfull afflictions"; his verbal catalogue underscores the multiple torments and ravenous savagery endured by early Christians for approximately three hundred years (until the time of Constantine): "some were scourged, some beheaded, some crucified, some burned, some had their eyes put out, some one way some another miserably consumed . . . "[20] The grim action-filled woodcut – the very first one at the end of the first volume of Foxe's text – is even more terrifying, conveying the energy and violence of savage persecution and blind fury as a king or emperor watches scenes of victims mutilated and mangled in a variety of horrifying ways.

When it comes to shocking acts of violence and torture, very little is left to the viewer's imagination in Foxe's woodcut. Besides showing victims about to be beheaded or burning alive, one part of the illustration shows a naked man whose flesh is being devoured by voracious lions; another part shows a man lying on the ground – his hands tied together and his face contorted in agony – as his persecutor presses one foot on the victim's chest and turns a drill that bores directly into the Christian man's right eye.

Here we may compare the brutal blinding of Gloucester in *King Lear*, a terrifying episode of violence dramatized on stage and almost too painful to watch in the theater.[21] Cornwall tears out the "vile jelly" of Gloucester's eyes as the latter, bound to a chair by his tormentors, appeals to the "wingèd vengeance" of the heavens (3.7.67) and asks for their help in response to such cruelty, while also appealing to the "Kind gods" (95) to forgive him just at that moment of anagnorisis ("O my follies!") when he recognizes that Edgar "was abused" (94) by the bastard Edmund. "Now, heaven help him!" cries out one servant as he observes Gloucester's disfigured and "bleeding face" (3.7.111), closing the vicious scene on a note that raises the possibility that providence, or an equivalent supernatural power, might intervene on the behalf of the miserable Gloucester. In their different mediums, both Foxe and Shakespeare depict a spectacle of extreme cruelty meant to generate the greatest emotional impact from readers or spectators. Foxe's illustration of sadistic violence sets the grim tone for some of the powerful physical images, including those of mutilated bodies, to follow in his great martyrological work – a reminder of what Foxe calls, at the beginning of his

[20] *Actes and Monuments* (London, 1570), NN1r, after p. 922; this is also the first illustration in the same series in the 1583 edition (see p. 780).

[21] As Janet Adelman observes, spectators in the theater are likely to close their eyes at this moment of terrifying cruelty, thereby reduplicating Gloucester's experience of darkness. Janet Adelman (ed.), *Twentieth-Century Interpretations of King Lear: A Collection of Critical Essays* (Englewood Cliffs, NJ: Prentice-Hall, 1978), p. 4.

massive work, the "violence of mens affections," raw human nature unreformed by God's grace or the working of the Bible.[22]

Yet Foxe's work depicting extreme and treacherous brutality also makes clear that as an evangelical Protestant he believed in a providential order in which there is "a special providence in the fall of a sparrow"; and that powerful godly perspective enabled Foxe, attempting to reveal the just hand of God's wrathful chastisement and punishment against wicked persecutors, to put the history of human violence and hatred in an apocalyptic perspective. While this world might indeed be "ruled by mans violence and wisedome," Foxe observes, the "happy succes of the other [was] euer ruled by Gods blessing and prouidence. The wrath & reuenging hand of God in the one, and his mercye vpon the other."[23] Shakespeare's great tragedy also depicts the "violence of mens affections" and their terrifying consequences. The difference, of course, is that Shakespeare sets *King Lear* in a pre-Christian world – one more distant in the past (as the Fool suggests) than that of the legendary Merlin and King Arthur[24] – where, ultimately and despite what some of the play's characters yearn to believe, there seems to be no providential order or divine justice at all, nor evidence of God's "wrath & reuenging hand." This enabled Shakespeare to write an unusually daring play in which, despite its frequent recourse to apocalyptic language, images, and overtones suggesting that the end of the world was at hand ("Is this the promised end?" Kent wonders at the end, "Or image of that horror?" as Edgar wonders [5.3.262–3]),[25] no kind of religious order or assurance of justice operates; in this tragedy there is no evidence that divine vengeance is ever executed, despite the language characters use to invoke it. Lear invokes (in a vehement exchange with Regan) "all the stored vengeances of heaven" to "fall" on Cordelia's "ingrateful top" or head and strike her "young bones," while he calls upon "nimble lightnings" to "dart [their] blinding flames / Into her scornful eyes!" (2.4.155–6, 158–9); Gloucester, when he is assaulted violently, believes that he "shall see" divine or "winged vengeance overtake" the brutal daughters of Lear (3.7.66–7). Even Albany, moved by the savagery meted out to Gloucester, can invoke "justicers" above who "speedily can venge" (4.2.79–81) when he hears that the cruel Duke of Cornwall has been slain by a servant. Yet the play reveals no evidence of

[22] "Foure Questions propounded," in *Actes and Monuments*, sig. *iiiir.

[23] *Actes and Monuments*, p. 49. [24] See the Fool's satirical prophecy at 3.2.77–94.

[25] On apocalyptic language and visions in the play, see Joseph Wittreich, *"Image of that Horror": History, Prophecy, and Apocalypse in "King Lear"* (San Marino, CA: Huntington Library, 1984). On figurations of apocalypse in *Lear*, see also Frank Kermode, *The Sense of an Ending: Studies in the Theory of Fiction* (Oxford University Press, 1979), pp. 82–3.

supernatural "judges" intervening and enacting vengeance – it is a man, indeed a "peasant" (3.7.83), who has slain Cornwall and nothing more, however heroically we may interpret this gesture of resistance.[26] Likewise, when Albany hears about the deaths of Goneril and Regan, he observes that "This judgment [is] of the heavens, that makes us tremble" (5.3.230); yet the play offers no evidence that "this judgment" has anything at all to do with the heavens, so that Albany's moralistic assertion partly rings hollow, even if he has become a more sympathetic figure at the end. Moreover, neither Fortune nor the gods can offer any consolation in the face of terrifying human anguish and violence, as Lear endures an ordeal of acute torment "upon the rack of this tough world" (5.3.313) or as Gloucester hopes that the gods will offer some help in response to the dreadful cruelty he endures.

Does this make Shakespeare, in this dark tragedy, an agnostic, a writer who believes that nothing is known or can be known of the existence and nature of God? Not necessarily. But it does mean that tragic drama enabled Shakespeare, a writer who was likely less doctrinaire in religion than the Protestant martyrologist Foxe, *to imagine* a world stripped of any kind of religious (as well as political) assurance, a world of intense and protracted suffering in which there is no ultimate role for providence as a force of justice, vengeance, or consolation in human affairs. And it does allow Shakespeare to represent dramatically a disturbing strain of religious skepticism.[27] Shakespeare's personal religious beliefs may remain elusive and the subject of speculation; nevertheless, it is unlikely that he could have written the devastating tragedy of *King Lear* had he been a fervent early modern providentialist like John Foxe. The medium of drama gave Shakespeare, who offers no evidence of being doctrinaire in religious matters, remarkable freedom when it came to exploring extremes of religious belief and uncertainty.[28] One need not assert that Shakespearean drama is secular – after all, the plays explore a wide range of competing or conflicting religious views and themes and are rich in biblical allusions[29] – to acknowledge that the early modern theater in London was a commercial venture whose

[26] On the political implications of this act of virtuous disobedience (and others) in *King Lear*, see Richard Strier, "Faithful Servants: Shakespeare's Praise of Disobedience," in Heather Dubrow and Richard Strier (eds.), *The Historical Renaissance: New Essays on Tudor and Stuart Literature and Culture* (University of Chicago Press, 1988), pp. 104–33.

[27] On the topic of Shakespeare and skepticism more broadly, see Graham Bradshaw, *Shakespeare's Scepticism* (Brighton: Harvester Wheatsheaf, 1987).

[28] Cf. Knapp, *Shakespeare's Tribe*, who argues for Shakespeare's alignment in his later years with a broad-based Erasmian Christianity and his toleration of beliefs and practices outside those tenents.

[29] For a major study of biblical allusions in Shakespeare, see Hannibal Hamlin, *The Bible in Shakespeare* (Oxford University Press, 2013).

performances were not dedicated to the worship of God.[30] Nonetheless, the early modern theater gave Shakespeare immense creative freedom "to explore any idea,"[31] including the *freedom* to explore religious or, indeed, even nonreligious perspectives that might clash with a mainstream providential point of view based on the notion of a deity who is directly and actively at work in the world.

The rest of this chapter examines the daring ways *King Lear* illustrates Peter Marshall's observation (made in Chapter 2 above) regarding Shakespeare's avoidance of clear (or even identifiable) confessional stances "in an age of confessional choices."[32] As I will argue, this religious avoidance also gave Shakespeare a crucial element of radical freedom and creativity as a dramatist when it came to early modern religion: it enabled him, in the case of *King Lear,* to write a great experimental tragedy about a savage world in which all religious assurances and appeals to supernatural powers are rendered bitterly ironic and ultimately uncertain.

## Supernatural powers and the "great confusion" of *King Lear*

*King Lear* deeply challenges a providential view of the world and universe in a culture that widely believed that God actively intervenes in human affairs to punish, chastise, test, and reward. In *King Lear* we find a cacophony of appeals by its characters to supernatural powers, including the "gods" or the "heavens." The wide range of appeals made by the play's characters to supernatural powers highlights the desperate and elusive attempts to comprehend human suffering and savagery, while calling attention to the radical and experimental nature of the play when it comes to positing any kind of religious and providential consolation or belief, or projecting a vision of any kind of interventionist deity.

If the play depicts a wide range of appeals to the gods and to the heavens, it offers no consistent view of their responses to human vulnerability and dreadful calamities: Are they vengeful? Are they indifferent to human misery? Are they supernatural powers ensuring human preservation? Since

30 See Anthony B. Dawson, "Shakespeare and Secular Performance," in Patricia Badir and Paul Tachnin (eds.), *Shakespeare and the Cultures of Performance* (Farnham: Ashgate, 2007), pp. 83–97, and the response to Dawson in Paul Stevens's Chapter 12 below, in which Stevens also engages with work by John Milbank and Charles Taylor on secularism. On modern secularization in relation to interpretations of early modern identity, see the acute account in Cummings, *Mortal Thoughts.*

31 See Stephen Greenblatt, *Shakespeare's Freedom* (University of Chicago Press, 2010), p. 1; Greenblatt's book contains acute observations on the ways Shakespeare was averse to absolutes, including, as this present volume further demonstrates, religious absolutes.

32 See p. 55 above.

the gods never intervene or respond in the tragedy (despite multiple efforts by the play's characters to invoke them), one is left with a sense that the gods are in fact contradictory projections of the human imagination as it responds to the pressures of physical, emotional, spiritual, and psychological extremity. At his most despairing moment, after he has been blinded and thrust out into the open country, Gloucester offers his bleakest doctrine: "As flies to wanton boys are we to the gods; / They kill us for their sport" (4.1.37–8). Yet this vision of the gods as callous and cruel is but one perspective and hardly a consistent one; elsewhere Gloucester can refer to the gods as "kind" or "ever-gentle" (3.7.35, 4.6.212), including at the moment of dramatic recognition when he suddenly understands that his elder son Edgar has been abused by the cunning, self-made Edmund: "Kind gods, forgive me that, and prosper him!" (3.7.95). As the despairing Gloucester faces "th' extreme verge" of Dover cliff, in a scene emblematic of the extremity of suffering, and expects to plunge to his death, he appeals to the heavens: "O you mighty gods! / This world I do renounce, and, in your sights, / Shake patiently my great affliction off" (4.6.34–6). Yet the gods never answer Gloucester. When Edgar speaks with Gloucester of his miraculous survival, after his apparent precipitous fall from Dover cliff, Edgar imagines that "the clearest gods" have "preserved" his "happy father" (4.6.72–4). Yet this is no more than a religious fiction, created by Edgar out of a sense of filial compassion and loyalty.

Lear too frequently appeals to the gods as though they might temper his behavior or bring about some kind of justice: for example, as a grieving, vulnerable old man stripped of his authority and meditating on the meaning of "true need," he appeals to the "heavens" and "gods" to give him patience, an appeal that carries both Job-like and Christian overtones (2.4.265–8; see Romans 5.3–4);[33] in the midst of the terrifying storm with its "bursts of horrid thunder," he refers to "the great gods" as though they and the storm itself (which assumes moral meaning in Lear's speech) might enact divine, apocalyptic wrath and justice on crimes yet unpunished (3.2.44, 47–58); or he refers to the heavens as "just" in his searing speech about poverty and social justice (3.4.29–37). Yet as usual the gods or heavens never answer his appeals nor intervene, so that readers or spectators of the play receive no assurance that they exist or (if they do) respond to human suffering, including Lear's Job-like affliction ("a man / More sinned against than sinning" [3.2.57–8]). In this way, Shakespeare constantly prompts readers or

[33] On *King Lear's* association with the Book of Job, see Steven Marx, *Shakespeare and the Bible* (Oxford University Press, 2000), pp. 59–78; Hamlin, *Bible in Shakespeare*, ch. 8.

viewers to question the limits of religious belief, including the role of supernatural powers in human life at moments of extreme calamity and crisis.

The loyal Kent, too, seems to have faith in the gods as protective deities. He appeals to the gods to protect Cordelia spurned by Lear ("The gods to their dear shelter take thee, maid" [1.1.183]), and in the mock trial scene he asks "the gods" to "reward" Gloucester's "kindness" (3.6.5). Yet appeals to the gods can be manipulated and put to darker purposes. The anarchic Edmund appeals to the "gods" to "stand up for bastards!" (1.2.22): he cynically flaunts the appeal to gods as protective deities in his world of Machiavellian self-invention – a world turned upside down and designed to serve his self-interests and cunning pursuit of power. Likewise, he refers to the "revenging gods" (2.1.46) as he engages in theatrical machinations aimed at convincing the easily duped and superstitious Gloucester that Edgar is a villain. Such references to the gods show that human invocations of supernatural deities can serve different and conflicting purposes, without ever confirming that supernatural deities truly intervene in human affairs.

In the last act of the play there seem to be more hopeful appeals to the gods, although these too can be seen as projections of the fragile human imagination responding to conditions of extremity and affliction. When Lear and Cordelia are prisoners, Lear imagines "the gods" throwing "incense" upon them as "sacrifices" (5.3.20–1); and just before this he envisions a happy ending that includes a fantasy in which he and his loving daughter might understand the mysterious workings of the world and its iniquities (see 2 Thessalonians 2:7) so that they "take upon's the mystery of things, / As if we were God's spies" (5.3.16–17), a passage that also leaves ambiguous whether Lear is referring to multiple pagan gods or to a single Christian one (in a play that nowhere else refers to the latter).[34] When Edgar finally defeats Edmund, he proclaims his true identity ("My name is Edgar, and thy father's son") and moralizes at this moment of triumph: "The gods are just, and of our pleasant vices / Make instruments to plague us" (5.3.169–70). Yet the play refuses to support any kind of simple moralizing based upon human projections of the gods and their justice. When Albany hears about the commission to hang Cordelia in prison, he proclaims "The

[34] For the allusion to 2 Thessalonians, see Foakes's note in the Arden edition on 5.3.16. On the question of whether the tragedy and its existential exploration of human suffering, providence, and justice can be understood in terms of a Christian perspective, including the notion of a "hidden God" stressed by Luther and Calvin, see Hamlin, *Bible in Shakespeare*, pp. 326–33 (cf. Elton, *"King Lear" and the Gods*); Shakespeare's tragedy, despite its biblical allusions and apocalyptic overtones, refuses any kind of clear-cut Christian reading.

gods defend her" (5.3.255), just a moment after he interprets the deaths of Goneril and Regan as the "judgment of the heavens" (5.3.230), and just a moment before the play's most devastating stage direction: "*Re-enter* LEAR, *with* CORDELIA *dead in his arms.*"

Other supernatural powers and celestial phenomena (which I will mention more briefly here) are likewise invoked to explain dramatic change or the descent into chaos, division, final judgment, and a sense of the end of the world. In early modern England, eclipses, for instance, were perceived as "providential tokens of future misfortune" and momentous events, including the subversion of kingdoms.[35] Gloucester envisions "late eclipses," signs of disorder in the cosmos, as signs of treasonous disorder in both the kingdom and the family, interpreting these cosmic events in an apocalyptic vein that evokes the terrifying mood of the play (1.2.96–106). Yet the cynical Edmund, who sees his father's notions as mere superstitious "foppery," qualifies Gloucester's apocalyptic interpretation and its potentially providential implications. He mocks astrological explanations ("an enforced obedience of planetary influence" and movements) – explanations which were often in competition with providential interpretations in early modern England[36] – and insists that "our disasters" are of our making and not to be explained "by a divine thrusting on" (1.2.109–16). Such clashing perspectives as these, voiced by Gloucester and Edmund, enable Shakespeare's play to provoke skeptical and unresolved questions about supernatural powers and celestial phenomena in relation to human calamities.

Appeals to the capricious Dame Fortune remind us that the play makes use of an ideological eclecticism when it comes to supernatural powers and phenomena as its characters attempt to find meaning in an unstable world full of misfortune. Medieval thinkers from Boethius to Dante may have placed Fortune in subservience to God, while Calvin and his providential English followers thought such compromise was anathema, dismissing heathenish but still prevalent concepts as "good luck" and "ill fortune" and referring to the goddess as nothing more than "a poeticall figment" and deceit.[37] Yet in *King Lear* the conceit of Fortune and her wheel highlights clashing perspectives: wishful thinking as well as the frustration of finding

[35] Walsham, *Providence*, pp. 167, 174. Cf. *King John*, 3.4.153–9.

[36] See, e.g., Keith Thomas, *Religion and the Decline of Magic* (New York: Charles Scribner's, 1971), ch. 12; Patrick Curry, *Prophecy and Power: Astrology in Early Modern England* (Princeton University Press, 1989); Walsham, *Providence*, pp. 23–5, 174–5, 328.

[37] See Walsham, *Providence*, pp. 20–2, citing English Protestant divines. For the "conceit" that good and ill luck are done by goddess Fortune, see William Gouge, *The Extent of Gods Providence,* in *Gods Three Arrowes* (London, 1631), p. 380; for Fortune dismissed as a poetical "figment," see Thomas Gataker, *Of the Nature of Lots* (London, 1619), p. 20.

hopeful signs in a world of human catastrophe and vicissitude. Put in the stocks and left alone at night, Kent appeals to the goddess – "Fortune, good night; smile once more; turn thy wheel!" (2.2.165) – and Edgar expresses hope ("esperance") that Fortune's wheel can only go up in times of calamity (4.1.2–6). Yet when a moment later Edgar sees his blinded, bloodied father, his assumptions about Fortune are brutally shattered: "World, world, O world! / But that thy strange mutations make us hate thee" (10–11). The goddess is likewise a point of reference for other characters: defeated and cast down, Cordelia imagines that she might "out-frown false Fortune's frown" (5.3.6), and even the Machiavellian Edmund, wounded by Edgar and dying at the end, confirms that the wheel of Fortune has come full circle, thereby indicating his self-defeating nature. If Fortune becomes one way for characters to explain the dramatic turn of events, the goddess in some sense remains "a poeticall figment" and a conceit – another projection of the human imagination desperately confronting a precarious world full of suffering and violence that "top[s] extremity" (5.3.206).

## Conclusion: we are "left darkling"

Given the foregoing discussion of supernatural powers and phenomena in *King Lear*, just how daring is its ending in terms of early modern notions of providential justice, order, and intervention? Shakespeare's immediate source, *The True Chronicle History of King Leir* (published 1605), with its combination of romance and legendary history, ends happily, unlike *King Lear*, as it highlights a providential order and interventionist deity that reinforce a final sense of justice and divine order. The Gallian King, who invades England and restores Leir to his throne, observes at the end about Leir and his mistreatment: "But God protected him from all their spight, / And we are come in iustice of his right." He also observes just before these lines that "we came in right, / And iust reuengement of the wronged King, / Whose daughters there, fell vipers as they are, / Haue sought to murder and depriue of life."[38] It is as though the Gallian King is himself an instrument of just providential revenge. At the very end, too, as "alarums . . . sound victory," and as Leir and Cordella enter for the last time, the King of Gallia proclaims to them: "Thanks be to God, your foes are ouercome, / And you againe possessed of your right." Moreover, he tells Leir to "Thank heauens, not me,"[39] just as Leir delivers the concluding speeches in which

[38] *The True Chronicle History of King Leir, and his three daughters, Gonorill, Ragan, and Cordella* (London, 1605), sig. I3v.

[39] Ibid., sig. I4v.

he expresses his deep gratitude for having his kingly title restored and for being reunited with his son and daughter.

Shakespeare's tragedy handles the ending very differently, offering no kind of assurance of providential order or supernatural intervention. No Christian God is invoked and there is no sense of "iustice" and reward. Instead, the ending is devastating as Lear enters for the last time with Cordelia in his arms – "She's dead as earth" (5.3.260), her father proclaims – and as Lear himself expires on stage. The contrast between the ending of Shakespeare's tragedy and the providential ending of *The History of King Leir and his three daughters* could not be more striking. In his suffering and rage Lear may refer to the heavens as though they might react to his profound grief ("O, you are men of stones! / Had I your tongues and eyes I'd use them so / That heaven's vault should crack" [5.3.256–8]). The apocalyptic language augments the play's final sense of devastation, as Kent and Edgar observe Lear in his intense emotional agony: "Is this the promised end?" observes Kent, as Edgar asks, "Or image of that horror?" Yet these apocalyptically inflected questions, with their implications of some kind of terrifying providential judgment and end-of-the-world scenario, yield no answers. Indeed, there is no sense that providence, even in the guise of pre-Christian gods, has played *any role* whatsoever in the devastating tragedy. We are left, at the end, with a profound sense of loss, suffering, and destruction in a godless world stripped of providential moral significance.

Shakespeare's experimental tragedy, written in an age saturated in providential thinking, thus leaves us with disturbing and unanswered questions: What if there might indeed be no providential order governing a pitiless world and universe? What if the notion of providential justice, chastisement, and punishment is nothing more than a chimera? Although *King Lear* powerfully dramatizes, at numerous points, poignant and moving expressions of human sympathy and fellow-feeling towards other suffering human beings ("Give me your arm," Edgar tells his suffering father in the Dover cliff scene, "Up – so. How is 't? Feel you your legs?" [4.6.64–5]),[40] this play denies any kind of providential certainty and comfort or any kind of

[40] There are numerous other important examples, including: Lear's pity for the Fool in the midst of the storm ("Come on, my boy. How dost, my boy? Art cold?" [3.2.66]); the servant "thrilled with remorse" (4.2.74) as he responds to Gloucester's cruel punishment; Albany's sympathy for the "poor" blinded Gloucester (4.2.81); Cordelia's grief at the news about Lear and the cruelty with which he has been treated by her sisters (4.3); Edgar's response to the despairing Gloucester as he faces the extreme edge of Dover cliff: "Give me your hand" (4.6.279; cf. 4.6.34ff.); Lear's advice to Gloucester that he "must be patient" in a world of pain (4.6.172–4); even Lear turning momentarily to others ("Pray you, undo this button. Thank you, sir") just after expressing intense bleakness ("Never, never, never, never, never!" [5.3.307–8]) at the very end.

religious consolation. And it does so in an age when providence and the intervention of the supernatural were, as we have seen, constantly invoked to explain cataclysmic events and divine responses to them. The play presents a world stripped of any certainty concerning supernatural powers (despite appeals to them, both good and demonic). If Shakespeare's plays often "clearly assume a world in which God is immanent,"[41] then one of his most daring achievements, at least as a playwright engaging with religious concerns, was to imagine in *King Lear* a godless or agnostic world.

This may tell us little about Shakespeare's own personal religious beliefs, which remain elusive, but it does tell us that he made use of the theater as a remarkably flexible and creative medium and space. In the hands of Shakespeare, it enabled daring religious freedom and speculation, as he tested a range of religious perspectives, some of them contradictory. Shakespeare could imagine a highly intellectual, introspective, and speculative Christian prince (in the case of Hamlet) who sees evidence of providence ("a divinity that shapes our ends"), even as he attempts to negotiate a world of Machiavellian duplicity that ultimately destroys him. Yet Shakespeare was equally capable of dramatically representing the possibility that, when it comes to misery and human beings gradually reduced to "bare, forked" animals, there might indeed be no God or supernatural powers which shape our ends and give them meaning and a coherent pattern. That does not necessarily mean that Shakespeare, judging by his most daring tragedy about extremes of human suffering, is a secular writer since his plays are saturated with religious references, language, and allusions; but it does mean that he was able to imagine a world where we cannot be sure of a supernatural order or the assiduous interventions of supernatural powers, despite the efforts of his characters to invoke these interventions. While we may never be able to pinpoint Shakespeare's own religious beliefs, it is hard to believe that the author of *King Lear* would have aligned himself with the zealous Protestantism of a John Foxe, himself a playwright who always maintained a providential perspective on the world of extreme human violence and savagery.[42] What we can say, however, is that the theater allowed Shakespeare the capacity to explore and test *both* religious and antireligious perspectives, including the limits of belief in the supernatural, with audacious freedom and imagination.

[41] Kastan, *Will to Believe*, p. 6.

[42] In this respect, Kastan seems persuasive when he observes that "religion is central in the plays, but Shakespeare is not a religious playwright," adding that it is "hard to argue that . . . his writings display the same kind of religious concern or commitment as Spenser's or Milton's verse." Ibid., pp. 6, 4.

CHAPTER 9

# "Another Golgotha"

*Ewan Fernie*

## I

This chapter explores and analyzes Shakespeare's most demonic play: *Macbeth*. It reads Shakespeare not so much via well-known sources and contexts such as James I's *Daemonology*, but in relation to the fundamental renegotiation with the Devil involved in Martin Luther's original "Reformation breakthrough." First, though, it considers St. Augustine's classical understanding of the demonic as privation, negation, decreation, and not-being, which itself offers a way into *Macbeth*'s empty heart.[1]

The prominent contemporary theologian (and founder of the Radical Orthodoxy movement) John Milbank writes, "Traditionally, in Greek, Christian and Jewish thought evil has been denied any positive foothold in being."[2] Indeed, evil is positively "the privation of being itself."[3] In the *Institutes*, Calvin writes, "But as the devil was created by God, we must remember that this malice which we attribute to his nature is not from creation."[4] And the orthodox Christian "privation theory" of evil entails the paradox which Jean-Luc Marion wittily observes: that the nonexistence of the Devil is the existence of the Devil![5] A privation theory of evil and the demonic is present in Zoroastrianism, the first recorded monotheistic religion, which conceptualized evil as the "non-good" brought into God's perfect creation via imperfect human choice. In the Judeo-Christian tradition, the theory features in the work of Jewish philosopher-theologians like

[1] For a fuller reading of both Luther and *Macbeth* along the lines suggested in this chapter, see Ewan Fernie, *The Demonic: Literature and Experience* (London: Routledge, 2012).

[2] John Milbank, "Darkness and Silence: Evil and the Western Legacy," in John D. Caputo (ed.), *The Religious* (Oxford: Blackwell, 2002), p. 277.

[3] Ibid.

[4] John Calvin, *Institutes of the Christian Religion*, trans. Henry Beveridge (Peabody, Massachusetts: Hendrickson Publishers, 2008), I.xiv.16, p. 98.

[5] See Jean-Luc Marion, "Le Mal en personne," in *Prolégomènes à la charité* (Paris: La Différance, 1986), pp. 11–43.

Maimonides in the Middle Ages, but it is associated above all with St. Augustine. Having left behind the Manichaean belief in an independent power of evil, Augustine struggled as a Christian theologian to understand how evil related to the comprehensive and perfect being of God. In his *City of God* (11.22), he concluded that there can be no natural evil, since all natures were created by God, and God only creates what is good. Yet this led to some improbable consequences, as Augustine himself recognized:

> One in which evil is present is a defective or faulty good; nor can there be any evil where there is no good. From this a strange result emerges. Since every being, insofar as it is a being, is good, when we call a defective being an evil being, we seem to be saying that what is good is evil, and that only what is good can be evil.[6]

One conundrum this entails is that, because the Devil is a creature, he is also good. Moreover, because God works good out of evil, evil is only evil apparently and temporarily.

What privation theory seems to *want* is a sort of bleaching out of evil, which, it suggests, is hardly evil at all, to the effect that the demonic also vanishes. Except that Augustine is perturbed by a recalcitrant and disturbing sense of evil's obstinate reality. When in *City of God* he says that evil takes its origin from the fact that man is made out of nothing, he is very close to recognizing not just the primordial negativity of human selfhood but also the "natural" opposition to God as the perfect being which follows from this.[7]

A great Christian theologian who struggled with this positive lure of the demonic was Pseudo-Dionysius the Areopagite. Dionysius nails demonic negativity in the following observation about demons: "They are called evil because of the deprivation, the abandonment, the rejection of the virtues which are appropriate to them. And they are evil to the extent that they are not, and insofar as they wish for evil, they wish for what is really not there."

[6] Augustine, *Enchiridion*, trans. Bernard M. Peebles, in *Writings of St. Augustine* (Washington, DC: Catholic University of America, 1947), vol. IV, p. 378; cf. *City of God*, trans. Henry Bettenson, intro. David Knowles (Harmondsworth: Penguin, 1972), 12.6. See also Terry Eagleton on Aquinas: "For Thomas Aquinas, the more a thing succeeds in realising its true nature, the more it can be said to be good. The perfection of a thing, he argues, depends on the extent to which it achieves actuality. Things are good if they flourish in the way appropriate to them. The more a thing thrives in its own peculiar way, the finer it is. Every being, considered as such, is good. And if God is the most perfect being of all, it is because he is pure self-realization. Unlike us, there is nothing that he could be that he isn't. So for Aquinas there is no such thing as a being which is bad." *On Evil* (New Haven, CT: Yale University Press, 2010), pp. 124–5. For an excellent discussion of Augustine and evil (and perversion), see Jonathan Dollimore, *Sexual Dissidence: Augustine to Wilde, Freud to Foucault* (Oxford: Clarendon Press, 1991), pp. 131–48.

[7] Augustine, *City of God*, 12.6, 14.13.

This is textbook privation theory, but Dionysius also wrote the following, apparently out of a sense of the danger of viewing evil simply as nonbeing, for does this not glamorize evil and even potentially associate it with God's own transcendence of mundane reality?

> Evil is not a being; for if it were, it would not be totally evil. Nor is it a non-being; for nothing is completely a non-being, unless it is said to be in the Good in the sense of beyond-being. For the Good is established far and beyond simple being and non-being. Evil, by contrast, is not among the things that have being, nor is it among what is not in being. It has a greater nonexistence and otherness from the Good than nonbeing has.[8]

But it is difficult to sustain a tidy demarcation between the nonexistence (of the demonic) and nonbeing (of God). And it doesn't help to characterize God's kind of nonbeing as "beyond-being," for nonexistence and nonbeing alike would seem to be beyond being. In its attempt to deny evil and hygienically separate the demonic from an omnibenevolent God, privation theory actually does the reverse, demonstrating their terrifying and confounding intermixture. Evil seems as metaphysical and transcendent as Good is.

All this leads us into the weird, fascinatingly and alluringly positive negativity of demonic evil, going beyond some of the most influential conceptions of evil in modernity. Kant's concept of "radical evil," for instance, isn't radical *enough* for the demonic. For radical evil in Kant is ultimate dedication to self-interest, but this can't account for the figure of the suicide bomber, who has so much torn into our contemporary world. As Joseph P. Lawrence writes, "He has sacrificed his very life in a way that Kant has denied is even possible."[9]

In her famous chapter on Adolf Eichmann's trial for his part in the Holocaust, "Eichmann in Jerusalem," Hannah Arendt coined the phrase "the banality of evil," proposing that "Eichmann was not Iago and not Macbeth, and nothing would have been further from his mind than to determine with Richard III 'to prove a villain.'"[10] No doubt evil is often banal, and after the Holocaust there are morally urgent reasons why its glamour or mystification have to be opposed. But even if what Arendt says

8 Pseudo-Dionysius, *Complete Works*, trans. Colin Luibheid (New York: Paulist Press, 1987), p. 85.

9 Joseph P. Lawrence, "Schelling's Metaphysics of Evil," in Alistair Welchman and Judith Norman (eds.), *The New Schelling* (London: Continuum, 2004), p. 172. Immanuel Kant's theory of evil makes up the first book of *Religion within the Limits of Reason Alone* (New York: Harper & Row, 1960), pp. 15–39.

10 Hannah Arendt, "Eichmann in Jerusalem," in *The Portable Hannah Arendt* (Harmondsworth: Penguin, 2000), p. 379.

of Eichmann is correct, the reference to Richard III, Iago, and Macbeth admits that evil isn't banal or essentially accidental as such. So here, in one of the most influential accounts of the worst atrocity of the twentieth century, Shakespeare's villains emerge as the placeholders for evil's recalcitrant mystery.

And we do seem to need some such conception of the mystery of iniquity for understanding Shakespeare's darkest play. After Macbeth's murder of Duncan, life in Scotland is reduced to the condition of Banquo's ghost, with "marowlesse" bones, cold blood, and absent speculation in its glaring eyes (3.4.95).[11] Particularly for the guilty murderer, whose special torment is that he alone is able to recover what life once was in heartbreaking moods of wistful elegy. Such evil is in part banal: "tomorrow and tomorrow and tomorrow" (5.5.19). But it is not altogether reducible to banality. Macbeth clearly remains the magnetic center of his play. Macduff, and still less Malcolm, can hardly compare with him.

## II

The preceding discussion suggests that what is perhaps the fundamental issue in *Macbeth* – the soul-shaking ambivalence of evil in the play – is related to one of the fundamental cruxes and problems of Christian theology. But I want to argue that *Macbeth* is more specifically historical than that, that it is perversely related to the Reformation breakthrough, and that it reveals the danger – even the strange pleasure – of a specifically aborted Protestantism.[12]

The reinvigorated faith of Luther's Reformation reinvigorates the Devil. Of course, as Jeffrey Burton Russell says, "The religious tensions, culminating in wars, between Catholics and Protestants and among varieties of Protestants promoted the sense that the Devil was lurking everywhere."[13] More than this, "now it was you versus the Devil: you alone, the individual, who had the responsibility for fending him off."[14] As Eamon Duffy observes, the Sarum baptism, and ceremonies such as Candlemas and Rogationtide, as well as holy artifacts and saintly intercessions, had traditionally offered protection from the demonic; but now all that was

[11] References are to *Macbeth*, ed. Nicholas Brooke (Oxford University Press, 1998).

[12] For a different perspective on Shakespeare's dramatic engagement with (and challenge to) some of the major issues of sixteenth-century Protestant theology, see Chapter 7 above.

[13] Jeffrey Burton Russell, *Mephistopheles: The Devil in the Modern World* (Ithaca, NY: Cornell University Press, 1986), p. 31.

[14] Ibid. But on this point, see also Nathan Johnstone, *The Devil and Demonism in Early Modern England* (Cambridge University Press, 2006), p. 2.

gone.[15] No wonder then that, as Russell writes, "the literary heroes of the age were Faust, standing alone at the midnight crossroads with Mephistopheles, and Macbeth alone on the blasted heath with the three witches. Isolation provoked terror, terror an exaggerated view of the Devil's power."[16] Heiko A. Oberman writes: "This *new* belief in the Devil is such an integral part of the Reformation discovery that if the reality of the powers inimical to God is not grasped, the incarnation of Christ, as well as the justification and temptation of the sinner are reduced to ideas of the mind rather than experiences of faith."[17] Luther himself writes: "If we do not have such a Devil, then we are nothing but *speculativi Theologi*, who handle their thoughts badly and speculate about everything with their reason, that it must be like this and that; just like the ... monks in the monasteries."[18] "For," he also writes, in his inimitable fashion, "I myself (if I, mouse dirt that I am, might mingle myself with pepper) have a great deal to thank my papists for, because they beat, belted, pressed, and frightened me so through the rampaging of the devil that they made rather a good theologian out of me, which I otherwise would not have become."[19]

And, according to Luther, the Devil is even more integral to the struggle for salvation than that suggests. Luther did not believe in self-justification – we cannot justify ourselves, we cannot earn happiness – we can only be *saved*. Saved *by* a savior; saved *from* ourselves. One of the most famous (or, rather, infamous) features of his life is that the *spiritus sanctus*, the Reformation breakthrough and his own salvation, came to him while he was sitting on the toilet. That toilet has recently been rediscovered by archaeologists in Wittenberg. Unlike the door to which Luther did not nail his 95 Theses – French troops burned that original down in 1760 – Luther's latrine hasn't proved much of a tourist attraction. "Its continued neglect is just as well," writes Diarmaid MacCulloch, "as its role in the Reformation story is myth, and based on a misunderstanding of the grammar in Luther's Latin reminiscence of his *Turmerlebnis* [tower experience]."[20] That's alright then. The fastidious distaste of the Luther heritage industry is underwritten by heavy-weight scholarship.

[15] See Eamon Duffy, *The Stripping of the Altars: Traditional Religion in England 1400–1580* (New Haven, CT: Yale University Press, 1992), pp. 280–3.

[16] Russell, *Mephistopheles*, p. 33.

[17] Heiko A. Oberman, *Luther: Man Between God and the Devil*, trans. Eileen Walliser-Schwarzbart (New Haven, CT: Yale University Press, 1982), pp. 104–5.

[18] Quoted ibid., p. 185.

[19] Martin Luther, *Luther's Spirituality*, ed. and trans. Philip D. W. Krey and Peter S. Krey, preface Timothy J. Wengert (New York: Paulist Press, 2007), p. 123.

[20] Diarmaid MacCulloch, *A History of Christianity* (Harmondsworth: Penguin, 2010), pp. 604–5.

However, even if it is unpalatable and unseemly, the myth that Luther was saved on the toilet may, in a Wildean sense, be truer than any literal truth. An old trope of leveling comedy is to imagine great men and women on the toilet; Luther may be the only one who is completely proof against such lavatorial attacks and not so much because he was a connoisseur of them himself as because he found salvation precisely where he was most debased. Indeed, in an important sense the Devil comes first in Luther. For, in terms of our ordinary, worldly experience, the Devil's reality is *primary*; it's what Reformation breaks through, both in the individual soul and in the life of the church. *Mouse dirt that I am*: Luther habitually thought of himself *sans* Christ in excremental metaphors. But, as Oberman writes, "No spot is unholy for the Holy Ghost; *this* is the very place to express contempt for the adversary through trust in the crucified."[21] As the killing king of negation, the Devil is especially king of the cloaca, where man cannot but viscerally recognize that his life is already involved with death, each turd a calling card from his own corpse. It is here we are lost and so it is here, if at all, that we must be saved. Which is precisely what the incarnation manages. For Luther, the child "wrapped in swaddling clothes, lying in a manger" is a sign that God has divested himself of omnipotence to redeem our mortality from original sin.

What a momentous turn-about! It is *not* in our most elevated moods and modes – *not* in our virtue – but in our viscerally realized degradation that our chance of salvation lies. For only when we utterly give up on ourselves are we suddenly opened, like a flower, to unexpected grace.

Luther seeks salvation in the depths, where we are abandoned, and if this means seeking it among the slops and specters of nonbeing in the toilet bowl, it equally means questing after it in sinfulness and sin. In fact, ontology is inseparable from spiritual ethics for Luther: the cloaca involves a physical confrontation with original sin. Luther's spirituality also involves an extraordinary embrace of sinfulness. According to the Reformer, a great part of our spiritual task is to *believe in sin*. He wrote in the Smalkald Articles (1537) that sin is so deep "that reason cannot understand it. It must be believed because of the revelation in the Scriptures."[22] Luther described the goal of Paul's great Letter to the Romans as "making sin *great*," affirming that "this letter is to affirm and state and *magnify* sin."[23]

[21] Oberman, *Luther*, p. 155.

[22] Quoted in Bernhard Lohse, *Martin Luther's Theology: Its Historical and Systematic Development*, trans. Roy A. Harrisville (Edinburgh: T & T Clark, 1999), p. 249.

[23] Quoted ibid., p. 69.

But it was from Wartburg Castle that Luther wrote to his younger colleague, Philipp Melancthon, the provocative words, "sin bravely."[24] This resonates with a lesser-known statement, a letter he wrote to Jerome Weller from the fortress at Coburg:

> My dear Jerome:
>
> You must believe that this temptation of yours is from the devil, who vexes you thus because you believe in Christ. For you see how secure and happy he permits the worst enemies of the gospel to be. Just think of Eck, Zwingli and others. It is necessary for all of us who are Christians to have the devil as an adversary and as an enemy. As Peter says, "Your adversary the devil prowls around," etc. (1 Pet. 5. 8).
>
> Excellent Jerome, you ought to rejoice in this temptation by the devil, because it is a certain sign that God is favorable and merciful to you.
>
> Sometimes one must drink more, play, or make nonsense, and even commit some sin in defiance and contempt of the devil in order not to give him an opportunity to make us too scrupulous about trifles. We shall be conquered if we worry too much about falling into some sin.
>
> Thus, if the devil should say, "Do not drink!" you should reply to him thus, "On this very account, because you forbid it, I shall drink, and, what is more, I shall drink a generous amount." Thus one must always do what Satan forbids. What do you think is my reason for drinking undiluted wine, talking freely, and eating more often, if not to torment and vex the devil, who decided to vex and toy with me. If only I could designate some token of sin, to deceive the devil, so that he might understand that I acknowledge no sin and am not conscious of any sin with respect to myself. When the devil seeks and vexes us thus, I say, we must set aside the whole Decalogue from the body and the soul. But when the devil throws our sins up to us and declares we deserve death and hell, then we ought to say, "Indeed, I confess that I deserve death and hell, but what afterwards? Will I therefore be condemned eternally?" By no means. For I know a certain one, who suffered and made satisfaction for me, and he is called Jesus Christ, the Son of God. Where he is, there I shall be also.
>
> Yours,
> Martin Luther[25]

[24] Quoted in Oberman, *Luther*, p. 320.

[25] See Martin Luther, *Letters of Spiritual Counsel*, ed. and trans. Theodore G. Tappert (Philadelphia: Westminster Press, 1955), pp. 85–7.

This is a low-key, vernacular, almost comic version of "sin bravely," with Luther responding to the temptation to drink by drinking the whole bottle, because the greater temptation is to believe in your own virtue. But lest we think that Luther is just toying with sins so trifling that we can barely think of them as real sins at all, it is worth turning to his Commentary on Galatians, where he praises Christ as the "greatest transgressor, murderer, adulterer, thief, rebel, blasphemer, &c. that ever was or could be in all the world."[26] The point is that Christ, by virtue of taking our transgressions on him, is in sin, and it is there that he brings us salvation. And, indeed, where else would we have it? We would have no need of it were it not for sin. Much as in his letter to Jerome, Luther writes elsewhere:

> When I awoke last night, the Devil came and wanted to debate with me; he rebuked and reproached me, arguing that I was a sinner. To this I replied: Tell me something new, Devil! I already know that perfectly well; I have committed many a solid and real sin. Indeed there must be good honest sins – not fabricated and invented ones – for God to forgive for His beloved Son's sake, who took all my sins upon Him so that now the sins I have committed are no longer mine but belong to Christ. This wonderful gift of God I am not prepared to deny, but want to acknowledge and confess.[27]

Note that, in the letter to Jerome, Luther associates self-security and happiness and holy pride with "the enemies of the gospel," with Eck and Zwingli, with those that he regarded as dangerously off-track in religion. The tricksy Devil tries to save us for himself by making us believe in our own morality. We can defeat him only by trying not to deserve anything other than death and Hell, recognizing that that is indeed, ineluctably, what we deserve and so casting ourselves on the mercy of God, which is the only thing that can save us. Luther's is an adrenalized spirituality of extraordinary opposed intensities: of the blackest gloom and doom suddenly irradiated with unearthly and unwarranted life. It is already intensely dramatic, not least because of the terrible risk involved. Resigning oneself to sin and death is the only way to overcome such things, but what if the gamble doesn't pay off, what if the rescuer *doesn't* stoop to scoop up the sinner? What if there is no rescuer?[28]

Luther goes so far, in his letter to Jerome, as to regard moral scrupulosity as Satanic. Elsewhere he said of himself and his fellow Reformers, "Life is as evil among us as among the papists," and "there are just as many bad

26 See Martin Luther, *Selections from his Writings*, ed. John Dillenberger (Garden City, NY: Anchor, 1961), p. 135.

27 Quoted in Oberman, *Luther*, pp. 105–6.

28 On Shakespeare's representation of a potentially godless world in another of his tragedies, see Chapter 8 above.

Christians among us as under the pope."[29] In the letter to Jerome, he even says we must tear "the whole Decalogue" (the Ten Commandments) out of our hearts. This is because "Christ has cancelled and torn in pieces the handwriting of our consciences,"[30] a statement that oddly resonates with Macbeth's "Cancel and tear to pieces that great bond / Which keeps me pale" (3.2.52–3). In fact, Christ has abolished conscience as such. As Oberman notes, when Luther defines a Christian as one who walks a "straight and narrow way," "this is not a reference to the 'straight gate' and the 'narrow way' of those monks and puritans who forgo the joys of life on the 'broad way' so as to maintain clear consciences. No, it is a difficult painful path because it leads to the near mystical experience of being torn out of one's conscience, the conscience that seeks peace in its own holiness." This is an extremely radical move because it tears morality itself out by the root. It goes well beyond the moral radicalism of our own time, which never dreams of stepping beyond conscience. As Oberman says further, "Centuries of Western formation of conscience must be overcome if saying yes to God means saying no to one's own conscience."[31] Lutheran salvation involves a scarcely thinkable passivity: "Why, do we then do nothing? Do we work nothing for the obtaining of this righteousness? I answer: Nothing at all." For Christ's gift takes us to a place utterly beyond morality. "Here no sin is perceived, no terror or remorse of conscience is felt; for in this heavenly righteousness sin can have no place: for there is no law, and where no law is, there can be no transgression" (Romans 4:15).[32]

By virtue of pure passivity – by what came to be known theologically as *imputation* – Luther gets his life back. But he had taken a terrible risk. *Sin bravely!* Nothing, perhaps, illustrates this better than Luther the ex-monk's marriage to Catherine of Bora, a runaway nun. At that time the consummation of a marriage was attested to by a witness at the bridal bed. Luther's was Justus Jonas, his closest friend. And Justus wept to witness Luther in bed with Catherine. Our modern, knee-jerk reaction is no doubt to applaud this entrance into active sexuality, but we need to recognize that this entails the world-historical failure of an effort to transcend merely mortal desires and indeed the whole cycle of death and generation with which they are involved.

I perhaps should break off to say at this point that I see Luther's life as nothing less than an event in western Christianity, indeed in western culture

[29] Quoted in Oberman, *Luther*, pp. 57 and 150.

[30] Martin Luther, *The Table Talk or Familiar Discourse of Martin Luther*, trans. William Hazlitt (London: David Bogue, 1848), p. 255.

[31] Oberman, *Luther*, p. 320. [32] Luther, *Selections from his Writings*, p. 105.

as such, and not just the beginning of the Reformation. It is instructive here to glance sideways for a moment at Catholic spirituality, at St. John of the Cross's mystic *via negativa* in *The Dark Night of the Soul*, which also involves a total renunciation of human worth and capacity in favor of God's grace.[33] But I say so only to demonstrate that a "Lutheran" perspective is for far more than Luther – or even Protestants – alone.

Luther always remained very aware of what a terrible risk he had taken, for himself and for others, writing that "[t]he devil often casts thus into my breast: How if thy doctrine be false and erroneous, wherewith the pope, the mass, friars and nuns are thus dejected and startled? *at which the sour sweat has drizzled from me.*"[34] In the event, his was a good death.

But *Sin bravely, magnify in sin, believe in sin*: these were great gifts of the great and pious doctor to the tragic dramatists of the early modern period, and they dared to go where he did not.

## III

It is no accident that Doctor Faustus works at Luther's university because Faustus's career exposes the demonic recklessness involved in the Reformation breakthrough: to participate in and affirm one's own abandonment to sin and negation is, at least temporarily, to hand oneself over to the Devil, even if all the while hoping and bidding for God's grace.

Protestantism can short-circuit, stopping in the midst of sin. Salvation does not always follow sin as day does night because, as Luther half understood, and Renaissance dramatists knew more vividly and fully, sin can be perversely attractive. Witness this famous moment from *Doctor Faustus*:

> Was this the face that launched a thousand ships,
> And burnt the topless towers of Ilium?
> Sweet Helen, make me immortal with a kiss.
>
> [*They kiss.*]
>
> Her lips suck forth my soul. See where it flies!
> Come, Helen, come give me my soul again.
>
> [*They kiss again.*]
>
> Here will I dwell, for heaven be in these lips,
> And all is dross that is not Helena. (5.1.91–7)[35]

[33] St. John of the Cross, *The Dark Night of the Soul*, ed. Halcyon Backhouse (London: Hodder & Stoughton, 1985).

[34] Luther, *Table Talk*, p. 268.

[35] Christopher Marlowe, *Doctor Faustus and Other Plays*, ed. David Bevington and Eric Rasmussen (Oxford University Press, 1995). References are to the A-text of the play.

Here Faustus chooses Helen even though she is a succubus. *Her lips suck forth my soul – see where it flies!* He is not disappointed by this. Spiritual death seems paradoxically to proffer another kind of immortality. *Give me my soul again; heaven be in these lips.* This sort of erotic Faustianism attains its fullest expression centuries later in Mozart's *Don Giovanni*, for whom overreaching erotic sin becomes the very savor and meaning of existence. But meanwhile Marlowe, in his *Doctor Faustus*, has discovered a major potential problem with the Reformation – if it leads into the cloaca, we might, perversely, discover that we like being there and choose a life of sinning bravely not as a cry to God to intervene, but rather for its own sake.

## IV

Faustus sins bravely, but his sinning is in part a superficial affair. The character who sins most bravely and terribly in all drama is surely Macbeth, or Macbeth and his "fiend-like queen" (5.7.99). *Macbeth* could have been a central text of reformed Protestantism – for who sins more bravely than Macbeth, who comes more to know himself as a sinner? What play more magnifies sin? But this tragedy of sin stops short; it does not set off the absolute freedom of grace by lavishing it on its tainted murderer: in a very different context, centuries later, it is Dostoevsky's *Crime and Punishment* that does this.

The true devil in Shakespeare's tragedy is perhaps Macbeth himself. Certainly, Lucifer is even more missing than Mephistopheles. And yet, it's made very clear that the stakes of the play include damnation, most famously when Macbeth yells in exultant defiance, "lay on Macduff / And damned be he who first cries 'Hold, enough!'" (5.7.63–4). He is attempting to turn damnation to his own purposes here, but Macduff has already said, when at last he set eyes on his great antagonist, "Turn hell hound, turn" (5.7.33). And Macbeth has lamented in soliloquy about how he had given "mine eternal jewel . . . to the common enemy of man" (3.1.67–8). Running in parallel to this is a more powerfully immanent metaphysics where, as we shall see, Hell is realized in and as Macbeth's Scotland; and in *Macbeth*, as is not the case in Marlowe's *Faustus*, there is no supernatural elsewhere to weaken this perception. This occasionally becomes explicit. If Lady Macbeth is "his fiend-like queen," Macbeth is "this fiend of Scotland" (5.7.99, 4.3.233). He isn't servant to Satan, he is attended by Seyton. And there is one textual indication that he has usurped not just Duncan but the Devil himself.

YOUNG SEWARD What is thy name?
MACBETH Thou'lt be afraid to hear it.
YOUNG SEWARD No: though thou call'st thyself a hotter name
Than any is in Hell.
MACBETH My name's Macbeth.
YOUNG SEWARD The Devil himself could not pronounce a title
More hateful to mine ear. (5.7.5–9)

Macbeth's is a hotter name than any in Hell, and more hateful than the Devil's own name. Faustus wanted everything and found that this paradoxically beggared him, but Macbeth shoots straight for the negative, exemplifying the pleasures of destruction, including self-destruction.[36]

*Macbeth* is in part a dramatic essay in the horrible excitement, in the life of sin, with the murder of Duncan in his bed standing in place of erotic

[36] It will be clear that the reading of *Macbeth* I am developing here moves in a different direction from recent historicist readings of the play as conservatively royalist. Henry Paul makes a pioneering link between Shakespeare's tragedy, demonology, and royalist politics in *The Royal Play of Macbeth* (New York: Macmillan, 1950). Stuart Clark notes that James I's own treatise, *Daemonologie*, is in part a statement about ideal monarchy; James presents witchcraft as the highest treason since it is "treason against God," "analogous to treason against the Prince" ("King James's *Daemonologie*: Witchcraft and Kingship," in *The Damned Art: Essays in the Literature of Witchcraft*, ed. Sydney Anglo [London: Routledge & Kegan Paul, 1977], pp. 156–7). Peter Stallybrass concurs that James's views "set ideological limits" to *Macbeth*, and that the representation of the demonic in the play serves in the way of "developing a particular conceptualization of social and political order" ("*Macbeth* and Witchcraft," in *Focus on Macbeth*, ed. John Russell Brown [London: Routledge & Kegan Paul, 1982], pp. 192, 201). Gary Wills argues that the play appeals to anti-Catholic sentiments in the wake of the Gunpowder Plot (*Witches and Jesuits: Shakespeare's "Macbeth"* [Oxford University Press, 1995]). Jans Frans van Dijkhuizen offers an importantly qualified view when he writes that "*Macbeth* stages a metaphorical expulsion of the forces of the demonic, represented by Macbeth and Lady Macbeth, from the body politic. In doing so, the play employs demonic possession as an emblem of the violation of sacred kingship. At the same time, *Macbeth* caters to James's skepticism towards demonic possession. Taken together, these factors suggest that the play is an exercise in politically orthodox, royalist demonology. But *Macbeth* also undermines orthodox demonological positions" (*Theatre: Demonic Possession and Exorcism in English Renaissance Drama, 1558–1642* [Woodbridge: D. S. Brewer, 2007], p. 140). We need, perhaps, to return to an older critical tradition for a recognition of just how subversive *Macbeth* is: see Helen Gardner, "Milton's 'Satan' and the Theme of Damnation in Elizabethan Tragedy," in Arthur E. Baker (ed.), *Milton: Modern Essays in Criticism* (Oxford University Press, 1965), pp. 205–17. I quote from Gardner below. Molly Smith engages with the "Augustinian concept of evil as incompleteness" but without following Macbeth's journey into evil and privation (*The Darker World Within: Evil in the Tragedies of Shakespeare and his Successors* [London: Associated University Presses, 1991], p. 16; see esp. ch. 2, "Evil as Nonbeing: Physical and Mental Fragmentation"). Ned Lukacher writes suggestively, "In *Macbeth* Shakespeare resumes his dwelling place near the default in Being and moves still closer to the silent play of the language of the daemon" (*Daemonic Figures: Shakespeare and the Question of Conscience* [Ithaca, NY: Cornell University Press, 1994], p. 163). I particularly recommend Simon Palfrey's "Macbeth and Kierkegaard," *Shakespeare Studies*, 57 (2004), 96–111, which touches on the play's relation to the Kierkegaardian "demonic."

consummation in the Macbeth marriage. Macbeth's reference to the rape of Lucrece in his bloody dagger soliloquy (2.2.55–6) underscores the connection between the sinful Macbeth's crime and erotic compulsion – both leading to self-destruction.

In an incisive and enlightening essay, Helen Gardner characterizes the demonic, in Milton, *Faustus*, and *Macbeth*, as a "rebellion against the essential fact of things," writing further that, in all these cases, "[t]he initial act is an act against nature, it is a primal sin, in that it contradicts the 'essential fact of things,' and its author knows that it does so."[37] This initial act is terrible in the modern sense of dispiritingly bad but also in that more spirited sense that shades into the sublime. It is very explicitly an act against being or creation and therefore demonic in that classical sense. Duncan's murder can't be grasped or understood; it involves a certain negative splendor, as though of some dreadfully flowering thing. In the extraordinary poetry of Macduff's reaction – Duncan's murder unblocks unwonted eloquence in the Thane of Fife – it is not merely an achievement, it's a great work of art. It also is a vision, one which brings the end in sight, a vision of "the great doom's image," of "death itself." At the same time it spells the end *of* sight: "destroy your sight / With a new gorgon." It is vision's consummation, or extinguishing. *We* never see it, or enter the killing chamber. And it is just as well since as Macduff intuits that, as with God, it is not possible to look upon it and live.

> Malcolm, Banquo,
> As from your graves rise up, and walk like sprites,
> To countenance this horror. (2.3.53–5)

It's as if the murder had pulled the plug on the world, draining all life from those left to witness it. Alternatively, when Donalbain asks, "What is amiss?", Macbeth answers for everyone, himself included:

> You are, and do not know't:
> The spring, the head, the fountain of your blood
> Is stopped, the very source of it is stopped. (2.3.72ff.)

In both cases, we are asked to imagine a world of men rendered not just dead but, as it were, drained and translucent. It's a weird thought, appropriately enough for this weird play, but also powerful testimony to the heart-stopping power of a masterpiece we shall never see, an absolute truth we shall never penetrate, even though it is, as the truth of death, the truth to which we ourselves are destined. *Macbeth* makes Duncan's death strangely

[37] Gardner, "Milton's 'Satan,'" pp. 206, 207.

and disturbingly desirable, as much in the mouth of his ultimate avenger as in the mouth of his murderer. And this speaks to and for the seduction of demonic negation, even in its most concrete form of murder.

*O horror, horror, horror* (2.3.64)! The act against "the essential fact of things" in *Macbeth* is extraordinarily comprehensive, reaching well beyond the destruction of the king. I have suggested that Duncan's murder is a sort of Baudelairean flower of evil because of the inalienable if negative splendor of its presentation in the play. In the course of the action it opens and opens like some rose of Hell, till it is seen in and encompasses almost everything. But Duncan's murder also acts as a ritualistic induction into a new existential or spiritual state, which is at once a state of death but equally and troublingly of more vivid life. To that extent, Macbeth's original criminal act does have the quality of the absolute he wishes for it; for a time at least, it indeed *is* the be all and end all.

It carries over into self-negation and self-murder for the murderers, and this is at once dreadful and dreadfully exciting. So much is revealed in Lady Macbeth:

> Come, you spirits,
> That tend on mortal thoughts, unsex me here,
> And fill me from the crown to the toe, top-full
> Of direst cruelty. Make thick my blood,
> Stop up th'access and passage to remorse,
> That no compunctious visitings of Nature
> Shake my fell purpose, nor keep peace between
> Th'effect and it. Come to my woman's breasts
> And take my milk for gall, you murd'ring ministers,
> Wherever, in your sightless substances,
> You wait on nature's mischief. (1.5.39–49)

Here is terrible energy and ecstasy, ecstasy of course meaning to stand outside oneself. Lady Macbeth, as it were, unzips and steps beyond what she is – steps beyond humankind, and thus beyond human kindness. The crushed skull of a breast-feeding baby is one potential effect of this; the actual effect is the murder of Duncan. And yet, there is something desperately grand and exhilarating about adventuring beyond all determinism, be it cultural, biological or moral, about voyaging out into a new life totally other to that merely creaturely order of life emblematized by the sleeping Duncan.[38] The implicit hope is that the life thereby gained will be what life

[38] Walter Clyde Curry writes that "without doubt these ministers of evil do actually take possession of [Lady Macbeth's] body" (*Shakespeare's Philosophical Patterns* [Baton Rouge: Louisiana State

really is, that it will "jump the life to come" in the form of all those predictable tomorrows (1.7.7). "Nothing is / But what is not" (1.3.142–3); and from the far shore of suffering new life and new creation beckon. Such is the terrible wager of this murder. A timid, superseded Macbeth says, "I dare do all that does become a man / Who dares do more is none" (1.7.47–8). But what *else* might he be? The murder of Duncan is also negatively grand in that it reduces its whole world to a condition of demonic ghastliness, where darkness does the face of earth entomb when living light should kiss it. Such events succeeding the murder in fact traumatically reveal and repeat it. When we are told of increasingly skinned and skeletal horses tearing into and devouring one another's flesh, we are seeing *into* "the great doom's image" (2.4.14–18).

Though we tend to think of *Macbeth* as a play that moves powerfully and fast towards its own catastrophe, it is in fact full of generalizations that intensify and entrench as much as they broaden the tragic effect because of their concrete precision and resonance with the original tragic deed. *Even like the deed that's done* (2.4.11). *Macbeth* gives us the world *as an image of murder*. The great bard or chronicler of this is the critically underrated Ross. As he puts it in his most agonized statement of the theme:

Alas, poor country,
Almost afraid to know itself. It cannot
Be called our mother but our grave; where nothing
But who knows nothing, is once seen to smile;
Where sighs and groans, and shrieks that rend the air
Are made, not marked; where violent sorrow seems
A modern ecstasy – the dead man's knell
Is there scarce asked for who, and good men's lives
Expire before the flowers in their caps,
Dying or ere they sicken. (4.3.165–74)

Here is the "death-drive" nationalized. All life, good, smiles, signification, and distinction fail. So pervasive are "sighs and groans and shouts that rend the air" as to be rendered meaningless and unremarkable. Death, indeed, scarcely merits more than a shrug. In this desert place, the only alternative to anaesthetized indifference is perverted pleasure, "a modern ecstasy" – I see twisted figures from Spanish paintings, Dali as well as El Greco, enacting a sexuality, a *religion* of sorrow. But such are the intense and swift transitions

University Press, 1959], p. 87); Curry further diagnoses Lady Macbeth's sleepwalking as a case of "somnambuliform possession" (p. 89). W. Moelwyn Merchant sees the episode as "a formal stage in demonic possession – though the implications of the statement are rarely if ever pursued . . . [T]he impact of the demonic invocation is reduced, both in critical reading and in our experience in the theatre" ("His Fiend-Like Queen," *Shakespeare Survey*, 19 [1966], 75).

of the *Macbeth* idiom that these images barely register – and they're gone. And then we are locked into a terrible vision of "good men's lives" – a phrase which blends life itself with the life of goodness – perishing before the flowers in their caps. Which is bad enough, but the strange, seemingly redundant – and so suggestively *dead* – half-line which succeeds it carries us right back into the dying. Or is it, this time, into the dying of the flowers? It's not clear, to the effect that we are *simultaneously* lost in the dying of good men and strangely lingering among their corpses, watching the blooms go out like lights in their hat brims. But then the *full* phrase, "Dying or ere they sicken," suggests something else: "good men's lives" are dying not just before the flowers in their caps but perhaps before the men even fall ill. The killing of Duncan in very concrete and particular ways appears to be dealing a sort of death blow in general.

And, as the above bears out, there is a terrible beauty in this. This is partly effected as a pathos of swiftness: as we have seen, images of violence are perfectly crystallized only to be succeeded, with equal instantaneity, by others. Even more troublingly, as in the last image – of good men's lives expiring before the flowers in their caps – it produces such cherishing detail as to suggest that the killing field may also be a primal scene and breeding ground of love. We will return to this.

What I am arguing for now is that the poetry of *Macbeth* is instinct with a creativity in destruction, investing the murderer not just with a world-changing destroying power, but a world-changing destroying power *in which strange life stirs*. This is particularly borne out in the following speech:

> The night has been unruly: where we lay
> Our chimneys were blown down, and, as they say,
> Lamentings heard i'th'air, strange screams of death,
> And prophesying with accents terrible,
> Of dire combustion and confused events,
> New-hatched to th'woeful time. The obscure bird
> Clamored the livelong night. Some say, the earth
> Was feverous and did shake. (2.3.55–62)

It suggests nothing so much as a terrible birth, as if Macbeth had strangely inseminated the world. Its evocation of labor resonates with the use of that word within the play: "sore labor's bath"; "the rest is labor which is not for you" (2.2.37, 1.4.45). The air seems to scream like a laboring woman, but one who is laboring to produce a monstrous birth of dire combustion and confused events. Things are *hatching*. Prophecy and metaphor both become uncannily and immediately true as "the obscure bird that clamors the livelong night." This is the soul-shaking creation – the *child* – of Macbeth's deed. And it seems to produce a horribly animating power elsewhere, as when the arm and hand of night strangles the traveling lamp; and the enveloping power of darkness smothers up breath in the face of a world which should be kissed and not killed. But the lines are arranged in strange apposition in the quoted passage: does the earthquake result from the obscure bird's clamor? Or is the earthquake the shudder in the womb, or the loins – one thinks of Yeats's "Leda and the Swan" – which precedes and is part of the process of its birth? The speech blurs and makes a mystery of causality, appropriately enough in a play for whose central murder Macbeth is and is not entirely responsible. Human wickedness ambivalently causes and is caused by a sublime, superpersonal, demonic life that is not at all exhausted by the witches and which remains just out of reach, beyond clear consciousness, just off stage.

My suggestion is that the poetry of *Macbeth* involves a certain terrible affirmation of the demonic negativity that Luther seeks to admit and even magnify so that the sinner gives up on him or herself and in desperation stakes everything on God's grace. This threatens to undo the whole teleology and movement of Protestantism towards salvation, exposing the Reformation breakthrough as a road which equally forks into Hell. I want to end by looking at a neglected speech of Macbeth's on the killing of the grooms, which takes us back to the strange relation already intimated between destruction and cherishing affection, between love and evil, giving a sinister indication of what might make the road to Hell terribly preferable to the better way:

> Who can be wise, amazed, temp'rate, and furious,
> Loyal and neutral, in a moment? No man:
> Th'expedition of my violent love
> Outran the pauser, reason. Here lay Duncan,
> His silver skin laced with his golden blood,
> And his gashed stabs looked like a breach in nature,
> For ruin's wasteful entrance: there the murderers,
> Steeped in the colours of their trade, their daggers
> Unmannerly breeched with gore – who could refrain,
> That had a heart to love; and in that heart,
> Courage, to make's love known? (2.3.110–20)

"Violent love" blends together love and murder, and to take these lines out of context is to realize a terrible thing: that the killing of Duncan is an erotic event. Silver skin laced with golden blood is seductive, luxurious, perversely iconic, altogether infused with a desire that blends amorous with religious flavors. And, in that context, the gashed stabs that gape for ruin's wasteful entrance associate the King with rape. Even when Macbeth is trying to express outraged horror at unnatural murder, his creepily beautiful language is at least partly in sympathy with it. Perhaps, then, when he killed the "murderers" he was, at a psychological level, wreaking virtuous punishment on himself. But, more importantly, the way he concludes the speech looks like the confession, the rhetorical question, of the murderer or rapist:

> who could *refrain*,
> That had a heart to love, and in that heart,
> Courage, to make's love known? (2.3.118–20; my emphasis)

Macbeth isn't a vulgarly ambitious man; it's striking that Shakespeare gives him no fantasies such as "the sweet fruition of an earthly crown" with which the ambitious Tamburlaine pleasures his self-conceit (*Tamburlaine the Great*, part 1, 2.7.29);[39] but in these strange lines surfaces the awful possibility that the murder of Duncan unlocks terrible and profound pleasures of destruction that are not unrelated to love.

It is difficult to know what this could mean. Except that love and admiration for Duncan in the play seems truly to be engendered in the prospect and aftermath of his murder, and not to precede this. Indeed, love in *Macbeth* in general seems to postdate the thought or fact of murder, with "pity like a new-born babe" emanating from that source (1.7.21), with the family love of Lady Macduff dramatized only in violation, even with Macbeth's wistful and acute love of his own life emerging only from the ruin he has made of himself. Like Faustus, Macbeth is hollowed out by his demonic behavior and life becomes for him quite empty, but somehow at the same time his dark voyage into sin remains a sort of supercharged moment of negativity that exceeds all forms of ordinary existence. *Macbeth* is a kind of perverse and empty apotheosis by means of which Shakespeare powerfully dramatizes the terrible risk involved in the new Protestant spirituality. For to participate in and affirm one's own abandonment to sin and negation always is, at least temporarily, to hand oneself over to the Devil, even if all the while one is hoping and bidding for God's grace. That grace has decayed or sickened in *Macbeth* is everywhere apparent and is exemplified, for instance, by the fact that English Edward's healing touch is called "the Evil" (4.3.146). Meanwhile Shakespeare's most demonic figure gathers to himself all the terrible truth of our "black and deep desires" and sinfully degraded condition (1.4.52). In this he is truly a spiritual hero. But

[39] Reference to Marlowe, *Doctor Faustus and Other Plays*, ed. Bevington and Rasmussen.

he does so without any hint or possibility of redemption. Macbeth is the most terrible icon of an abortive Protestantism. If Shakespeare intended to "memorize another Golgotha" (1.2.40), as a teasing and neglected phrase from the tragedy has it, here there is no rising but crucifixion alone. And what is worse, there is life, albeit of the darkest and most opaque kind, to be had in the Place of the Skull.

Here, it would seem, sin bravely is pursued to its most terrible conclusion.

CHAPTER 10

# *Shakespeare and wisdom literature*

*Michael Witmore*

Steven Marx, in his study of Shakespeare and the Bible, calls Shakespearean tragedy a form of wisdom literature, linking these plays to a tradition of sapiential writing stretching at least as far back as the wisdom books of the Hebrew Old Testament and the Apocrypha.[1] Arguing this point through a close reading of *King Lear* and the Book of Job, Marx demonstrates how the theological and moral concerns of ancient wisdom literature take shape within the narrative arc of Shakespearean tragedy. *King Lear* is an apt choice for Marx: the trials of the play's two main protagonists, Lear and Gloucester, mirror those of Job, the latter the most complex narrative subject of the Hebrew and Christian wisdom traditions. Like their biblical counterpart Job, Lear and Gloucester move from prosperity to utter desolation. Only after they have arrived at the bitter, empty-handed end of knowledge does each man approach something like the beginning of wisdom. Extending Marx's analysis, one might argue that characters in other Shakespearean tragedies pass through this same arc of metaphysical exhaustion. Hamlet, for example, when faced with a bewildering series of accidental events, finally loosens his calculating grip on events, embracing instead the mysteries of providence.[2] Ophelia, on the other hand, herself a victim of the same mischances, finds these mysteries intolerable. Othello and Macbeth push up against the limits of their own singular knowledge, each finding

I am grateful to Gail Kern Paster, Barbara Mowat, and David Loewenstein for their invaluable comments on this chapter prior to its revision.

[1] See Steven Marx, *Shakespeare and the Bible* (Oxford University Press, 2000), as well as Hannibal Hamlin, "The Patience of Lear," in Ken Jackson and Arthur F. Marotti (eds.), *Shakespeare and Religion: Early Modern and Postmodern Perspectives* (Notre Dame, IN: University of Notre Dame Press, 2011), pp. 127–60. The wisdom books include Job, Proverbs, Psalms, Ecclesiastes, and Song of Songs from the Hebrew Old Testament, and Wisdom and Ecclesiasticus from the Apocrypha.

[2] On the conflicting religious views in *Hamlet*, especially concerning the questionable status of providence in human events, see Chapter 1 above.

that his understanding – of a wife, of events foretold in prophecy – is disastrously incomplete.

Marx's readiness to read Shakespeare's plays as a form of wisdom literature seems to me fundamentally correct, although this approach may strike some readers as dated. In our post-Foucauldian age, we are reluctant to entertain a difference between knowledge and wisdom since the latter implies a form of truth that defies historical formalization. As presented in the biblical tradition, wisdom is the intellectual and cultural negative of those historically specific "discourses" and "epistemes" that have occupied literary and cultural studies for the last three decades. Almost by definition, wisdom stands outside of any specific genealogical or institutional context.[3] James Crenshaw, a scholar of biblical wisdom literature, acknowledges the deliberately vague intellectual underpinnings of wisdom when he argues that proverbs, the traditional conduit for wisdom, derive their power from an "incommunicable quality" that lends them paradigmatic force.[4] Quoting Cervantes, Crenshaw defines the proverb as "a short sentence founded upon long experience, containing the truth." But if proverbs contain such truths, then those truths must persist beyond any specific historical, institutional, or even documentary context. Indeed, the power of proverbial wisdom to transcend context – to advance that which is true "time out of mind" – stems precisely from its *lack* of any clear genetic history or originating context. Of wisdom, it is sufficient to say that it is the product of long experience, even if we cannot say what those experiences were.[5]

One needn't take wisdom at its word, however. Removed as it is from the specifics of history, what early moderns call wisdom seems nevertheless to be intimately connected with life. Its role is obvious in the lived drama of human deliberation and action, for example when a reason must be given for a certain course of action (prudential wisdom), or when the course of obscure events must be explained or predicted (providential or divinatory wisdom). As a deliberative practice, wisdom thus leaves an historical trace at precisely those moments when a society engages in more or less ritualized forms of justification – of the ways of "God to man" certainly, but also, of

[3] This genealogical ambiguity allows critics of historicist approaches to literature such as Harold Bloom to argue that wisdom is precisely what great literature carries from one historical context to the next. See Bloom's *Where Shall Wisdom Be Found?* (New York: Riverhead Books, 2004).

[4] James L. Crenshaw, *Old Testament Wisdom*, 3rd edn. (Louisville, KY: Westminster Press, 2010), p. 62.

[5] See Chapter 13 below, which focuses on and explores a similar kind of contrast or tension in Shakespeare's plays between truth/wisdom/faith on the one hand and mere historical fact or correctness on the other.

the ways of one person to another.[6] For the purposes of my inquiry, then, wisdom is a practice with its own cultural history and value: it is a means whereby individuals are accommodated to groups, and groups to their own imagined or remembered histories. Sitting somewhere between ethics, folklore, and religion, wisdom encompasses a whole range of reason-giving activities that extend beyond those we would recognize as explicitly religious, activities that center on the search for, and sanctioned application of, time-honored generalizations to the particulars of a contingent life world.

In the early modern period, this quasi-ritualistic process of reasoning out life's contingencies is mediated through print. Drawn from Christian and classical literary forms, printed collections of "wise" proverbs constitute both a distinct literary genre and a rapidly developing print commodity. Such collections sell widely in this period, in part (as we will see) because they provide readers with the "matter" of their arguments when they needed to justify an action or simply make a witty point. Shakespeare would have known wisdom literature well; its preoccupations shape both his own theatrical practice and the context in which his plays are interpreted. But the popularity of printed wisdom literature, rooted partially in religious traditions, should not suggest that wisdom is sought only between the covers of a book. That literature's claim on early modern life grows out of its status as a practical adjunct to action: wisdom serves those who wish to become skilled in applying or repurposing proverbs (written and spoken) at moments of choice. By exploring the nature of this literature – its material form and uses – I wish to provide here a much fuller sense of how wisdom leaves its mark on the culture of the late sixteenth and early seventeenth centuries.[7] We can recognize this mark, I believe, without attempting to resolve, once and for all, whether wisdom is a concept, genre, or cultural practice. Likely it is all three.

Because it is more than a mode of knowledge production or discourse, then, the historical study of wisdom that I wish to undertake will range across cultural domains that are often treated as distinct. As a practice, wisdom designates both a semiformalized reservoir of received knowledge and – more actively – a form of lived inquiry, one that engages the body, environment, and mind in much the same way that sacred meditation

[6] Justification here implies an appeal to a validating, because communally recognized, authority; whenever the *need* for such authority appears in speech or print, "wisdom" stands ready in the wings.

[7] I leave aside here the vatic, numinous forms of wisdom so frequently discussed in neo-Platonic literatures of the period; so too the wisdom of eschatological prophecy.

practices do.[8] The products and process of such inquiry must necessarily overlap, issuing in a distinct way of living and coping with contingency, the latter a perennial theme of wisdom literature of the sacred variety. Because it is a lived form of inquiry, wisdom generates a body of statements that can never quite be systematized into a field of knowledge or *scientia*: thus, the need for collections of suggestively incomplete proverbs that present them in no particular order.[9] Unlike more formal and so impersonal modes of thought, wisdom is intimately tied to experience, albeit experience of a particular sort. The kind of situations that seem to generate wisdom are those that exhaust prudential and practical modes of reflection. Only when one is forced to cope with the contingencies of "life," as Lear must do in Shakespeare's tragedy, does the value of wisdom clearly appear. The play suggests that in recognizing that value ("Take physic, pomp"), one gains wisdom for oneself; in making this suggestion, *King Lear* becomes a part of the wider wisdom culture I will be exploring, even if it refuses any explicitly religious context for such an insight.[10]

As the subsequent discussion will show, wisdom practices of the period encourage individuals to interpret the meaning of these unexpected outcomes with the help of proverbs, thus demonstrating the wisdom of the individual who can productively match saying to situation.[11] The most structured version of this experience is the lottery, a practice (as I will explain) that engages moral judgment by forging unexpected links between proverbs and the situations they might plausibly describe. The casket lottery

[8] One model for this hybrid intellectual-experiential form of inquiry can be found in Brian Stock's *After Augustine: The Meditative Reader and the Text* (Philadelphia: University of Pennsylvania Press, 2001), ch. 7. In attempting to broaden this model beyond the reader's experience of a book, I have found useful the work of book historians (see note 22 below), the work of Evelyn Tribble (her *Cognition in the Globe: Attention and Memory in Shakespeare's Theater* [New York: Palgrave, 2011]), and that of anthropologist Timothy Ingold. For the latter, see his *Perception of the Environment: Essays on Livelihood, Dwelling and Skill* (New York: Routledge, 2000) and *Being Alive: Essays on Movement, Knowledge and Description* (New York: Routledge, 2010).

[9] John Considine points out that early modern wisdom practices resemble those Stoic *hypomnemata* that Foucault, late in his career, associated with ancient regimes of self-cultivation or "arts of oneself." See John Considine, "Wisdom-Literature in Early Modern England," *Renaissance Studies*, 13.3 (1999), 325–42; and Michel Foucault, *Ethics: Subjectivity and Truth*, ed. Paul Rabinow, trans. Robert Hurley et al. (New York: New Press, 1997), pp. 207–22.

[10] William Shakespeare, *King Lear*, 3.4.38. All quotations from the plays of Shakespeare are drawn from Barbara Mowat and Paul Werstine (eds.), *Folger Shakespeare Editions*, as they appear online at www.folgerdigitaltexts.org (accessed August 20, 2013). On the absence of Christian providence in the play, see Chapter 8 above.

[11] Often these situations cannot be comprehended under a single rule. See *Nicomachean Ethics*, trans. H. Rackham (Cambridge, MA: Harvard University Press, 1975), 1.3 and 6.3–4; John M. Cooper, *Pursuits of Wisdom: Six Ways of Life in Ancient Philosophy from Socrates to Plotinus* (Princeton University Press, 2012), ch. 3.

for Portia in *The Merchant of Venice* is perhaps the best-known Shakespearean example of the lottery staged as a moral test, but there are others, most notably the love contest in *King Lear*. I will explore each of these Shakespearean examples in the next two sections, arguing that their significance as wisdom practices, while complex, can be explained with reference to real early modern lotteries staged outside of the theater – practices that mechanically link proverbs to "prizes" and, in so doing, offer a sort of contrived occasion for moral reflection. This extratheatrical discussion will focus on two representative examples of lotteries involving proverbs: a state-sponsored "lotterie" introduced during the reign of Elizabeth I, and a later "lottery book" by George Wither that recasts popular wisdom practices in codex form. If we recognize the links between Shakespeare's theatrical scenes and a lively set of wisdom practices involving proverbs, we gain access to a set of powerful early modern intuitions about how wisdom is related to experience. Experience, these practices suggest, is the great teacher of wisdom because it confronts individuals, sometimes terrifyingly, with what they do not and cannot foresee.

Shakespeare and his contemporaries understood the intimate relationship between contingency, chance, and wisdom, seeing proverbs as a kind of verbal fragment in which the great puzzle of the world could be contained.[12] As an antidote to habit or ignorance, contingency was the stone on which many early moderns thought judgment could be honed – precisely because the path of experience, unlike the progress of ideas, is made crooked by chance or fortune.[13] This link between chance and wisdom would become more powerful in the sixteenth century as popular printed accounts of shocking or unexpected events provided a steady flow of exemplary "accidents" to which proverbial wisdom could be applied.[14] Shakespeare alludes to this tradition in *Hamlet*, glossing the common proverb "murder will out" in Hamlet's exclamation that "murder . . . will speak / With most miraculous organ" (2.2.622–3). *Hamlet*, of course, is a play where the glibness of proverbs is mocked. Yet even if proverbs fail as guides to judgment, their repeated invocation suggests that they retain a certain currency on stage. In

12 On the ancient and early modern understanding of proverbs as fragments, pieces of wisdom to be joined to a situation, see Richard Harp, "Proverbs, Philosophy, and Shakespeare's *The Merchant of Venice* and *King Lear*," *Ben Jonson Journal*, 16 (2009), 197–215.

13 Early moderns would vigorously debate whether or not chance events could be subsumed by some underlying logic (which only God could originate and understand). See Michael Witmore, *Culture of Accidents: Unexpected Knowledges in Early Modern England* (Stanford University Press, 2001). See also Alison Shell, *Shakespeare and Religion*, Arden Shakespeare (London: Bloomsbury 2010), ch. 4.

14 On the profusion of printed accounts of providential mishaps, see Alexandra Walsham, *Providence in Early Modern England* (Oxford University Press, 1999), pp. 96–106.

the context of early modern playgoing more generally, the act of selecting a play to patronize based on its title might itself be viewed productively in the context of the quasi-divinatory practices of early modern wisdom culture. As I argue at the end of this chapter, early modern playgoers may well have considered the proverbial titles of plays themselves – for example, *As You Like It*, *What You Will*, *All Is True* – as counterfoils in a lottery that would distribute theatrical entertainment to those choosing wisely (if blindly) among uncertain offerings.

## Early modern wisdom collections and arts of "construction"

Until recently, there has been no systematic attempt to understand what might have counted as wisdom literature in the period. Critics are only just beginning to explore broader intuitions about the relationship between knowledge and experience that serves as the crucial, unstated link between this growing literature and the actual wisdom practices of which they were a part.[15] Shakespeare was aware of such practices and modeled them in his plays. As Morris Palmer Tilley demonstrates, the plays are filled with proverbs, the mainstay of wisdom literature.[16] Frequently these short phrases are invoked by characters in order to place the dramatic action in some moral context. Polonius's litany of old saws is a nod to this tradition, but it does little to show wisdom "in action," so to speak. For this more interpretively active process of application or "construction," whereby a brief utterance such as a proverb is invoked to make sense of an ambiguous or unexpected situation, Shakespeare turns to another domain of early modern wisdom practices, that of the lottery.

The practice of casting or drawing lots has a long and rich history in Europe. As practiced in Shakespeare's England, these events focus attention on the value and meaning of contingency by manufacturing "unforeseen outcomes" in a reliable and semiritualized fashion.[17] Lotteries thus play a quasi-divinatory role in early modern culture, submitting the moral deserts of individuals to a process so arbitrary or inscrutable (for example, the blind

[15] For the exception, however, see the following section. Studies of wisdom as a concept, rather than of wisdom literature the genre, are plentiful prior to the post-structuralist turn, exploring the range of meanings – from Aristotelian *phronesis* and prudential reasoning to divine or mystical insight – comprehended within it since antiquity. See, for example, Eugene Rice, *The Renaissance Idea of Wisdom* (Cambridge, MA: Harvard University Press, 1958).

[16] See Morris Palmer Tilley, *A Dictionary of Proverbs in England in the Sixteenth and Seventeenth Centuries* (Ann Arbor: University of Michigan Press, 1950). See also William Dent, *Shakespeare's Proverbial Language* (Berkeley: University of California Press, 1981).

[17] See C. L'Estrange Ewen, *Lotteries and Sweepstakes* (London: Heath Cranton, 1932).

drawing lots from a container) that the outcome of that process can be seen as a kind of "verdict" on those deserts. This process begins to unfold on a national scale when the monarch institutes the selling of lots to be drawn for prizes, something which first occurs in England in 1567. The formal lottery, however, is simply a version of more widely diffused practices of cultivating wisdom, practices that seek to manufacture unexpected events for the purpose of moral reflection. One might think, here, of Hamlet's sudden realization about the forces of providence that follows upon his chance encounter with pirates on his way to England. The utter improbability of this turn of events points him toward the metaphysical convictions he expresses (however nihilistically or convincingly) in the final act of the play.

In the late 1990s lexicographer John Considine attempted to provide a comprehensive definition of the wisdom literature which had become a popular genre of print during the late sixteenth and seventeenth centuries.[18] Noting that the genre has its origins in ancient Near Eastern cultures and is developed in the Hebrew Old Testament, Considine shows that the characteristic features of wisdom literature can be found in collections of Anglo-Saxon gnomes and riddles, which are in their turn succeeded by medieval compilations of wise sayings taking a range of encyclopedic and verse forms.[19] This genre was by no means exclusively religious. Humanist methods of commonplacing, for example, added a powerful historical dimension to the tradition, focusing students and learned readers on short fragments or *sententiae* which could be gathered into "tables" for subsequent reuse. Ann Moss, Anthony Grafton, Lisa Jardine, Heidi Brayman Hackel, William Sherman, and Mary Thomas Crane have all shown how this deliberate practice of gathering the "flowers" or "posies" from one's reading expressed important ideas about the value of imitation and adaptation, particularly with respect to classical sources.[20] The last two decades have brought considerable nuance to our understanding of what we might call a hermeneutics of redisposition that was employed by early modern readers – a process whereby texts could be segmented, excerpted, or in some other material sense disposed for reuse in other contexts of reading and interpretation. Considine's vital contribution to this discussion has been to offer a generic definition for wisdom literature that

[18] Considine, "Wisdom-Literature," 325–42. [19] Ibid., 326–7.

[20] See Ann Moss, *Printed Commonplace-Books and the Structuring of Renaissance Thought* (Oxford: Clarendon Press, 1996); Anthony Grafton and Lisa Jardine, "'Studied for action': How Gabriel Harvey Read his Livy," *Past & Present*, 129 (1990), 30–78; Heidi Brayman Hackel, *Reading Material in Early Modern England: Print, Gender, and Literacy* (Cambridge University Press, 2005); William H. Sherman, *Used Books: Marking Readers in Renaissance England* (Philadelphia: University of Pennsylvania Press, 2009); and Mary Thomas Crane, *Framing Authority: Sayings, Self, and Society in Sixteenth-Century England* (Princeton University Press, 1993).

provides a clear reference point for such practices. According to him, wisdom texts are collections of iterable "verbal units": they are "instructive collections of brief sententious statements, arranged in a roughly arbitrary series."[21]

The preference for an arbitrary, rather than principled, arrangement of these fragments suggests that it is the compressed nature of proverbial utterances that makes their loose arrangement a powerful spur for reflection. The contents of the biblical books of Proverbs or Ecclesiastes, for example, need not be read in sequential order. Whatever verbal units they contain are exempt from any distinct narrative context of application. "Like a war club, a sword, or a sharp arrow is one who bears false witness against a neighbor" (Proverbs 25:18). Any number of real or fictional protagonists can become the subject of this sentence. Once an engaged reader supplies that subject, the proverb has (in early modern parlance) been "constructed": an interpretation and judgment has been applied through the proverb to the actions it now describes. Proverbs are interpretively capacious, and so capable of occupying potentially *any* position within a wisdom text, because they are relatively indifferent to the specifics of persons and situations to which they might be applied. A proverb or any other short utterance so collected is deliberately incomplete, such that the possible meanings of a proverb are expanded as it is applied to new situations, even – or especially – to situations encountered *at random*, since these will tend to up-end the natural tendency of the interpreter to consider only the obvious situations to which the proverb applies.

Collections of proverbs, posies, sentences, gnomes, and apothegms are among the most popular genres of early modern print: they were more widely read than texts written in continuous prose.[22] John Heywood's *Dialogue conteiyning the number in effect of all the prouerbes in the english tongue* appeared in 1546 and went through ten editions before 1640; Udall adapted the indispensable *Adages* of Erasmus in 1542 in his *Apothegmes* (this and other adaptations of the *Adages* went through twenty editions); Baldwin's *A treatise of Morall Phylosophie, contaynyng the sayinges of the wyse* is issued twenty-four times after its first publication in 1547. Shakespeare encountered works like these in his early education, for example, the *Sententiae periles* of Leonard Culman and the *Sententiae* of Publilius Syrus, both wisdom collections that were popular during the period.[23] And,

[21] The Book of Job is an obvious exception, one which Considine recognizes as such.

[22] Considine, "Wisdom-Literature," 329.

[23] On Shakespeare's specific use of Culman and Publilius, see Charles G. Smith, *Shakespeare's Proverb Lore: His Use of the Sententiae of Leonard Culman and Publilius Syrus* (Cambridge, MA: Harvard University Press, 1963).

of course, a range of writers adapted these texts to their own ends. Francis Bacon's *Essays*, for example, can plausibly be argued to extend the tradition of wisdom collections into the realm of continuous prose.[24] Shakespeare learned to think proverbially in this culture, one in which printers served up tens of thousands of proverbs to literate individuals who wanted to "salt" their own speech and writings with them.

The pervasiveness of proverbs in the printed codex offered Shakespeare something else: a way of thinking about the vast mobility of wise sayings that links their variable interpretability to the waywardness of Fortune. Most obviously, proverbs exist to help individuals cope with the vicissitudes of chance and Fortune, offering pragmatic or metaphysical guidance depending on how they are interpreted. Because they are hermeneutically flexible, proverbs can be applied to almost any situation – even situations which, because they have come about by chance, could not have been foreseen. Nowhere is this link between chance, proverbs, and interpretation illustrated more clearly than in the casket "lottery" of *The Merchant of Venice*, where Portia's future husband is identified via a contest in which each of her suitors interprets a chosen proverb and, in doing so, justifies his claim to her hand. The idea of a lottery seems to refer to the fact that the process of selecting the prize (Portia) cannot be mastered from the outset because the link between the clues on the caskets and their contents is unclear. As with any situation in which chance or Fortune is seen to operate, such outcomes can be interpreted as the result of some overriding providence, as they are in *Hamlet*.[25] The idea of structuring Portia's courtship as a lottery, however, seems more of a paternal legacy in the play when it is first presented by Nerissa:

> NERISSA Your father was ever virtuous, and holy men at their deaths have good inspirations. Therefore the lottery that he hath devised in these three chests of gold, silver, and lead, whereof who chooses his meaning chooses you, will no doubt never be chosen by any rightly but one who you shall rightly love. (1.2.27–33)

The presence of such a lottery on stage is not unusual in Renaissance drama: Jonson employs lotteries in *Cynthia's Revels* and *Poetaster*, while Chapman stages a lottery in the opening scene of *An Humorous Day's Mirth* in which "posies" or short poetic sayings are inscribed on randomly distributed trinkets.[26] What is significant about Shakespeare's use of this trope is the

[24] Considine, "Wisdom-Literature," 330. [25] Witmore, *Culture of Accidents*, ch. 4.

[26] George Chapman, *An Humorous Day's Mirth*, ed. Charles Edelman (Manchester University Press, 2010). See also Act 1, scene 1 in Thomas Kyd, *The Spanish Tragedy*, ed. T. W. Ross (Berkeley: University of California Press, 1968).

way he spatializes the practice of inscribing proverbs on disparate objects – customarily slips of paper or trinkets – and makes it fodder for a theatrical performance. The *mise en scène* is critical. Staged in the recess of the playing space ("draw aside the curtain"), Portia's suitors encounter a series of three caskets, each inscribed with a "posey" or proverb. Most likely adapted from a 1595 edition of the *Gesta romanorum*, the scene takes crucial advantage of the physical barrier presented by each of the caskets – gold, silver and lead – to the discovery of their contents,[27] contents which the suitors must infer by constructing the proverb, making *themselves* the subject of each statement:

> *[Enter Portia with Morocco and both their trains.]*
> *Portia* Go, draw aside the curtains and discover
> The several caskets to this noble prince.
> *[A curtain is drawn.]*
> Now make your choice.
> *Morocco* This first, of gold, who this inscription bears,
> "Who chooseth me, shall gain what many men desire";
> The second, silver, which this promise carries,
> "Who chooseth me, shall get as much as he deserves";
> This third, dull lead, with warning all as blunt,
> "Who chooseth me, must give and hazard all he hath."
> How shall I know if I do choose the right?
> *Portia* The one of them contains my picture, prince,
> If you choose that, then I am yours . . . (2.7.1–15)

If the choices here were entirely obvious, both the drama of the scene and the point of the lottery would vanish. Suitors must choose between gaining what many men desire, getting as much as one deserves, or giving and hazarding all that one has. That choice will depend upon an individual suitor's interpretation of the words "what," "much," and "all." When the chosen casket opens, an almost divinatory judgment will have been passed on the aptitude of a given suitor, a judgment based on the construction the suitor himself gives of the available inscriptions.

Yet like the early modern lotteries I discuss below, the one in *The Merchant of Venice* is susceptible to fixes. Portia's comments preceding Bassanio's deliberation, for example, combined with the song accompanying the scene, can be seen as tilting things in Bassanio's favor. Shakespeare

[27] Shakespeare's source from the *Gesta romanorum* refers in each instance to a casket upon which has been engraven or "insculpt" a "posey." See William Shakespeare, *The Merchant of Venice*, ed. J. R. Brown (London: Methuen, 1955), appendix 5.

has already weighted the dice in some abstract sense, scripting both the choices and the reasons given for them. Nerissa has pointed out, moreover, that Portia is the prized lot that will "no doubt never be chosen by any rightly but one who you shall rightly love." There is no shortage, then, of forces within or outside the fictional frame of the play that might motivate the link between a suitor and an individual casket. For the process to be theatrically and morally salutary, however, the lottery must turn on something that at least *appears* to be contingent: the reasoned choice of a suitor who construes aloud his moral deserts.[28] Character differences among the suitors, the riddling incompleteness of the proverbs, even the physical barrier that separates the suitor from his prize, all contribute to the sense that the outcome of the game "could have been otherwise."

I emphasize the contingency of the casket lottery because it is both dramatically engaging and also crucial to the wisdom practice being enacted here on stage; to the extent that the inscriptions are ambiguous, each suitor's choice becomes something more than a foregone conclusion. We can appreciate this dramaturgical feature of *The Merchant of Venice* without offering a final interpretation of its densely textured engagement with Old Testament wisdom culture – present at the end of the play in Portia's performance as the "new Daniel" – and the narrative of Christian conversion which, as Barbara Lewalski has shown, Portia's judgments help effect.[29] Critics cannot easily resolve the dueling perspectives that follow from Portia's juxtaposition of Old Testament proverbs and the New Testament rhetoric of "mercy." This should not be surprising, as the play offers spectators interpretive prompts such as proverbs that are themselves verbally iridescent, capable of taking on different hues. Like the proverb itself, the fabric of scriptural, ethnographic, and political allusion in *Merchant* suggests a religious allegory that is fundamentally unstable. The causes of that instability can be more fully understood by connecting the use of proverbs in the play to contemporary wisdom practices. These practices turn experience itself into a contest, and proverbs into the pivot on which a contestant's fortunes turn.

[28] Contingent here does not mean random (although a random event must obviously be contingent). Human choices and future events are contingent, at least from a bounded (human) perspective, because they are too complex to be predicted or foreseen. See Witmore, *Culture of Accidents*, chs. 1–2.

[29] On this issue, see Janet Adelman, *Blood Relations: Christian and Jew in "The Merchant of Venice"* (University of Chicago Press, 2008); James Shapiro, *Shakespeare and the Jews* (New York: Columbia University Press, 1997); D. M. Cohen, "The Jew and Shylock," *Shakespeare Quarterly*, 31 (1980), 53–63; and Barbara K. Lewalski, "Biblical Allusion and Allegory in *The Merchant of Venice*," *Shakespeare Quarterly*, 13 (1962), 327–43.

## Wisdom, Fortune, and the lottery of experience

Early modern lotteries make frequent use of proverbs, perhaps because proverbs – and the wisdom they are supposed to contain – are themselves something one is supposed to cling to in a world subject to Fortune. The contest between wisdom and Fortune is long-standing; it was developed in the Stoic revival of the Renaissance and handled with particular subtlety in the writings of Machiavelli and Montaigne, both of whom give Fortune substantial sway over the realm of experience.[30] Montaigne famously adopts a posture of skepticism toward a world that can only be known through the senses – experience providing too great a variety to be subsumed under any single governing idea. As Hans Blumenberg points out, Montaigne the skeptic understands that "man's imagination is constrained by the limits of his experience."[31] The partial or incomplete nature of experience thus puts a permanent limit on knowledge for Montaigne, who nevertheless finds in it a variety that furnishes endless opportunities for reflection. "The scholars distinguish and mark off their ideas more specifically and in detail," Montaigne writes, yet "I speak my meaning in disjointed parts, as something that cannot be said all at once and in a lump." Especially in the realm of human action, there is too much diversity to be comprehended under systematic categories.[32] Montaigne's manner of coping with the variability of experience – his feel for the almost insensible ways in which it commits individuals to idiosyncratic ideas – pairs strongly with his reliance on ancient *sententiae*: the latter, in their flexible incompleteness, hug the camber of life's path and provide modest supports for the skeptical observer. The variability of Fortune, which Montaigne encounters in the crooked byways of experience, is thus essentially a goad to reflection and perhaps moral courage; proverbs are the prosthetic that he and others will use to

30 As Machiavelli famously writes, "Fortune is a woman," an association analyzed in depth in Hanna Fenichel Pitkin, *Fortune is a Woman: Gender and Politics in the Thought of Niccolo Machiavelli* (University of Chicago Press, 1999).

31 His best-known thoughts on the topic appear in "Of Experience" and "An Apology for Raymond Sebond," for which see *The Complete Essays of Montaigne*, trans. Donald Frame (Stanford University Press, 1965). See also Hans Blumenberg, *The Genesis of the Copernican World*, trans. Robert M. Wallace (Cambridge, MA: MIT Press, 1987), p. 629; and Martin Jay, *Songs of Experience: Modern American and European Variations on a Universal Theme* (Berkeley: University of California Press, 2006), ch. 1.

32 "Of Experience," p. 824. Francis Bacon, discussed below, makes a similar appeal for the value of incompleteness, both in the context of the maxim and the aphorism. See Brian Vickers, *Francis Bacon and Renaissance Prose* (Cambridge University Press, 1968), pp. 61–70; and Lisa Jardine, *Francis Bacon: Discourse and the Art of Discovery* (Cambridge University Press, 1974), p. 177.

cope in such a landscape, arriving at what Montaigne regards as the ultimate contingency: death.[33]

Montaigne's essentially defensive posture here – his emphasis on coping rather than overcoming – contrasts with more active attempts to outdo, or at least harness, Fortune by simulating its most disruptive effects. As we will see in a moment, this more activist approach to wisdom is built into early modern practices of bibliomancy, a popular divinatory use for the collections of proverbs being produced in volume during the period. It is worth noting, however, that the practice of simulating chance events – on stage, in the world – has its own intellectual pedigree in the period. The underlying idea is present well before it is formulated by Francis Bacon, who in the *Novum organum* (1621) argues that "experience . . . if taken as it comes is called accident [*casus*]; if it is deliberately sought, is called experiment [*experimentum*]." No stranger to the collection of maxims and aphorisms in the service of productive action (moral, physical, and judicial), Bacon seeks exhaustively to configure and so "try" human encounters with the world in ways that will provoke or precipitate unexpected discoveries:

> if many useful discoveries have been made by some chance [*casu quodam*] or through some favourable circumstance [*per occasionem*], by men who were not looking for them and were engaged on some other matter, then no one can doubt that much more would be discovered by men who were actively engaged in looking for them, and doing so in a methodical, not an impulsive or desultory way.[34]

Bacon's natural philosophy represents a pivotal episode in the longstanding battle between wisdom and Fortune in the domain of experience. Far from banishing chance from the world, he seeks to co-opt its powers by simulating its unpredictable turns and, in doing so, shaking out possibilities for action that would otherwise remain hidden. By submitting deliberately to chance – engaging it exhaustively in a comprehensive regime of experiment or trial – he believes that the insensible grip of ignorance, itself the product of the limits of one's own experience, will lose its hold on the imagination.[35] Far from trying to banish dame Fortune, Bacon would prefer to imitate and perhaps become her.[36]

33 For more on Montaigne's skepticism and his possible influence on Shakespeare, see Chapter 7 above.

34 Francis Bacon, *Novum Organum*, trans. Peter Urbach (Chicago: Open Court, 1994), pp. 112–13. For the Latin, see Francis Bacon, *Novum Organum*, ed. Thomas Fowler (Oxford University Press, 1878), p. 312.

35 The critique of imagination's tendency to leap ahead of experience, which might furnish grounds for the reformulation of beliefs, is embodied in Bacon's theory of the Idols. See *Novum Organum*, trans. Urbach, pp. 53–68.

36 See Witmore, *Culture of Accidents*, ch. 5.

This same inclination to simulate (by systematically exhausting) the variability of Fortune is expressed in the early modern practice of lotteries and, more explicitly, in the use of lottery books. In the case of both formal lotteries and the use of individual lottery books – the latter so called because they invite readers to navigate their contents by chance – an aleatory process is used to pair a wise saying, proverb, or posey with a particular moral or material desert. Texts employed in early modern divinatory wisdom practices include the Christian and Hebrew bibles (in the practice known as *sortes biblica* or *sortes sanctorum*), Virgil (*sortes Virgilianae*), and Homer (*sortes Homerica*).[37] While the English monarch only began sponsoring lotteries in the mid sixteenth century, English readers (alongside continental ones) would have been familiar with bibliomancy, the art of seeking advice by randomly opening a book to a given passage. The *locus classicus* for the practice is found in Augustine's *Confessions* 8.12, where the narrator's conversion is prompted by a child's half-heard command to "take, read" [*tolle, lege*] a random biblical passage.[38] Jonson's *Poetaster* adapts the procedure of *sortes Virgilianae* for the stage (5.2) when Caesar selects at random a passage from the works of Virgil and commands the poet to perform it for the court.[39] The text so "chosen" reproves the excesses that have dominated behavior thus far in the play, affirming the aptness of randomly selected texts for the diagnosis of moral ills.

The proverb's role in bibliomancy is literally built into what is known as a "lottery book" (*Loßbuch* in German), a text first introduced in northern Europe that is meant to be navigated discontinuously rather than read serially, usually with the help of a device known as a *volvelle*.[40] A volvelle is a kind of paper spinner attached to a printed, radial dial on the page of a book; functioning as a sort of random number generator, the volvelle plays a crucial role in George Wither's *Collection of Emblemes* (1635), an early English lottery book that encourages its user to plot an aleatory course through its contents.[41] Unlike the casket scene in *The Merchant of Venice*,

[37] See William Klingshirn, "Defining the 'Sortes Sanctorum': Gibbon, Du Cange, and Early Christian Lot Divination," *Journal of Early Christian Studies*, 10 (2002), 77–130.

[38] Augustine, *Confessions*, trans. R. S. Pine-Coffin (Harmondsworth: Penguin, 1961), p. 177.

[39] Ben Jonson, *Poetaster*, ed. Tom Cain (Manchester University Press, 2006), p. 141.

[40] Examples include Jan David, *Veridicus Christianus* (Antuerpiæ: Apud Ioannem Moretum, 1601) and *Ein gar kurzweilich Loßbuch* . . . (Collen: Heinrich Nettessem, 1586). On discontinuous reading and the codex, see Peter Stallybrass, "Books and Scrolls: Navigating the Bible," in Jennifer Anderson and Elizabeth Sauer (eds.), *Books and Readers in Early Modern England: Material Studies* (Philadelphia: University of Pennsylvania Press, 2002), pp. 42–79.

[41] Collections of proverbs could, of course, be used without such a device by randomly opening the text and reading the first item that strikes the eye.

where the suitors begin with a proverb that is linked to a prize, the user of Wither's *Collection* is launched on his or her journey entirely by chance. Closing their eyes, readers are expected to rotate a pair of spinners in order to determine their pathway through the book. This pathway has two components, the first specified by a volvelle that generates a number between 1 and 56 (corresponding to a series of epigrams assembled into four discrete "books" or sections), the second by a volvelle specifying which of those four books should be consulted. Of the epigrams in these "books," fifty correspond to full emblems, which the reader goes on to consult, but six confront the reader with what is known as a "blanck," which is essentially a dead end. A typical blank reads as follows (p. 61):

> Your Fortune, hath deserved thank,
> That she, on you, bestowes a Blank,
> For, as you nothing good, have had;
> So, you, have nothing, that is bad.

Like a series of caskets that cannot all be opened at once, the pages of Wither's *Collection* are, by virtue of the physical affordances of the codex, "closed" to one another once a given opening has been made. Although certainly not original, the design of Wither's *Collection* shows the degree to which blind encounters with proverbial wisdom – and the notion that proverbs were themselves *links* to prizes of a sort – was a compelling idea for English readers, compelling enough to be formalized into an elaborately structured reading experience.[42]

There is another link between this sort of bibliomancy and the wisdom practices that Shakespeare chose to simulate on stage. The possibility that readers might end up with a "blanck" – the "nothing" dealt by Fortune in the example above – links the meditative practice formalized in the *Collection* to the communal lotteries introduced during Elizabeth's reign. Lotteries had a shaky start in England, and were first greeted with a skepticism that persisted through the beginning of the seventeenth century.[43] Elizabeth introduced a formal lottery in a series of royal proclamations beginning in August 1567, proclamations that promised prizes to those who were willing to purchase what amounted to 400,000 available lots or

[42] In "To the Reader," Wither glosses the process as follows: "if any one shall draw a Lot wherein his Secret vices are reproved; or some good Counsels proposed, which in his owne understanding are pertinent to his welfare, let not such as those, pass them over as meere Casualties to them."

[43] Ewen, *Lotteries*, p. 29.

tickets offered at a price of 10s each.[44] An array of sumptuous prizes appears in a surviving woodblock print that accompanied the proclamation. In order to attract "adventurers" to the lottery, the royal proclamation emphasized that the lottery contained no "Blankes."[45] Designed to yield at least a modest reward for every purchased lot, Elizabeth's lottery seemed designed to avoid the situation described above in Wither, where the game stops once an unlucky outcome has been drawn. The possibility that a lottery might yield such a dead end is one Shakespeare will entertain when he stages his own lottery in the opening scene of *King Lear*.

Manuscript sources suggest how Elizabeth's lottery was conducted: once the prizes had been "published," collectors were sent throughout England and Ireland to sell lots to "adventurers."[46] This process was highly disorganized. The actual drawing of the lots was delayed by over a year and comprised only a meagre twelfth of the lots available to be sold, the sale requiring the distribution of books of numbered lots which could be bought in varying quantities, each numbered lot being given to the purchaser while the counterfoil, labeled with the adventurer's "devise" or "poesie," remained with the collector. When the lottery was finally "read" or drawn at St. Paul's after much delay, the process itself took sixteen weeks. Each of the approximately 33,000 lots actually purchased had to be duplicated twelve times so that the full 400,000 counterfoils containing the owners' posies could be deposited into the lot-shuffling box or wheel. This innovation could not have encouraged faith in the process, nor could the accompanying expediency of reducing the prizes – drawn from a second box or wheel – by another twelfth. Even the idea that there were no blanks in the lottery was a stretch: while there were 29,505 prizes to be had (though at one-twelfth their original value), a remaining 370,495 lots returned a small fraction of the original investment for the lot, effectively representing a loss.[47]

One can imagine the drudgery of pulling lots from each of these receptacles and matching adventurers with their now reduced prizes.[48] Surviving records of the poseys and prizes illustrate the kinds of texts that were used to declare the hopes of individuals and even civic guilds who bought them.[49]

44 While this is the first formal lottery sponsored by the monarch, it is clear that other lotteries must have been in existence prior to this point. See ibid., p. 57.

45 *A very rich lotterie generall, without any blanckes, contayning a great number of good prices* . . . (Henrie Bynneman, [1567]).

46 Ewen, *Lotteries*, pp. 46–8. 47 See ibid., pp. 62–3.

48 On the process of drawing lots from two drums simultaneously, see ibid., p. 81.

49 See Alfred John Kempe (ed.), *Manuscripts and other rare documents illustrative of some of the more minute particulars of English history, biography and manners* . . . (London: John Murray, 1836), pp. 207–15.

The riddling quality of some recalls the enigmatic inscriptions on the caskets in Shakespeare's later play:

> What chaunce to me befall
> I am content withal.
>
> I hope to hear the trumpet sound,
> A lot worth to me a thousand pound.
>
> Fain would I have,
> Though nothing I crave.
>
> All is well that endeth well.
>
> First learne, then discerne.
>
> Let the arrow flie.

Other poseys were less high-minded, and some were glib: "The chancel is in decay," for example, or "The head of a snake with garlick, is good meate," or "Priestes love pretie wenches." Even the most prosaic examples of lottery poseys, however, possess the kind of interpretive incompleteness that is a hallmark of wisdom utterances and proverbs, suggesting that the 1567–9 lottery was viewed by some as an exercise in divination, one that matched the lottery's material deserts with the compressed expression of each adventurer's claims. What is dramatized much later in *The Merchant of Venice*, then, is this process of making wisdom through interpretation: instead of digesting that wisdom into words on the page, however, the play reverses the process, harnessing the play of contingency and proverbial incompleteness for a drama of decision.

## *King Lear* and the wisdom play

*The Merchant of Venice* participates in this broader wisdom culture, a culture that takes its cue from wisdom literature but is in fact part of a widely dispersed set of wisdom practices that revolve around the seemingly arbitrary pairing of proverbs with material and social rewards. Such pairings must, on some level, be arbitrary – they must occur in ways that *cannot* be immediately foreseen – since the point of these processes is to outsmart the human tendency to bias any form of inquiry or adventure in one's own favor. One can imagine a situation in which the soon to be disappointed suitor Morocco encounters a full description of his life and moral worth, down to the smallest detail and then chooses this particular option: nothing would be ventured, because no uncertainty exists in the description. "Who chooses me shall gain what many men desire" is far better if the lottery is to function like a bet.

A formal lottery turns this process of assigning rewards to words into a competition; interpreted as such, the opening scene of *King Lear*, which represents the "division of the kingdom" into lots that will be distributed to Lear's family, is itself a powerful, if disturbing, example of the wisdom practices discussed up to this point. Freud was one of the first readers to associate the casket lottery in *Merchant* with the love test in *Lear*, an association motivated by their common structure: in the first, a man chooses between three caskets; in the second, between three women.[50] The scenes are just as intelligible, however, as Shakespearean adaptations of the early modern lottery and the belief that underlies them: that there is some value to be gained in submitting one's interests to an arbitrary, or at least inscrutable, process that pairs them with certain rewards. There is at least one biblical precedent for reading the love test specifically as a lottery: in chapter 26 of the Book of Numbers, Moses is given a divine commandment to divide the land of Israel by lot after conducting a census. The episode is described as follows in the Geneva Bible:

> 52 And the Lord spake unto Moses, saying,
>
> 53 Unto these the la[n]d shal be deuided, for an inherita[n]ce, according to the no[m]ber of names. [Marginal note: "or, persons"]
>
> 54 To manie thou shalt give the more inherita[n]ce, and to fewe thou shal give lesse inheritance: to everie one according to his number shalbe given his inheritance.
>
> 55 Notwithsta[n]ding, the land shal be divided by lot: according to the names of the tribes of their father thei shal inherit:
>
> 56 According to the lot shal the possession thereof be devided betwene manie & few.[51]

The instructions here anticipate one of the principles already seen in European lotteries occurring much later, assigning rewards proportionally on the basis of numerical participation (more land to the larger tribes who, in effect, have larger pools of lots). This principle of quantitative proportioning translates into *Lear*'s contest of speeches, where claims and

[50] Sigmund Freud, "The Theme of the Three Caskets," in Philip Rieff (ed.), *Character and Culture* (New York: Collier Books, 1963), pp. 67–79.

[51] *The Bible and Holy Scriptures Conteyned in the Olde and Newe Testament* (Geneva: Rouland Hall, 1560), p. 74. The land is actually divided, according to this divine prescription, by Joshua (Joshua 10:23), who assigns the two largest portions by lot to the tribes of Judah and Joshua, apportioning the balance to the remaining tribes. The Geneva Bible depicts this division on a map (pp. 102–3).

assertions represent portions of love. The rhetoric of quantity that dominates these speeches is well developed, serving to underscore the unhappy overlap between the apportioning of land and love in Lear's kingdom. As the Arden editor of the play, R. A. Foakes, has noticed, these quantities are ventured in response to an invitation to what appears to be a lottery. When Lear turns to Cordelia and asks, "what can you say to draw / A third more opulent than your sisters'?" (1.1.94–5), his telling use of the verb "draw" suggests the context in which to read the king's pairing of daughters with his lands. Foakes follows the Folio reading for the verb in this clause (Q1 reads "win"), asking in the gloss below, "as in a lottery?"

Certain other features of the play associate the love contest with lotteries and wisdom practices, an association that is more explicit in the version of the play surviving in the Folio. Before the love contest begins, Lear says that he is going to reveal his "darker purpose," namely that he intends to divide the kingdom into three portions, having decided now to "publish / Our several daughters' dowers" (1.1.46–7). These lines, again unique to the Folio, are spoken after Lear has received a map of the kingdom, the latter functioning like one of the broadsides through which the prizes from a lottery were "published" (see above).[52] As the contest unfolds, the first two daughters lay claim to what they hope will be the greater of the prizes represented on the map. Regan alludes to this hope when she begins her appeal, saying "I am made of that self mettle as my sister / And prize me at her worth" (1.1.76–7, Q and F). Lear is assumed to be assigning the prizes in the contest by "prizing" or valuing the words of his daughters, a reading France advances when he accepts Cordelia's hand even though she is "unprized" (1.1.301): "thy dowerless daughter, king, thrown to my chance, / Is queen of us, of ours and our fair France" (1.1.297–9, Q and F). Lear, then, is the one who assigns a particular lot to each daughter-adventurer who represents her claim through words, as well as the one who then matches those lots with the claims, as if drawing them from a drum. When Cordelia ventures "nothing" in this process, Lear draws a blank and pairs it with this damning posey: "Nothing will come of nothing. Speak again" (1.1.99). The First Folio adds an echoing repetition of Cordelia's first response, suggesting a break in the formal reading of the lottery and perhaps a cheat: contrary to convention, Cordelia is being offered a second draw. The additional lines

[52] Another lottery, documented only in an excerpt from the register of the Privy Council, was held in Westminster for a period of six months in 1604, a year before the presumed composition of Shakespeare's play. See Ewen, *Lotteries*, p. 68.

allow the staged lottery to realize more fully, then, what must be the pivotal moment of the "reading" Shakespeare is alluding to in this scene.

That "reading" of the lots is a grim farce, as grim in its underlying psychological meaning as the assumption that Lear's daughters can actually exchange quantities of love for quantities of land. Participants shoulder an additional layer of forced belief in this scene when lots are exchanged for love. In pleading their cases, Lear's daughters must appear not only to agree to the terms of the contest and its underlying assumptions about love and dynastic entitlement, but also, and more subtly, to agree with the assumption that Lear is not morally responsible for the outcome, since he assigns rewards by lot. What some of Shakespeare's audience would recognize as a wisdom practice has thus become an empty pageant of sorts – a punishing one, since the aged child who is conducting it (Lear) is the one who needs wisdom the most.[53] The remainder of *King Lear* will explore the ways in which wisdom fails to accompany experience, a condition that the Fool, alluding to a common proverb, diagnoses with brutal precision: "Thou shoudst not have been old till thou hadst been wise" (1.5.43–4). Delivering a stream of seemingly disconnected but also highly suggestive commonplace utterances, the Fool advances the play's perverse engagement with early modern wisdom culture. He is an oracle without divinity.

The complete absence of providence in the play, an absence that began to preoccupy critics around the second half of the twentieth century, might thus be linked to the failure of this initial gambit of faith – that of resolving the future of the kingdom in a kind of divinatory lottery whose principle of operation is as impersonal as it is arbitrary. While this is not the only context in which to interpret the various failures dramatized in the play – failures of providence, self-knowledge, political prudence, and familial love – the tragic course of *Lear* suggests that the very wisdom practices that the early modern period found so compelling have lost their force, or at least have lost their force for Shakespeare. Perhaps this is why the play's last speaker, Albany or Edgar, refuses to offer anything like a proverbial gloss on its contents: as if by chance, a Christ-like Cordelia has been killed. The gods preside over a slaughter of creatures that might just as well be flies. In its intensity of feeling and the suffering it provokes, *Lear* simultaneously invites a process of reflexive proverbial "construction" – an application of a phrase like "ripeness is all" to the events it unfolds – while at the same time suggesting that these insights

[53] Lots were typically chosen by children, who were understood to be "simple" and so unable to comprehend or bias the process of selection. (The classical source for the practice is Cicero, *De Divinatione*, book II.) A Lear who is aged, in second childhood, may be fulfilling a similar purpose.

have no foreordained value, lacking as they are in divine sanction. This is, perhaps, an appropriate if paradoxical point on which to balance a play such as *Lear*, one that summons up an array of religious, political, and commercial contexts in which to think about wisdom only to withdraw from any confident assertion about its availability for use.

Shakespeare's adaptation of wisdom practices shows a subtle awareness of what went into these practices – an awareness, that is, of his culture's emerging faith in the power of unexpected outcomes both to jog the faculties and to prod those faculties toward proverbial wisdom. Shakespeare seems to have lacked faith that such wisdom would always be found, but he understood its grounds, particularly the conviction that unexpected events challenge the poverty of one's prudential and moral imagination. He may even have felt that plays are themselves a kind of wisdom literature, not because they contain a fund of proverbial wisdom that can be digested in Polonius-like fashion, but because they provoke a uniquely engaged, constructive thinking with the intensity of the situations they depict. It is one thing to read in a commonplace book that "ripeness is all." It is quite another to look, with Edgar, on his ruined father and hear these words ring with something like truth.[54]

A more specifically early modern understanding of Shakespeare's plays as wisdom literature would involve thinking of them, again with reference to the practices I have been describing here, as "prizes" to be matched with proverbs. We do not yet understand how the titles of early modern plays are connected with their contents, and the lottery is one context in which to begin thinking about this relationship. On several occasions, Shakespeare gave his plays proverbial titles or subtitles that may have been used to advertise the plays: *As You Like It*; *What You Will* (the subtitle of *Twelfth Night*); *Measure for Measure*; *All's Well that Ends Well*; *All Is True* (the subtitle of *Henry VIII*). Possibly those who went to see a play performed were themselves engaged in a kind of lottery, adventuring their income on the basis of a short proverb that was being used to advertise a play.[55] (The practice is not unique to Shakespeare, of course, and early modern play titles

[54] A number of the chapters in this volume similarly entertain the idea that whatever religious "message" Shakespeare's plays may be trying to communicate, central to his method is the goal of inspiring his audience to take a more active, conscientious, participatory, and/or faithful role in the religious fictions they are watching. See especially Chapters 11 and 12 below.

[55] If proverbial titles were printed with some visual sign representing a particular theater, then playbill advertisements might have born some resemblance to the pages of emblem or lottery books. On advertising plays and the use of images on playbills, see Tiffany Stern, *Documents of Performance in Early Modern England* (Cambridge University Press, 2009), pp. 36–62.

range from the outright proverbial – as in Middleton's *Women Beware Women* – to something that more resembles a motto, adage or a posey [*Westward Ho!*, *The Devil is an Ass*, *The Case is Altered*].)[56] Like Portia's caskets, plays advertise themselves with titles. The familiarity of such proverbial titles, then, may serve a function similar to that of the poseys inscribed on the counterfoils in formal lottery: such phrases are the placeholder for what the adventurer hazards, here the playgoer's time and money staked on the promise of entertainment.

That playwrights certainly recognized such theatrical "adventuring" is witnessed by Ben Jonson, who alludes to this type of investment – linking it specifically to a lottery – in the induction to *Bartholomew Fair*. Here the Scrivener lays out the specifics of a covenant that holds between auditors and author. Auditors buy tickets to plays like they do lots. Some spend more on seats, some less. Depending on the outlay, they purchase a greater or lesser right to censure the play:

> **Scrivener** . . . It shall be lawful for any Man to judge his six
> penn'orth, his twelve penn'orth, so to his eighteen pence,
> two shillings, half a crown, to the value of his place:
> provided always his place get not above his wit. And
> if he pay for half a dozen, he may censure for all them
> too, so that he will undertake that they shall be silent.
> He shall put in for censures here, as they do for lots at
> the lottery: marry, if he drop but sixpence at the
> door, and will censure a crown's worth, it is thought
> there is no conscience, or justice in that. (Induction, 102–12)[57]

Jonson, acutely sensitive to the judgments of his critics, ridicules the value of those judgments by linking them to the amount ventured in a lottery, suggesting that a playgoer's opinion is as variable as chance itself. If censure takes the form of a proverbial construction, it will be hard to know what links proverb to prize.

Plays titled with proverbs are thus part of this contingent process that links expectation – what is ventured through attendance at a play – with a particular desert, here advertised by an enigmatic phrase that serves as a lure to entertainment. As the Scrivener's remarks above suggest, the value of

[56] On the early modern practice of writing interludes to illustrate proverbs, see Harp, "Proverbs, Philosophy"; Paula Neuss, "The Sixteenth-Century English 'Proverb' Play," *Comparative Drama*, 18 (1984), 1–18; and Marjorie Donker, *Shakespeare's Proverbial Themes: A Rhetorical Context for the "Sententia" as "Res"* (Westport, CT: Greenwood Press, 1992).

[57] Ben Jonson, *The Selected Plays of Ben Jonson*, vol. II, ed. Martin Butler (Cambridge University Press, 1989).

what Shakespeare or any other writer introduces into this early modern lottery of playgoing is as unpredictable as the crowd who must judge it. Not everyone who attends *All's Well That Ends Well*, for example, will be convinced that the title truly describes the play's conclusion. But like all proverbs, the "poseys" that Shakespeare "publishes" in the titles of his plays can be interpreted in a number of ways, inviting the auditor to a kind of *What You Will* banquet of interpretation. Sometimes, the plays succeed in delivering intelligible, even eloquent situations that fit the worldly wisdom they seem to convey. And sometimes, as in the case of *Lear*, the lottery cannot possibly pay off. A blank is drawn, the proverb fails.

Shakespeare's adaptation of early modern wisdom practices shows us how pervasive these practices were and the depth of their theatrical power when staged as a communal ritual. That ritual did not need to rise to the level of sacred divination, even if divinatory practices were themselves becoming more popular (particularly in godly circles).[58] For, as the popular lottery run by Elizabeth demonstrates, one could adapt the procedures of such practices to less obviously religious ends. Words like "practice," applied here to structured encounters with wisdom texts, allow us to move between spheres that are not yet historically distinguishable into the "secular" and the "religious."[59] Indeed, the search for wisdom as *practiced* during this period suggests a productive ambiguity between the spheres of private contemplation, civic fundraising, and theatrical entertainment. What remains important about the interplay of wisdom literature with drama is the lively sense, present both in Wither's *Collection* and the plays we have examined, that the search for wisdom advances through the productive linkage of what one has lived to what one has read. Like Shakespeare's theater, then, wisdom is a practice inseparably linked with words that bear witness to experience, words that – in their abrupt concision – show the signs of long and pointed use.

58 Oliver Cromwell is known to have cast lots in connection with military decisions. See Barbara Donagan, "Understanding Providence: The Difficulties of Sir William and Lady Waller," *Journal of Ecclesiastical History*, 39.3 (1988), 433–49.

59 On the difficulty of making this distinction between the "secular" and the "religious," see the introduction to Brian Cummings, *Mortal Thoughts: Religion, Secularity and Identity in Shakespeare and Early Modern Culture* (Oxford University Press, 2013). Opposition to the "secularization" thesis emerges, most powerfully, in Hans Blumemberg's *Legitimacy of the Modern Age*, trans. Robert M. Wallace (Cambridge, MA: MIT University Press, 1985). See also Chapter 12 below.

CHAPTER 11

# *Awakening faith in* The Winter's Tale

*Richard McCoy*

By the end of *The Winter's Tale*, the play's long-penitent hero, King Leontes, is not only reunited with his abandoned, lost daughter, Perdita, but also with the queen he so grievously wronged, Hermione. Astonishingly, the wife he thought he had killed with his insanely jealous suspicions returns to life and forgives him. She turns out to have been alive all along while he mourned her loss and his guilt for sixteen years. Her survival and return are as much of a surprise to the audience as they are to Leontes. That surprise is intensified by her presentation as a statue that appears to come to life. Paulina, the character orchestrating this seeming miracle, tells Leontes that she can "make the statue move indeed, descend, / And take you by the hand," but, before she does so, she says, "It is required / You do awake your faith."[1] Her command includes onlookers in the audience as well as those on stage, and it raises several critical questions: what kind of faith does Paulina require of us, and what does it mean to believe in this play's climax? More broadly, what does faith in Shakespeare and his plays mean and how does it alternately resemble and differ from religious belief?

The faith that Paulina demands of her spectators can certainly feel like religious belief. Like all Shakespeare's late plays, *The Winter's Tale* is suffused with hints of higher, supernatural forces at work behind both its painful and felicitous reversals. After hearing that his son is dead, Leontes concludes that "Apollo's angry, and the heavens themselves / Do strike at my injustice" (3.2.143–4), and he prays to the god to "pardon / My great profaneness 'gainst thy oracle" (3.2.151–2). Reunited with her daughter Perdita, Hermione prays that the "gods, look down / And from your sacred vials pour your graces / Upon my daughter's head" (5.3.122–4). Gods and goddesses actually do descend near the end of *Pericles* and *Cymbeline*, and

[1] *The Winter's Tale* (5.3.88–9 and 94–5), in Stephen Greenblatt et al. (eds.), *The Norton Shakespeare* (New York: W. W. Norton, 1997); all references to Shakespeare's plays are to this edition unless otherwise noted.

the happy outcome of *The Tempest* is declared "A most high miracle" (5.1.180) bestowed "by immortal providence" (5.1.192). The late Victorian scholar Edward Dowden was one of the first to call these late plays "Romances," and he discerns in them a strong religious vision. Dowden sees them as being part of a pattern of recovery from despondency in the tragedies that ultimately placed Shakespeare "On the heights" and let him regain faith in a providential power:

> In these 'Romances' . . . a supernatural element is present; man does not strive with circumstance and with his own passions in darkness; the gods preside over our human lives and fortunes, they communicate with us by vision, by oracles, through the elemental powers of nature. Shakespere's faith seems to have been that there is something without and around our human lives, of which we know little, yet which we know to be beneficent and divine.[2]

The other contemporary term for these late plays was tragicomedy, and in her discussion of the genre Joan Hartwig suggests that an "affirmation of divine control is a signal characteristic."[3] More recently, Raphael Lyne suggests that "a supernatural register is never far away, and often intervenes strongly. They are wondrous in two senses: first, they are improbable (and they make an issue of their patent fictionality); and second, they are miraculous in a more religious sense – they bring to mind the actions of gods, and of God."[4]

This intricate blend of the fictitious and the miraculous in the late plays makes it hard to know what to believe. Marina's cure of her father balances an "artificial feat" with "sacred physic" in *Pericles* (21.61–3), leaving the hero to ask "who to thank / Besides the gods for this great miracle" (22.80–1). Even with *deus ex machina* descents in *Pericles* and *Cymbeline*, the happy ending depends less on gifts from the gods than on the merely human virtues of fidelity, forgiveness, and good fortune. In *The Tempest*, Prospero describes his "rough magic" as a "potent art" (5.1.50), but in *The Winter's Tale* the magic of the last scene is qualified by suspicions that "we are mocked with art" (5.3.68). Nevertheless, feelings of mystery and reverence remain powerful in this play. When Perdita kneels before a statue that resembles a Madonna enshrined in a lady chapel, she evokes older religious customs, and when she rebukes those who would call it

[2] Edward Dowden, *Shakespere* (London: Macmillan, 1893), p. 60.

[3] Joan Hartwig, *Shakespeare's Tragicomic Vision* (Baton Rouge: Louisiana State University Press, 1972), pp. 19–20.

[4] Raphael Lyne, *Shakespeare's Late Work* (Oxford University Press, 2007), p. 3. Lyne sees the irony of these late works as a qualification of a tendency towards religious faith (pp. 7–8).

"superstition, that / I kneel and then implore her blessing" (5.3.43–4), she subtly protests against their suppression. Accordingly, several critics read *The Winter's Tale* as a kind of belated miracle play, suffused by nostalgia for banned medieval mysteries and traditional religious practices. Phebe Jensen argues that "*The Winter's Tale* can be seen to insist that the power of theatrical, sculptural, and literary art is grounded in an aesthetics of representation and transformation rooted in Romanist ritual."[5] Michael Wood extends his argument for Shakespeare as a recusant by claiming that *The Winter's Tale* has a "clear religious undertow with an unmistakably Catholic resonance" and moves "beyond the insufficiencies of art" to greater religious themes of love, redemption, and resurrection.[6] Sean Benson acknowledges that Hermione's revival is not a real resurrection but still insists that "this does not obviate the parallel" with Christ's resurrection, claiming that the sense of "faith" in this play is "preeminently religious."[7] Sarah Beckwith also acknowledges that Hermione's resurrection is not real, describing it as an "ordinary" miracle sustained by what Calvin dismisses as "merely human imagining"; but she also argues that "In Shakespeare's version of resurrection, it is the agencies of both art and religion, of religion working through the agencies of theatrical art, that have become essential."[8] For Beckwith, art alone cannot sustain genuine faith, and she dismisses mere notions of the willing suspension of disbelief as "cognitivist" and "incoherent."[9] This assumption seems deeply mistaken to me. Samuel Taylor Coleridge's concept of "the willing suspension of disbelief for the moment, which constitutes poetic faith" is paradoxical but hardly incoherent, and it is far from simply "cognivitist."[10] On the contrary, it requires a degree of

[5] Phebe Jensen, "Singing Psalms to Horn-Pipes: Festivity, Iconoclasm, and Catholicism in *The Winter's Tale*," *Shakespeare Quarterly*, 55 (2004), 279–306; 306. See also Michael O'Connell, who sees the play's focus on the statue as a temptation to Catholic idolatry, in *The Idolatrous Eye: Iconoclasm and Theater in Early-Modern England* (Oxford University Press, 2000), pp. 141–4. By contrast, Julia Reinhard Lupton argues in *Afterlives of the Saints: Hagiography, Typology, and Renaissance Literature* (Stanford University Press, 1996) that *The Winter's Tale* simultaneously is "tainted by signs of Catholicism" (p. 177) and "smashes the Catholic idols in order to extract their fascinating power" (p. 217). See also Mimi Still Dixon, "Tragicomic Recognitions: Medieval Miracles and Shakespearean Romance," in Nancy Klein Maguire (ed.), *Renaissance Tragicomedy: Exploration in Genre and Politics* (New York: AMS Press, 1987), pp. 56–79 (p. 77).

[6] Michael Wood, *In Search of Shakespeare* (New York: Basic Books, 2003), p. 320.

[7] Sean Benson, *Shakespearean Resurrection: The Art of Almost Raising the Dead* (Pittsburgh, PA: Duquesne University Press, 2009), pp. 159–60.

[8] Sarah Beckwith, *Shakespeare and the Grammar of Forgiveness* (Ithaca, NY: Cornell University Press, 2011), pp. 145, 143, 138.

[9] Ibid., pp. 144–5.

[10] Samuel Taylor Coleridge, *Biographia Literaria*, ed. James Engell and W. Jackson Bate, *The Collected Works of Samuel Taylor Coleridge*, Bollingen series 7 (Princeton University Press, 1969–2002), part II, p. 6.

engagement and good will that makes poetic faith a serious emotional, intellectual, and moral endeavor.[11]

For me, Coleridge's reflections on Shakespeare's plays and the power of theatrical illusion offer a far better explanation of the faith awakened by *The Winter's Tale* than any fundamentally religious interpretation of the play. Indeed, in my book *Faith in Shakespeare* I make poetic rather than religious faith the basis for belief in all of Shakespeare's plays.[12] There are certainly strong parallels between poetic and religious faith, and Coleridge recognizes both their similarities and differences. For him, good will is a point where poetic faith and religious faith converge, and religious belief requires as much strength of will as the willing suspension of disbelief. Coleridge was a deeply religious man with a keen interest in theology.[13] He was also an influential religious thinker whose ideas have deep roots in the Reformation, and that makes his insights into the power of Shakespeare's plays especially valuable. In his *Essay on Faith*, Coleridge defines faith as fidelity to God and says it "subsists in the Synthesis of the Reason and the Individual Will. By virtue of the latter, therefore, it must be an *energy* ... it must be a total, not partial, a continuous, not a desultory, or occasional, Energy: and by virtue of the Former, i.e. Reason, Faith must be a Light, a form of Knowing, a Beholding of Truth."[14] Coleridge's definition anticipates what William James calls "the will to believe," but it also resembles earlier, Reformation conceptions of faith.[15]

During the Reformation, faith in God became the supreme virtue and *sine qua non* of human salvation. From Luther onwards, reformers preached that faith alone saves because no merely human work could ever secure salvation. Calvinism saw the Elect as Christianity's counterpart to the Old Testament's Chosen People, and the doctrine of predestination takes faith alone as a means to redemption for granted. Since faith is a gift of God given only to those chosen through no merit of their own, divine omnipotence always trumps human impotence and sin. In his poem "The Holdfast,"

[11] See Richard Harter Fogle's discussion of the "good will" required of the spectator in "Coleridge on Dramatic Illusion," *Tulane Drama Review*, 4 (1960), 33–44 (38).

[12] Richard McCoy, *Faith in Shakespeare* (Oxford University Press, 2013).

[13] See James Engell, *The Creative Imagination: Enlightenment to Romanticism* (Cambridge, MA: Harvard University Press, 1981), p. 332; and Thomas McFarland, "The Origin and Significance of Coleridge's Theory of Secondary Imagination," in Geoffrey Hartman (ed.), *New Perspectives on Coleridge and Wordsworth* (New York: Columbia University Press, 1972), pp. 195–246, esp. p. 203.

[14] Coleridge, "Essay on Faith," in H. J. Jackson and J. R. de J. Jackson (eds.), *Shorter Works and Fragments* (Princeton University Press, 1995), *Collected Works*, vol. XI, part II, pp. 843–4.

[15] William James, *The Will to Believe and Other Essays in Popular Philosophy* (New York: Dover, 1956); James and Coleridge both emphasize what James calls the "passional and volitional ... root of all our convictions" (p. 4), and this same volition is required in the willing suspension of disbelief.

George Herbert tries on his own initiative to "trust in God to be my light," but then discovers "ev'n to trust in him, was also his."[16] Resignation to the depravity of the human will and the futility of human effort firmly subordinated works to faith while also exacerbating anxiety about salvation. Nevertheless, as Max Weber discovered long ago, predestination paradoxically promoted a rigorous work ethic whereby "God helps those who help themselves."[17] A comparable paradox is manifest in many Reformation tracts and sermons on faith and works. Their authors exhort their readers to strenuous and willful exertion and also anticipate James's "will to believe." One Elizabethan tract insists that "a strong faith sendeth forth earnest requestes, as a foeble faith vttereth cold & formall praiers."[18] Another tract duly subordinates works to faith but then makes faith an aggressively proactive endeavor: "Faith apprehendeth (and so cannot works) and thereby we take hold on Christ his passion and death . . . Faith now being the instrument wherewith we take hold on Christ, assureth vs that wee are elected."[19] A Jacobean treatise argues that "Christian Faith, although immediately infused by God without anie cooperation of man doth not exclude, but rather more necessarily require[s] precedent humane endeuours for the attaining of it."[20] Even as the author asserts the supremacy of faith over works, he still insists that faith does not preclude work, works, or "working in matters of our salvation"; ultimately, faith becomes the supreme work since "true faith is the soule of Good workes."[21]

For Coleridge, faith's basis in divine revelation is also informed by a Reformation awareness of the ambiguities of figurative discourse. In a treatise on the problem of belief in Scripture, he complains:

> It is among the miseries of the present age that it recognizes no medium between *Literal* and *Metaphorical.* Faith is either to be buried in the dead letter, or its name and honors usurped by a counterfeit product of the

[16] George Herbert, "The Holdfast," in F. E. Hutchinson (ed.), *The Works of George Herbert* (Oxford: Clarendon Press, 1967), p. 143.

[17] Max Weber, *The Protestant Ethic and the Spirit of Capitalism*, trans. Talcott Parsons (New York: Charles Scribner, 1958), p. 115.

[18] William Fulke, *A comfortable sermon of faith, in temptations and afflictions* (London, 1574), sig. Ci.v.

[19] H. D., *A godlie and fruitfull treatise of faith and workes. Wherein is confuted a certaine opinion of merit by workes, which an aduersary to the gospell of Christ Iesu, held in the conference, had in the Tower of London* (London, 1583), p. 20.

[20] Thomas Jackson, *Iustifying faith, or The faith by which the just do liue. A treatise, containing a description of the nature, properties and conditions of Christian faith. With a discouerie of misperswasions, breeding presumption or hypocrisie, and meanes how faith may be planted in vnbeleeuers* (London, 1615), p. 279.

[21] Ibid., pp. 278, 192.

mechanical understanding, which in the blindness of self-complacency confounds SYMBOLS with ALLEGORIES.[22]

One of his so-called *Lay Sermons*, this work argues that faith in the Bible requires its reader to move beyond rigidly literal-minded readings or contrived allegorical abstractions. For Coleridge, symbols are the compromise solution, constituting the proper "medium between *Literal* and *Metaphorical*" as well as a medium of divine revelation. The symbols, images, and figures in biblical discourse are not identical with what they symbolize, but, for Coleridge, they are "consubstantial with the truths, of which they are the *conductors*."[23] For Coleridge, symbols acquire an almost sacramental significance in both Scripture and poetry, and his discussions of them often highlight parallels between religious and poetic faith.[24] Coleridge also wrote extensive commentaries on a large number of Reformation theological works, from Luther's *Table Talk* through the Book of Common Prayer to writings of both Jesuits and Puritans. His annotations of John Donne's sermons reaffirm his notion of the symbol as a "medium between *Literal* and *Metaphorical*" by insisting on "the true definition of a Symbol as distinguished from the Thing on one hand, and from a mere metaphor or conventional exponent of a Thing on the other"; he then adds, "Had Luther mastered this great Idea, this Master-Truth, he would never have entangled himself in that most mischievous Sacramentary Controversy or had to seek a murky Hiding-hole in the figment of Consubstantiation."[25]

Coleridge recalls here the Reformation's most divisive and dangerous theological conflict, and he expresses the same desire for a *via media* solution, a solution ardently pursued throughout the earlier period. As one early modern historian puts it, controversies over the Eucharist

[22] Coleridge, *The Statesman's Manual*, in R. J. White (ed.), *Lay Sermons*, *Collected Works*, vol. VI, p. 30. Paul de Man tries to turn this "valorization of symbol at the expense of allegory" against Coleridge and claim that he and other Romantics consequently fail "to distinguish between experience and representation of this experience" (Paul de Man, "The Rhetoric of Temporality," in *Blindness and Insight: Essays in the Rhetoric of Contemporary Criticism*, rev. 2nd edn. [Minneapolis: University of Minnesota Press, 1983], p. 188). Such condescension is unwarranted since Coleridge consistently takes pains to distinguish between the symbol and the thing it represents.

[23] Coleridge, *Statesman's Manual*, vol. VI, p. 29.

[24] See Mary Anne Perkins on Coleridge's conception of words as "living powers" akin to the divine *Logos* in her chapter on Coleridge as "Religious Thinker" in Lucy Newlyn (ed.), *The Cambridge Companion to Coleridge* (Cambridge University Press, 2002), pp. 187–99 (p. 192). See also Lucy Newlyn, *Coleridge, Wordsworth, and the Language of Allusion* (Oxford University Press, 2001), p. 135.

[25] Coleridge, *Marginalia*, ed. George Whalley, in *Collected Works*, vol. XII, part 2, p. 280. For a discussion of Coleridge's views on the Eucharist, see Nicholas Halmi, *The Genealogy of the Romantic Symbol* (Oxford University Press, 2007), pp. 110–19 and 127–32.

"produced the sharpest and most bitter disagreements between reformers who on many other topics were basically at one."[26] Protestants were united in their rejection of Catholic beliefs in Christ's "real presence" in the sacrament as a pernicious delusion, but they were divided over alternatives. Martin Luther quickly advanced beyond criticisms of church corruption to attack the belief that "the mass is a good work and a sacrifice" as "the most wicked abuse of all" in *The Babylonian Captivity of the Church.*[27] Yet Luther retained a belief in a physical presence in the Eucharist that others tagged "consubstantiation." Ulrich Zwingli did not accept this position and argued for a purely spiritual and symbolic presence: "The sacraments we esteem and honour as signs and symbols of holy things but not as though they themselves were the things of which they are the signs."[28] Luther and Zwingli persisted in their differences at a Protestant summit meeting in Marburg in 1529, and their meeting ended in deadlock. John Calvin objected to both their positions, criticizing Luther for positing "the sort of local presence that the papists dream about" while objecting to Zwingli for reducing the sacraments to mere abstractions and denying their "reality and efficacy."[29] Calvin's disciple and successor, Theodore Beza, put these objections more succinctly by charging Luther and Zwingli with reducing the Eucharist to "either transubstantiation or a trope."[30] Calvin and his followers sought and found a *via media* through this false dichotomy by embracing what Kilian McDonnell calls the "doctrine of the efficacy of the sacramental signs."[31]

English reformers soon embraced this idea of the Holy Sacrament's semiotic rather than metaphysical efficacy. Protestants no longer saw the sacrament as an *opus operatum* with intrinsic supernatural powers. They

26 Euan Cameron, *The European Reformation* (Oxford: Clarendon Press, 1991), p. 161.

27 Martin Luther, *The Babylonian Captivity of the Church*, trans. A. T. W. Steinhauser, revised by Frederick C. Ahrens and Abdel Ross Wentz in Abdel Ross Wentz and Helmut T. Lehman (eds.), *Luther's Works: Word and Sacrament*, 54 vols. (Minneapolis, MN: Fortress Press, 1959), vol. XXXVI, pp. 35–6.

28 Ulrich Zwingli, *Exposition of Faith* (1530), cited by G. R. Potter, "Zwingli and Calvin," in Joel Hurstfield (ed.), *The Reformation Crisis* (New York: Harper & Row, 1965), p. 34.

29 Jaroslav Pelikan, *The Christian Tradition: A History of the Development of Doctrine: The Growth of Medieval Theology, 600–1300*, 5 vols. (University of Chicago Press, 1978), vol. IV, pp. 186 and 192–3. See also Brian Gerrish, *Grace and Gratitude: The Eucharistic Theology of John Calvin* (Minneapolis, MN: Fortress Press, 1993), pp. 104–6 and 140–5. Resolving these disputes was not easy, nor was finding a *via media*; as Gerrish says, Calvin sometimes "seemed to stumble between the rival opinions of Luther and Zwingli rather than to harmonize them" (p. 10).

30 Cited in Pelikan, *Christian Tradition*, vol. IV, p. 201.

31 Kilian McDonnell, *John Calvin, the Church, and the Eucharist* (Princeton University Press, 1967), p. 243. See also Christopher Elwood's discussion of Calvin's theory of "sacramental signification" in *The Body Broken: The Calvinist Doctrine of the Eucharist and the Symbolization of Power in Sixteenth-Century France* (Oxford University Press, 1999), pp. 61–71.

believed its powers depended on the good faith and good will of the recipient. In rejecting transubstantiation, they concluded that sacramental change no longer occurred in the elements of the Eucharist, transforming the bread and wine into the body and blood of Christ. Instead, the change took place in the heart and soul of the recipient. As archbishop of Canterbury under Edward VI, Thomas Cranmer promoted this reception theory of the Eucharist in liturgical reforms and theological treatises. His Book of Common Prayer replaces the Mass and belief in a sacrifice with an emphasis on commemoration of the Lord's Supper and celebration of Holy Communion.[32] Cranmer also wrote an extended refutation of the doctrine of transubstantiation that argues that "although Christ be not corporally in the bread and wine, yet . . . he is effectually present, and effectually worketh not in the bread and wine, but in the godly receivers of them."[33] He also insists that "the real conversion is in him that receiveth the sacraments; which real conversion is inward, invisible, and spiritual."[34] The change was thus not metaphysical or material but subjective and psychological, prompting an inner, emotional transformation. As Christopher Cocksworth puts it, in Cranmer's reception theory of the Eucharist "the effective potential of the Sacrament was a product of its affective force."[35] This affective force is emphasized in a tract called "A Communicant Instructed," where the sacrament is described as "neither a *commixtion* of *persons* nor an vnion of *substances*, but a *confederation* of our *affections* and *concatenation* of our *wils*: there it shall appear in the *consociation* of our *persons*."[36]

The potency of the Sacrament's spiritual and emotional effects clearly depends on the reformers' belief in the efficacy of signs and symbols. In his study of Tudor liturgy and literature, Timothy Rosendale convincingly argues that the Book of Common Prayer "pivots around a newly stressed faith in the power of representations," including human and merely poetic representations.[37] These liturgical reforms thus reflect an awareness of

[32] For an illuminating discussion of the evolution of Cranmer's Eucharistic theology, see Diarmaid MacCulloch, *Thomas Cranmer: A Life* (New Haven, CT: Yale University Press, 1996), pp. 181–3, 354–5, 378–405, and 614–16.

[33] Thomas Cranmer, *An Answer to a Crafty and Sophistical Cavillation devised by Stephen Gardiner*, in John Edmund Cox (ed.), *Writings and Disputations . . . Relative to the Sacrament of the Lord's Supper* (Cambridge: Parker Society, 1894), 15.34–5.

[34] Ibid., 15.271.

[35] Christopher J. Cocksworth, *Evangelical Eucharistic Thought in the Church of England* (Cambridge University Press, 1993), p. 29.

[36] Robert Hill, "A Communicant Instructed," in *The Path-way to Pietie* (1606; London, 1629), p. 230.

[37] Timothy Rosendale, *Liturgy and Literature in the Making of Protestant England* (Cambridge University Press, 2007), p. 8.

profound affinities between poetic and religious faith.[38] The Prayer Book's prefatory discussion "Of Ceremonies" concedes that they "had their beginning by the institution of man" but maintains their value as a reminder of our "duty to God by some notable and special signification."[39] Cranmer firmly believed that the liturgy he helped to devise could sustain this "special signification," and his commitment to the ultimate truth of symbols was so strong that he gave his life to affirm it. When Mary I succeeded her brother, Edward VI, and launched her counter-reformation, Cranmer was stripped of office and put on trial for heresy. When he insisted that "Christ did use figurative speech in no place more than in his sacraments, and specially in his supper," he was accused of reducing the sacraments to mere figures of speech and empty symbols; indeed, one of his inquisitors responded "whosoever saith that Christ spake by figures, saith that he did lie," but Cranmer stood by his position and disdainfully told his opponents they did not understand tropes.[40] Cranmer's adversaries saw figures of speech as at best empty symbols and at worst deceitful fictions, but he saw them as our only effective means of grasping truths otherwise ineffable and incomprehensible. Cranmer thus anticipates Coleridge's argument in one of his *Lay Sermons* that a symbol "partakes of the Reality which it renders intelligible" and becomes "a living part in that Unity of which it is the representative."[41]

Coleridge's discussion of symbols in Shakespeare also recalls these intense Reformation controversies over the real presence. In his *Notebooks* he writes that it is

> Hard to express that sense of the analogy or likeness of a Thing which enables a Symbol to represent it, so that we think of the Thing itself – & yet knowing that the Thing is not present to us. Surely, on this universal fact of words & images depends by more or less mediations the *imitation* instead of *copy* which is illustrated in very nature *shakespearianized* / – that Proteus Essence that could assume the very form, but yet known & felt not to be the Thing.[42]

[38] For more on the parallels between poetic and religious faith, especially the close affinities between Shakespeare's staged representations of religious ritual and the actual church rites of the Elizabethan Settlement, see Chapter 12 below.

[39] John E. Booty (ed.), *The Book of Common Prayer 1559: The Elizabethan Prayer Book* (Charlottesville: University of Virginia Press, 1976), pp. 18–19.

[40] Thomas Cranmer, *Disputations at Oxford*, in Cox, *Writings and Disputations*, 15.401. Rosendale discusses this exchange as evidence of Cranmer's shift from a literal to a figurative conception of the Eucharist. *Liturgy and Literature*, p. 106.

[41] Coleridge, *Statesman's Manual*, vol. VI, p. 30.

[42] Kathleen Coburn (ed.), *The Notebooks of Samuel Taylor Coleridge*, 5 vols. (London: Routledge, 1957–2002), vol. II, p. 274.

He elaborates on this distinction between imitation and copy in subsequent lectures, arguing that Shakespeare's plays are "an *imitation* of reality not a *Copy* – and that Imitation is contra-distinguished from Copy by this, that a certain quantum of Difference is essential to the former, and an indispensable condition and cause of the pleasure, we derive from it; while in a Copy it is a defect, contravening its name and purpose."[43] He illustrates this distinction by citing the Chorus in *Henry V* who repeatedly distinguishes between the great events of Agincourt and the actors' feeble efforts to represent them. Coleridge writes that, since there is no possibility that the theater's "narrow ~~stage~~ Cockpit may hold 'The vasty fields of France,'" the Chorus must ask our help in envisioning its epic battles.[44] Coleridge explains this collaborative process as one that works "by the Art of the Poet and the Actors, and with the consent and positive Aidance of our own Will" to provide the "means to this chief end – that of producing and supporting this willing Illusion."[45] To sustain that "willing Illusion," *Henry V*'s Chorus must resort to what he calls "a crooked figure" (15) to "bring forth / So great an object" (10). Similarly, Christians rely on humble, even degrading figures – a lamb, bread, a cross – to comprehend God's infinite might.

Nevertheless, the prologue to *Henry V* is also a point where the differences between religious and poetic faith are made clear. The Chorus may yearn for "a muse of fire, that would ascend / The brightest heaven of invention," but he laments that his "flat, unraisèd spirits" cannot rise above their "unworthy scaffold" (*Henry V*, Prologue 1–2, 9–10). *Henry V* is not a godly work in the manner of *Paradise Lost*, nor does the Chorus attempt anything like Milton's confident invocation of the Holy Spirit and "Heav'nly Muse."[46] Shakespeare's inspiration is earthbound, not celestial, and even then he seems apprehensive that it will fail. The Chorus worries that the players' efforts "shall much disgrace / With four or five most vile and ragged foils, / Right ill-disposed in brawl ridiculous / The name of Agincourt" (4.0.49–52). At the same time, despite these fears of bathos, the eloquence of his speeches still enables us to "sit and see, / Minding true things by what their mockeries be" (4.0.52–3). It is a wonderfully

[43] Coleridge, *Lectures 1808–19: On Literature*, ed. R. A. Foakes, 2 vols., *Collected Works*, vol. II, p. 264. Foakes points out in his note on this passage that Coleridge "never tired of insisting upon this distinction" and calls attention to similar passages in lecture 4 in the 1808 series (vol. I, p. 83) and lecture 3 in the 1811–12 series (vol. I, p. 223).

[44] Ibid., vol. II, p. 267. [45] Ibid., vol. II, pp. 266–7.

[46] John Milton, *Paradise Lost*, I.6 and 13, in Merritt Y. Hughes (ed.), *Complete Poems and Major Prose* (New York: Odyssey Press, 1957).

ambiguous command that grasps the core paradox of the willing suspension of disbelief. Shakespeare's "mockeries," like Coleridge's "Illusions," are intensely engaging and illuminating, but they are also transparently fictitious. And while they can convey "true things," the truths they represent do not require the religious conviction that cost Cranmer his life.

Cranmer's martyrdom also makes the difference between religious and poetic faith clear. This preeminent Tudor churchman and reformer's ideas about the Eucharist as a figure changed over the course of his career, and, under threat of death, he supposedly recanted his presumed heresies.[47] Nevertheless, he was still condemned to be burned at the stake, and at the end he repudiated these disavowals from the pulpit and his pyre, thrusting the hand that signed his *Recantacyons* into the flames. Faith in God ultimately demands this moment of truth and allows no doubts or evasions – or "equivocations," in the term used in Shakespeare's time.[48] As the philosopher of religion Anthony Kenny explains, "The common characteristic of faith in almost all religious traditions is its irrevocability. A faith that is held tentatively is no true faith. It must be held with the same degree of certainty as knowledge"; and, Kenny adds, "In some traditions the irrevocability of faith is reinforced by the imposition of the death penalty for apostasy, which is the abandonment of faith."[49] Of course, from the apostate's perspective, apostasy is the ultimate truth and, like Cranmer, one must be prepared to die for it. Then and now, the commitment required by religious faith is unconditional and a matter of life and death. By contrast, faith in Shakespeare allows a respite from such inexorable and lethal confessional pressures and presents within its alternative theatrical space a far more congenial, tolerant, and humane alternative. His plays exult in the ambiguity and circumspection condemned by many contemporaries as equivocation. They also allow for the open-mindedness later praised by John Keats as "negative capability" that is an ability to accept "uncertainties, Mysteries, doubts" rather than striving for absolute and positive conviction.[50] The appeal of such an alternative must have been strong at a time when religious beliefs could have such dire consequences.

[47] In his biography of Cranmer, MacCulloch discusses *Cranmer's Recantacyons* (*Life*, pp. 584–600) and Cranmer's final repudiation of them (*Life*, p. 603).

[48] Shakespeare's Porter in *Macbeth* famously describes "an equivocator, that . . . could not equivocate to heaven" (2.3.8–10), a presumed reference to Father Henry Garnet who wrote a defense of equivocation.

[49] Anthony Kenny, "Knowledge, Belief, and Faith," *Philosophy*, 82 (2007), 381–97 (394).

[50] John Keats, "Letter to George and Thomas Keats (December 21, 27 (?), 1817)," in Douglas Bush (ed.), *Selected Poems and Letters* (Boston, MA: Houghton Mifflin, 1959), p. 261.

Shakespeare's theater relies on and cultivates many of the same responses developed by Reformed religion. His plays awaken a faith that requires strenuous effort, good will, and a will to believe. They depend on a figurative discourse that does not pretend to present "the Thing itself" but still allows us "to think of the Thing itself" while "knowing that the Thing is not present to us." And the participation they require sustains a sense of solidarity and communion that approximates the "*confederation* of our *affections*" and "*consociation* of our *persons*" ascribed to the Eucharist. These affinities between poetic and religious faith have led some critics to ascribe a fundamentally religious function to Shakespeare's plays. In *Shakespeare's Tribe*, Jeffrey Knapp treats them as "godly enterprises" and assigns them a "sacramental purpose."[51] Knapp argues that the Chorus in *Henry V* presents the play as a "theatrical sacrament," sustained "not only with the inward participation of the audience but also with the sense of charity and communal endeavor that such participation is supposed to inspire."[52] Knapp draws here on Joel Altman's influential essay on *Henry V*, which claims that the play achieves a kind of "transubstantiation of 'presence' and ... the royal presence" by enlisting our "active participation."[53] There are, as I have noted, strong parallels between theatrical fellowship and reformed ideas of Holy Communion, but assigning these plays a "sacramental purpose" pushes those similarities too far. Plays are not a means to divine grace or redemption, much less a "transubstantiation" or presentation of a real "presence." On the contrary, they present themselves deliberately as mockeries and illusions.

Art's mockery is emphasized throughout *The Winter's Tale*'s final scene. Before unveiling the supposed statue of Hermione, Paulina tells Leontes and the other onlookers to "prepare / To see the life as lively mocked as ever / Still sleep mocked death" (5.3.18–20). Mockery can be defined simply as an imitation, and the *Oxford English Dictionary* cites the lines from *Henry V* about "Minding true things by what their mockeries be" (4.0.52–3) as an example of this relatively neutral meaning. Paulina seems to be telling us to expect a remarkably lifelike image of the late queen. At the same time, the *OED* entry adds that its connotation is "depreciative" and suggestive of "an

51 Jeffrey Knapp, *Shakespeare's Tribe: Church, Nation, and Theater in Renaissance England* (University of Chicago Press, 2002), pp. 2 and 19.

52 Ibid., p. 138.

53 Joel B. Altman, "'Vile participation': The Amplification of Violence in the Theater of *Henry V*," *Shakespeare Quarterly*, 42 (1991), 1–32 (19 and 24). See also Anthony B. Dawson, "Performance and Participation," in Anthony B. Dawson and Paul Yachnin, *The Culture of Playgoing in Shakespeare's England: A Collaborative Debate* (Cambridge University Press, 2001), pp. 45 and 37–8.

outrageous or ludicrous simulation," and the self-deprecation of the Chorus also carries that association. Mocking can also mean to deride and deceive, as well as to tantalize and disappoint, and Leontes' use of the term evokes these more disturbing implications. Leontes is impressed by the sculptor's skill as he gazes on his wife's statue, but he is uneasy about its effect: "The fixture of her eye has motion in't, / As we are mocked with art" (5.3.67–8). The statue's "lively" appearance stirs hopes for a Pygmalion-like transformation, but a fear that "we are mocked with art" anticipates that such hopes must be dashed. As the scene develops, the dramatic ironies of Leontes' fears ramify. As the statue begins to move, it becomes clear that we are gazing not on an artwork but on the still living, if wrinkled and older, Hermione. Her *tableau vivant* is, in the words of Polixenes, "an art / Which does mend Nature – change it rather; but / The art itself is Nature" (4.4.95–7). Hermione's survival reverses and allays Leontes' apprehensions: art does not mockingly simulate life but instead life imitates and mocks art with its greater vitality.

Many critics conclude that the final scene firmly subordinates art to life.[54] Yet Shakespeare still believes in art's value even when he discounts or mocks it. In *The Winter's Tale*, as in *Henry V*, we can mind "true things by what their mockeries be," even if these ingenious fictions entail distortion and deception. In the final scene of *The Winter's Tale* we are tricked and "mocked with art" in two ways. The first trick is the spectacle of a statue that turns out to be a living person and actor. The second involves the plot twist of Paulina's artful lie that laid the groundwork for this artful *coup de théâtre*. But the impact of this scene depends on the transformation and participation of the protagonist. Paulina makes that clear by demanding Leontes' consent before proceeding: "I have thus far stirred you; but I could afflict you farther" (5.3.73–4). Leontes agrees, "For this affliction has a taste as sweet / As any cordial comfort" (5.3.76–7). She then presents him and every onlooker, including all of us in the audience, with a choice:

Either forbear,
Quit presently the chapel, or resolve you
For more amazement. If you can behold it,
I'll make the statue move indeed, descend,
And take you by the hand. But then you'll think –

[54] See e.g. Charles Frey, *Shakespeare's Vast Romance: A Study of "The Winter's Tale"* (Columbia: University of Missouri Press, 1980), p. 93. Leonard Barkan offers a far more balanced and accurate assessment of the relation of art and life in Shakespeare in "'Living sculptures': Ovid, Michelangelo, and *The Winter's Tale*," *ELH*, 48 (1981), 639–67, esp. 663–4. See also Edward Tayler, *Nature and Art in Renaissance Literature* (New York: Columbia University Press, 1964).

Which I protest against – I am assisted
By wicked powers. (5.3.85–91)

Leontes replies, "What you can make her do / I am content to look on; what to speak, / I am content to hear" (5.3.91–3), but that response is insufficient. Contentment is too meager, implying that one is not unwilling to do something or prepared to settle for something inadequate. Merely looking on and listening will not suffice, so Paulina asks for a more active and intense effort.[55] Here too she includes us in her demands; as Stanley Cavell points out, a "transformation is being asked of our conception of the audience of a play, perhaps a claim that we are no longer spectators, but . . . participants."[56] While forswearing the "wicked powers" of necromancy, Paulina also makes it clear that she cannot make the statue move by her powers alone. She demands what Shakespeare always demands at these pivotal moments of incredibility in his plays: "It is required / You do awake your faith" (5.3.94–5).

The faith required here is poetic faith, or the willing suspension of disbelief, rather than a religious belief in a divine power or sacred purpose. Poetic faith requires the active and energetic participation of every onlooker, on stage and in the audience. With our help and good will, she can finally tell Hermione to "Descend. Be stone no more. Approach. / Strike all that look upon with marvel. Come / . . . Bequeath to death your numbness, for from him / Dear life redeems you" (5.3.99–103), and Hermione steps down from her pedestal. Hermione's recovery is not a real resurrection of the dead. Her transformation from a statue to a person is a trick that requires a more profound transformation of Leontes. "Dear life redeems" her because the passage of life and time has also redeemed Leontes' once diseased imagination. Right after swearing that Hermione was killed by Leontes' cruelty and insisting that his crimes' effects were irreversible, Paulina scorns his sudden remorse and hope that "she will recover" (3.2.148) by daring him to try to save her:

If you can bring
Tincture or lustre in her lip, her eye,
Heat outwardly or breath within, I'll serve you
As I would do the gods. (3.2.202–5)

[55] Frey, in *Shakespeare's Vast Romance*, astutely observes that Paulina says, "Not 'if you *will* behold it' but 'if you *can*,'" implying more rigorous demands on Leontes' capacities and energies (p. 161).

[56] Stanley Cavell, *Disowning Knowledge in Seven Plays of Shakespeare* (1987; Cambridge University Press, 2003), p. 218.

By the play's end, after sixteen years of atonement under her supervision, Leontes is so profoundly transformed that such a miracle is possible – but it is a psychological rather than divine miracle. Previously carried away by jealousy, his thoughts were wholly destructive; but now, stirred by remorse and renewed desire, his thoughts are so life-affirming that he can indeed help restore Hermione's color, warmth, and breath; "O, she's warm" (5.3.109), Leontes exclaims as he takes hold of her hand. As this stirring climax unfolds, we see that her seeming resurrection requires not divine intervention but only the change of heart that comes with repentance and renewed love. After his morbid jealousy has wrought its worst effects, Leontes realizes, "I have too much believed mine own suspicion" (3.2.149). Now repentant, he also realizes that he was "transported by my jealousies / To bloody thoughts and to revenge" (3.2.156–7). His prolonged repentance and the passage of time subsequently move him and his thoughts from bad faith to good. Sixteen years later, as he gazes on his wife's image, Paulina repeats his verb, rendering this passage of time and the movement of his mind literal when she says, "My lord's almost so far transported that / He'll think anon it lives" (5.3.69–70). Just as his desperate "Affection" once made the worst "possible things not so held" (1.2.140–1), so now his restored and healthy affections make possible an affirmation of the best but most precarious possibilities: forgiveness, restoration of lives thought irrecoverably lost, and another chance at happiness.

Paulina's trick not only restores a marriage blighted by jealous suspicions, but also allows the audience a truly astonishing happy ending. We believe in this extraordinary outcome because it never pretends to be an actual miracle, just as Shakespeare's art never mocks us by pretending to be completely real or plausible. He rejects copies or simulacra so realistic that, like Giulio Romano's statue, they "would beguile Nature of her custom" (5.2.89). What *The Winter's Tale* offers instead is manifest fictions, which Coleridge calls illusions or imitations. Shakespeare repeatedly acknowledges and stresses their differences from reality. Paulina is the first to concede the absurdity of this outcome: "That she is living, / Were it but told you, should be hooted at / Like an old tale. But it appears she lives" (5.3.116–18). Paulina's contrast between telling and appearing highlights the difference between this scene and its predecessor while affirming the power of theatrical spectacle. The talkative gentlemen in the previous scene could only recount events "so like an old tale that the verity of it is in strong suspicion" (5.2.26) and taunt us with losing "a sight which was to be seen, [and] cannot be spoken of" (5.2.38–9). In the final scene we move from mere narrative to a sight that strikes "all that look upon with marvel" (5.3.100).

In the earlier scene the statue is said to be so lifelike "that they say one would speak to her and stand in hope of answer" (5.2.91–2), and the scene largely consists of questions and extended answers. In the final scene, once the statue turns out to be Hermione in the flesh, there are even more pressing questions, with Camillo asking, "If she pertain to life, let her speak too" (5.3.114), and Polixenes adding, "Ay, and make manifest where she has lived, / Or how stol'n from the dead" (5.3.115–16). Hermione in turn wants to know how her daughter has survived since she has "preserved" herself "to see the issue" (5.3.128–9). Paulina's cryptic reply turns aside further discussion and refuses to give answers: "There's time enough for that, / Lest they desire upon this push to trouble / Your joys with like relation" (5.3.129–31). Her first response that "it appears she lives" is no less enigmatic, but, for those whose faith is awakened, it must suffice.[57] Faith in *The Winter's Tale* accepts the truth of seeming and mockeries, even if they lack plausible explanations. Even as they remind us that appearances can deceive, Shakespeare's plays also affirm that at moments like this, seeing can be believing.

Theater generally asks us to believe what we see on its stages, even while recognizing that all its sights are illusions; the Greek root, *theatron*, means "seeing place." We must also accept our own active part in the plays shown, one that requires us to awaken our faith in illusions. Leontes has the last word in *The Winter's Tale*, and he is finally prepared to accept the truth of appearances as well as his part in the play. When gripped by his mad fury, he scorned the honorable appearance of "her without-door form" (2.1.71). He also fiercely rejected both his part and that played by his wife. Raging against Hermione, he urged all to "Look on her, mark her well. Be but about / To say she is a goodly lady" (2.1.67–8). He repudiated the truth of her appearance and insisted that it was a lie. By the play's end he has fully recovered from his madness, a madness that drives him to a radical skepticism and homicidal disenchantment. He is now charmed by his wife's

[57] A. D. Nuttall deems "it appears she lives" an "unanswerable reply" in *William Shakespeare: The Winter's Tale* (London: Edward Arnold, 1966), p. 58. I find Nuttall's discussion of this scene's peculiar ambiguities especially persuasive: "the audience cannot relax into the easy cynicism of 'seeing through the charlatan' since the most beautiful and wonderful thing is happening before its eye; Hermione who was lost is found; Leontes' broken heart is healed" (p. 54); the outcome moves beyond "the cheaply theatrical supernatural to the immense natural miracle" (p. 55). Kenneth Gross offers a similarly subtle analysis of this final scene, describing it as "a return to the commonplace, and at the same time a recuperation of theater. The faith to be awakened is partly the faith that the cheap stage trick was performed in good faith," but this resolution still presents a "real difficulty" that results from offering "neither self-evident faith in magic nor the quiet comforts of disenchanted irony." See his *The Dream of the Moving Statue* (Ithaca, NY: Cornell University Press, 1992), p. 109.

wrinkled beauty and says he could stand gazing upon her image for "twenty years," joining his daughter as "a looker-on" (5.3.84–5).

Perhaps most significantly, Leontes accepts both play and play-acting in *The Winter's Tale*'s very last words. His daughter is at least ambivalent about play-acting and submits to her role reluctantly, conceding that "the play so lies / That I must bear a part" (4.4.637–8). Nevertheless, she still plays along, intermittently enjoying her roles as they "change my disposition" (4.4.135). Eventually she triumphs in her royal role and confirms what another character calls the "truth of your own seeming" (4.4.636). In the play's first part Leontes is utterly horrified by the prospect of playing a role, and he bitterly objects to the parts assigned to his wife and himself by her presumed duplicity. He urges his son to "Go play, boy, play. Thy mother plays, and I / Play too; but so disgraced a part, whose issue / Will hiss me to my grave" (1.2.188–90). He seems as appalled as Macbeth is by the prospect of becoming a "poor player / That struts and frets his hour upon the stage" (5.5.23–4). By the end he happily accepts his part in the play and even joins Paulina in giving directions. Leontes is almost as curious about Paulina's mysterious means and methods as some of the others. He remarks that, while she lost her spouse in his service, "Thou hast found mine, / But how is to be questioned" (5.3.139–40). Nevertheless, he is not only prepared to wait for answers, but he also suggests that he and everyone else must finally provide their own. Accordingly, rather than asking Paulina for answers, he simply directs her to

> Lead us from hence, where we may leisurely
> Each one demand and answer to his part
> Performed in this wide gap of time since first
> We were dissevered. Hastily lead away. (5.3.153–6)

Answers will come not from some revelation of hidden or higher truths but rather from each character accepting and answering to the part each performed in the play. *The Winter's Tale* makes the same demands on its audience, for faith in Shakespeare also requires our imaginative participation and willing suspension of disbelief in an illusion. Awakening our faith requires that we too answer to our part in the play.

CHAPTER 12

# Hamlet, Henry VIII, *and the question of religion: a post-secular perspective*

*Paul Stevens*

Two of the most famous responses to Shakespeare and Fletcher's *Henry VIII* are those of Sir Henry Wotton in 1613 and Jane Austen in 1814. Wotton's response is better known than Austen's, but Austen's, so I want to suggest, may ultimately be of more value. Writing a few days after the play's performance at the Globe Theater on June 29, 1613, Wotton, as everyone familiar with the play knows, characterized it as overly ceremonial and pretentious – its scenes were "set forth with many extraordinary circumstances of pomp and majesty," so much so that its final effect was to make "greatness very familiar, if not ridiculous."[1] Indeed, so contemptuous was he that he seems to have taken considerable pleasure in the way the play's hubris was rewarded with a fire-storm: in his letter to Sir Francis Bacon's nephew, Edmund, he is clearly delighted that the elaborate stage effects, the "chambers" or stage cannons deployed to announce King Henry's arrival at Wolsey's masque set off a fire that burned the theater to the ground "within less than an hour" (II, p. 32). But Wotton's judgment on the play, a critique that has shaped so much modern criticism, may not be as reliable as it is usually taken to be. First, it is not clear how much of the play he could have actually seen if the fire was ignited in the first act, and second, even if he did see the play, he may not have been the most disinterested observer. Ambitious, often obsequious and disingenuous, Wotton loved a good story. His nickname was "Signor Fabritio" and he was considered dangerously unreliable even by his closest friends: as the judicious news-gatherer and letter writer, John Chamberlain, wrote in October 1612, "my good old friend Fabritio will never leave his old trade of being a fabler, or, as the devil

I am grateful to Martin Dawes, David Loewenstein, Deidre Lynch, and Lynne Magnusson for their responses to this chapter.

[1] Letter to Sir Edmund Bacon, July 2, 1613, in Logan Pearsall Smith, *The Life and Letters of Sir Henry Wotton*, 2 vols. (Oxford: Clarendon Press, 1907), vol. II, p. 32.

is, father of lies."[2] In June 1613 Wotton's career was in tatters: he was still in disgrace with the king for a notorious indiscretion and only intermittently employed by him. "Touching Fabritio," wrote Chamberlain's friend, Dudley Carleton, "the devil owed him a shame and now he hath paid him."[3] At the time of the play's performance, then, Wotton was a professional courtier with a notorious tendency to fabricate, watching a theatrical representation of the court life from which he had just been excluded. Jane Austen's situation was more than a little different. Although it is unlikely that she ever saw Shakespeare and Fletcher's play performed, her reading of it in *Mansfield Park* seems strikingly more engaged and discerning than Wotton's; in fact, her response to the play, to which I will return at the end of this chapter, suggests what many would call a "post-secular perspective."[4]

## Shakespearean individualism and the post-secular

Until very recently, "secular" was a term that would have attracted very little attention. Within the space of just over a decade, however, "secular" and its various cognates have once again become key words, but this time with a new edge. For many intellectuals, the "decline" of religion in the West has increasingly come to be questioned or relativized – that is, it is now felt to be not so much a matter of progress as simply one of change. The secular itself is no longer seen as our natural or authentic state – what John Milbank calls "the perennial destiny of the West," always there "gestating in the womb of Judeo-Christianity" – but simply another way of being in the world.[5] Indeed, the secular, so Milbank feels, is "constituted or *imagined*" every bit as much as the religious understanding of things it is supposed to have superseded. It is not simply a process of stripping away or desacralizing, but one of active construction. The immediate advantage of this insight is that it

[2] Quoted in the entry for Wotton in the *Dictionary of National Biography* (London, 1900), 63:53.

[3] Letter to John Chamberlain, December 14, 1612, in Maurice Lee, Jr. (ed.), *Dudley Carleton to John Chamberlain, 1603–1624: Jacobean Letters* (New Brunswick, NJ: Rutgers University Press, 1972), p. 136. The indiscretion which "much clouded" Wotton's prospects of royal favor was what Izaak Walton called his "pleasant definition" of an ambassador: "An Embassadour is an honest man sent to lie abroad for the good of his country" (quoted in Geoffrey Hill's chapter on Walton and Wotton, "Caveats Enough in their own Walks," in Kenneth Hayes [ed.], *Collected Critical Writings* [Oxford University Press, 2008], p. 215). The king was not amused.

[4] Whether or not Austen ever saw a performance of *Henry VIII* is moot even though Henry Crawford's remarks in *Mansfield Park* are very suggestive: "I once saw Henry the 8th acted – Or I have heard of it from somebody who did – I am not certain which" (p. 335). Austen is quoted from Jane Austen, *Mansfield Park*, ed. Tony Tanner (1814; Harmondsworth: Penguin, 1985).

[5] John Milbank, *Theology and Social Theory: Beyond Secular Reason* (1990; Malden, MA: Blackwell, 2006), quoted from p. 9.

allows us much less restricted access into the contingency and indeed the alterity of sixteenth- and seventeenth-century culture. That culture ceases to be merely "early" modern or just a prelude to the triumph of the secular; it becomes something else. Armed with this insight, the present looks considerably less familiar; and so for thinkers like Milbank, the age in which we now live seems less "postmodern" or "late capitalist" than "post-secular."[6] What is most undesirable about the present from this postsecular perspective is laid out with great force by Charles Taylor, first in such sketches as his 1991 book *The Malaise of Modernity*, and then in his much more ambitious 2007 work *A Secular Age*.[7] The particular malaise of modernity that he considers most problematic is, somewhat ironically, precisely the individualism a literary critic like Harold Bloom and innumerable others would see as the glory of Shakespeare, indeed the characteristic central to the playwright's "invention of the human."[8]

For Bloom, the human is essentially literary: people are truly human only to the extent that like all the great characters of modern literature, from Hamlet to Anna Karenina, they can be said to possess inner selves or personalities, that is, an inward life that develops rather than simply changes. It develops because beings who are truly *human*, whether literary characters or real people, are individuals who possess agency or autonomy in the very specific form of the ability to reflect on and "reconceive themselves" (*Shakespeare*, p. xvii). We could not even imagine ourselves as human, Bloom feels, without the precedent of Shakespearean interiority. Life imitates art. In insisting on individual agency or autonomy as an historical *invention*, however, Bloom has learned from the "French Shakespeare" (p. 9), the cultural materialism or Foucault-inspired new historicism he affects to despise – but only, of course, to attempt its co-optation.[9] His aim is to reassimilate "social invention" or "cultural construction" back into the

6 Besides Milbank, see, for instance, Alain Badiou, *Saint Paul: The Foundation of Essentialism*, trans. Ray Brassier (Stanford University Press, 2003); Terry Eagleton, *Reason, Faith, and Revolution* (New Haven, CT: Yale University Press, 2009); Jurgen Habermas et al., *An Awareness of what is Missing: Faith and Reason in a Post-Secular Age*, trans. Ciaran Cronin (Cambridge: Polity Press, 2010); Feisal G. Mohamed, *Milton and the Post-Secular Present* (Stanford University Press, 2011).

7 Charles Taylor, *The Malaise of Modernity* (Toronto: Anansi, 1991) and *A Secular Age* (Cambridge, MA: Harvard University Press, 2007).

8 Harold Bloom, *Shakespeare: The Invention of the Human* (London: Fourth Estate, 1999).

9 Both the British cultural materialism and the American new historicism of the 1980s were focused on the attempt to demystify the autonomous individual subject, a cultural construct which they felt to be at the heart of modern-day liberal humanist ideology. See, for instance, Stephen Greenblatt, *Renaissance Self-Fashioning: From More to Shakespeare* (University of Chicago Press, 1980); Jonathan Dollimore, *Radical Tragedy: Religion, Ideology and Power in the Drama of Shakespeare and his Contemporaries* (Brighton: Harvester Wheatsheaf, 1984); Catherine Belsey, *The Subject of Tragedy: Identity and Difference in Renaissance Drama* (London: Routledge, 1985).

familiar realm of individual creativity and through Shakespeare to reassert a very old-fashioned conception of Romantic individualism. His heroes, the characters from whom he derives his own much proclaimed, capacious humanity, are Hamlet and Falstaff. Hamlet is especially important because "Hamlet and Western self-consciousness," he feels, "have been the same for about the last two centuries of Romantic sensibility" (p. 420). Life does indeed imitate art, he might insist, but it is our art, our creativity, and like Milton's Satan we know no time, at least not since Shakespeare, when we were not as now, "self-begot" and "self-raised / By our own quickening power" (*Paradise Lost* 5.859–61).[10] Indeed, for Taylor, this is the blind alley of secularism, and Bloom and his heroes exemplify the intractable nature of the secular bounded or "buffered" self (*Secular Age*, p. 37).

For Taylor, Bloom's autonomous subject or unfettered consciousness is anything but free; it is bounded or buffered not because it denies the social invention or cultural construction of human subjectivity, but most importantly and much more tragically because it obscures the experience of religious *transcendence* – that is, it denies access to the "enchanted" world of powers and spirits, the reality outside the frame or prison-house we have constructed through the power of our own unaided human reason (*Secular Age*, p. 38). When discussing Hamlet, Bloom talks much of transcendence, but he doesn't mean the supernatural, the world of spirits, those "wondrous strange" things not dreamt of in Horatio's philosophy; he means the way Shakespeare invents in Hamlet an individual mind able both to define the limits of understanding and at the same time to go beyond them, gesturing towards the modern existentialist conviction that consciousness, even while it stands alone in the universe, is endless in its creativity.[11] This is what really moves us, says Bloom: "we worship (in a secular way) this all-but-infinite consciousness" (*Shakespeare*, p. 421). For Taylor, nothing could better illustrate the idolatry of "the self-sufficiency or exclusive humanism . . . at the heart of secularity" (*Secular Age*, p. 19). From Taylor's religious perspective, Hamlet is, in fact, unusually sensitive to moments of real transcendence, to the "imbrication of secular and higher times" (pp. 861, 58–9), but when he asks the existentialist question for which he is best

[10] Milton's poetry is quoted from *John Milton: The Major Works*, Oxford World Classics, ed. Stephen Orgel and Jonathan Goldberg (1991; Oxford University Press, 2008); hereafter references to *Paradise Lost* are cited in the text as *PL*.

[11] Both Bloom and Stephen Greenblatt, the antagonist Bloom seems reluctant to name, are deeply rooted in the popular existentialism of the 1940s and 1950s: see Paul Stevens, "Pretending to be Real: Stephen Greenblatt and the Legacy of Popular Existentialism," *New Literary History*, 33 (2002), 491–519.

remembered – "To be, or not to be" – he arrogates to himself the kind of authority that denies him access to the *fullness* of any reality outside that constructed by his own powers of reason. This is certainly how Milton, one of Shakespeare's most astute readers, interprets Hamlet in *Paradise Lost*. In Shakespeare's play, Hamlet reviles conscience or consciousness for inhibiting action: "Thus conscience makes cowards of us all, / And thus the native hue of resolution / Is sicklied o'er with the pale cast of thought" (3.1.84–6).[12] In Milton's poem, however, these lines are recalibrated to suggest how, in the case of Adam, the ability of Hamlet's consciousness or the overactive cast of thought to inhibit action is less important than its capacity to deny him access to the evidence of things not seen and the freedom of God's grace. The newly fallen Adam is more than willing to "take arms against a sea of troubles" (3.1.59) – he already finds himself in "a troubled sea of passion" (*PL* 10.718) – but as he exercises his formidable forensic skills he can find no assurance of things hoped for: "O conscience, into what abyss of fears / And horrors hast thou driven me; out of which / I find no way, from deep to deeper plunged!" (*PL* 10.842–4). Only with prevenient grace, only with Eve's memory of God's word, his curse on the serpent remembered as a promise, do our first parents find a way out of what Taylor would call their disenchanted state.[13] By casting Adam as Hamlet, Milton does a number of things: first, he anticipates Taylor's conviction that the unaided reason of the bounded self denies us faith, and second, in doing this, he exploits what many, even in the seventeenth century, would consider an emphatically secular text for a religious purpose.

For both Bloom and Taylor, a Shakespearean play like *Hamlet* (1601) stands at the fulcrum of the West's turn to the secular; it allows them to construct grand narratives in which the one idealizes what the other laments. A later, much less well-known play like *Henry VIII* (1613), however, confuses the issue – it has no place in Taylor's scheme and Bloom quite explicitly finds it a "puzzle" he cannot solve (*Shakespeare*, p. 691). While the play in its oddness, in its characters' relative lack of inwardness, its emphasis on ceremony, and its disappointingly episodic structure, complicates both their master narratives, it also encourages us to think about things other than individualism. From a more expansive post-secular perspective, specifically one less focused on the problems of individualism, the play, in a way

[12] *Hamlet* is quoted from William Shakespeare, *The Tragedy of Hamlet, Prince of Denmark*, ed. Edward Hubler, Signet Classic Shakespeare (New York: New American Library, 1963).

[13] For more on this, see Paul Stevens, *Imagination and the Presence of Shakespeare in "Paradise Lost"* (Madison: University of Wisconsin Press, 1985), pp. 227–8.

that might surprise Taylor, comes alive – its central religious concerns are dramatically thrown into relief. In order to develop this line of thought, I want to make three principal points: first, that the creators of the play (especially Fletcher, I suspect) want to do something more than entertain their audience, something more than simply aestheticize the accidents or outward shows of religion for pleasure and profit; second and most importantly, that in doing so, as their redaction of English Reformation history seeks to articulate what Holinshed calls the "grace" of truth, their play often seems to be responding to the form and pressure of the Church of England's liturgy, reversing the usual practice of the commercial theater exploiting religion and actually seeking what the Book of Common Prayer calls a "Godly unity"; third and finally, that this in turn suggests why *Henry VIII* and Jane Austen's *Mansfield Park* stand in such a mutually illuminating relationship about what it means to be human. Let me return to *Hamlet* and begin my argument with what many consider to be the relentlessly secularizing power of theatrical performance.

## *Hamlet* and the limits of irrepressible performance

In a major essay ultimately consonant with the grand narratives of Bloom and Taylor, Tony Dawson switches the emphasis from individual to social invention and so presents the case for the secularity of Shakespeare and the commercial theater with renewed force.[14] While fully acknowledging the quality of the scholarship evident in Shakespeare studies' recent turn to religion, Dawson feels it to be fundamentally misconceived. Central to his argument is a vision of the early modern theater as an increasingly autonomous institution with its own protocols and practices. It is above all a commercial venture, secular and secularizing, relentlessly turning all it touches, "the rags and bones of culture," to its own independent, institutional purpose ("Shakespeare and Secular Performance," p. 86) – you paid your penny and entered a space not dedicated to religion or the worship of God but to pleasure or entertainment: a domain that was predominantly "aesthetic and affective" (p. 85). Not only was its purpose secular, but more importantly in *performance*, its principal mode of communication, it was irredeemably alien to all authoritative discourse, not least the sacred discourse of religion – for the truth is that no authoritative discourse could withstand the essentially unstable dialogism of theatrical performance, the

[14] Anthony B. Dawson, "Shakespeare and Secular Performance," in Patricia Badir and Paul Yachnin (eds.), *Shakespeare and the Cultures of Performance* (Farnham: Ashgate, 2007), pp. 83–97.

constant play of competing and contradictory voices, the ever present possibility of parody or ridicule. No matter how the words were written down, no one could predict or control how they might be performed. In this particular vision of the theater, Dawson deepens the perspectives of Bloom and Taylor, because for him the volatility of performance so feared in the Queen's 1559 proclamation, the unpredictability of the theater's capacity for social invention, is not an alternative to but very much a function of the individualism that preoccupies Bloom and Taylor. Indeed, for Dawson, performance and the new religion of Protestantism appear as interrelated manifestations of the same revolutionary emphasis on the individual's thoughts and experiences. Following John C. Sommerville, he argues that Protestantism itself, in its individualism, in the way it effects a radical transformation from "religious culture" to "religious faith," is most usefully understood as another, analogous secularizing movement: it is in fact, in Sommerville's phrase, a "secularizing religion" ("Shakespeare and Secular Performance," p. 86).[15] As Protestantism breaks consensus and privatizes the individual's relation with God, so, the implication is, the commercial theater, to the extent that it is religious at all, breaks with doctrine and produces its own multiple, *ersatz* forms of religion. The epiphanic moments it offers are real but not other-worldly: its moments of "sweaty transcendence" are truly uplifting but ultimately "temporary and provisional" (p. 87); they are matters of artifice, the stuff that dreams are made on.

Dawson's characterization of Protestantism as a "secularizing religion" is highly problematic; even with some chronological "modification" (p. 87), it is a paradox that any sixteenth- or seventeenth-century Protestant of whatever persuasion would have found incomprehensible. The distinctions between culture and faith, community and individual, are too imprecise to capture the complexity or extraordinary force of reformed religion – reliance on these distinctions, in its presentist telescoping or reduction of the past into the same grand narrative of individualism imagined by Bloom and Taylor, obscures the revolutionary alterity of historic Protestantism. To be specific, because of its preoccupation with individualism, Sommerville's thesis does violence to the reformers' profoundly other-worldly emphasis on the freedom of God and to so many ordinary people's renewed sense of his immediate presence in the world. That that presence was not magical, fantastical, or "wondrous strange," but the active work of grace, that it

[15] See John C. Sommerville, *The Secularization of Early Modern England: From Religious Culture to Religious Faith* (Oxford University Press, 1992), p. 8.

might be made known through Scripture, whether read by the individual in private or heard by the community in public worship, and through an increasing array of other media all intended to retell Scripture's truly wondrous story of Christ's death and impossible resurrection, hardly makes Protestantism secular or secularizing. Indeed, it suggests that early modern English audiences, all of whose members were familiar to some degree or other with the divine service of the Church of England, might have felt that theatrical transcendence was not always as this-worldly, temporary, and provisional as Dawson contends. An avid playgoer like young Milton, for instance, was explicit on this point. Growing up in a godly household that was musical and theatrical, his father a trustee of the Blackfriars playhouse, the young poet recorded his sense of what the theater could do in his 1632 poem introducing the second folio of Shakespeare's works, "On Shakespeare." Exactly like divine Contemplation or "holy passion" in "Il Penseroso," Shakespeare, so Milton claimed, had the power to astonish us; that is, even while simply being read his plays had the power to produce a kind of religious ecstasy, to enable us to transcend the this-worldly and make us "marble with too much conceiving" (line 14).[16] When one considers the larger traditions of English religious drama, the immediate success of his own Ludlow *Maske*, the didactic design of the early Reformation theater of Foxe and Bale, or the popularity of biblical plays in the commercial theater well into the early seventeenth century, Milton may not be as exceptional or as unrepresentative an indicator of what early modern audiences felt or wanted as is usually claimed.[17] None of this, it might be argued, seriously disrupts Dawson's central point about the instability of theatrical performance, but even here there is room for serious qualification.

Dawson is particularly convincing in showing how secular a play *Hamlet* is, especially in the way it resists the implications of its own religious allusions. The play may be "rife with religious reference" ("Shakespeare and Secular Performance," p. 90), he says, but none of it adds up to a coherent exposition of Christian doctrine. The Prince's increasing "religious calm" (p. 90), for instance his pointed allusion to the Gospel's declaration that there is "special providence in the fall of a sparrow" (5.2.220–1), is not quite

[16] This point is developed in Paul Stevens, "Subversion and Wonder in Milton's Epitaph on Shakespeare," *ELR*, 19 (1989), 375–88; it is followed up in Charles Whitney, *Early Responses to Renaissance Drama* (Cambridge University Press, 2006), esp. pp. 256–70, and Aaron Kunin, "Shakespeare's Preservation Fantasy," *PMLA*, 124 (2009), 92–106.

[17] On the persistence of religious drama into the seventeenth century, see Beatrice Groves, *Texts and Traditions: Religion in Shakespeare, 1592–1604* (Oxford: Clarendon Press, 2006), pp. 10–25.

what it appears to be. In the Gospel itself, in the fuller context of Matthew 10, Christ's words offer a remarkable insight into the terrifying otherness of God's presence in the world; the demands that Christ places on his disciples argue anything but calm. Yes, no sparrow will fall without God knowing it (Matthew 10:29), but Christ's disciples are offered this particular reassurance, first, somewhat ironically – "Fear ye not therefore, ye are of more value than many sparrows," if not all (10:31) – and, then, only in the context of Christ's demand that they take up arms against the rotten state of the everyday world: "Think not," he admonishes them, that "I am come to send peace on earth: I came not to send peace, but a sword. For I am come to set a man at variance against his father, and the daughter against her mother," and you, the agents of my word, "shall be hated of all men for my name's sake" (10:34–6, 22). If the overall action of the play seems to parody and distort Matthew 10 – perhaps most strikingly in the way the appearance of the ghost caricatures Christ's declaration to his disciples that "the spirit of the Father speaketh in you" (10:20) – Hamlet's allusion in the final act goes further, reducing the Gospel's sense of transcendence to a stoic commonplace on the inevitability of death, one whose primary function is dramatic or aesthetic. His words are meant to set up the climax of the play's bloody ending: "if it be now, 'tis not to come; if it be not to come, it will be now; if it be not now, yet it will come. The readiness is all" (5.2.221–4). Hamlet's words here ignore the divisiveness of Christ's fervor and bring the audience together, so Dawson feels, as a harmonious community "under the idea of a special design that affects us all equally" (p. 91). Like Hamlet, the audience readies itself for the end, but in their reduction of Scripture, what Shakespeare's words tell even the most religious members of the audience is that the play's special design is not God's but the playwright's. This is a persuasive argument – it does much to explain Bloom's sense that Hamlet's reaction to providence is ultimately one of indifference or "disinterestedness" (*Shakespeare*, p. 429). But in highlighting the secular direction of the tragedy, it needs to be emphasized, Dawson also makes it clear that the play's text is not entirely at the mercy of its performance. The words matter: they have considerable power in controlling the stability of the performance, and this is not merely a case of orchestrating competing voices. The point is, of course, that the play's text has the capacity to tell both its audience and its actors, to a greater or lesser extent, how the play is to be performed and experienced. As Dawson's own argument implies, as it effectively sacrifices its fundamental premise for a much less important gain, the secularity of *Hamlet* is not simply a matter of irrepressible performance, but of textual design, of Shakespeare's cunningly directed, articulate energy. In this, Dawson's Shakespeare begins to look a lot like Shakespeare's own fictional playwright-cum-producer, Hamlet.

In producing *The Murder of Gonzago*, the Prince has very clear ideas on how it is to be performed and what effect he wants to achieve. In order to catch the conscience of the King, to show him the exact "form and pressure" of his crime (3.2.25), he wants to reduce the contingency of performance to a minimum. He wants the players to speak and comport their bodies according to specific guidelines: "Speak the speech, I pray you, as I pronounced it to you," do not "saw the air too much with your hand," and do not tear "a passion to tatters" or out-herod Herod. There should be a precise consonance between text and performance: "Suit the action to the word, the word to the action" (3.2.1–15). Above all, the players are not to extemporize in such a way that they prejudice some truth or "necessary question of the play" the playwright might want to be considered (3.2.40–5). These questions or issues of the play are crucial for Hamlet. He idealizes the kind of play that might seem like "caviary to the general" (2.2.447), too choice for the general public, but need not be. He remembers a dramatization of *Aeneid* 2, which he and others "whose judgments in such matters cried o'er the top of mine" (2.2.448–9) thought excellent, "well digested in the scenes, set down with as much modesty as cunning" (2.2.449–51). The cunning and paradoxically well-tempered representation of the atrocity of Priam's murder is likely to provoke a particular reaction. This example of a well-directed play substantiates Hamlet's memory that "guilty creatures sitting at a play / Have by the very cunning of the scene / Been struck so to the soul that presently / They have proclaimed their malefactions" (2.2.601–4). In this kind of work, the play's mimetic and aesthetic dimensions are entirely subordinate to its pragmatic end – it works like a speech act, an authoritative discourse designed to effect specific ends. Here, in *The Murder of Gonzago*, those ends are political and moral, but in another play they might just as well be religious. And in *Henry VIII*, so I want to suggest, that is what Shakespeare and his collaborator, John Fletcher, set out to do. In a period that witnessed the sudden death of England's hope in Prince Henry (November 1612) and its renewal in the marriage of Princess Elizabeth (February 1613), between what Sir Henry Wotton calls "our griefs and our jollities,"[18] they set out to produce a play in the commercial theater that had something of the force of liturgy, an act of praise emerging out of the flux of English history in which members of the audience might cease to be individuals and be brought together in a godly unity to experience the

[18] Letter to Dudley Carleton, February 25, 1613, Pearsall Smith, *Life*, vol. II, p. 14.

presence of God's grace in the history of their national community. While the political or nationalist dimension of this move is not unfamiliar, the distinctiveness of its religious orientation continues to remain elusive.[19]

## *Henry VIII* and the grace of truth

The critical consensus since the middle of the nineteenth century has been that *Henry VIII* is the collaborative work of Shakespeare and Fletcher.[20] For many, the play witnesses a generational shift in the life of Shakespeare's company, for after 1613, as Gordon McMullan suggests, "Fletcher seems to have settled into Shakespeare's role as chief playwright of the King's company."[21] In their prologue the elder and younger writers speak as one, but, of more importance for the present argument, they seem unusually anxious about the play's reception. Like Hamlet with *The Murder of Gonzago*, they clearly want a particular effect. They want to control expectations and reduce the contingency of performance. Accordingly their prologue offers the audience specific instructions, insisting that this *Henry VIII* will not be like Samuel Rowley's earlier version of the king's reign, *When You See Me* (1604).[22] If you come to "hear a merry, bawdy play," the prologue admonishes its audience, "A noise of targets, or to see a fellow / In a long motley coat guarded with yellow," you will be disappointed (prologue 14–16). This play is "weighty," "serious," and "sad," designed to arouse "pity" – working such "noble scenes as draw the eye to flow" (1–7). Most importantly, clownish improvisation will not be allowed to prejudice "our chosen truth," for we would not forfeit either "our brains" or our reputation for truth-telling (17–20). A little earlier, as if speaking directly to Dawson, the prologue insists that the purpose of the commercial theater is not exclusively aesthetic or affective – it is not simply about make-believe, producing spectacle or arousing pity, but may bring the audience to a knowledge of the truth – "Such as give / Their money out of hope they

[19] On the play's nationalism, see Annabel Patterson, "'All is true': Negotiating the Past in *Henry VIII*," in R. B. Parker and S. P. Zitner (eds.), *Elizabethan Theater: Essays in Honor of S. Schoenbaum* (Newark, DE: University of Delaware Press, 1996), pp. 147–66.

[20] *Henry VIII* is quoted from William Shakespeare, *King Henry VIII, or All is True*, ed. Jay L. Halio (Oxford University Press, 2000). For the collaboration debate, see Gordon McMullan (ed.), *King Henry VIII (All is True)*, Arden Shakespeare (London: Bloomsbury, 2000), esp. pp. 180–99, and Halio (ed.), *King Henry VIII*, pp. 16–24.

[21] Gordon McMullan, "John Fletcher (1579–1625)," *Oxford Dictionary of National Biography* (www.oxforddnb.com).

[22] In his *Narrative and Dramatic Sources of Shakespeare*, vol. IV (New York: Columbia University Press, 1962), pp. 437–51, Geoffrey Bullough is illuminating on the relation between the two plays.

may believe, / May here find truth, too" (7–9). Hence the play's emphatic subtitle, *All is True*. While the play aspires to the status of an authoritative discourse, what specific truth the prologue has in mind is not immediately clear. It first focuses on truth as mimetic verisimilitude. Like the prologue in Shakespeare's *Henry V*, it first claims to offer an accurate account of English history; it offers to bring England's noble dead back to life: "Think ye see / The very persons of our noble story / As they were living; think you see them great / And followed with the general throng and sweat / Of thousand friends" (25–9). In a celebrated passage from *Pierce Penniless* (1592), Thomas Nashe explains the value of this kind of theatrical resurrection, what Dawson calls the theater's "sweaty transcendence." Especially in those plays "borrowed out of our English Chronicles," says Nashe, "our forefathers' valiant acts, that have long lain buried in rusty brass and worm-eaten books, are revived" and our forefathers themselves are "raised from the grave of oblivion, and brought to plead their aged honours in open presence." The resurrection may be feigned, but it is extraordinarily effective in promoting heroic virtue: what more than this, he asks, could serve as "a sharper reproof to these degenerate effeminate days of ours."[23] In *Henry VIII*, however, the prologue ups the ante and implies that this kind of theatrical transcendence might articulate a truth deeper and more other-worldly than national valor. Most immediately, it points to the contingency of all "earthly glory" (1.1.14): think you see the very persons of our noble story in all their greatness and "then," the prologue insists, "in a moment, see / How soon this mightiness meets misery" (prologue 29–30). But as the play proceeds, so its engagement with the complexity of this truth intensifies and the contentious historical matter of the King's reign is ordered, reduced through the play's stylized repetitions to suggest an overarching pattern of falling from power, coming to grace, and knowing God's truth.

## *Mightiness meeting misery*

Although he feels defeated by the strangeness of *Henry VIII*, Bloom is acute in recognizing how "remarkably unified" the play is (*Shakespeare*, p. 685). It comprises four distinct but interrelated narratives of mightiness meeting misery, those of Buckingham, Queen Katherine, Wolsey, and Cranmer – four "heraldic pictures with beautiful voices," says Bloom (p. 685). As each one ends so the next begins. It is through these narratives that the primary

[23] Quoted from Thomas Nashe, *The Unfortunate Traveller and Other Works*, ed. J. B. Steane (Harmondsworth: Penguin, 1971), pp. 112–13.

but curiously unforegrounded story of Henry and Anne Boleyn is presented. What Bloom finds most disappointing about these speaking pictures is that none of their central characters is "endowed with any inwardness" (pp. 685–6); none of them reveal the kind of self-reflexive interiority or internal development that he considers essential to the invention of the human. The narrative sequencing of events is "processional," and the overall impact of the play is alien and premodern – it marks "a reversion," he says, "to pre-Shakespearean theater" (p. 686). Bloom's response is striking not so much because he exaggerates the characters' lack of inwardness but because he shows so little interest in what may well have been much more important for the members of an early seventeenth-century audience – that is, the sustaining presence of God's grace in the story of its country, even in the scandalous story of Henry VIII and his second wife. For each of the four heavily stylized narratives that constitute the play is emphatic in describing the limits of human agency and repeating a climactic, often surprising act of grace. All four narratives are stories, however imperfect, of the key characters learning the kind of patience that will enable them to perform forgiveness and reconciliation. Against the worldly noise of bewilderingly contingent history, of rumor, slander, and misinformation, far from rendering "greatness very familiar, if not ridiculous," as Wotton contends, the play clearly labors to see a design and articulate a rhythm. Unlike *Hamlet*, the implications of the play's biblical allusions are not ironized but carefully deployed to mark out the force of a truth beyond human agency.

In the opening story, Buckingham's angry determination to expose the corruption of Wolsey, the drama of his imminent struggle with the "venom-mouthed" Cardinal (1.1.120), is suddenly cut short; he is rendered powerless, and the emphasis falls on the patience and consequent grace with which he struggles to accept the injustice of his arrest and conviction for treason. This *agon* is now made to seem more important than the original one of contesting the Cardinal's arbitrary rule. On his arrest, in a way that a modern audience might find wooden or frustrating, Buckingham immediately submits: "The will of heav'n / Be done in this and all things," he says, "I obey" (1.1.209–10). Scripture speaks through him, and his quotation from Matthew 6:10, "Thy will be done in earth, as it is in heaven," alludes to the Lord's Prayer at the beginning of the Book of Common Prayer. It is then almost immediately echoed by his son-in-law Abergavenny as if his refrain were a response from the Litany: "The will of heaven be done and the King's pleasure / By me obeyed" (1.1.215–16). In Buckingham's final speech there are moments when the memory of the liturgy continues to reassert itself and the Duke loses his identity in that of the psalmist: invoking Psalm 141:2, "Let my prayer be set before thee as incense; and the lifting up of my hands as the evening sacrifice," he urges his friends to "Make of your prayers one sweet sacrifice / And lift my soul to heaven" (2.1.78–9). It is made clear in the report of the Duke's trial that this continued piety has not come easily. The gentlemen who report the trial and who constitute a projection of the play's imagined audience are intensely concerned that he should succeed and behave with grace: for a moment he spoke in "choler, ill and hasty," says one of the gentlemen, but then to everyone's relief "he fell to himself again and sweetly / In all the rest showed a most noble patience" (2.1.35–7). Finally, he forgives all – his custodians, his enemies, and most importantly his hasty and, at this stage of the play, pitiless King: "May he live / Longer than I have time to tell his years; / Ever beloved and loving may his rule be" (2.1.91–3). Buckingham's gracious end is far from perfect – his final speech still contains "too many curses" (2.1.138) for the liking of the first gentleman – but it is paradigmatic: it substantiates the Duke's nobility, offers aid and comfort to the King's peace, and it suggests the degree to which patience is both a cause and consequence of grace. Echoing so many scriptural fragments from the Book of Common Prayer and especially its companion publication, the Psalter, Buckingham's end exemplifies what Queen Katherine will later idealize as a good death (4.1.9–11).[24] And it is these good deaths that punctuate the processional progress of the performance, unfolding what the play's key source, Holinshed, calls "the grace of truth."[25]

## *The grace of truth*

This phrase is more significant than it sounds. Not only does it imply the capacity of truth to provide a surplus of good will, to bring peace and reconciliation to the kingdom, but much more radically it acknowledges God's freedom: it suggests that truth is not within our unaided power to possess – that it is, in fact, a matter of grace, the gift of God. We cannot know truth without his intervention and, as the continual echoing of the Psalms suggest, this is precisely the understanding that all the fallen finally come to recognize. Faced with execution, Buckingham reflects on his fate: "When I came hither I was Lord High Constable / And Duke of Buckingham – now,

[24] For the relation between the BCP and the Psalter, see Brian Cummings (ed.), *The Book of Common Prayer: The Texts of 1549, 1559, and 1662* (Oxford University Press, 2011), pp. 783–5. Quotations from the BCP are taken from this edition.

[25] Holinshed's *Chronicles* are quoted from vol. IV of Bullough's *Sources of Shakespeare*; here from vol. IV, p. 463.

poor Edward Bohun. / Yet I am richer than my base accusers, / That never knew what truth meant" (2.1.103–6). Stripped of "such furniture as suits / The greatness of his person" (2.1.100–1), the truth he will now seal with his blood is not simply his continued loyalty to the King but this knowledge of his nakedness or powerlessness in the world. The treachery of his servants and tragic history of his family is incomprehensible, and yet, he says, bringing a commonplace to life, "Heaven has an end in all" (2.1.125). When false friends "fall away / Like water from ye" (2.1.130–1), his lament only confirms God's agency and the efficacy of the psalmist's prayer: let the wicked "melt away as waters which run continually" (Psalm 58:7). The recurrent echoing of the Psalms clearly has a purpose. Wolsey, for all his wickedness, is made to articulate the same kind of truth in a similar way. Having inexplicably recovered a "still and quiet conscience," with only his robe and "integrity to heaven" to call his own, his most famous lines are made to answer the psalmist's prayer, "Cast me not away in time of age" (Psalm 71:9): "Had I served my God with half the zeal / I served my King, He would not in mine age / Have left me naked to my enemies" (3.2.381, 453–8). While Cranmer at the height of his ordeal, like Buckingham and Wolsey, is stripped of his dignity and made "but a private man again" (5.2.89), the nakedness of Queen Katherine is evident in the way her trial is made to imitate the suffering of Job. She stands before the King "a most poor woman" and demands of him, "In what have I offended you" that you should "take your good grace from me?" (2.4.13, 16–20). Like Job, she is a servant without blemish, "lost among ye, laughed at, scorned" (3.1.106), but at the height of her persecution by her "counselors," Wolsey and Cardinal Campeius, at the height of their attempt to persuade her to deny the truth and acknowledge the incestuous, illegal nature of her marriage to the King, she remains immovable and remembers Psalm 7:8, "The Lord shall judge the people," and, even more poignantly, Job 19:25, "I know my redeemer liveth": "Is this your Christian counsel?" Katherine demands of her self-styled friends, "Out upon ye! / Heaven is above all yet; there sits a judge," a vindicator, that "no king can corrupt" (3.1.98–100). The insistent presence of the Psalms in the play seems to suggest that history is only there to illustrate Scripture. And Scripture is there throughout the play.

The most difficult part of England's chronicle history the play struggles to represent in terms of God's truth, perhaps not entirely successfully, is the King's motivation in precipitating his tragic divorce from Queen Katherine.[26] The problem English Protestants have to deal with is that

[26] For more on *Henry VIII*'s depiction of Henry's motives for divorcing Katherine, see Chapter 13 below.

the immediate occasion of the Church of England's Reformation is the relationship between Henry and Anne Boleyn. If the play's four stories of "mightiness meeting misery" focus on the limits of human agency, then the central story of Henry and Anne reveals the unlimited, intensely active power of God's agency, that is, the sheer force by which his grace moves in mysterious ways, utterly indifferent to human plans and designs. The play allows the world's cynical view of their relationship full scope. Slander flourishes (2.1.153–4); malice in the form of Wolsey, so rumor tells us, possesses the King "with a scruple" (2.1.156–8); and the pricking of the King's conscience, so Suffolk claims, is entirely a matter of sexual desire: it's not so much that "marriage with his brother's wife / Has crept too near his conscience," he tells us, but that his conscience has "crept too near another lady" (2.2.15–17). Even the King himself keeps confusing his tender conscience with tender bedfellows (2.2.140–3). This worldly view is exacerbated by the way the play alters its source in Holinshed and has Henry meet Anne before the divorce proceedings begin. But there is a countervailing narrative which, far from denying the sexuality of the King's desire, struggles to transume it. Against this cloud of unfaithful witnesses, the play insists on Anne's innocence. Anne's cynical and salacious fellow lady-in-waiting, the old Lady, inadvertently identifies Anne's virtue with that of the Queen: Anne is corrupt, she claims, because every "woman's heart" is venal, drawn to "eminence, wealth," and "sovereignty" (2.3.28–9). But the example of the Queen gives the lie to this self-serving generalization and intimates that in Anne's feelings for the Queen and contempt for the old Lady she may be made of sterner stuff, indeed the same stuff as the Queen: "Good Lady," she says to her venom-mouthed companion, "Make yourself mirth with your particular fancy," but "leave me out on't" (2.3.101–3). In her compassion and modesty, her "beauty and honour," however tragic and confused the historical circumstances, Anne is made to appear a fitting successor to Katherine – "a gem / To lighten all this isle" (2.3.75–9). Similarly, highly sexualized as the context of the King's conversion narrative remains, nothing quite prepares us for its force.

As Henry tells the story, his conversion originates in the marriage negotiations for his daughter Mary, a conversation which appears to predate his meeting with Anne. It overtakes him like a tempest: it "shook / The bosom of my conscience, entered me, / Yea, with a spitting power, and made to tremble / The region of my breast" (2.4.178–81). The language is that of *spiritus*, the breath of God, the central metaphor of Scripture from the divine wind of Genesis (1:2) to the "rushing mighty wind" of the Pentecost (Acts 2:2). In the play, it is the same tempest that sweeps away the earthly glory of the Field of Cloth of Gold, the "hideous storm" that shreds the false "garment of this peace" (1.1.89–94). If the King's very real desire for Anne is not denied, it appears to be co-opted and made merely a part of God's design. The King begins his narrative by offering to defend Wolsey against the rumor accepted as fact by the Queen that he had initiated and encouraged the divorce. The King would justify him – "will you be further justified" (2.4.159)? In this, the King touches on one of the most sensitive terms of the Reformation. Justification by faith alone means that in justifying God or believing in his justice, we justify ourselves.[27] So here, in denying the world's truth and offering Wolsey the "grace of truth," the King's confessional speech act seems designed to realize the descent of grace it describes. As in any classic Protestant conversion narrative, the King is moved by the Word, the breath of God unexpectedly manifesting itself in the very human words of the Bishop of Bayonne, for the Bishop's suspicion that Henry had married "our brother's wife" (2.4.178) raises the horror of Leviticus 20:21: "And if a man shall take his brother's wife, it is an unclean thing: he hath uncovered his brother's nakedness; they shall be childless." Overwhelmed by the tempest which these words constitute, the King suddenly comes to understand the reason for his lack of a male heir, to see a truth whose "sharp thorny points" (2.4.221) make him "reek" under their oppression; they overrule his will and so drive the play's re-presentation of English history forward to its climax.

### *God shall be truly known*

There is, of course, no way of being absolutely sure of either Anne's innocence or the King's integrity – it requires some kind of faith, specifically the suspension of disbelief that the play's ending encourages its audience to make. The play's ending, the longed-for birth and baptism of a child, England's "sacred" Queen Elizabeth, throws everything else into perspective. "Let me speak, sir," says Cranmer, "For heaven now bids me, and the words I utter / Let none think flattery, for they'll find 'em truth" (5.4.14–16). They will find them "truth" because Cranmer's future is the audience's present and in the festival mood of early 1613 London, England's present peace and prosperity is meant to confirm the substance of the Archbishop's act of faith. Out of so many stories of mightiness meeting misery there

[27] See the insightful analysis in Brian Cummings, *The Literary Culture of the Reformation: Grammar and Grace* (2002; Oxford University Press, 2007), esp. pp. 88–101. See also his *Mortal Thoughts: Religion, Secularity, and Identity in Shakespeare and Early Modern Culture* (Oxford University Press, 2013).

emerges a design, the play's "chosen truth" (prologue 18). Out of England's troubled past, the King's great matter and the sexually ambiguous nature of his conversion, the divorce and the Job-like suffering of the old Queen, comes regeneration – a new queen, one whose fruitful promise is realized in the greater glory of her daughter, the future Queen Elizabeth and in Elizabeth's own "star-like" male successor, the present king. Henry VIII finally has his son. "God shall be truly known" (5.4.35), says Cranmer, and known in the providential history of the nation, because in the root of Anne, in the maturing of the Elizabethan settlement, England has come to realize the peace and prosperity of the Davidic kingdom, the biblical age so idealized by the Church of England's early seventeenth-century divines from Hooker to Lancelot Andrewes – those divines who will eventually come to be seen as the creators of a specifically "Anglican" church, divines whom Joseph Hall calls the "wonder of the world" as he addressed the *flos cleri Anglicani* at St. Paul's in 1624.[28] It is Protestant England as this first United Kingdom, the realm of David and Solomon, that the play is celebrating, not the militant or apocalyptic radicalism of those who still restlessly seek, in Hooker's derisory words, to further "the Lord's discipline."[29] Queen Elizabeth fulfills the promise of 1 Kings 4:25, "And Judah and Israel dwelt safely, every man under his vine and under his fig tree, from Dan even to Beer-sheba, all the days of Solomon," for "In her days every man shall eat in safety / Under his own vine what he plants and sing / The merry songs of peace to all his neighbours" (5.4.32–5). Similarly, King James fulfills the promise of Psalm 92:11–12, "The righteous shall flourish like the palm tree: he shall grow like a cedar in Lebanon. Those that are planted in the house of the Lord shall flourish in the courts of God," for the King "shall flourish / And like a mountain cedar reach his branches / To all the plains about him." The present audience, the audience of 1613, our "children's children," shall "see this and bless heaven" (5.4.52–5). It is too easy to overemphasize the political and dismiss all this as the flattery Cranmer fears it might be taken for – mere performance or *ersatz* religion in the service of royal propaganda. It is too easy because what the ending strives to throw into relief more than anything else is not the human agency of great princes or even heroic individuals but a universal truth, in this case God's

[28] Hall is quoted from Patrick Collinson, *The Religion of Protestants: The Church in English Society, 1559–1625* (Oxford: Clarendon Press, 1982), p. 92. On the Davidic kingdom, see Achsah Guibbory, *Christian Identity, Jews and Israel in Seventeenth-Century England* (Oxford University Press, 2010), pp. 60–82.

[29] Hooker's *Laws of Ecclesiastical Polity* is quoted from *The Folger Library Edition of the Works of Richard Hooker*, ed. W. Speed Hill, 7 vols. (Cambridge, MA: Harvard University Press, 1977–98), vol. 1, p. 2.

freedom in the form of grace shaping and sustaining the fate of the community.

All the principal characters, whether Catholic queens or Protestant martyrs, come to show grace in the very specific form of peace and reconciliation – in patience, humility, and emphatically against their will. The glory of monarchy itself is entirely dependent on the grace of truth not being withdrawn from it – otherwise it is doomed to turn into the vanity of the Field of the Cloth of Gold. For this reason, the King's historical desire for Anne is represented as a story of prevenient grace, and his closing rescue of Cranmer is figured as an act of royal subjection: "if a prince / May be beholden to a subject," Henry confesses, "I / Am for his love and service so to him" (5.2.189–91). That is, out of his love I have become a subject to my servant. Monarchy is justified as a conduit or function of grace. It is this recurrent abnegation of independent human understanding and agency that appears so disappointing and alien to Bloom and his sense of what it means to be human. As the play's epilogue suggests, the example of the saintly Queen Katherine is especially important in establishing its centrality. When she comes to her end, she appears for a moment like Hamlet determined to set it down and remember Wolsey's unspeakable guilt, his "unbounded stomach" (4.2.34). But checked by her lowly servant, her "honest chronicler," Griffiths, she comes to acknowledge the cardinal's virtues and so bless her enemy: "Whom I most hated living, thou hast made me, / With thy religious truth and modesty, / Now in his ashes, honour. Peace be with him" (4.2.72–5). And then, ironically invoking Patience, the virtue as much as her actual lady-in-waiting, she says, "Patience, be near me still and set me lower" (4.2.76). It is out of this example of abnegation or stillness, of humility or being set lower, that the playwrights seem to imagine that their ceremonial history will succeed: if the good women in the audience will show pity, imitate the grace or "merciful construction" of the Queen (epilogue 10), then so will all "the best men" (13) and with that the play will have its desired effect. It is ultimately out of this God-given surplus that the "wonders" (5.4.55) of both Cranmer's prophecy and the play itself will be realized. However anticlimactic and weak the metatheatrical epilogue is, the play itself is not. And it is the seriousness with which it strives to reorder and so transcend what Alain Badiou would call the "facticity" of history, the intractable contingency of this history in particular, that makes the difference.[30]

[30] Badiou, *Saint Paul*, p. 45.

It is as if the play were rerooting the theater's secular exploitation of the Christian doctrine of grace, so evident in Shakespeare's late romances, back into a religious understanding of the recent past. Who would have thought that out of so many stories of confusion and failure, there should emerge such peace and prosperity? History is made to transform the credulity of fictional characters like *The Tempest*'s Gonzalo into something substantial by showing how the relation between past and present confirms the efficacy of faith, providing a very real "assurance of things hoped for" (Hebrews 11:1). In this, it argues for the presence of God in the world; it offers a perception of transcendence, the whole action of the play turning on a sense of the universe being, in Charles Taylor's terms, "porous" or open to the divine. In this sacralizing drama, this specifically proto-Anglican play, that openness, it needs to be emphasized, is not imagined in terms of magic or Taylor's "enchantment" but in terms of Scripture, and Scripture often inflected through memories of the liturgy. Liturgy is as important as it is because even for so many Protestants committed to the principle of *sola scriptura*, "spiritual life," as Brian Cummings suggests, still needs to "find an expression in bodily performance" (*Common Prayer*, p. 750). That is, the liturgy enables the believer to perform his or her relation to the transcendence of the Word in Communion or as part of a public community.[31] The sacraments celebrated in the liturgy, says Hooker, are "heavenlie ceremonies" ordained as outward shows or "markes whereby to knowe when God doth imparte the vitall or saving grace of Christ."[32] *Henry VIII* is as much Shakespeare's play as Fletcher's, but the critical influence in its liturgical turn may well have been that of the late Bishop of London's son.

## The coronation of Queen Anne and the liturgy of the Prayer Book

John Fletcher was born into a distinguished ecclesiastical family, his grandfather Richard becoming Vicar of Cranbrook in Kent in 1561, and his father (also Richard) rising to much greater eminence as the Bishop of London in January 1595.[33] Over the course of the later sixteenth century the careers of

[31] On the relation between ceremony and community, see Achsah Guibbory, *Ceremony and Community from Herbert to Milton* (Cambridge University Press, 1998), esp. pp. 11–43.

[32] Hooker, *Laws* v.57 (vol. 11, p. 245).

[33] During his time at Cambridge, Fletcher the dramatist seems to have been destined for the ministry. In 1593 he became a Bible clerk at his college, Corpus Christi, and as such his principal task was to read the lessons at divine service. Two points seem especially significant about Fletcher's religious background. First, his father's career anticipates the pattern of "mightiness meeting misery" so evident in the play. In other words, its theme comes close to home, and it is hard to imagine Fletcher not

Fletcher's father and grandfather epitomize the progress of many English Protestants from what Patrick Collinson calls "primitive Protestantism" towards "a kind of Anglicanism."[34] At the heart of this proto-Anglicanism, no matter how radical individual members might be in doctrine, was an enduring commitment to the liturgy of Thomas Cranmer's Book of Common Prayer.

The purpose of the liturgy, like that of the play's "chosen truth," is, as the real Cranmer says in his 1549 preface to the Prayer Book, the "advauncement of godliness" (p. 4), that God should be truly known. The liturgy should be so ordered that "the whole Bible (or greatest part thereof) should be read over once in the yeare" (p. 4). The Psalms, in particular, should not be divided up, some read and some "utterly omitted" (p. 4), but so ordered that all one hundred and fifty of them could be heard over the course of each month at Matins and Evensong. Most importantly, the liturgy should be performed in such a way that it would have an *affective* impact. Both clergy and the people should feel moved: the clergy should be "stirred up to godliness" and the people "inflamed with the love of his true religion" (p. 4). The liturgy will effect this by dramatizing or performing Scripture. If Shakespeare and Fletcher's play has an obvious ceremonial quality, then equally, the ceremony of the liturgy has a strong theatrical bias. The *Book of Common Prayer*, says Cummings, is a "performative book, more like a play-text than like a novel in the way we must approach it as readers," its various rubrics functioning "a little like the stage-directions in a Shakespeare play" (*Prayer Book*, p. xxxiv). "Then the Priest turnyng hym to the Altar, shall saye or syng, playnly and distinctly, this prayer folowynge" (p. 29), reads a typical rubric. In performing this prayer, he becomes its living embodiment. At the same time, Cranmer is acutely aware of the dangers of performance: he knows full well that "no ordre can be so perfectly devised" that for some, out of "ignoraunce and infermitie, or els of malice and obstinacie," it will not be "misconstrued, depraved, and interpreted in a wrong part" (p. 667). He is therefore careful to reduce the contingency of performance by giving precise instructions on how prayers, readings, and ceremonies are both to be carried out and, in some cases, how exactly they are to be understood. Above

remembering his father's fall as he worked on *Henry VIII*. Within two months of becoming Bishop of London, Richard Fletcher fell out of favor with Queen Elizabeth for marrying a second wife. He was banished from the Queen's presence and only reluctantly allowed to continue in office. But he bore his disgrace with patience and over the course of a year was finally forgiven just before his death in June 1596. See Brett Usher, "Richard Fletcher," *ODNB*.

34 Patrick Collinson, "Cranbrook and the Fletchers: Popular and Unpopular Religion in the Kentish Weald," in *Godly People: Essays on English Protestantism and Puritanism* (London: Hambledon Press, 1983), pp. 399–428 (p. 422).

all, he is concerned, just as the play is, that performance in articulating God's truth should not be divisive; it should produce peace and reconciliation, "a godly unitie" (p. 19), avoiding "all matters and occasyon of dyscension" (p. 38). Just as in the play, the fictional Cranmer and his Catholic enemy, Gardiner, are made to embrace and bless each with "a true heart / And brother-love" (5.3.205–6), so in the Prayer Book the real Cranmer struggles over and over again to reconcile the sensitivities of old and new with "brotherly charitie" (p. 667). My point is that the spirit of the liturgy, however fitfully, animates the play. The performance of Holy Communion in the Prayer Book is especially sensitive, and although quite different in its immediate significance, something of its form and pressure is evident in one of the play's ceremonial high points, its representation of Queen Anne's coronation.

What is striking about Cranmer's rubrics is that although the main aim of the Prayer Book is to foreground the Word, enormous attention is still paid to ceremony. The most contentious issue in the ceremony of Communion is that of kneeling to receive the bread and wine. In 1552, in response to the objections of the Scots minister John Knox, Cranmer added a long paragraph to the Prayer Book known as "the Black Rubric" to avoid dissension and explain exactly what was to be understood by kneeling. It is not an act of adoration, he declares – there is no question of transubstantiation, of worshipping either "the Sacramentall bread or wyne there bodily received" or "anye reall and essential presence there beeying of Christes naturall fleshe and bloude" (p. 667). It is an act of reverence, signifying "the humble and gratefull acknowledging of the benefites of Chryst" (p. 667). In kneeling, communicants are meant to act out and so formally realize the reception of the grace made possible through Christ's sacrifice, the implication being that ceremony, Cranmer says, stirs up the mind and edifies the participant by "some notable and special signification" (p. 215). Spiritual life needs to find expression in bodily performance. At the climax of the play's representation of the coronation of Queen Anne, there is a similar emphasis on kneeling.

As the chorus of gentlemen makes clear, the public occasion of the Queen's coronation is meant to counterpoint that of Buckingham's trial: if "that time offered sorrow," then this offers "general joy" (4.1.6–7). Out of that sorrow comes a happiness that was utterly unforeseen. As the high point of the trial is Buckingham's gracious speech act, so the high point of the coronation is the new Queen's gracious act of communion. After the elaborate procession to Westminster Abbey is formally enacted on stage, the coronation itself is described at third hand by a third gentleman whose only appearance in the play this is. His emphasis falls on the relation between the Queen and the people, first the fruitfulness of their union and then something else. The King is entirely absent and she bears his sovereignty in her own right.[35] Having entered the Abbey, so we are told, "her grace sat down" on a chair of royal state opening or "opposing freely / The beauty of her person to the people" (4.1.67–70). Their reaction is electric: the free-flowing and regenerative force of "her grace" is registered in the noise the people make – the rushing sound of "a stiff tempest": "Great-bellied women" shake and everyone, men and their wives, all are "woven / So strangely in one piece" (4.1.74, 78–83). The Queen and her people have become one. But this highly sexualized, metaphoric communion is immediately transmuted into something different. At its climax she turns to God and kneels:

> At length her grace rose, and with modest paces
> Came to the altar, where she kneeled and saint-like
> Cast her fair eyes to heaven and prayed devoutly. (4.1.84–6)

At this moment, so the kneeling suggests, she redirects the affect of the people to God; they are incorporated with her in "a humble and gratefull acknowledging of the benfytes of Chryst" (*Prayer Book*, p. 667). Before she is finally crowned by Cranmer, before receiving the symbols of sovereignty, she subjects herself to the people: then she "rose again and bowed her to the people" (4.1.87). Monarchy is certainly being idealized, but only as it is imagined in the Prayer Book, as a conduit for and very much subject to God's grace: "Almightie and everlasting God," the coronation audience might have prayed, "wee bee taught by thy holy worde, that the heartes of Kynges are in thy rule and governaunce, and that thou doest dispose, and turne them as it semeth best to thy godly wisedom: We humbly beseche thee, so to dispose and governe" this, the heart of our new Queen (*Prayer Book*, p. 21). Let her be moved by the grace of God's truth.

How effective the immediate impact of the play was is not clear. Although records before 1660 are inadequate and despite Wotton's dubious testimony, it seems to have enjoyed increasing success.[36] The success of the play continued throughout the eighteenth century and Jane Austen was clearly influenced by the increasing focus on Queen Katherine and her internal sufferings. Actresses like Mary Porter, for instance, worked hard to intensify the effect of the character's inwardness: "the suppression of her

[35] The King was not entirely absent for the historical ceremony of June 1, 1533, but observed from a specially erected gallery. See Diarmaid MacCulloch, *Thomas Cranmer: A Life* (New Haven, CT: Yale University Press, 1996), pp. 94–6.

[36] See, for instance, Halio, *Henry VIII*, pp. 45–7.

tears when she reproached the Cardinal," says Thomas Davies in 1784, "bespoke a tumultuous conflict in her mind, before she burst into the manifestation of indignity she felt in being obliged to answer so unworthy an interrogator."[37] Austen's reading of the play in *Mansfield Park*, however, offers a much more rigorously expansive perspective than the contemporary theater's tendency to turn *Henry VIII* into the kind of Shakespearean tragedy Bloom might expect and admire. Like John Fletcher, Jane Austen was also the child of an Anglican clergyman, and her response to the play brings me to the heart of my argument.

## *Mansfield Park* and the stillness of Queen Katherine

Austen clearly loved the play and she gives it a prominent role in her great novel *Mansfield Park* (1814). Her choice of a play about Henry VIII is most obviously a joke at the expense of the novel's own inconstant Henry, Henry Crawford. More importantly, however, the play becomes the occasion of an animated discussion about how to improve both the understanding and affective impact of the Church of England's liturgy. The discussion is deeply ironic. The novel's central character, the modest but perceptive Fanny Price, has been reading *Henry VIII* to her less than acute aunt, Lady Bertram. When they hear Fanny's persistent suitor, Crawford, and her cousin, Edmund Bertram, approaching, Fanny nervously breaks off. Crawford picks up the book and continues the reading, playing all the roles, lighting "with the happiest knack" on "the best scene, or the best speeches of each" (pp. 334–5). His performance is mesmerizing. Even the reluctant Fanny is captivated, and Edmund, a newly ordained minister, is inspired to consider how the "distinctness and energy" of such a dramatic reading might be applied to the liturgy – how it might "have weight in recommending the most solid truths" (p. 337). Crawford concurs: "Our liturgy has beauties which not even a careless, slovenly style of reading can destroy; but it has also redundancies and repetitions, which require good reading [if they are] not to be felt [as such]" (pp. 337–8). The irony, to which only the sensitive Fanny seems privy, is that the actorly Crawford is far more interested in the performance than the significance of either the play or the liturgy. While neither the value of dramatizing the liturgy nor sacralizing drama in plays like *Henry VIII* is in doubt, Crawford's constancy is. In his consummate acting skills and irrepressible delight in performance, in his restless self-fashioning, he is a caricature of rootless, autonomous agency: as

[37] Quoted ibid., p. 49.

Fanny had noticed much earlier, he "was every thing to every body, and seemed to find no one essential to him [self]" (p. 309). Unlike Crawford, Fanny "lights" on nothing. When Edmund and Crawford interrupt her and Lady Bertram, she has been reading one particular speech, Wolsey's great act of remorse. His final, gracious act of faith is not a matter of "sweaty transcendence"; it has had a profound impact on both her and her aunt. It has calmed Fanny, and when Edmund and Crawford enter both ladies appear to be in a state of "deep tranquility" (p. 334). Fanny had only got to the middle of the Cardinal's speech, but she may well have ended on this exhortation: "Still in thy right hand carry gentle peace / To silence envious tongues. Be just, and fear not" (3.2.446–7). Here at his end Wolsey speaks out of the wisdom of Queen Katherine, immovable in her righteousness, and the mystery of Jane Austen's least popular heroine is that she exemplifies the "still and quiet conscience" (3.2.381) that Wolsey attains only at the end of his life and to which the play *Henry VIII* constantly returns. As Queen Katherine remembers Job and the Psalms, so Fanny remembers the play and remains immovable in her discriminating sense of what the truth is. Early in the novel this stillness, the particular way of being in the world that protects Fanny from the unmoored agency of players like Crawford, is located in the chapel at Mr. Rushworth's great house at Sotherton.

The chapel is immediately distinguished for its simplicity. It was "a mere, spacious, oblong room fitted up for the purpose of devotion" (p. 114), a place where "silence and stillness reigned in it with few interruptions throughout the year" (p. 117). Like the Protestantism of the Church of England itself, the chapel negotiates a middle way between what Austen might imagine to be extremes of religious practice, between Roman Catholicism, on the one hand, and religious individualism, on the other. The chapel seems to have been conceived as a place of refuge during the reign of England's last, aggressively Catholic king, James II, a holy place where the Rushworth household could worship in peace as a community – not as individuals in their closets but at the same time away from the parish church. "It is a handsome chapel," says Mrs. Rushworth, "and was formerly in constant use both morning and evening. Prayers were always read in it by the domestic chaplain, within the memory of many. But the late Mr. Rushworth left it off" (p. 115). Crawford's sister, the quick but worldly Mary, misses the elegiac tone: "Every generation has its improvements," she responds tartly. But Fanny sees the point and immediately seizes on the liturgical ideal Mrs. Rushworth's remarks intimate: "There is something in a chapel and chaplain so much in character with a great house, with one's ideas of what such a household should be! A whole family assembling for the purpose of prayer, is fine!" (p. 115). In response to Mary's continued skepticism, Edmund joins Fanny in defending the value of communal worship, emphasizing entirely in the spirit of the Book of Common Prayer the singular value "of place and example" in avoiding distraction and rousing "better feelings" (p. 116). In Evelyn Waugh's *Brideshead Revisited* (1945), the chapel at Sotherton is appropriated for Roman Catholicism. While both texts are concerned with Charles Taylor's transcendence, what the particular stillness of the two chapels signifies is quite different. At Brideshead, it simply means emptiness. That is, unless the presence of the Holy Spirit is made manifest in the sanctuary lamp, the chapel's stillness only evokes the desolation of the Book of Lamentations: *Quomodo sedet sola civitas* – "How doth the city sit solitary" (Lamentions 1:1).[38] At Sotherton, however, stillness, "deep tranquility" or "gentle peace," is of intrinsic value; it doesn't stand in opposition to, but welcomes the sound of prayers "both morning and evening," in the liturgy of Matins and Evensong. When read through the novel's relation to *Henry VIII*, Fanny's stillness reveals its specifically religious roots in the drama of Buckingham, Queen Katherine, Wolsey, and Cranmer. It is true that when read through such bewilderingly different perspectives as the Crawfords' vitality, the Prices' poverty, or, most disturbingly, the slavery on which the prosperity of Mansfield Park itself rests, Fanny's stillness might look, at the very least, like complacency, but when read through *Henry VIII* it suggests a discourse not *necessarily* at odds with any of these perspectives: a discourse consumed with the desire for the kind of truth – "that principle of right," "that just consideration of others, that knowledge of [one's] own heart" (p. 119) – which might resist the erosion of value and anchor all moral relations. In this, her stillness points to the way the Bible's wisdom literature, especially Job and the Psalms, sustains Shakespeare and Fletcher's characters. "Stand in awe, and sin not," says Psalm 4:4, "commune with your own heart . . . and be still." Tanner senses this dimension of the novel when he concludes that Fanny "suffers in her stillness. For righteousness sake" (p. 32). In this, says the novel, she "should be justified" (p. 438).[39]

For Harold Bloom, and of course for most of us, *Hamlet* remains at the center of our profoundly relativistic, skeptical culture: however embedded the play is, in fact, in seventeenth-century religious culture, it is difficult not to feel its secular power, its ability to tell us who we are and what it means to

38 See Evelyn Waugh, *Brideshead Revisited* (Harmondsworth: Penguin, 2000), p. 225, where the theme of *Quomodo sedet sola civitas* first begins to be articulated.

39 For more on Shakespearean drama and biblical wisdom literature, see Chapter 10 above.

be human. It is part of our "constitution," as Henry Crawford might put it (p. 335) – not just an Englishman's, but any secular person's.[40] *Henry VIII* is much harder to appreciate. What I have been trying to suggest is not simply that the play is a sacralizing drama, something more than the "the rags and bones" of a religious culture reassembled to please a secular crowd, but a subject for postsecular inquiry. For the play models a different way of being in the world – most importantly, a different way of being human from the one Bloom claims Shakespeare invented in his plays. It idealizes a truth beyond relativism; when read in relation to the much later *Mansfield Park*, it points not necessarily to religion itself but to what Alain Badiou calls the "transcendent neutrality" of the universal. Queen Katherine and her descendant, Fanny Price, are no less capable of inwardness or self-reflection than the Prince, but they exemplify something more than Bloom's self-regarding worship of our own "all-but-infinite consciousness." They exemplify a way of being whose goodness does not depend on the endless idealization of human agency and our instrumental reason, but rather on a universal or truth, a transcendent signified, which with all its difficulties might enable us to go beyond our selves.

40 See Stephen Greenblatt, "Racial Memory and Literary History," *PMLA*, 116 (2001), esp. 50–1, for a characteristically stimulating but also nationalist, American reading of this passage.

CHAPTER 13

# *Converting Henry: truth, history, and historical faith in* Henry VIII

*Michael Davies*

## I

My conscience first received a tenderness,
Scruple, and prick, on certain speeches uttered
By th' Bishop of Bayonne, then French Ambassador,
Who had been hither sent on the debating
A marriage 'twixt the Duke of Orleans and
Our daughter Mary. I'th' progress of this business,
Ere a determinate resolution, he –
I mean the Bishop – did require a respite
Wherein he might the King his lord advertise
Whether our daughter were legitimate,
Respecting this our marriage with the dowager,
Sometimes our brother's wife. This respite shook
The bosom of my conscience, entered me,
Yea, with a spitting power, and made to tremble
The region of my breast, which forced such way
That many mazed considerings did throng
And pressed in with this caution. First, methought
I stood not in the smile of heaven, who had
Commanded nature that my lady's womb,
If it conceived a male child by me, should
Do no more offices of life to't than
The grave does to the dead. For her male issue
Or died where they were made, or shortly after
This world had aired them. Hence I took a thought
This was a judgement on me that my kingdom,
Well worthy the best heir o'th' world, should not
Be gladded in't by me. Then follows that
I weighed the danger which my realms stood in
By this my issue's fail, and that gave to me

For lending me their ears, eyes, and wisdom while preparing this chapter, sincere thanks are owed to Carina Vitti, Greg Walker, and Nick Davis.

Many a groaning throe. Thus hulling in
The wild sea of my conscience, I did steer
Toward this remedy, whereupon we are
Now present here together – that's to say
I meant to rectify my conscience[1]

This speech of King Henry VIII's may well be one of the most significant in the canon of Shakespeare's works in terms of what it could signal about Shakespeare's relationship as a dramatist to early modern religion.[2] On one level, as commentators have often observed, it stands at the center of *Henry VIII*'s fascination with "conscience," a keyword that encircles and patrols the King's thinking here just as it orbits and frames the play's action as a whole.[3] These words are important, moreover, because they appear to give human shape in the play to the magisterial origins of the Henrician Reformation. They lay bare (or so it might seem) the political and religious convictions behind Henry's decision to end his marriage of twenty years to Katherine of Aragon, his "Sometimes . . . brother's [i.e., Arthur's] wife" (2.4.178). This dramatic moment would lead historically to the fall of Wolsey, the break with Rome, and the Great Supremacy, the legislation for which established Henry VIII as Supreme Head of the Church of England, thereby instituting a much grander historical narrative: that of the English Reformations.[4]

So much is obvious. What seems to have eluded critical notice is the way in which this speech makes central to *Henry VIII* a type of confession we would not usually expect to find in any play by Shakespeare: that of the evangelical (or, as it would later become known, the "Puritan") conversion

[1] *King Henry VIII, or All is True*, ed. Jay L. Halio (Oxford University Press, 1999), 2.4.167–200. All further references are to this edition.

[2] Scholars who recognize *Henry VIII* as a play coauthored by Shakespeare and Fletcher agree that Shakespeare contributed 2.4 in its entirety. On the play's authorship, see Brian Vickers, *Shakespeare, Co-Author* (Oxford University Press, 2002), pp. 331–402, 433–45, 480–91; *King Henry VIII*, ed. Gordon McMullan, Arden Shakespeare (London: Bloomsbury, 2000), pp. 180–99, 448–9.

[3] See Paul Bertram, "*Henry VIII*: The Conscience of the King," in Reuben Arthur Brower and Richard Poirier (eds.), *In Defense of Reading* (New York: E. P. Dutton, 1962), pp. 153–73; Frank V. Cespedes, "'We are one in fortunes': The Sense of History in *Henry VIII*," *English Literary Renaissance*, 10 (1980), 413–38; Alan R. Young, "Shakespeare's *Henry VIII* and the Theme of Conscience," *English Studies in Canada*, 7 (1981), 38–53; Susannah Brietz Monta, "'Thou fall'st a blessed martyr': Shakespeare's *Henry VIII* and the Polemics of Conscience," *English Literary Renaissance*, 30 (2000), 262–83.

[4] Peter Saccio, *Shakespeare's English Kings: History, Chronicle, and Drama*, 2nd edn. (Oxford University Press, 2000), pp. 227–8. On English reformations (as opposed to the English Reformation), see Christopher Haigh, *English Reformations: Religion, Politics, and Society under the Tudors* (Oxford: Clarendon Press, 1993).

account.[5] For the King's monologue here – the longest in the play – is an admission not just of his "scruple" but of a particular (and particularly Protestant) kind of transformation, recalled within what might be termed a testimony of "experience." Henry's statement in Act 2, scene 4 reads like an oral spiritual autobiography typical of the kinds of confession expected of members of seventeenth-century (often separatist) congregations of godly "saints."[6] Quite characteristically, it is a somewhat hesitant first-person narrative in which a faltering "I" and its tentative "methought" unsettle the more strident royal "we" and "our." Here, Henry's "mazed considerings" bear witness to what appears to be the early stages of a "morphology of conversion," a process of spiritual change beginning with an all-important conviction of sinfulness: that "spitting power" which "entered" Henry suddenly and, as he puts it, "made to tremble / The region of my breast."[7] The nautical language of Henry's spiritual ardor – his "hulling in / The wild sea of my conscience" – likewise cements this account firmly to the evangelical tradition. Such experience is defined authentically, it seems, by the vicissitudes encountered by godly converts amid "flouds of temptation" that can easily "over-whelme the poore distressed, doubting, despairing and drowning soule."[8] Like John Bunyan, another, later English convert whose "*castings down, and raisings up*" amid his own inward storms are recollected in *Grace Abounding to the Chief of Sinners* (1666), Shakespeare's Henry finds himself "mazed" by a painful conviction that he stands no longer "in the smile of heaven."[9]

5 *Henry VIII* is often regarded as devoid of anything specifically "Protestant": see, for example, Cespedes, "Sense of History," 414; Brietz Monta, "Polemics of Conscience," 276; Frederick O. Waage, Jr., "*Henry VIII* and the Crisis of the English History Play," *Shakespeare Studies*, 8 (1975), 297–309 (300). As Linda McJ. Micheli has noted, "Most writers have perceived little emphasis on religion in the play" (*Henry VIII: An Annotated Bibliography* [New York: Garland, 1988], p. xix). G. Wilson Knight, in idiosyncratic fashion, has strenuously argued otherwise: see *Shakespeare and Religion* (London: Routledge & Kegan Paul, 1967), pp. 5–7, 31–8, 75–82, and *The Crown of Life* (London: Methuen, 1965), pp. 256–336.

6 On the importance of confessions of experience in this context, see especially Edmund S. Morgan, *Visible Saints: The History of a Puritan Idea* (New York University Press, 1963); Patricia Caldwell, *The Puritan Conversion Narrative: The Beginnings of American Expression* (Cambridge University Press, 1983); Kathleen Lynch, *Protestant Autobiography in the Seventeenth-Century Anglophone World* (Oxford University Press, 2012).

7 The phrase "morphology of conversion" comes from Morgan, *Visible Saints*, pp. 66–73, 90–2.

8 Vavasor Powell, from the preface to an early collection of such testimonies, *Spiritual Experiences of Sundry Beleevers* (1653), p. ii. On nautical imagery in English literary and religious writings, see Michael Davies, "Shaping Grace: The Spiritual Autobiographies of John Bunyan, William Cowper, and John Newton," *Bunyan Studies*, 12 (2007), 36–69.

9 In the famous "game-at-Cat" episode recounted by Bunyan, it is "as if" he sees "the Lord Jesus looking down . . . very hotly displeased with me." He is "put to an exceeding maze" by it all. *Grace Abounding to the Chief of Sinners*, ed. Roger Sharrock (Oxford: Clarendon Press, 1962), p. 10.

What is so striking, then, about Henry's speech in 2.4 is just how faithfully it reproduces the shape of a religious experience common to the Protestant tradition from Martin Luther to John Newton, and from William Perkins to William Cowper. On the one hand this is a tradition that connects Henry's suffering and its sudden "spitting power" to that most archetypal of conversions, Paul's on the road to Damascus, while on the other it centers him in the language of "new birth."[10] When Henry confesses to suffering from a "groaning throe" brought on by his newly burdened conscience, this allusion to the pangs of pregnancy may signal a crisis over the king's "manliness," as Gordon McMullan has argued.[11] Yet it also testifies, perhaps more directly, to his laboring or "travailing" in an implied spiritual rebirth. Such Protestant "experience" would not have been beyond Shakespeare's reach. In their popular tracts and sermons, Calvinist divines since at least the 1580s had been extolling the virtues of a practical piety that would focus on individual repentance and personal reformation as a means of national conversion towards godliness and "amendment of life."[12] "The power of grace doth beget in a regenerate man, a watchfulnesse, care and conscience of smaller offences, of secret sins, of sinfull thoughts" and "of all occasions of sinne," Robert Bolton would advise in *A Discourse on the State of True Happiness* (1611), "whereas the formall hypocrite . . . makes no conscience of them at all, holding it a point of precisenes to be too conscionable."[13] In this context, Shakespeare's conscience-bound Henry VIII seems to step forward in 2.4 as an ideal witness to the Protestant "power of grace," as Bolton puts it. His words appear to epitomize how "the soule of Gods child, comming fresh out of the pangs and terrors of his new-birth" is humbled "under the mightie hand of God, by a sight and sense of his sinnes."[14] As the Protestant pun that introduces Henry's confession at the beginning of his speech indicates, in this way will the king be "justified" (2.4.159).

There is, of course, a significant obstacle to accepting this presentation of Henry VIII in terms of what G. Wilson Knight has described as the play's

[10] On Paul's conversion as a Reformation "archetype" (and "anti-type"), see Brian Cummings, *The Literary Culture of the Reformation* (Oxford University Press, 2007), pp. 366–72, 388–9.

[11] Gordon McMullan, "'Thou hast made me now a man': Reforming Man(ner)liness in Henry VIII," in Jennifer Richards and James Knowles (eds.), *Shakespeare's Late Plays: New Readings* (Edinburgh University Press, 1999), pp. 44–6.

[12] Dewey D. Wallace, Jr., *Puritans and Predestination: Grace in English Protestant Theology, 1525–1695* (Chapel Hill: University of North Carolina Press, 1982), pp. 43–61; Patrick Collinson, *The Elizabethan Puritan Movement* (London: Jonathan Cape, 1967), pp. 464–5.

[13] Robert Bolton, *A Discourse on the State of True Happiness* (1611) (Short-Title Catalogue [hereafter STC] 3228), p. 72.

[14] Ibid., p. 71.

"poetry of conversion": is it "true"?[15] In a play for which the alternative (or perhaps even original) title is, famously, *All Is True*, how are we to read this dramatic rendition of the origins of English Reformation?[16] Is it, for instance, "true" historically? Did it really happen? Did Henry undergo some kind of conversion: a personal reformation, that is, which would result in national reformation? And would he have spoken these words? Yet, even if he had, would that make them "true" in the sense of genuine and sincere? Are we really to believe, in other words, that Shakespeare's Henry VIII is motivated to seek a divorce because of a sharp "prick" in his "conscience"? Or were Henry's marital misgivings spurred by a rather different kind of "prick": that is, by "the historical reality of Henry's sexual, corporeal desire for Anne [Boleyn]"? Is it in fact "fact" that "one of the major events of English history [i.e., the Henrician Reformation] ultimately had its genesis" not in the tender conscience of a converting king but, more shamefully, "in Henry's loins"?[17]

What should we take as the "truth" here? In which version of "history" are we to put our faith? The purpose of this chapter is to illustrate not only how natural it is for us to ask such questions of *Henry VIII*, but also how imperative it is for us to do so. How we see Shakespeare's Henry – whether as God-fearing man and proto-Protestant monarch, or as nascent tyrant and philandering crook – may be determined, to a large degree, by whether we believe he is speaking the truth in Act 2, scene 4. How we receive Henry's words about his conversion is key in this respect. Our reaction to them may well shape – as it has done for so many of the play's critics and commentators – whether we see the play as sympathetic or cynical towards Henry, and indeed whether the drama betrays a denominational bias in its historiography; that is, whether *Henry VIII* presents the king in a way that could be thought of as either "Catholic" or "Protestant."[18] The fact that *Henry VIII*

[15] Wilson Knight, *Crown of Life*, p. 282.

[16] On *All Is True* as the play's original title, see Stanley Wells and Gary Taylor, *William Shakespeare: A Textual Companion* (Oxford University Press, 1987), pp. 28, 618–19.

[17] Thomas Betteridge, "Henry VIII and Popular Culture," in Mark Rankin et al. (eds.), *Henry VIII and his Afterlives: Literature, Politics, and Art* (Cambridge University Press, 2009), pp. 208–22 (p. 212).

[18] See Robert S. Miola, "Shakespeare's Religion," *First Things*, 138 (May 2008), 25–30 (25). For "Catholic" readings of the play, see, e.g., Peter Rudnytsky, "*Henry VIII* and the Deconstruction of History," *Shakespeare Survey*, 43 (1990), 43–57; and David N. Beauregard, *Catholic Theology in Shakespeare's Plays* (Newark: University of Delaware Press, 2008), pp. 136–44. E. A. J. Honigmann has referred to the "attitude" of *Henry VIII* as "uncompromisingly Protestant" in *Shakespeare: The "Lost Years"*, 2nd edn. (Manchester University Press, 1998), p. 125, whereas Roland Mushat Frye has indicated the play's perceived Protestantism by pointing to its Catholic censorship by Father William Sankey, SJ, around 1641–51: see *Shakespeare and Christian Doctrine* (Princeton University Press, 1963), pp. 275–93. Claire Asquith regards the play as Protestant "propaganda," being "a brilliant imitation of

has been read as both Catholic and Protestant in its sympathies (and sometimes as both simultaneously) suggests, along with its generic hovering between "History" and "Romance," why the image of the tempest serves appropriately as one of the play's crucial organizing metaphors.[19] For, as Philip Edwards has indicated, the language of struggling at sea, brilliantly employed in Henry's speech in 2.4, communicates "equivocation" and "hesitation" rather than "control": it signals "uncertainty" in the turbulent wake of literary interpretation.[20]

It is the play's "uncertainties and hesitations," as Peter Sahel has likewise described them, that I aim to navigate in this chapter, particularly in relation to Henry's surprising conversion narrative in 2.4.[21] Not only are ambivalence and irony central to our experience of the play, they are also a defining aspect of the play's employment of "history."[22] By continually asking us to test our sense of what happens in the play – what we are seeing and hearing with our own eyes and ears – against what we already know (or at least what we think we know) about Henry's reign, *Henry VIII* appears to remain "true" to history. It does so, however, even while encouraging us to question and ultimately to abandon what early modern reformers and Protestants referred to as a "historical faith" in the events selectively dramatized within it. It is in recognizing the play's immersion in some distinctly early modern Protestant ways of thinking about Henry's Reformation, and especially its mistrust of any faith in past events that may be termed merely "historical," that we can see how *Henry VIII* presents the "truth" of its "history" as unfixed and unstable, perhaps even untrue. It does so, moreover, while asserting throughout that what is being staged before our eyes nevertheless is, as the prologue reinforces, "All . . . True." To establish how the play works in such paradoxical and indeed startlingly experimental terms, we need to look again at the King's speech in 2.4 – the history

Shakespeare's work" produced entirely by Fletcher (*Shadowplay* [New York: PublicAffairs, 2005], pp. 276–8). For a denominationally more balanced reading, see Jean-Christophe Mayer, *Shakespeare's Hybrid Faith: History, Religion and the Stage* (Basingstoke: Palgrave Macmillan, 2006), pp. 131–51.

19 As is often noted, references to tempests, shipwreck, and sinking can be found throughout: e.g., 1.1.92; 2.1.50–2, 61; 3.1.148, 163; 3.2.438; 4.1.74; 4.2.21. On the play's generic complexity as history and/or romance, see Raphael Lyne, *Shakespeare's Late Work* (Oxford University Press, 2007), pp. 15–17, 111–14; Howard Felperin, "Shakespeare's *Henry VIII*: History as Myth," *SEL*, 6 (1966), 225–46.

20 Philip Edwards, *Sea-Mark: The Metaphorical Voyage, Spenser to Milton* (Liverpool University Press, 1997), pp. 4, 6.

21 Pierre Sahel, "The Strangeness of a Dramatic Style: Rumour in *Henry VIII*," *Shakespeare Survey*, 38 (1985), 145–51 (147).

22 On the ways in which *Henry VIII* privileges contradiction, irony, and a "double vision" of "history" and "truth," see especially Lee Bliss, "The Wheel of Fortune and the Maiden Phoenix of Shakespeare's *Henry VIII*," *ELH*, 42 (1975), 1–25; Barbara Kreps, "When All Is True: Law, History and Problems of Knowledge in *Henry VIII*," *Shakespeare Survey*, 52 (1999), 166–82.

behind which will remain the focus of this chapter – in order to ask once more that key question: in what sense is it "true"?

## II

Perhaps the first thing to acknowledge about Henry's speech in Act 2, scene 4 is the legitimacy of its claim to "truthfulness" through a literal – that is, letter-for-letter – fidelity to its most likely principal source: the second, revised edition of Holinshed's *Chronicles* (1587).[23] Although Shakespeare takes "many liberties" with events and their chronology in the play,[24] nevertheless the near verbatim treatment of Holinshed as the basic material for key scenes and passages, as well as some of the more elaborate stage directions in *Henry VIII*, is almost unique among Shakespeare's English histories. As numerous commentators have noted, the play appears to be at times little more than "Holinshed versified."[25] Act 2, scene 4 is one of those times. When Henry offers his reasons for questioning the legitimacy of his marriage, we might be pressed to accept it as "true" partly because of the closeness with which Shakespeare follows almost word-for-word the corresponding passage in the 1587 *Chronicles*: with its story of the "Bishop of Baion" and the query raised over Mary's legitimacy; its sense of "Gods indignation" being suddenly "conceived within the secret bottome" of Henry's soul; and its memorable image too of the King's "conscience" being "tossed in the waves of a scrupulous mind."[26] The result is a play that becomes almost obsessively punctilious about conveying historical "truth" by remaining, in certain places, doggedly faithful to the "letter" of history, or at least to Holinshed's well-known version of it.

The "spirit" of this dramatic method and of the history that it purports to lay before us is more difficult to fathom. Although the structure and content of Henry's speech in 2.4 mirror almost exactly those of the 1587 *Chronicles*, any notion that it presents an incontestable or unitary "truth" can be challenged by the smallest of our historical doubts. In this instance, a simple but significant problem arises from the fact that in Holinshed, and thus too in 2.4 of *Henry VIII*, Henry's reference to the Bishop of Bayonne is

[23] See Geoffrey Bullough (ed.), *Narrative and Dramatic Sources of Shakespeare*, 8 vols. (London: Routledge & Kegan Paul, 1957–75), vol. IV, pp. 435–510.

[24] Kenneth Muir, *The Sources of Shakespeare's Plays* (London: Methuen, 1977), p. 286.

[25] Judith H. Anderson, *Biographical Truth: The Representation of Historical Persons in Tudor-Stuart Writing* (New Haven, CT: Yale University Press, 1984), p. 131; R. A. Foakes (ed.), *Henry VIII*, 3rd edn. (London: Methuen, 1968), p. xxxvii.

[26] Raphael Holinshed, *The Third Volume of Chronicles* (1586) (STC 13569), pp. 907–8.

historically almost certainly a mistake. The bishop in question would have been Gabriel de Grammont, bishop of Tarbes, who led the French embassy on this occasion in 1527, not Jean du Bellay, bishop of Bayonne.[27] Such an error may appear to be entirely harmless, of course, but it can also serve to invite a certain skepticism towards the trustworthiness of the history being presented. J. J. Scarisbrick, Tudor historian and preeminent biographer of Henry VIII, is in fact deeply dubious about the whole story of this conjugally inquisitive bishop, as recounted by Henry at Blackfriars in 1529: "It is incredible that an ambassador would have dared to trespass upon so delicate a subject as a monarch's marriage," he notes, "least of all when he had come to negotiate a treaty with that monarch" (in this case over Mary's marriage to the Duke of Orleans).[28] Aside from the arrival of the Bishop of Tarbes in England in 1527, which rules him out as the possible prompter of Henry's "scruple" (as the king was already taking steps to prosecute the divorce by that point), Scarisbrick adds that "another account of the beginnings of the story, given by Henry in 1528, says that doubts about Mary's legitimacy were first put by the French to English ambassadors in France – not by the bishop of Tarbes to his English hosts."[29]

Henry either makes a mistake in referring to the Bishop of Bayonne in his "scruple" speech, as it is reported (or perhaps misreported?) in Holinshed (and then subsequently dramatized in *Henry VIII*); or, as Scarisbrick seems to be implying, the King was fabricating the entire thing. It might be objected, of course, that few audience members in either 1613 or today would actually recognize this historical error over which bishop did what to set Henry on the course of his conscientious conversion. Yet we could still wonder, as Scarisbrick does, how any experienced ambassador could drop such a resounding clanger before a king with whom he is attempting to broker a diplomatic deal. We would not need to be that well versed in the minutiae of Tudor history to sense that something about Henry's story fails to ring true in this respect. Yet, still, why should such things matter? Why should we care? If Bohemia can develop a conveniently fatal coastline in *The Winter's Tale*, then surely we should be able to accommodate in *Henry VIII* some small discrepancy over which bishop said what to the King, even in a

[27] George Cavendish, *The Life and Death of Cardinal Wolsey*, ed. Richard S. Sylvester (Oxford University Press and London: Early English Text Society, 1959), p. 228 n. 83/5. In Edward Hall's account it is neither the Bishop of Bayonne nor Tarbes but, more simply, "one of the chiefe cou[n]sailors to the Frenche kyng" who is said to have raised the problem of Mary's legitimacy: *The Union of the Two Noble and Illustre Famelies of Lancastre & Yorke* (1548) (STC 12721), fo. clxxx, and see fos. clxxix–xxxiii.

[28] J. J. Scarisbrick, *Henry VIII*, new edn. (New Haven, CT: Yale University Press, 1997), p. 153.

[29] Ibid., pp. 153–4.

play with the provocative title *All Is True*. But in *Henry VIII* such things *do* matter. For if the detail about the Bishop of Bayonne indicates even the slightest flicker of unreliability or falsehood on either Henry's or Holinshed's part, then the entire integrity of Henry's confession at Blackfriars in 1529 (dramatized so faithfully in 2.4) is called into question. As a result, we may not know whether to take anything as "truthful" in this speech nor, more to the point, where to locate the source of Henry's troubled "conscience." If not in a sincere conviction that his marriage has offended God, from whence might Henry's "scruple" be said, truthfully, to have its origin?

The play itself seems to make it relatively easy to answer this question: in the King's desire for the eminently lustworthy Anne Boleyn. This is a woman whose physical presence in the play is marked by an attractiveness that men find simply irresistible: they are compelled to kiss Anne practically on sight in *Henry VIII*. Wherever she goes, charged sexual energies are detonated into explosive moments of either bawdy punning or riotous, even orgiastic festivity (none of which bodes well in hindsight, of course, given the charges that would lead to her execution).[30] As commentators have been aware, it is because the play has Henry meet (and fall for) Anne in Act 1, scene 4, long before he declares anything about his "tender conscience," that it becomes hard for us to see the King's confession in 2.4 (which, naturally, makes no mention of Anne) as sincere or truthful. As a result, "conscience," even by 2.4, becomes a troublingly sullied word in *Henry VIII*: shorthand for the King's sexual proclivities rather than his piety.[31] If read cynically, moreover, Henry's words about "conscience" in 2.4 would confirm a scathingly skeptical view of *Henry VIII* overall when it comes to its claims about "truth" because, as Frank Cespedes has argued, everything in the play appears to be "structured to . . . underline Henry's hypocrisy."[32] Henry's speech in 2.4 thus becomes symptomatic and paradigmatic in these terms. It offers an "unflattering" image of Henry, we might conclude, whose "erratic self-defense" on the basis of "conscience" evinces no more, as Hugh M. Richmond has put it, than his "own guilty awareness of his dishonorable motives" and, indeed, "the appalling moral and political confusion into which he has betrayed himself."[33]

30 See, e.g., 1.4, 2.3, and 4.1.42–83, for comments on which see Wilson Knight, *Crown of Life*, pp. 303–4.

31 See Cespedes, "Sense of History," 425; Brietz Monta, "Polemics of Conscience," 275.

32 Cespedes, "Sense of History," 426.

33 H. M. Richmond, "Shakespeare's *Henry VIII*: Romance Redeemed by History," *Shakespeare Studies*, 4 (1968), 334–49 (343), and see further H. M. Richmond, *King Henry VIII: Shakespeare in Performance* (Manchester University Press, 1994), pp. 4, 24. The skeptical view of Henry's speech in 2.4 has a long pedigree: see James Spedding, "Who Wrote Shakespeare's *Henry VIII*?", *Gentleman's Magazine*, n.s. 34 (Aug. 1850), 115–23 (117).

Such an approach has led some commentators, perhaps inevitably, to read the play as "Catholic" in both its historiography and its "implicit theological positioning."[34] It is easy to see why. On the one hand, *Henry VIII* appears to champion Katherine's cause as a pious wife and loyal papist over and above Henry's as a conscientious and heirless king, making the abandoned wife, mother, and queen the emotional focus of the play.[35] On the other, as Peter Rudnytsky has argued, its chronology appears to adhere to that of sixteenth-century "Catholic" histories of the divorce. Because "Henry's desire for Anne arises before the bruiting of the rumor of his divorce," Rudnytsky notes, then Shakespeare effectively "undermines the official version" of Henry's alleged "motives" for the divorce. The reason for the conspicuous "implausibility" of Henry's "unconvincing" speech in 2.4 can now be explained quite easily: it is because "Shakespeare upholds a *Catholic* perspective on the divorce," Rudnytsky posits, one that subverts "[t]he 'Protestant' reading of the play" by locating Henry's "scruple" not in a wounded conscience but, more accurately, in the lust, greed, and villainy that are, in truth, at the root of this power-hungry king's "true feelings."[36]

But can we be sure – historically speaking – that Henry VIII's "scruple" was no more than a smoke-screen for baser, carnal desires, as is so often assumed? As Diarmaid MacCulloch has indicated, there may be good reason for us to regard Henry's words about "conscience" as sincere, making it historically misguided, as Lacey Baldwin Smith likewise has argued, "to accept politics and lust as the central motives behind the divorce."[37] As a king who "took time off from the pleasures of hunting and war not only to read theology voraciously, but to write it," MacCulloch argues, and who would turn to "theological activity for comfort in successive great crises of his life," Henry's "efforts to rid himself of the Aragon marriage were fatally complicated from the beginning by his obstinate refusal to see the question

34 Beauregard, *Catholic Theology*, p. 137.

35 The view that the play treats Katherine more sympathetically than any other character, fueling speculation that Shakespeare himself was a Catholic, has a long tradition: ibid., p. 141; Velma Bourgeois Richmond, *Shakespeare, Catholicism, and Romance* (New York: Continuum, 2000), pp. 201–6. For readings that challenge this tradition, see Waage, "Crisis of the English History Play," 298; Mayer, *Shakespeare's Hybrid Faith*, pp. 137–41.

36 Rudnytsky, "Deconstruction of History," 49–51, 53, 55.

37 Diarmaid MacCulloch, "The Religion of Henry VIII," in David Starkey (ed.), *Henry VIII: A European Court in England* (London: Collins & Brown, 1991), pp. 160–2, and both MacCulloch's introduction and chapter "Henry VIII and the Reform of the Church" in his edited volume *The Reign of Henry VIII: Politics, Policy and Piety* (Basingstoke: Palgrave Macmillan, 1995), pp. 1–11 and 159–80; Lacey Baldwin Smith, "A Matter of Conscience," in Theodore K. Rabb and Jerrold E. Seigel (eds.), *Action and Conviction in Early Modern Europe: Essays in Memory of E. H. Harbison* (Princeton University Press, 1969), pp. 32–51 (p. 32).

as anything else than theological: a confrontation between his own sin and an angry God."[38] As Eric Ives puts it, "the vital point is that Henry believed" such things.[39] It would be a mistake, then, simply to assume that Henry's "conscience" was in reality motivated only "by statecraft or sex, or some combination of the two." Inseparable from the King's recognition that his "dynasty was barren, his wife old and infertile" was a sincere belief that "he had inadvertently broken God's commandment" in marrying the wife of his deceased elder brother, Arthur, "and thereby incurred divine wrath."[40]

Such views recognize the importance of taking Henry's "scruple" seriously rather than accepting axiomatically that it served as a mask for "mere selfishness or cynical diplomacy."[41] Yet the point here is not to presume that Henry was driven solely by his "scruple" to act as he did in divorcing Katherine but, more simply, that Henry *may* have been prompted to do so, at least in part, by what *may* have been a genuinely pricked "conscience." The truth of the King's "great matter" is, after all, still very much open to debate. If, for example, we were to share Scarisbrick's skepticism about Henry's "scruple" originating from a conversation with a French ambassador when negotiating the marriage of Mary then, equally, we would have to admit that we can never know the full truth of its genesis. Scarisbrick pragmatically proposes that "[i]t is very likely that Henry himself was the author of his doubts" about his marriage, rather than Wolsey or any other advisor-confessor, and that he "may have begun to entertain" them "as early as 1522 or 1523."[42] Others accept that "the precise origins of the divorce remain obscure" and that it is impossible to say whether Henry's conscientious reasons for wanting to end his first marriage were sincere or not.[43] As Henry Angsar Kelly has put it succinctly, "Henry's mind in the matter has remained a mystery."[44]

It seems just as difficult for historians to determine the truth about what might otherwise seem the most obvious and well-known of "facts" about the divorce and the beginnings of Henrician Reformation: the role played by Anne Boleyn. Was the love (or lust) she inspired in Henry the proper cause of it all? Perhaps not. According to Scarisbrick, "the scruple may already have acquired firm roots" in Henry's mind long before "Anne

38 MacCulloch, "Reform of the Church," pp. 162–3.
39 Eric Ives, *Anne Boleyn* (Oxford: Blackwell, 2004), p. 84.
40 Smith, "Matter of Conscience," pp. 39, 42–3.
41 MacCulloch, "Religion of Henry VIII," p. 160. 42 Scarisbrick, *Henry VIII*, pp. 154, 151–4.
43 Virginia Murphy, "The Literature and Propaganda of Henry VIII's First Divorce," in MacCulloch (ed.), *Reign of Henry VIII*, pp. 135–58 (p. 135).
44 Henry Ansgar Kelly, *The Matrimonial Trials of Henry VIII* (Stanford University Press, 1976), p. 1.

Boleyn captured the king," particularly as "the chronology of Anne's rise is impossible to discover exactly."[45] Though a firm believer in the idea that Henry's "true reason" for divorcing Katherine "may well have been his passion for Anne," nevertheless G. W. Bernard admits that "precise and specific information on the circumstances and the timing" of Anne's appearance on Henry's sexual radar "is hard to find."[46] Regardless of uncertainties surrounding the "chronology" of Henry's "advancing conviction" about the sinfulness of his marriage to Katherine, David Loades has argued recently that "what is reasonably certain is that Anne Boleyn had nothing to do with it": "Anne Boleyn was not a factor in the early stages of these doubts," he asserts, and in any case "we do not know how they arose."[47] By contrast, Thomas Betteridge is convinced "that Anne Boleyn, and Henry's desire for her, played a significant role in the Reformation's course": "at a fundamental level," he proposes, "the reason Henry decided his marriage to Catherine was not legitimate was undoubtedly because of his desire to marry Anne Boleyn."[48]

## III

What, then, is the "truth" of the king's "great matter"? If we appear to have come full circle in asking this question then this is because it is almost impossible to decide what the "truth" is in this case. Like Shakespeare's Henry, we find ourselves amid "many mazed considerings," unsure of which course to "steer" when "hulling" in the historically choppy waters of the king's "conscience." On this basis alone we can begin to see how the title *All Is True* is both playfully ironic and philosophically intriguing. Even the briefest consideration of the king's "scruple" reveals, as the play seems determined to show, how "history" is hardly the same as, or a reliable source of, "truth." What is clear, however, is that in presenting both the history of the divorce and its participants as unfathomably complex and contradictory, *Henry VIII* remains entirely true to the spirit of *uncertainty* that characterizes this history. This is an uncertainty typical not just of modern historical assessments of the divorce, of course, but also of contemporary sources for *Henry VIII*: those sixteenth-century histories labeled by

45 Scarisbrick, *Henry VIII*, pp. 154, 149.

46 G. W. Bernard, *The King's Reformation: Henry VIII and the Remaking of the English Church* (New Haven, CT: Yale University Press, 2005), pp. 14, 4.

47 David Loades, *Henry VIII* (Stroud: Amberley, 2011), pp. 184, 191; David Loades, *Henry VIII: Court, Church and Conflict* (Kew, London: National Archives, 2007), p. 206.

48 Betteridge, "Henry VIII and Popular Culture," p. 212.

Rudnytsky as "official" and "Protestant."[49] Historians as reformed as John Foxe and as loyal to Henry VIII as Edward Hall evidently found it difficult to account for the divorce and the beginnings of Reformation in unambiguous ways or with entirely unalloyed admiration for the king. The "truth" of such things is navigated uneasily by these writers as something fractured and fractious rather than unitary or straightforward.[50] Yet the fact that such "Protestant" histories would betray a deep ambivalence about Henry VIII should not surprise us. As MacCulloch puts it, "King Henry was a difficult figure for the victors of the English Reformation to celebrate," and the writings of Hall, Foxe, and Holinshed reveal this fact implicitly and even, at times, explicitly.[51] Contrary to Rudnytsky's convictions, then, Shakespeare need not have been a follower of "Catholic" histories to regard Henry's dubious behavior over his "scruple" with skepticism: the uncertainty and ambivalence current in *Henry VIII* are also present in the play's "Protestant" historical sources.[52]

Nowhere does this hesitation over the "truth" of Henry's "conscience" become more complex historiographically than in Holinshed's *Chronicles*, the publication history of which reveals something important about the textual instability of "truth" in the period. Whereas the first (1577) edition of Holinshed's *Chronicles* offers a remarkably brief story of the emergence of Henry's scruple, providing a truncated version of the king's "conscience" speech before the legates at Blackfriars in 1529, the second (1587) edition of the *Chronicles* provides a much longer and more detailed rendition.[53] In fact, the two versions – those of the 1577 and 1587 editions – are entirely different. The reason for this discrepancy is straightforward. The 1587 *Chronicles* offers a version carefully revised by Abraham Fleming, "the chief editor of the second edition": an "aggressively anti-Catholic" and polemically "strenuous Protestant."[54] It was Fleming who replaced the sparse account of the Blackfriars trial in the 1577 *Chronicles* with one much richer in detail taken from a source published three years after the first edition of

49 Rudnytsky, "Deconstruction of History," 50.

50 MacCulloch, "Introduction," p. 4. On Foxe's views of Henry, see also David Loades, "John Foxe and Henry VIII," *John Foxe Bulletin*, 1 (2002), 5–12. On Hall and the problems of telling the "truth" of the origins of Henrician Reformation, see Thomas Betteridge, *Tudor Histories of the English Reformations, 1530–83* (Farnham: Ashgate, 1999), pp. 55–68.

51 MacCulloch, "Introduction," p. 8.

52 Anderson, *Biographical Truth*, pp. 134, 136.

53 Raphael Holinshed, *Chronicles of England, Scotlande, and Irelande* (1577) (STC 13568), pp. 1550–2; Holinshed, *Third Volume of Chronicles*, pp. 907–8.

54 Annabel Patterson, "'All is true': Negotiating the Past in *Henry VIII*," in R. B. Parker and S. P. Zitner (eds.), *Elizabethan Theater: Essays in Honor of S. Schoenbaum* (Newark: University of Delaware Press, 1996), pp. 147–66 (p. 156).

Holinshed's *Chronicles* appeared: John Stow's *Chronicles of England* (1580).[55] It is from Stow that the 1587 Holinshed's *Chronicles* takes verbatim Henry's "scruple" speech at Blackfriars, with its erroneous reference to the Bishop of Bayonne, alongside the queen's act of kneeling as she pleads her case before Henry, just as these details (among many others) are replicated in 2.4 of *Henry VIII*.

More interesting and also more important, though, is the fact that both Stow and the second, revised edition of Holinshed's *Chronicles* – the 1587 text more than likely consulted by Shakespeare – offer us their histories of Henry's "conscience," and the "scruple" speech in particular, by way of what might be termed a historiographical transplant. For the "scruple" speech as it appears in 2.4 of *Henry VIII* finds its true source, transmitted via the *Chronicles* of Stow and Holinshed, in one of the most famous "Catholic" accounts of the divorce, and one famously committed to telling the "truth" and yet which remains characterized by "ambiguity and irony": George Cavendish's (then unpublished) narrative of *The Life and Death of Cardinal Wolsey*.[56] It is, in fact, in Cavendish's account that all of the details of Holinshed's version of Henry's speech about his "conscience" find their proper origin: from the more personal tone and hesitant style of Henry's speech here, to his exoneration of Wolsey, and even his mistaken reference to the Bishop of Bayonne. It is in Cavendish's report that Henry declares how it was that his "scrupulous conscience" (a phrase repeated at least three times) received a "doubtful prick," which "bred" and "pricked, vexed, and troubled so my mind, and so disquieted me, that I was in great doubt of God's indignation." It is Cavendish too who first recalls how Henry confessed to having been "troubled in waves of a scrupulous conscience," while suffering "in despair of any male issue."[57]

As an eye-witness present at many such occasions, moreover, Cavendish carries authority. As such, both Stow and Fleming would naturally be keen to preserve the historical fidelity offered by Cavendish's narrative as a reliable first-hand account of the proceedings at Blackfriars. What they are less keen to preserve, and so carefully excise, is Cavendish's hostility toward a Henry whose hypocrisy is presented as transparent and disgusting. Passages "critical of the Protestant position" are thus deleted.[58] There is no sense in the *Chronicles* of Stow and Holinshed, for example, of a Henry who

[55] John Stow, *The Chronicles of England* (1580) (STC 23333), pp. 959–65.

[56] Anderson, *Biographical Truth*, p. 136. See Richard S. Sylvester and Davis P. Harding, eds., *Two Early Tudor Lives* (New Haven, CT: Yale University Press, 1962), pp. 1–193 (pp. 4, 82–9). All quotations refer to this edition. On Cavendish's treatment of "truth," see Anderson, *Biographical Truth*, pp. 27–39.

[57] Sylvester and Harding, *Two Early Tudor Lives*, p. 86.

[58] Anderson, *Biographical Truth*, p. 136.

is frankly desperate to discover "whether I might take another wife in case that my copulation with this gentlewoman [i.e., Katherine] were not lawful; which," Cavendish records Henry as averring, "I intend not for carnal concupiscence."[59] The king protests too much here, we might think. In Cavendish's chronology, we should remember, Henry's "conscience" emerges as a problem, as it does in *Henry VIII*, only after he has met his "sweetheart," Anne Boleyn (2.1.97).[60] In Holinshed, as in Hall and Foxe, this timing is not contradicted or denied: more delicately, it is rendered more mysterious and yet concurrent with other developments and events happening at this time.[61]

If we were left in any doubt of Cavendish's intention to paint Henry in the worst light of villainy and hypocrisy possible, we need only note that Cavendish's most damning condemnation of the king comes immediately before his account of the legatine divorce trial at Blackfriars. "Is it not a world to consider the desire of wilful princes," Cavendish asks, "when they fully be bent and inclined to fulfil their voluptuous appetites ... ? And above all things," he asserts, "there is no one thing that causeth them to be more wilful than carnal desire and voluptuous affection of foolish love":

> The experience is plain in this case, both manifest and evident, for what surmised inventions hath been invented, what laws have been enacted, what noble and ancient monasteries overthrown and defaced, what diversities of religious opinions hath risen, what executions hath been committed, how many famous and notable clerks hath suffered death, what charitable foundations were perverted from the relief of the poor unto profane uses, and what alterations of good and wholesome ancient laws and customs hath been tossed by will and wilful desire of the prince, almost to the subversion and desolation of this noble realm.[62]

Cavendish's history of the divorce, one in which the Henrician Reformation has its disastrous origins in "this pernicious and inordinate love" of Henry for Anne Boleyn,[63] is one that neither Stow nor the more militantly Protestant Fleming would replicate in their Elizabethan *Chronicles*. Yet the transplanting of entire passages, such as the Blackfriars trial of 1529, from Cavendish's history into their chronicle accounts of Henry's divorce has important implications for how we view the later incorporation and reworking of such material in *Henry VIII*. For although neither Fleming nor Stow could commit to presenting a "Catholic"

[59] Sylvester and Harding, *Two Early Tudor Lives*, pp. 86–7. [60] Ibid., pp. 98, 124.

[61] See Holinshed, *Third Volume of Chronicles*, pp. 907–8. See also Hall, *Famelies of Lancastre & Yorke*, fos. clxxxiiiv–clxxxiiii, and John Foxe, *Actes and Monuments* (1583) (STC 11225), pp. 1049–55.

[62] Sylvester and Harding, *Two Early Tudor Lives*, p. 81. [63] Ibid., pp. 81, 30–1.

perspective on the Blackfriars trial or on the origins of Henry's "scruple," nevertheless Cavendish could still offer them more detail – more "truth" – with which to augment their own versions of history, versions in which Cavendish's depiction of Henry as an outright hypocrite is largely erased. In fact, when transferred to the *Chronicles* of Stow and Holinshed, and from thence into *Henry VIII*, Henry's words about his "conscience," although derived from Cavendish, appear to be those of a much more sincerely conscientious king. At the very same time, though, they are also the words of someone about whom we might feel deeply uncertain. In this way Cavendish's account of Henry's "scruple" is, in effect, converted by Stow and Fleming, though not merely from one kind of ethical absolutism to another, that is, from "Catholic" to "Protestant." Rather, this conversion of history is effected by the reshaping of Cavendish's unbending moral certainty about Henry as a voluptuous tyrant into a more flexible and open-minded *uncertainty* over what the king's "true" motives were at Blackfriars in 1529. It is this uncertainty that is subsequently dramatized so faithfully in 2.4 of *Henry VIII*.

## IV

The Protestant tradition of privileging ambivalence – perhaps even skepticism – towards Henry VIII's conscience reaches its apogee, one could argue, in *Henry VIII*. This is a play, after all, in which the king's encounter with Anne Boleyn in 1.4, long before his "conscience" is openly exercised, generates nothing like any absolute certainty about the king's motives for wanting a divorce, as the "Catholic" tradition would purport. Instead, it generates an even deeper, more radical *uncertainty* about them as mixed and contradictory. Far from dictating to its audiences an inflexibly "Catholic" view of Henry as religious charlatan and marital scoundrel, what *Henry VIII* reflects – and that to which it remains steadfastly "true" throughout – is something arguably much more complicated: a more enlivening, more lifelike, and (in Anderson's sense of the term) more "truthful" *hesitancy* about Henry's ethical character.[64] The king's behavior is thus almost impossible to nail down in the play, either morally or historically. It has been easy, of course, for commentators to assume that *Henry VIII* must be written against "official" "Protestant" histories of the Henrician Reformation. Yet, as we have seen, the aim of such histories seems to be one of ensuring that that which is unknown and uncertain remains a key

64 Anderson, *Biographical Truth*, pp. 130, 134.

element of the story, a part of the fabric of historical "truth" itself. Critics who attempt to assert that the play's treatment of Henry's "conscience" is either entirely sincere or wholly suspect are bound equally to come undone in this respect. The truth is that it is difficult to know how to categorize with any degree of certainty what *Henry VIII* offers in its treatment of Henry's "scruple" or indeed of his "Reformation" generally – sincerity or cynicism? As Lee Bliss has put it, we may have to accept both options "as possible, and even as equally true."[65]

How, then, can we understand Shakespeare's treatment of history and its complex relationship to "truth" in *Henry VIII*? Why is "history" so concertedly and yet disconcertingly divorced from what is "true" in this play? Understandably, these are the questions that have troubled and fascinated the play's critics.[66] As has been hinted at throughout this chapter, however, one way to understand *Henry VIII* is to see it as something which, at almost every turn, excites but then punctures and deflates our "faith" in the "truth" of the history it presents. The play solicits but then demolishes our faith in the historical veracity of the events and persons it stages. In this sense, what might be standing behind *Henry VIII*'s employment of "history" could well be a simple yet particularly "Protestant" idea: that of "historical faith," the Reformed pedigree of which is important for us to acknowledge when fathoming the "truthfulness" of *Henry VIII*.[67] Although the term was originally formulated by the German Reformer Philip Melancthon, William Tyndale was the first English writer to employ "historical faith" in his debates with Sir Thomas More around 1530.[68] Tyndale argued that any faith received passively from the church alone, rather than arising from the personal experience of the believer, was no more than "historical" in nature. It was something acquired by human means only, requiring no more than superficial assent from the participants and an acknowledgment that the stories of Scripture had actually happened and that its persons existed historically. For Tyndale, the "faith" propagated by Papists could never be anything more than "historicall" because it simply "hangeth of the

65 Bliss, "Wheel of Fortune," 7.

66 As well as the many examples already cited in previous notes, see also Anston Bosman, "Seeing Tears: Truth and Sense in *All Is True*," *Shakespeare Quarterly*, 50 (1999), 459–76; and Thomas Healey, "History and Judgement in *Henry VIII*," in Richards and Knowles, *Shakespeare's Late Plays*, pp. 158–75.

67 On the place of "history" in early modern English thought, see D. R. Woolf, *The Idea of History in Early Stuart England* (University of Toronto Press, 1990), esp. pp. 3–76, and *Reading History in Early Modern England* (Cambridge University Press, 2000), esp. pp. 3–131.

68 See David Weil Baker, "The Historical Faith of William Tyndale: Non-Salvific Reading of Scripture at the Outset of the English Reformation," *Renaissance Quarterly*, 62 (2009), 661–92.

trueth and honestie of the teller, or of the comen fame and consent of many. As if," he goes on to say, "one told me that the turke had wonne a citie, and I beleved it," having been "moved with the honestie" of the teller alone. Such belief was distinct from what Tyndale calls "felynge faith," which is "as if a man were there present whan it was wonne" and whose first-hand experience of it means that "all the worlde coude not turne him from his faith." Using another notable analogy, Tyndale explains the difference thus: "Even likewise if my mother had blowen on hir finger and told me that the fire wold burne me," then, he asserts, "I shuld have beleved hir with an historicall faith, as we beleve the stories of the worlde . . . And so I shuld have done, if she had tolde me that the fire had bene cold and wold not have burned, but," he notes, "assone as I had put my fingre in the fire, I shuld have beleved not by the reason of hir but with a felynge faith."[69]

This primacy of a faith centered in the experiential and "felt" conviction of a spiritual "Truth," one that would be said to exist beyond the commonly accepted historical facticity of the Bible as a proper record of ancient happenings and persons, would become a cornerstone of scriptural interpretation and soterial doctrine in the Reformed tradition. Divines and preachers from Theodore Beza and Jean Calvin to William Perkins and, even later, John Bunyan would repeat a mantra concerning these two kinds of faith: the "historical" kind – which could be held by anyone, even ungodly hypocrites, reprobates, and devils – and a "true" or "saving" faith, which read Scripture as a communication of something deeper than mere history, recognizing it as a vehicle for "Truth" beyond historical facts alone and rooted in the transhistorical promises of salvation.[70] As the means whereby "credence is yeelded to the History of Gods word" but without the believer being "any whit the better affected . . . either to love God, or feare him, or trust in him the more for his faith," as William Gouge would put it, "historical faith" was, for many Reformed English divines, simply no "faith" at all.[71] To read the Bible as if it were simply a chronicle of events was not enough: its "Truth" transcended

69 William Tyndale, *An Answere unto Sir Thomas Mores Dialogue* (Antwerp, 1531) (STC 24437), fos. xxix–xxx (fo. xxixv). For More's response, see *The Second Part of the Confutacion of Tyndals Answer* (1533) (STC 18080), fos. cccxlviii–cccxlix, ccclxxviii, ccccxiii–ccccxv.

70 Miles Coverdale, *A Goodly Treatise of Faith, Hope, and Charitie* (1537) (STC 24219:5), "Preface," fo. i(verso); Theodore Beza, *The Treasure of Trueth* (1576) (STC 2049), sig. FV(verso); Jean Calvin, *An Abridgement of the Institution of Christian Religion* (1585) (STC 4429), pp. 138–9; William Perkins, *An Exposition of the Symbole or Creed of the Apostles* (Cambridge, 1595) (STC 19703), p. 6; John Bunyan, *The Doctrine of the Law and Grace Unfolded* (1659), in *The Miscellaneous Works of John Bunyan*, 13 vols., gen. ed. R. Sharrock (Oxford: Clarendon Press, 1976–1994), vol. I, pp. 134–5.

71 William Gouge, *The Whole-Armor of God* (1619) (STC 12123), p. 208.

"history" and indeed canceled its relevance as "history" alone. The message, not the story, is what would matter most.

Recognizing this Protestant idea of "historical faith" may enable us to recalibrate our understanding of the fraught and sometimes paradoxical tension between "truth" and "history," as well as their separation, in *Henry VIII*, given that so much in the play fissures and splits upon that which might be termed historically "true." As we have seen, some "facts" about Henry's divorce and the beginnings of the Henrician Reformation, including the sincerity of the king's "scruple," are simply too obscure ever to be verifiable. As a result, the "history" of *Henry VIII* resists even the most basic kind of "historical faith" in its characters and events simply because the historical "truth" of such things is just too unreliable, too unstable, too entangled in what Tyndale refers to as "the stories of the worlde" and "the comen fame and consent of many" to uphold anything like an unquestionably "true" historicity. In this respect it seems typically ironic of the play to present a king who, wounded in his conscience over the sinfulness of his first marriage, claims to have undergone a conversion into a "feeling faith" of sorts in 2.4. In reality, the historical Henry VIII was probably capable of no more than "story" faith: "historical faith," that is, in its crudest form.[72] Historians from Hall to Scarisbrick can easily accept that, whatever prompted Henry's desire for divorce, it resulted in his political "conversion" and "reformation" as a ruler: he cast off his old man, Wolsey, and asserted himself more independently as his own king.[73] Yet, given Henry's life-long rejection of the most fundamental tenet of Reformed doctrine, justification by faith alone, few would believe in the conspicuously evangelical "conversion" Shakespeare's Henry claims to have undergone in 2.4.[74] As such, Shakespeare's subtle enhancement of the language of Protestant transformation in Henry's "scruple" speech has a very strange effect: it makes Henry's identification with Protestantism stronger and yet draws attention to just how doubtful that identification would always be.

By ensuring that no certain or fixed "truth" can be yielded by "history," *Henry VIII* subverts, it would seem, some of the Tudor English chroniclers' grander ambitions to provide their readers with sources of historical "truth"

[72] Scarisbrick, *Henry VIII*, pp. 406–7.

[73] Hall, *Famelies of Lancastre & Yorke*, fos. clxxxiii(verso)–iiii; Scarisbrick, *Henry VIII*, pp. 245–6, 248, 326, 386–90.

[74] See Scarisbrick, *Henry VIII*, pp. 399–408; Bernard, *King's Reformation*, pp. 228–43.

as reliable and indeed as true as the Scriptures themselves.[75] This strategy may explain why the play is so full of sea-changes: those sudden, self-erasing reversals to both character and plot that complicate what is true and what is not.[76] All that which is "now best" is shown to be, almost in the same breath, "now worst" in *Henry VIII* (1.1.29), and vice versa, whether in recounting the "fierce vanities" of the Field of Cloth of Gold (1.1.54) or in dramatizing Wolsey's conversion from arch-villain to sincere penitent who feels his "heart new opened" (3.2.367). The play's most conspicuous dramatization of this cancellation of history as a source of "truth" comes climactically, of course, in Cranmer's prophecy (5.4.14–62). For this is a speech without any historical source or precedent, spoken before a king who may not even have attended the occasion at which it is delivered: the christening of his daughter, Elizabeth. Cranmer's vision here serves, too, to complete that which, historically speaking, almost certainly did not occur: Henry's spiritual regeneration, marked in the play by the king's inspired but "entirely unhistorical" words, "Thou hast made me now a man" (5.4.64).[77] What Cranmer's vision reveals, moreover, is something profoundly awful for Henry. It shows him the utter pointlessness of his attempts, both within and beyond the events dramatized in the play, to secure a male heir to continue the Tudor dynasty. What is foreseen instead is that which the audience already knows: the death of the most long-reigning Tudor monarch, the childless "virgin" (5.4.60), Elizabeth I, and with her the royal Tudor line.[78]

By the end of *Henry VIII*, Cranmer's very different kind of "Truth" – being that on which, he states, both Elizabeth and England will be nursed and nourished (5.4.28) – triumphs not because of the vicissitudes of history but entirely, it would seem, in spite of them. Cranmer's "Truth" is, then, like that image of the "phoenix" (5.4.40) so figuratively central to the larger rhetoric of his prophecy: it is something that rises against the self-defeating and "fruitless" nature of historical ambition, whether Henry's or Wolsey's. Cranmer's final promise of a phoenix-like pattern of regeneration for England thus offers "an escape from the endless repetitions of history" and the "immutable recurrence" of history's pointless victories and

75 Annabel M. Patterson, *Reading Holinshed's Chronicles* (University of Chicago Press, 1994), pp. viii–x: Patterson quotes Fleming as stating in the 1587 edition of Holinshed's *Chronicles* that "Chronicles approach next in truth to the sacred and inviolable scripture" (pp. viii and 277 n. 1).

76 In Chapter 5 above Beatrice Groves notes a similar disconcerting emphasis on unexpected "sea-changes" in one of Shakespeare's earlier history plays, *King John*. She, too, reads these reversals as challenging mere historical "correctness" in favor of a more uncertain, diverse, and profound sense of truth.

77 Saccio, *Shakespeare's English Kings*, p. 225.

78 Ibid., pp. 224–5.

defeats.[79] In the face of Cranmer's "Truth," "history" in *Henry VIII* is shown – to borrow one of the play's own tropes of self-consuming non-progression – to "outrun" itself and, indeed, to "lose by over-running" the very thing toward which it runs (1.1.141–3): the "truth."

## V

What is revealed to be of "transcendent importance" throughout *Henry VIII* is never "history," but an idea of "Truth" beyond history, although it is a "Truth" that, as Thomas Betteridge remarks of Hall's writing of the Henrician Reformation, "endangers the very principle on which" the play's "historiography is predicated": that of "all" being "true."[80] Because the historical "truth" cannot be known in *Henry VIII* or separated from Tyndale's "comen fame of many" and "the stories of the worlde," then the "truth" that it asserts in the end must be "ahistorical and asocial": something more akin, in the terms of Cranmer's prophecy, to "the truth of the gospel" and the deeper faith that truth requires of believers, a truth beyond a recognition of mere "historical" facts alone. As with Hall's treatment of history, so too must *Henry VIII* assert its "truthfulness" by "writing around or through the official records of the past" in order to produce a "Truth" of a very different quality, purpose, and nature: that of Cranmer's elegiac vision.[81] Cranmer's divining of Elizabeth's reign thus has the strangely vertiginous effect of sweeping aside the struggles of Tudor history entirely, revealing the bloody and messy years between the birth of Elizabeth I and the accession of James I to be strangely irrelevant to its final assertion of "Truth." In this sense, Cranmer's prophecy performs another, crucial kind of conversion at the end of the play. It transforms civil or secular history into a narrative of "sacred reality," as David Scott Kastan has termed it: one that privileges a "transcendent" notion of "Truth" that remains "unconditional and unchanging," indeed, beyond "history."[82]

It goes without saying that Shakespearean drama is not usually considered to work in the ways outlined in this chapter: that is, as subtly but determinedly "Protestant" in design and effect, staying paradoxically true to the "letter" of its historical sources while requiring audiences and readers to discern an alternative "spirit" within its treatment of historical events and persons. Nor, perhaps, could any other Shakespeare play be viewed as if it

79 Bliss, "Wheel of Fortune," 17, 20, 23. 80 Betteridge, *Tudor Histories*, p. 67.
81 Ibid., pp. 67–8.
82 David Scott Kastan, *Shakespeare and the Shapes of Time* (London: Macmillan, 1982), p. 137.

were another of Stanley Fish's "self-consuming artifacts": as a seventeenth-century text, that is, that seeks to achieve a "conversion" in the "perceptual habits" of its audiences through strategies that ask them to "discover the truth for themselves" through a form – in this case, that of "history" or "chronicle" – which becomes "the vehicle of its own abandonment."[83] It is in just this way, however, that *Henry VIII* "points away from itself to something its form cannot capture," appealing, as Cranmer's prophecy exemplifies, to the "values" of a "progressively widening vision," the "truth" of which lies beyond any "version of reality yielded by the senses" alone.[84]

If *Henry VIII* can be read in the ways I am suggesting, this could leave us with a formidably different version of "late" Shakespeare. For this would be a dramatist who, even at the very end of his career, remained remarkably attuned to contemporary discourses of early modern religion: beyond, that is, an often alleged nostalgia for the rituals and beliefs of the "Old Faith," but also beyond a more limited, because secular, rootedness in questions of "religious" court politics and Jacobean factionalism.[85] The Shakespeare of *Henry VIII*, by contrast, coauthors a play which looks back carefully upon the perplexing origins of the Henrician Reformation but which senses, too, a future about to unfold: a turbulent and indeed revolutionary future in which, during the fifty years following *Henry VIII*'s first performances, ordinary men and women would increasingly undergo Henry's kind of "Puritan" conversion experience and put their narratives of such experience into print. They would also bring questions of "conscience" – that keyword of seventeenth-century British history and politics – to bear directly on their dealings with secular and ecclesiastical authorities in the name and spirit of "true" Reformation. Such is the future Shakespeare seems to be sensing and peering into intently in his final play, *Henry VIII*.

83 Stanley Fish, *Self-Consuming Artifacts: The Experience of Seventeenth-Century Literature* (Berkeley: University of California Press, 1972), p. 3.

84 Ibid., pp. 4, 7.

85 For a different reading of *Henry VIII* that shares a number of this chapter's larger thematic concerns, see Chapter 12 above. On "Catholic" rituals and beliefs in the late plays and Romances, see Ruth Vanita, "Mariological Memory in *The Winter's Tale* and *Henry VIII*," *SEL*, 40 (2000), 311–37; and Richmond, *Shakespeare, Catholicism, and Romance*. On Henry VIII and the religious politics of the Jacobean court, see Mark Rankin, "Henry VIII, Shakespeare, and the Jacobean Royal Court," *SEL*, 51 (2011), 349–66.

CHAPTER 14

# *Shakespeare's non-Christian religions*

*Matthew Dimmock*

It has become almost proverbial that one searches in vain for non-Christian religion in the majority of Shakespeare's dramatic corpus. When compared with the geographically wide-ranging imaginations of his contemporaries – and with Christopher Marlowe in particular – Shakespeare's drama, it is argued, rarely looks beyond the bounds of Christendom to the old worlds of the East or the new worlds to the West.[1] The two primary "exceptions" in this regard are *The Merchant of Venice* (*c.* 1596) and *Othello* (*c.* 1603), but even they are often considered reticent and elusive in dramatizing non-Christian religion. A Shakespeare industry which globalized and secularized the "national bard" in the twentieth century has by turns fretted over and celebrated these plays as controversial, atypical, even political. Recent scholarship has followed suit, with the New Historicist rediscovery of "virtually every marginalized Other that passed through early modern England" leading to the disproportionate scrutiny of Othello, Shylock, and their potential contexts.[2]

Yet dramatizing any kind of religion on the professional stages of late sixteenth- and early seventeenth-century England was a complex proposition; doubly so in the case of religious practice.[3] The late suppression of the suspiciously Roman Catholic Corpus Christi plays prompted legislation that prohibited the counterfeiting or representation of "the Ma(jest)ye of God the Father, God the Sonne, or God the Holie Ghoste or the administration of either the Sacramentes of baptisme or of the Lordes Supper" or "anythinge plaid which tende to the maintenaunce of superstition or

[1] A. L. Rowse's comment that in this regard Shakespeare, "that quiet countryman," was "the least engaged writer that ever was," suggests that this perception is of long standing. *The Expansion of Elizabethan England* (London: Macmillan, 1955), p. 177.

[2] James Shapiro, *Shakespeare and the Jews* (New York: Columbia University Press, 1997), p. 86.

[3] See Chapter 12 above for more on the current critical debate about the degree to which religious practices (particularly Christian ones) were made a part of early modern English theatrical productions, and the questionable nature and purpose of such staged rites.

idolatrie or which be contrarie to the lawes of God [and] of the realme."[4] The effect this had on the depiction of non-Christians and their religion is unclear, but it was certainly uneven: although it was a source of widespread fear and fascination, there was no stage depiction of Christian-Muslim conversion until Robert Daborne's *A Christian Turn'd Turk* (1612), whereas Robert Greene could depict "Turks" and "Moors" prostrate before an antiquated fire-breathing idol of "Mahomet" in his *Alphonsus of Arragon* (*c.* 1587).[5] Tracing religion on the early modern stage is further complicated by its ephemerality; often minimal directions make the role of props, costume, and gesture difficult to recover.[6]

There are, however, many different religious systems and practices present in Shakespeare's plays, and they are engaged in more subtle and various ways than is commonly acknowledged. The pantheon of classical deities is regularly presented, and witchcraft occupies a prominent place, both of which are folded into non-Christian religions in provocative ways. In the often parodied cauldron scene in *Macbeth*, for instance, amongst a cascade of ingredients that include "poisoned entrails," "scale of dragon," "Witches' mummy," and a range of animal parts, we find the "Liver of blaspheming Jew," a "Nose of Turk," and "Tartar's lips" (4.1.5, 22–9).[7] Scholars tend to gloss such references as constituent parts of a cumulative register of barbarity that fixes the weird sisters beyond the province of Christ, signaling an encroaching and infernal other world, but these specific elements are not, unlike some of the sisters' other props, simply ephemeral exotica.

That it is the liver of a "blaspheming Jew" demonstrates how even an apparently offhand reference might signal religious difference – here presumably a reference to the Jews' bitter and defining unwillingness to acknowledge the divinity of Christ.[8] There are similar examples elsewhere

4 Declaration of the Diocesan Court of High Commission at York, quoted in Glynne Wickham, *Early English Stages, 1300 to 1600*, vol. I, 1300–1576 (London: Routledge & Kegan Paul, 1966), p. 115.

5 Conversion is described in comic detail by Basilisco in Thomas Kyd's *Soliman and Perseda*, however. On the rich and bizarre ritual concocted by Daborne, see Matthew Dimmock, "Materialising Islam on the Early Modern English Stage," in Sabine Schülting, Sabine Lucia Müller, and Ralf Hertel (eds.), *Early Modern Encounters with the Islamic East: Performing Cultures* (Farnham: Ashgate, 2012), pp. 115–34.

6 One prominent attempt to explore the life of costumes and props on the early modern stage is Jean MacIntyre, *Costumes and Scripts in the Early Modern Theaters* (Edmonton: University of Alberta Press, 1992).

7 Unless otherwise noted, all references to the plays of William Shakespeare are taken from *The Norton Shakespeare*, ed. Stephen Greenblatt et al. (New York: W. W. Norton, 1997). It has been argued that this particular scene may have been added by Middleton.

8 The many elements of the stereotype of the Jew and its history in England are notably discussed in Shapiro, *Shakespeare and the Jews*, and Anthony Bale, *The Jew in the Medieval Book: English Antisemitisms, 1350–1500* (Cambridge University Press, 2007).

in the Shakespearean canon: Falstaff protests that if he is not telling the truth, he is "a Jew else, an Hebrew Jew" (*1 Henry IV* 2.5.165); Launce demands that Speed accompany him to the alehouse, for "if not, thou art an Hebrew, a Jew, and not worth the name of a Christian" (*Two Gentlemen of Verona* 2.5.44–5); and Benedick reflects upon Beatrice, "If I do not love her I am a Jew" (*Much Ado About Nothing* 2.3.231–2). Understood on a proverbial level, such shorthand references work antithetically, aligning the singular "Jew" with Christian sin – specifically, in these examples, with lying, incivility, and a lack of charity. The result is a paradox – the Jew is absolutely opposed to the Christian, as sin is to virtue, but every Christian has the potential "to Jew." The Jew, denied subjecthood, becomes a phantom of the Christian psyche.[9]

Although they seem undifferentiated in the sisters' incantation, "Turks and Tartars" (particularly the former) carry quite different connotations in this Shakespearean shorthand, and appear more frequently, than "the Jew." They can be barbarous, as when the Duke of Venice urges Christian sympathy, unlike "stubborn Turks and Tartars never trained / To offices of tender courtesy" (*Merchant of Venice* 4.1.31–2). "The Turk" can also take his place alongside "the Jew" in a Christian psychodrama: so Hamlet can ponder whether "the rest of my fortunes turn Turk with me" (*Hamlet* 3.2.253–4), and Margaret can intervene in a discussion about marriage by cautioning Beatrice, "Well, an you be not turned Turk, there's no more sailing by the star" (*Much Ado About Nothing* 3.4.37–8). Most references make "the Turk" – almost invariably singular and male – emblematic of a violent, vast, and anti-Christian power that threatens Christianity from without; Richard ironically asks the Lord Mayor of London, "think you we are Turks or infidels?" (*Richard III* 3.5.39), and in *Richard II* the Bishop of Carlisle anachronistically couples contemporary "Turks" with medieval "Saracens" as he reflects upon Norfolk's glorious crusading exploits, "For Jesu Christ in glorious Christian field, / Streaming the ensign of the Christian cross / Against black pagans, Turks, and Saracens" (4.1.84–6).

In a manner characteristic of Shakespeare's history plays, the reassuring certainties of a crusading past collapse inwards in the turmoil of civil strife, so "Peace shall go to sleep with Turks and infidels" (*Richard II* 4.1.130), and the new King Henry V must reassure his brothers that "This is the English,

[9] For an intriguingly similar exploration of the unexpected intersections of Good and Evil and Self and Other in sixteenth-century religious thought, and for a more extended analysis of *Macbeth* specifically, see Chapter 9 above, where Ewan Fernie discusses among other things how Luther's Protestantism posed new and fundamental challenges to the long-standing Augustinian "privation theory" of evil.

not the Turkish court" (*2 Henry IV* 5.2.37).[10] Henry then externalizes this defining opposition between Christian and Islam by mapping it onto intra-Christian conflict with France.[11] The frequency of such references reflect the prominence of the Ottoman Empire in the late sixteenth-century world, but also the continuing existence – however antiquated or ambivalent – of an idealized Christian identity and the displacement of vice onto non-Christian adversaries.

One further related context for the presence of Jew, Turk, and Tartar body parts in the weird sisters' cauldron is the theater itself. By the first performance of *Macbeth* all three had been prominent figures on the English stage. A merchant-usurer named Gerontus had appeared in Robert Wilson's *Three Ladies of London* (1581), and Stephen Gosson mentions a play (no longer extant) titled *The Jew* which depicted "the greediness of worldly choosers, and bloody minds of usurers" in 1587.[12] Marlowe's vicious, comic, and influential *Jew of Malta* was written in or around 1590, and was followed by Thomas Dekker's lost *Josef, the Jew of Venice* (1593) and Shakespeare's own *Merchant of Venice* (*c.* 1596).[13] The figure of the Turk had been even more popular than that of the Jew – twenty or more "Turk plays" followed the first part of Marlowe's *Tamburlaine* (1587), and Tartar emperors (the Mongol descendants of Genghis Khan) had been the celebrated protagonists of the now lost two parts of *Tamar Cam* (1592).[14] The early modern English stage was crowded with non-Christian figures which, aside from these "stock" examples, included a procession of Moors, Amazons, Pigmies, Cannibals, and many others. Although records suggest increasing numbers of non-Christians arriving on English shores in this period, it seems likely that the weird sisters' ingredients, as with most of Shakespeare's references to Jews, Turks, and Tartars, are not simply experiential but are instead

[10] Fratricide upon the accession of a new emperor was established practice in the Ottoman Empire of this period and was widely reported in English books and pamphlets.

[11] The mirroring of Anglo-French and Christian–Muslim conflicts in the history plays is explored further in Jerry Brotton, "Shakespeare's Turks and the Spectre of Ambivalence in the History Plays," *Textual Practice*, 28.3 (2014), 521–38.

[12] Stephen Gosson, *The School of Abuse* (1587), p. 43, quoted in Jonathan Burton, *Traffic and Turning: Islam and English Drama, 1579–1624* (Newark: University of Delaware Press, 2005), p. 220.

[13] Burton, *Traffic and Turning*, p. 257.

[14] The plot book of *The First Part of Tamar Cham*, although now lost, was transcribed in the early nineteenth century and is reproduced in Walter W. Greg (ed.), *Henslowe Papers: Being Documents Supplementary to Henslowe's Diary* (London: A. H. Bullen, 1907), pp. 145–8. A list of "Turk plays" is presented as an appendix in Burton, *Traffic and Turning*, p. 257.

theatrically self-reflexive, drawing upon a semiotic system that dealt in emblems, resonances, and oppositions.[15]

## Shakespeare's Judaism

On those occasions when Shakespeare chose to engage with Judaism or Islam in a more sustained way, the theatrical context is essential since it demonstrates how he imitated, nuanced, or rejected the dramatic language used elsewhere to conjure non-Christian religion for early modern playgoers. The creation of a character like Shylock is clearly a more complex undertaking than the blunt references to Jews scattered through the canon, and although there are obvious connections, Shakespeare repeatedly plays with the assumptions embedded in that shorthand. Continuity is most obviously manifest in separation – following the lead of Marlowe's Barabas, Shylock articulates a keen sense of his own difference and that of his "tribe" (1.3.106) in specifically "racial" terms.[16] In an early modern context, "race" began to assume some of the connotations of ethnicity and innate difference that it would carry in a post-Enlightenment period, but it is most often used to indicate genealogy. When Barabas and Shylock both affirm their particular descent from "father Abram" (1.3.156) in opposition to the Christians, who are "Hagar's offspring" (2.6.42), they assert a biblical distinction between the two sons of Abraham, Isaac (born of Sarah) and Ishmael (born of Hagar), and make claim to be God's chosen people – disputing the tradition which identified Christians as the true inheritors of Isaac and Abraham.[17]

Unlike contemporary biological-genetic conceptions of race, this is an explicitly religious distinction, one that generates a stage Judaism distinct from and antagonistic towards Christianity. At root is a denial of Christ's divinity, about which Shylock is explicit from his first entry, referring to "your prophet the Nazarite" (1.3.28) and his own "sacred nation" (1.3.43) in

[15] Records of non-Christians in England are collected and analyzed in Imtiaz Habib, *Black Lives in the English Archives, 1500–1677* (Farnham: Ashgate, 2008), and Nabil Matar, *Islam in Britain, 1558–1685* (Cambridge University Press, 1998). The intertwining of different non-Christian religions might also include Roman Catholicism: this is most notably present in the idolatry and witchcraft of *Alphonsus of Arragon*, but even the witches' incantation in *Macbeth*, with its opening invocation of a kind of thaumaturgical time and elaborate ritual, might hint at anti-Catholic polemic, an element that might be heightened (as in *Alphonsus*) in performance through the use of props, costume, and gesture.

[16] It is worth noting here how the word "tribe" used by both Shylock and Barabas to refer to Jews and Judaism is, in biblical terms, explicitly religious.

[17] The most engaging recent discussion of "race" in an early modern context appears in the introduction to Ania Loomba and Jonathan Burton (eds.), *Race in Early Modern England: A Documentary Companion* (Basingstoke: Palgrave Macmillan, 2007), pp. 1–36.

an aside heard only by the audience. In *The Jew of Malta* Barabas's tone is similar – he insists that "all are heretics that are not Jews" (2.3.317), castigating the "swine-eating Christians" as an "unchosen nation, never circumcised" (2.3.7–8) and as "Philistines" (2.3.233).[18] For Christian audiences, this foundational difference between their own scripturally affirmed status as the new Israelites, the "chosen," and Jews' erroneous claims to the same, animates every element of the stage Jew's characterization. It is affirmed in Shylock's unwillingness to eat, drink, or pray with Christians (1.3.31–2); in his profession of usurer (linking him to earlier stage Jews and itself an uneasy reflection on new economic realities); in references to the indelible mark of circumcision; and in the play's familial dynamic – like Barabas, Shylock has no living wife or son, but only a daughter of marriageable age (a "most sweet Jew" [2.3.11]), offering a neat formula for assimilation as if the stage Jew were a problem to be solved.[19]

It is to this fiction of competing narratives of the "chosen" that remnants of an earlier Christian mythology of Judaism are attached. In Marlowe's play the incorporation of that mythology is a darkly comic reflection on irrational prejudice, as when Friar Bernardine promises to reveal Barabas's crime: Friar Jacomo's immediate assumption is that the Jew has "crucified a child" (3.6.49), an accusation that surfaces in a number of medieval cases.[20] Shakespeare similarly places elements of this opprobrious tradition in the mouths of Christian accusers: thus Shylock is referred to as a dog or cur on eight occasions and as a devil on four, the latter reflecting Judas's identification as the devil in John 6:70 and the Jews' as the children "of [their] father the devil" in John 8:44.[21] When the prospect of Jewish cannibalism is raised, however, it comes obliquely from Shylock himself, who will go to supper with Bassanio and Antonio "in hate, to feed upon / The prodigal Christian" (2.5.14–15). Some critics, most prominently James Shapiro, have found in Shylock's demands for a pound of Antonio's flesh an intersection of such "Jew-libel" mythology with early modern anxieties about circumcision as a defining mark of difference: that the cut is a kind of circumcision, and "Shylock will cut his Christian adversary in that part of the body where

18 All references to Marlowe's plays are taken from Christopher Marlowe, *The Complete Plays*, ed. Mark Thornton Burnett, Everyman series (London: J. M. Dent, 1999).

19 Norman Jones, *God and the Moneylenders: Usury and Law in Early Modern England* (Oxford: Blackwell, 1989), pp. 145–74.

20 One such example is "Little Saint Hugh" of Lincoln: for the narrative and its wider dissemination, see Richard Utz, "The Medieval Myth of Jewish Ritual Murder: Toward a History of Literary Reception," *The Year's Work in Medievalism*, 14 (1999), 22–42.

21 Discussed in Bale, *Jew in the Medieval Book*, p. 11.

the Christians [following St. Paul] believe themselves to be truly circumcised: the heart."[22]

Despite the presence of earlier libel motifs, the invocation of Judaism on the early modern stage was not dependent on them. There was an established costume for the Jew – Shylock refers to his "Jewish gaberdine" (1.3.108), and there are repeated references to Barabas's apparently prominent nose (2.3.177) as well as the possibility of red beards and distinctive hats (referred to by Barabas at 4.4.78–9) – although critics do not agree on exactly how it was constituted. Regardless of the exact clothing used, as Eva Johanna Holmberg has noted, we should recognize that "an audience was aware that what they were seeing were English people portraying Jews."[23] So when Shylock enters the stage with Bassanio at the start of Act 1, scene 3, or Barabas is revealed in his counting house at the opening of *The Jew of Malta*, an audience would make certain assumptions about the nature and role of their characters that are then affirmed by the immediate association established between money, usury, and Jewishness, the biblical encoding of their difference, and subsequent allusions to a medieval mythology. But beyond a sense that it was a religion that disputed the foundations of Christianity, what does *The Merchant of Venice* show us of Judaism?

As it turns out, very little; for, in a strictly literal sense, neither Shakespeare's play nor *The Jew of Malta* contains any Judaism. Although both refer to groups of Jews meeting at synagogues, there is no religious practice (which may well have been impossible given the prohibitions on staging Christian religion, as noted above). In its absence – and in the absence of any stage directions that might indicate a specifically "Jewish" language of gesture – Judaism is almost entirely constituted through reference to Scripture, and it is here that Shakespeare diverges from Marlowe and dramatic convention. Barabas's language and points of reference are suffused with the early books of the Christian Old Testament, corresponding to the Torah and Prophets in the Hebrew Bible. His allusions to "Old Abram" (1.1.105) and to Cain and Adam (3.4.33) come from Genesis. He laments his fate in reference to the plagues of Egypt and the Passover, calls upon "thou, that with a fiery pillar led'st / The sons of Israel through the dismal shades" (2.1.12–13), and reminds his audience of when "heaven rained manna for the Jews" (2.3.253) – all referring to Exodus. His

[22] Shapiro, *Shakespeare and the Jews*, p. 127.

[23] Eva Johanna Holmberg, *Jews in the Early Modern English Imagination: A Scattered Nation* (Farnham: Ashgate, 2012), p. 114. Robert I. Lublin asserts Marlowe's lasting influence on the costume of subsequent stage Jews in his *Costuming the Shakespearean Stage: Visual Codes of Representation in Early Modern Theater and Culture* (Farnham: Ashgate, 2011), pp. 157–61.

identification of the Jews as a "scattered nation" (1.1.120) comes from Deuteronomy, his comment that he is "not of the tribe of Levi" (2.3.18) from Joshua, and his promise to lend Mathias a "comment on the Maccabees" (2.6.157) refers to an apocryphal book, further distancing him from Anglican Protestantism and associating him with the Roman Catholicism of the Knights of Malta. Marlowe even constructs the names of Barabas's associates from the Old Testament – Kirriah Jairim and Obed (1.1.123–4) are taken from Joshua and Chronicles, while Ithamore may be derived from Ithamar, one of Aaron's sons in Exodus.[24]

Marlowe therefore deliberately cultivates Barabas as a creature of the Old Testament, using well-known Mosaic and Abrahamic narratives alongside deliberately obscure passages (even for an audience well versed in the Bible). The division this implies between a backward-looking, literalist Judaism and the play's Christian characters is only enhanced, in the first scene of Jewish–Christian confrontation, by the Maltese Knights' explicit use of the New Testament. Ferneze refers to Matthew 27:25 – in which the Jews accept responsibility for the death of Christ by exclaiming "His blood be on us, and on our children" – when he justifies his actions against the Jews of Malta through reference to his "sufferance" of their "hateful lives, / Who stand accursed in the sight of heaven" (1.2.63–4), a defense reinforced by the First Knight's assertion of the same "first curse" later in the scene.[25] Such references point to the true irony of this scene: its playfully transgressive recreation of the trial of Christ before Pilate, with Barabas, both the Maltese Jew and his biblical namesake, standing in for Jesus (a parallel that can be heightened in performance). In response to what he sees as hypocritical Christian sermonizing on the rejection of worldly covetousness, Barabas turns again to the Old Testament, reminding those who have just confiscated his goods of the words of Exodus 20:15: "Thou shalt not steal" (1.2.128–9).

Judaism in *The Jew of Malta* is a montage of Old Testament motifs that is comprehensible to an audience and has a kind of grudging legitimacy by virtue of its biblical origins, but which is implicitly obsolete as a system of belief due to its supercession by the Christian New Testament. For Marlowe, this ambivalence, carefully built into his particular stage Judaism, allows a sustained critique of the debasement of religion when in

[24] This section builds on the notes in Burnett's edition of Marlowe's *Complete Plays*, esp. p. 592, and in David Bevington and Eric Rasmussen's edition of *Doctor Faustus and Other Plays* (Oxford University Press, 1995), p. 454.

[25] At 1.2.110: "your first curse fall heavy on thy head."

the service of power and wealth. This critique spares neither Jew nor Christian, although ironically it does spare the "Turk," and the Knights of Malta are so conspicuously Roman Catholic that any moral lessons for Protestant England are only implied.[26] The "Hebrew" religion is therefore a satirical device, one structured around a characteristically playful use of archetype.

Aside from the near inevitable hints at parallels between Barabas and his fortunate namesake and with the betrayer-devil Judas, Job is another particularly prominent paradigm.[27] Job was a wealthy man of Uz, whose goods Barabas enumerates in typically assiduous fashion (following the Bible once again): "seven thousand sheep, / Three thousand camels, and two hundred yoke / Of labouring oxen, and five hundred / She-asses" (1.2.185–8). Responding to a challenge from Satan regarding the nature of Job's faith, God repeatedly tests Job with afflictions, taking everything he has, and still Job does not curse God in return; ultimately his faith is rewarded with greater riches. When Barabas's fellow Jews suggest he might alleviate his suffering at the Christians' hands by reflecting on the example of Job, he dismisses their suggestion, asserting that Job's wealth was nothing compared to his. But then he curses the day he was born in language that follows Job's own curse very closely (1.2.194–201; Job 3:1–6). Having lost his wealth, Barabas then proceeds to follow Job's example by regaining his riches not once but twice – raising the possibility that he in fact might be, as he insists, one of God's chosen nation.

That provocative possibility is of course dashed in Barabas's elaborate death, and here too we find Marlowe toying with an Old Testament archetype. The Book of Esther (which precedes the Book of Job) tells the story of Haman who, having gained favor with King Ahasuerus, plots to have his enemy Mordecai hung on a gallows "fifty cubits high" (Esther 5:14). When his treachery against the honest Mordecai is discovered, Haman is hanged on the very gallows he had prepared for his enemy (Esther 7:9–10), just as Barabas is drowned in the same cauldron he intended for Selim-Calymath. The irony is that Haman, on whose actions Barabas's final plot is surely based, was renowned as an enemy of the Jews, since Mordecai was a prominent Jew. If this is more than a dark joke on Marlowe's part, it may be

[26] Marlowe's playfully positive characterization of the Ottoman prince Selim-Calymath is further discussed in Burton, *Traffic and Turning*, pp. 221–2.

[27] The role of Job in *The Merchant of Venice*, *Othello*, and in Venetian society is analyzed in considerably more detail in Julia Reinhard Lupton, "Job in Venice: Shakespeare and the Travails of Universalism," in Laura Tosi and Shaul Bassi (eds.), *Visions of Venice in Shakespeare* (Farnham: Ashgate, 2011), pp. 105–21.

intended to effectively deny Barabas's Judaism any connection with the Israelites of the Old Testament, whose legitimate inheritors were, it was often claimed, English Protestants. Instead, Barabas and his Judaism are connected to a biblical emblem of evil in a dynamic familiar from the great religious cycles of medieval drama.[28]

Superficially, Judaism in *The Merchant of Venice* looks very similar. Shylock's religion is similarly comprised of echoes of the Old Testament: aside from the lineage implied by "father Abram" (1.3.156), he describes Launcelot as a "fool of Hagar's offspring" (2.6.42), he shadows the apocryphal Ecclesiasticus 34:22 ("He that taketh away his neighbour's living slayeth him") in the lines "you take my life / When you do take the means whereby I live" (4.1.372), and he references Genesis 32:10 in swearing "by Jacob's staff" (2.5.35).[29] Jacob is presented by Shylock as a kind of justificatory archetype in his discussion with Antonio over the legitimacy of interest (1.3.68–86, on which more below). Both Barabas and Shylock have a Mosaic insistence on the word of "law" (4.1.141); both lose their wealth in the manner of Job; and it could be argued that, like Barabas and the biblical Haman, Shylock is ultimately hoist by his own petard. However, unlike *The Jew of Malta*, in which Barabas's Old Testament theology is rigorously juxtaposed against the New Testament theology of that play's Christian characters, the religious divisions of *The Merchant of Venice* are far less distinct.[30]

The breakdown of any easy opposition on the basis of faith is demonstrated in the disguised Portia's inability to distinguish which "is the merchant here, and which the Jew" (4.1.169) in her entrance to the court scene, and is in part a consequence of Shakespeare's decision to place Shylock not at the center of the play (as Marlowe had done with Barabas) but on the periphery, both in the number of lines he speaks and in his minimal role in the Portia–Bassanio love match. Shakespeare required something different from his staged Judaism, and its contours shifted as a result. Unlike Barabas in *The Jew of Malta*, a play in which scripture is used to justify violence and rapacity, Shylock is the most conspicuously religious

28 See, for example, the discussion in John Tolan, *Saracens: Islam in the Medieval European Imagination* (New York: Columbia University Press, 2002), pp. 129–31.

29 This section builds on the detailed notes in John Russell Brown (ed.), *The Merchant of Venice*, Arden Shakespeare (London: Methuen, 1955), pp. 26, 51–2, 119.

30 This emphasis on the rather unique religious ambiguity in Shakespeare's plays accords with David Bevington's and Peter Marshall's views above; this chapter, though, ultimately sees Shakespeare's representation of non-Christian religions, despite their being subtler and more understated than his contemporaries', as effectively concretizing and reinforcing the Christian beliefs and practices endorsed in these same plays.

figure in *The Merchant of Venice*. No other character directly quotes scripture, and Shylock's theological corpus unusually includes both Old and New Testaments. He is acutely aware, for instance, of the Christians' defining belief in the divinity of their prophet "the Nazarite" (1.3.28), but his reference to the "fawning publican" (1.3.36) probably comes from Luke 18:10–14; his insistence that "My deeds [be] upon my head" (4.1.201) stems from Matthew 27:25 (the same passage quoted by Ferneze and the First Knight above); and his assertion that the Jews are "the stock of Barabbas" (4.1.291) reflects the events narrated in Mark 15:6–15. The last two of these references suggest that Shakespeare turned to those passages in the Gospels traditionally used to assert Jewish responsibility for the crucifixion of Christ not to emulate Marlowe but to allow Shylock to damn himself and his religion, in keeping with the intensely Christian emphasis on mercy and prayer in the court scene. Paradoxically, it is through the expression of his religion in this scene that Shylock comes to tacitly acknowledge – and again in some sense replay – the truth of that defining accusation, paving the way for his final conversion.[31]

Earlier in the play the difference between Christians and Jews is not marked by divergent Old and New Testament positions or soteriology. Instead it is based on the differing exegesis of shared scripture: a departure which emphasized the theological proximity of the two religions but also demonstrated the well-documented "literalism" of Jewish interpretation and its confutation.[32] When Shylock is negotiating with Antonio for the loan of three thousand ducats, they fall to disputation concerning the justification for usury (an issue prominent in late sixteenth-century England). In proposing the example of Jacob and Laban's sheep (from Genesis 30:25–43), Shylock asserts a biblical precedent for interest, since Jacob manipulated pregnant ewes to produce "parti-coloured lambs" that would be his.[33] In scornful opposition, Antonio asserts that only the power of God could bring such a thing about, pointing out to Bassanio that the "devil can cite Scripture for his purpose" (1.3.94). Here shared scripture provides the basis for negotiation – and differing interpretations prove no barrier to commerce – but after marveling at Shylock's ingenious reading of this episode, an audience is left with Antonio's image of Judaism as a "goodly apple rotten at the heart" (1.3.97).

[31] The various forms in which accusations of Jewish complicity in the crucifixion of Christ appear in early modern writings are discussed in Shapiro, *Shakespeare and the Jews*, *passim*.

[32] Ibid., p. 127.

[33] This exchange is considered at greater length in Andrew Hadfield, "Shakespeare and Republican Venice," in Tosi and Bassi, *Visions of Venice*, pp. 67–82.

Less obvious as an example of disputation, but more in keeping with the Haman archetype, is the use of Daniel in the court scene. The scene begins with Shylock's exclamation approving Portia (disguised as Balthasar) as "A Daniel come to judgement, yea, a Daniel! / O wise young judge, how I do honour thee!" (4.1.218–19). This is a straightforward acclamation of Portia's apparent probity, in reference to the Apocryphal "History of Susanna" in which the young Daniel (whose name translates as "God is my judge") intervened to convict the two elders that were about to falsely condemn Susanna for adultery. As Shylock reads it, he is the wronged Susanna, the "daughter of Israel" (Susanna 48), and his Christian antagonists the false witnesses. Later, as Portia's manipulation of the terms of Shylock's contract and the law become clear, it is Graziano who taunts Shylock in return: "A second Daniel, a Daniel, Jew!" (4.1.328) and "A second Daniel, still say I, a second Daniel!" (4.1.335). The unrestrained glee with which Graziano uses Shylock's own terms of reference in triumph over him can obscure his divergent reading of the same scripture. In Graziano's use of Daniel the primary identification of Portia–Balthasar as the embodiment of righteous justice remains, but it is Antonio who becomes the innocent and wronged Susanna, and Shylock the false elders – an identification made all the more forceful in the way that, like Haman and Barabas, the elders' own actions condemn them (Susanna 51–8). Once again Jews are responsible for their own downfall and obsolescence.

Shakespeare's recreation of Judaism for the early modern stage is thus primarily a scriptural construction, built from a tissue of quotation, reference, and archetype in order to create the appearance of a coherent theology, but one that is always already past, defeated by the truth of Christ. In the apparently casual references that litter his dramatic works, Shakespeare uses Jews and Judaism in a theatrical shorthand to signal sin and non-Christian contrariness. When involved in a more sustained dramatization, Marlowe had constructed a world of basic religious oppositions debased by human greed, in which Judaism became almost as provocatively valid as the Maltese Knights' Roman Catholicism. In *The Merchant of Venice* the contradictions and disputations that Shakespeare carefully embeds in his sophisticated stage Judaism cause any theological coherence or validity to unravel as the play progresses. In drawing on dramatic precedent and the Bible, but offering a shared scriptural language whose valid interpretation is always a Christian prerogative, Shakespeare creates a Judaism that is neither a viable alternative to Christianity nor (in a Marlovian sense) satirical. Instead, his Judaism is made subservient to the plot and structure of a comedy that ends in the sanctification of a double Christian marriage.

## Shakespeare's Islam

Act 2, scene 4 of *2 Henry IV* features the first entrance into the play of Falstaff's ensign, identified on the title page of the play's first quarto as "swaggering Pistol."[34] His arrival is anticipated by Falstaff, Mistress Quickly, and Doll Tearsheet, and here again he is described as a "swaggerer" and "the foul-mouthedest rogue in England" (2.4.60–1). Following his entrance and some initial bawdy banter, he engages in an argument with Doll and soon begins spouting a series of short, self-aggrandizing speeches typical of his "choler" (2.4.138). Pistol's ridiculously affected speeches here quote directly from (and parody) the hackneyed rhetoric of a particular genre of drama popular in the late 1580s and early 1590s. The lines "Have we not Hiren here?" (2.4.136), "hollow pampered jades of Asia" (2.4.141), and "feed and be fat, my Calipolis" (2.4.155) represent clichéd extravagance, and each comes from a popular play. The first is presumed to quote George Peele's lost *The Turkish Mahamet and Hiren the Fair Greek* (dated by Jonathan Burton to 1588), one of a series of plays in different languages on the "Irene" (or Hiren) myth; the second, Marlowe's *2 Tamburlaine* (again probably from early 1588); and the third, Peele's *The Battle of Alcazar* (*c.* 1589).[35] Each belongs to moments of tension and dramatic spectacle, and all are set in non-Christian locations against the epic backdrop of Islamic–Christian conflict.[36] These partially remembered and recycled quotations are made all the more absurd by the banality of the context in which Pistol uses them – he has just been involved in a tavern brawl with a prostitute – and they fit the mock-heroism that characterizes the Eastcheap scenes and that offers such a rich counterpoint to the play's aristocratic court scenes (later in the same scene Falstaff is celebrated by Doll as "valorous as Hector of Troy, worth five of Agamemnon, and ten times better than the Nine Worthies" [2.4.196–7]).

[34] William Shakespeare, *The second part of Henrie the fourth continuing to his death, and coronation of Henrie the fift. With the humours of sir Iohn Falstaffe, and swaggering Pistoll* (London: Valentine Simmes for Andrew Wize and William Aspley, 1600).

[35] Burton, *Traffic and Turning*, p. 257.

[36] These plays and their context have been recently studied in Burton, *Traffic and Turning*; Matthew Dimmock, *New Turkes: Dramatizing Islam and the Ottomans in Early Modern England* (Farnham: Ashgate, 2005); Nabil Matar, *Islam and Britain*, and *Turks, Moors and Englishmen in the Age of Discovery* (New York: Columbia University Press, 1999); Linda McJannet, *The Sultan Speaks: Dialogue in English Plays and Histories about the Ottoman Turks* (Basingstoke: Palgrave Macmillan, 2006); Benedict Robinson, *Islam and Early Modern Literature: The Politics of Romance from Spenser to Milton* (Basingstoke: Palgrave Macmillan, 2007); and Daniel Vitkus, *Turning Turk: English Theater and the Multicultural Mediterranean, 1570–1630* (Basingstoke: Palgrave Macmillan, 2003).

So why does Shakespeare choose to invoke these particular plays? Certainly each one Pistol refers to can be characterized as part of a distinctive genre of "Turk plays," a term put forward by Daniel Vitkus and Mark Hutchings to denote those plays that followed hard upon the success of *1 Tamburlaine*.[37] There are records of at least fifteen examples (and there were likely more) between 1587 and 1596, when Shakespeare's *Merchant of Venice* was probably first performed, and they are the product of a complex intermixture of circumstances ranging from the immediate success of Marlowe's play and the collaboration and competition between rival companies that followed; the Anglo-Ottoman relationship that had been established around 1580 and celebrated in print by Richard Hakluyt in 1589; the continuing repercussions of the Ottoman conquest of Constantinople in 1453 and westward expansion thereafter; the visibility (and desirability) of goods from Asia and North Africa in London streets and households; and simmering post-Reformation conflict with Spain.[38] The result was, as Hutchings writes, that "even occasional playgoers were familiar with visual or verbal images of the Ottoman Empire: whether at inns prior to the ban in 1594 or subsequently at the Rose, Curtain, Swan, or Theater, and then at the end of the century at the Globe and Fortune, companies maintained a repertoire of 'Turk plays.'"[39] Their names help to conjure up their rich associations with non-Christian geographies and potentates, as well as the militarized, tension-filled environment in which they were created, staged, and restaged: plays like the first and second parts of *Tamar Cham*, *The Capture of Stuhlweissenburg*, *Selimus*, and *The Battle of Alcazar*.

Pistol's repeated quoting of these plays in *2 Henry IV* is thus a reaction to the ubiquity of the "Turk type" and the language associated with it: his much mocked "fierceness" as a "counterfeit cowardly knave" (5.1.66) who "cannot avouch" in his "deeds" any of his "words" (5.1.69–90) is a comic version of the epic protagonists of the "Turk plays." The fact that he garbles these quotations into nonsense – "hollow pampered jades of Asia" rather than "holla," "Cannibal" rather than "Hannibal," and the nonsensical mixture of "Trojan Greeks" – indicates furthermore that such characters and language had become something of a joke by the late 1590s; that, despite

37 Daniel Vitkus (ed.), *Three Turk Plays from Early Modern England* (New York: Columbia University Press, 2000); Mark Hutchings, "The 'Turk Phenomenon' and the Repertory of the Late Elizabethan Playhouse," *Early Modern Literary Studies*, special issue 16 (2007), 1–39.

38 Hutchings, "'Turk Phenomenon'"; Susan Skilliter, *William Harborne and the Trade with Turkey, 1578–1582* (Oxford University Press, 1977); Dimmock, *New Turkes*, pp. 87–9.

39 Hutchings, "'Turk Phenomenon,'" 6–7.

the odd revival, the "Turk play" as a theatrical genre had had its day. Some critics have gone further, arguing that these passages reveal another aspect of the shifting relationship between Shakespeare and the ghostly influence of Marlowe; Robert Logan, for instance, has suggested that in his characterization of Pistol, Shakespeare "took advantage of the comic richness latent in the Marlovian prototype" and that "Pistol's role as a comic Tamburlaine seems to be his chief reason for being."[40] Or alternatively, as Jerry Brotton has suggested, Pistol's reference to a series of "Turk plays" is a further sign of the ways in which Shakespeare's history plays in particular are haunted by the "spectre" of Islam.[41] It is certainly the case that Tamburlaine's bombast and braggadocio had been a primary element in those characters that appeared thereafter – Muly Hamet in *Alcazar*, Mahamet in *The Turkish Mahomet*, and Tamburlaine himself, as well as in a range of "Grand Turks" on the stage. But its comic potential was also quickly exploited. Basilisco in *Soliman and Perseda* (thought to be by Thomas Kyd) is a prominent example; and, solely in a Shakespearean context, Logan has suggested Hotspur from *1 Henry IV*, Samson in *Romeo and Juliet*, and the Prince of Morocco in *The Merchant of Venice* as examples of this role; and there are also Jonson's later Volpone and Sir Epicure Mammon.[42]

Pistol is therefore a recognizable comic caricature, part of (but also a response to) the "Turk play" tradition. But Islam is not a central element of this caricature, nor of Pistol's original quotations. To ridicule the "Turk play" does not seem to require reference to Islam. Pistol's muddled recreation of himself as a thundering epic hero is absurd, perhaps all the more so since he repeatedly identifies himself with non-Christian characters – and Turks on the Elizabethan stage were associated with bombastic excess – but the role Pistol thinks he is assuming here is not an explicitly Muslim one. Of the three characters Pistol quotes, only one, Peele's Turkish sultan Mahomet, seems to have been unequivocally Muslim, like those dramatic sultans – the Amuracks, Amuraths, Bajazeths, and Solimans – that followed. While both Tamburlaine and Muly Hamet are associated with Islamic lands, neither are explicitly Muslim – Hamet veers towards a kind of pagan polytheism, while Tamburlaine acknowledges "Mahomet" whom he once "thought a God" (*2 Henry IV* 5.1.174), but burns the Alcoran in defiance of him.[43] None of the later comic braggart examples,

[40] Robert Logan, *Shakespeare's Marlowe: The Influence of Christopher Marlowe on Shakespeare's Artistry* (Farnham: Ashgate, 2007), p. 157.

[41] Brotton, "Shakespeare's Turks." [42] Logan, *Shakespeare's Marlowe*, p. 157.

[43] There is further discussion of this episode in Dimmock, *New Turkes*, pp. 156–9.

not even *Merchant*'s Prince of Morocco, are explicitly Muslim either, with the possible exception of Kyd's Basilisco, who comically converts to Islam without realizing it.[44] There has been some debate about the nature of Shakespeare's Morocco: is he, as Logan has argued, a "comic characterization" of a "Tamburlainian warrior hero," or is he, as Jonathan Burton has alternatively suggested, a dignified and noble alternative to "the stereotype of the lascivious, blustering" stage Turk?[45] He is certainly a subject of the Ottoman Sultan, and is dressed "all in white" – his costume presumably including a turban (as stipulated in some modern editions) – and he is certainly grandiloquent in the Tamburlaine mould; but beyond the implications of costume, nowhere does he deliberately articulate a Muslim identity. I want to suggest that Shakespeare's unwillingness to unequivocally characterize Morocco as a Muslim is related to his turning away from the "Turk play" genre, as suggested by Pistol's comic manglings.

This turning away can only be explained through a more detailed consideration of the curious nature of Islam on the early modern English stage. It is important to recognize that for most early modern English readers there was in fact no such thing as "Islam" but only "Mahometanism," an important conceptual and verbal distinction that highlights how the Islamic faith was understood as basically the heretical inverse of the Christian one, with the all too human Mahomet rather than Christ as its central deity. Mahomet was imagined as a false prophet, a cynical manipulator of his followers, a fabricator of miracles: manipulative, lascivious, and violent, a "juggling" mortal who fraudulently performed divinity. For those who read or heard them (such material was a popular source for sermons), such scurrilous details of Mahomet's life were confirmed by a considerable and authoritative body of printed and manuscript material, the early examples of which affirmed the notion that he was an idol, a version that would linger on in the romance tradition.[46]

For the stage, however, Mahometanism was a different entity, and dramatists seem to have struggled to find a suitable way to materialize it. In *Tamburlaine* and the "Turk plays" that followed, Mahometanism was itself a performance, designed to generate what Jonathan Sell has identified as an "exophoric representation," the deliberate creation of a sense of

44 Thomas Kyd (?), *The tragedye of Solyman and Perseda* (London: Edward Allde for Edward White, 1592), sig. G2r.

45 Logan, *Shakespeare's Marlowe*, p. 156; Burton, *Traffic and Turning*, p. 208.

46 The division of Christian notions of Islam as monotheistic or as idolatrous is considered by Norman Daniel in *Islam and the West: The Making of an Image*, 2nd edn. (Oxford: Oneworld, 1993), pp. 239–40.

wonder by depicting a realm beyond the audience's geographical and cultural realities.[47] In these plays a Turkish identity is typically signaled by stage properties, themselves borrowed from continental prints and costume books – robes, the turban, the falchion (or scimitar), and often the mustache. This costume might also signal a Mahometan identity (just as the word "Turk" might act as a synonym for "Mahometan" in certain contexts), but the two could also be distinct. In another indication of how much writers depended on Christianity as a model, it was the invocation of Mahomet that was the most common means of indicating Mahometanism – such as Bajazeth's vow by "Ye holy priests of heavenly Mahomet, / That, sacrificing, slice and cut your flesh, / Staining his altars with your purple blood" (*1 Tamburlaine*, 4.2.2–4). These characters perform their veneration of Mahomet, and do so in exaggerated ways, as in Tamburlaine's hubristic rejection of Mahomet. It is as if Mahometanism, this heretical system, had to be shown to be false through its gross theatricalism, an extension of the juggling theatricality of its founder. But this too was not consistent. Mahomet often took his place in a classical pantheon of gods (suggesting again an uncertainty as to how to dramatize Mahometanism), or as a demonic figure, or even, as in Greene's *Alphonsus of Arragon*, as a "brazen idol" breathing flames and prophesying to his followers. It was further possible for a staged "Turk" not to invoke Mahomet at all and thus immediately to be identified as a sympathetic character, like Corcut in Greene's *Selimus*.[48] This chaos of possible Mahometanisms, all performance and bombast, with no one seemingly clear about what exactly Mahomet and his religion might be, became increasingly ridiculous and unsustainable. Certainly Greene's idol of Mahomet's head, referred to in contemporary verse as "Mahomet's Poo," gained a kind of absurd comic notoriety.[49] If we recognize that this was the specific context in which Shakespeare came to write, it hardly seems surprising that staging Mahometanism was something the savvy playwright tried to avoid.

Yet while Shakespeare never wrote a "Turk play" per se (that is, if we discount for the purposes of this chapter the suggestion that *Titus* or *2 Henry VI* are kinds of "Turk play"), the "Turk motif" nevertheless appears in at

[47] Jonathan Sell, *Rhetoric and Wonder in English Travel Writing, 1560–1613* (Farnham: Ashgate, 2006), p. 16.

[48] Corcut is discussed further in Dimmock, *New Turkes*, pp. 175–7, and is mentioned in this context in Burton, *Traffic and Turning*, p. 109.

[49] This poem, "A Farewell," is reproduced alongside Peele's companion piece, "An Eclogue Gratulatory," in David Horne (ed.), *The Life and Minor Works of George Peele* (New Haven, CT: Yale University Press, 1961), vol. 1, pp. 220–30.

least thirteen of his plays.[50] As I have suggested, this may simply have been a question of timing: that what we tend to recognize as the mature Shakespeare from the later 1590s onwards came after the initial popularity of the post-Tamburlaine "Turk play" and developed as a reaction to its fading. There was probably no commercial pressure to create such a play, whether from company or audiences. Yet its traces remain throughout his work, and it is perhaps more accurate to talk of Shakespeare being haunted by the "Turk play" than by Islam. This is a useful distinction to make, simply because those instances we find in Shakespeare that do refer to Moors or Turks seem to intentionally step back from the stale bombast associated with the "Turk play" in which a confused, unstable, and hyper-theatrical vision of Mahometanism was embedded. Instead, Shakespeare innovates by doing something that seems counterintuitive, and which no "Turk play" had consistently done: he answers the uncertainties and failures in the vision of Mahometanism presented in the "Turk play" by *down-playing* it. After the hundreds of references to Mahomet that appear in the "Turk plays," the lack of reference to Mahomet by Morocco, or in the context of the Ottoman threat in *Othello* or more generally in Shakespeare, is suggestive of a new and different direction.

That Shakespeare's only explicit reference to Mahomet comes in a play like *1 Henry VI* is therefore revealing. The Dauphin's exclamation to Joan, "Was Mahomet inspired with a dove? / Thou with an eagle art inspired then" (1.2.140-1), is a curiously ambivalent statement since in the countless times this story was told in early modern English sermons and books, it was invariably a vehicle for absolute condemnation: the tale of Mahomet's mere fabrication of a miracle by inserting peas in his ears to attract a dove, a dove then falsely identified as the Holy Spirit, was read as a sure sign of a lack of divinity and a damning disproof of Mahometanism. Yet Shakespeare's use of the story is either ironic – celebrating Joan while nodding to an audience's knowledge of this myth and its implications for her characterization – or it is almost provocatively relativistic, recognizing without explicit condemnation what inspired Mahomet, and thus what inspires Mahometans. Either way it is unusual in terms of early modern writing about Mahometanism.

So it is perhaps the case that Shakespeare's decision not to explicitly acknowledge Mahomet or Mahometanism in *Othello* or through the Prince of Morocco is less theatrical innovation than it is a recognition of how culturally literate audiences had become after the post-Tamburlaine "Turk play" phenomenon, in ways they had not been in the late 1580s. It might

50 Hutchings, "'Turk Phenomenon,'" 5.

also suggest that Shakespeare was more interested in emphasizing "Moroccanness" and "Ottomanness" or "Turkishness" – a set of characteristics relating to culture or ethnicity that might include but are not defined or dominated by religion. That Shakespeare chooses to refer specifically to the "turbanned" and "circumcised" nature of the Turk whom Othello remembers encountering in Aleppo (5.2.362–5) indicates that religion is still an important factor, but this turn to alternative signifiers of Mahometanism rather than conventional references to Mahomet suggests Shakespeare's unease at how contested Mahomet's status and nature had become.

## Conclusion

Shakespeare's various allusions to the two Abrahamic non-Christian religions indicate an awareness of their dominant forms in early modern English culture but also an unwillingness to blindly reproduce those forms. Instead, both Judaism and Islam are pushed back to the fringes of his plots and there reconstituted, threatening but insubstantial. Shakespeare chooses to no more than hint at the religious practices associated with either, nor does he address the vexed questions regarding the status of Mahomet. And he does not bind the two religions together in infamy, a common move by his contemporaries. Rather, the two are kept deliberately distinct: the Jew a debased and anachronistic interlocutor whose religion is designed to be recognizably and intrinsically invalid; the Mahometan denied either scriptural congruence or religious coherence, embodied in the martially aggressive male.

These non-Christian religions are used to underpin a structural emphasis on Christianity in plays like *The Merchant of Venice* and *Othello*, in which their largely unrealized presence throws the Christian values and virtues of the protagonists (or their lack) into sharp relief: the skewed dynamic of the casket test is perhaps the obvious example. The Venetian and wider Mediterranean setting of both plays parallels this formal element. In these terms, in constructing his stage Judaism and Islam as constituent elements of a specifically Christian worldview, Shakespeare signals an engagement with an Erasmian abstraction of Turks to Christian sins, and leans towards a Calvinist Protestant universalism in which Muslims and Jews are simply misguided Christians awaiting their shepherd, an influential view endorsed in the Book of Common Prayer.[51]

[51] Erasmus, "A Most Useful Discussion Concerning Proposals for War Against the Turks" (1530) (also known as "De Bello Turcico"), in Dominic Baker-Smith (ed.), *Collected Works of Erasmus* (University

In dramatizing Islam and Judaism at all, however, Shakespeare had to respond to their semantics within theatrical culture and to the contested, crude, and contradictory forms in which both Jews and Mahometans had been hitherto represented. It is to this context, rather than to any detailed theological engagement, that we must look to find non-Christian religion in Shakespeare. This was a playwright establishing an audience and a reputation in a crowded marketplace, and his depiction of non-Christian religion is intrinsically theatrical: there is no evidence that he looked beyond his Bible and some continental histories and romances for source material, indicating either a lack of interest in or a lack of access to sources that delineated religious belief (let alone any detailed reading or intuitive sense of Jewish theology, the Qur'an, or Sufism, as some have suggested).[52] Instead, a search for non-Christian religion in Shakespeare's work reveals a playwright responding directly and with nuance to the ways Judaism and Islam were already encoded in the playhouse, and doing so with a keen sense of changing theatrical fashions, audience tastes, and the constraints of form. On those few occasions when Shakespeare does attempt to signal the existence of a non-Christian belief system in anything more than an off-hand, polemical fashion, what we glimpse is absolutely defined by its "not-Christianness," a device subservient to character and plot. It is Shakespeare's decision to render non-Christian religion as background rather than foreground that sets him apart from the bombast of the 1580s and early 1590s and his contemporaries, and shows us a playwright in the making. This fruitful and complex engagement would present new directions for his work and for the theater in the decades that followed.

of Toronto Press, 2005), vol. LXIV, pp. 201–66. Further discussion of this aspect of Erasmus's text can be found in Dimmock, *New Turkes*, pp. 20–1. Jean Calvin, *The Institution of Christian Religion*, trans. Thomas Norton (London, 1561), fo. 105r. *The book of common prayer* (London, 1559), sig. G8v. See also Brian Cummings (ed.), *The Book of Common Prayer: The Texts of 1549, 1559, and 1662* (Oxford University Press, 2011), p. 317.

52 See, for example, the later work of Martin Lings and those influenced by him.

# *Afterword*

*Brian Cummings*

In 1998 Harold Bloom described Shakespeare's works as a "secular scripture."[1] Whatever view may be held about Bloom's general theory about Shakespeare and the invention of the "human," he sums up a twentieth-century consensus that is eloquently and compellingly expressed in 1904 by A. C. Bradley in his classic work, *Shakespearean Tragedy*:

> The Elizabethan drama was almost wholly secular; and while Shakespeare was writing he practically confined his view to the world of non-theological observation and thought, so that he represents it substantially in one and the same way whether the period of the story is pre-Christian or Christian.[2]

Throughout the twentieth century the prevailing view of Shakespeare was that he was to be interpreted and studied outside of a religious context, that he saw the world in a "non-theological" way.

In part, as in Bradley, this was an observational stance based on a reading of the texts. None of Shakespeare's plays takes a biblical subject, for instance, for its plot. There is no outwardly devotional or doctrinal theme. However, Bradley also participated in a theory of literature that with increasing rigidity founded itself on a division between the secular and the religious. This was not, in Bradley's case, out of any antireligious bias. In 1907–8 he delivered the Gifford Lectures at Glasgow on the subject of "Ideals of Religion." Through an exploration of spirit, mind, idealism, truth, reality, and good and evil, he aimed to understand what religion is, and what human needs it seeks to satisfy. However, it was part of Bradley's religious idealism to distinguish firmly in a philosophical sense between poetry and religion. Poetry is part of his explanation of what he calls "the

1 *Shakespeare and the Invention of the Human* (London: Longman, 1998), p. 3, borrowing a phrase from Northrop Frye.

2 A. C. Bradley, *Shakespearean Tragedy: Lectures on Hamlet, Othello, King Lear, Macbeth*, 2nd edn. (London: Macmillan, 1905), p. 25.

inadequacy of natural religion."[3] The religious is a transcendent world which is separate from the manufactured and fictive language of poetry.

Bradley's writing on Shakespeare and on religion coincided with the first development of English Literature as an academic discipline. Indeed, he was the first person to hold the chair of Literature at Liverpool University, and was later offered (but declined) the first chair of English Literature at Cambridge.[4] It can be argued that the very identification of the "literary" as a distinctive subject is part of a struggle to see literature as an emergent force in culture which comes about through a dissociation from religion. In Matthew Arnold's *Culture and Anarchy* (1869), culture arises out of a separation from religion, and thus acquires its capacity to restore society: "Religion says: The kingdom of God is within you; and culture, in like manner, places human perfection in an internal condition, in the growth and predominance of our humanity proper."[5] Literature appears where angels fear to tread. A theory of secularization, in this sense, lies at the origin of the study of English as a discipline. The absence of religion from the plays of Shakespeare is therefore not incidental, but axiomatic to the emergence of modernity. From Bradley in 1904 to Bloom in 1998, Shakespeare's exceptionalism lies in this capacity to explain a secular view of culture as postreligious.

It is something of an irony that the first stirrings of an alternative view of religion in Shakespeare came with New Historicism. In despite, that is, of an aggressively Nietzschean rejection of the lure of theology, New Historicist studies acknowledged the power of religious languages and fantasies in early modern culture. This often took the form of a repeat of the secularization thesis – religious ideology fails and is replaced by tragedy as a radical critique – but it allowed by the back door a sense of how the religious is inscribed in Shakespeare.[6] This was followed at the turn of the twentieth century by a seemingly quite opposite movement. Long-standing biographical rumors about Shakespeare's residual Catholicism combined with an interest in religion as a form of covert and suppressed political identity. Various shades of recusancy allied Shakespeare's plays

[3] Bradley, *Ideals of Religion: Gifford Lectures Delivered at the University of Glasgow in 1907* (London: Macmillan, 1940), p. 56.

[4] G. K. Hunter, "Bradley, Andrew Cecil (1851–1935)," *Oxford Dictionary of National Biography* (www.oxforddnb.com).

[5] *Culture and Anarchy*, ed. John Dover Wilson (Cambridge University Press, 1971), p. 47.

[6] See Jonathan Dollimore's review of his own work in *Radical Tragedy: Religion, Ideology, and Power in the Drama of Shakespeare and his Contemporaries*, 3rd edn. (Durham, NC: Duke University Press, 2004), p. l.

with a current of clandestine opposition to the prevailing norms of culture and orthodoxy.

In time, this trend in Shakespearean studies became identified with a more general form of "religious turn" in early modern literary analysis.[7] The "religious turn" had some unpredictable results. In some features it became the antithesis of the "linguistic turn" from which it derived its name. Religion returned Shakespeare to the habitus of human and social subjectivity. Especially in the "Catholic Shakespeare" argument, religion became a kind of proxy coat of transcendental personal identity, wresting literature back from deconstruction. In other forms, by a deeper irony, it was a restoration of the secularization thesis. The deconsecrated forms of medieval religion were given an afterlife in the maimed rites of the Elizabethan theater. Shakespeare lamented their disappearance but also sealed their loss.

Behind the more obviously controversial claims of the "religious turn" in Shakespeare studies, therefore, lie deeper ruptures concerning historicism and personal identity. And behind these, it may be argued, is a conflict about interpretation and meaning, one which continues to haunt the very definition of what literary study claims to be. Bloom avers that to tie Shakespeare to the particularity of religious confessionalization is to assume that plays can only be interpreted in a specific, historicized way. Whereas (in his view) it is the special quality of Shakespeare's work, or indeed of any literary work, not to be quantifiable in this way. At the same time, his sterling defense of a secular Shakespeare has coincided with a vexed discussion among the social sciences over whether the "secularization thesis" has prevailed at all.[8] While literary study long assumed that the horizon of modernity looked out on a secular realm, the newest forms of literary theory call this entire paradigm into question. Shakespeare is now as likely to be seen through the lens of political theology as of secular evangelism or enfranchisement.[9]

What the chapters in this volume collectively show, however much they are invested in such a theorization, is that definitions of both "religious" and "secular" are in urgent need of revision. In this way the initial energies of the "religious turn" have some unexpected trajectories. David Bevington takes Shakespeare firmly out of narrow confessional politics; Matthew Dimmock

[7] Ken Jackson and Arthur F. Marotti, "The Turn to Religion in Early Modern English Studies," *Criticism*, 46 (winter 2004), 167–90.

[8] Peter Berger (ed.), *The Desecularization of the World: Resurgent Religion and World Politics* (Grand Rapids, MI: Eerdmans, 1999).

[9] Graham Hammill and Julia Reinhard Lupton (eds.), *Political Theology and Early Modernity* (University of Chicago Press, 2012).

out of the assumption that religious equals Christian. Within the terms of the Reformation controversy, meanwhile, Peter Marshall, in discussing the residual Catholicism of Elizabethan Warwickshire, and Felicity Heal, in reassessing the emergent public Protestantism of Shakespeare's London, both reveal how much more hybrid and volatile religious identities were in post-Reformation England than was once assumed. Conferring a religious identity on Shakespeare need not mean straitjacketing the plays to a particular confession. In that way, the plurality of the theater or of the literary is not threatened by the religious, but enriched by it.

In a different direction, Peter Lake and Adrian Streete realign the forces of religious and secular intellectual history. The history of ideas, as much as the history of literature, has recently been in the throes of a difficult divorce from the secularization thesis. The seventeenth-century revolutions in scientific and political thought are both subject to religious revisionism, though not without contention.[10] Primary in the continuing secular camp have been the proponents of classical republicanism. Lake, working in the tradition of mapping neo-Roman political culture against Puritan and Catholic forms of resistance theory, finds less a chasm between classical and Christian thinking than a form of mutual stress. In that way, Bradley's assumption that a Roman garb means always a nontheological framework is misplaced. Similarly, Streete shows how Lucretian atomism is vexed with Christian anxieties about death and dissolution rather than offering an escape.

Other chapters in this volume take specific plays and show how the religious historicization of Shakespeare's work does not need to be tied to a confessional motivation. One of the interesting aspects of this is that plays which have sometimes proved resistant to historical interpretation, whether through neglect (*King John* here examined by Beatrice Groves, *Henry VIII* by Michael Davies and Paul Stevens) or through overfamiliarity (*A Midsummer Night's Dream* in the hands of Alison Shell, *King Lear* of David Loewenstein), can come to mean something rich and strange through the intervention of the peculiar alchemy of religious identity.

However, the largest lesson of all that emerges from this book is the falseness of the dichotomy between the religious world and the secular world. It is one of the binding assumptions of the secularization narrative that the secular is a hermetically sealed concept of opposition. The paradox

10 Peter Harrison, *The Fall of Man and the Foundations of Science* (Cambridge University Press, 2009); Eric Nelson, *The Hebrew Republic: Jewish Sources and the Transformation of European Political Thought* (Cambridge, MA: Harvard University Press/Belknap Press, 2010).

is that it thus conjures into existence a category which did not have meaning until the idea of the secular. The "religious" in modern parlance is a term which is effectively forced to equal "nonsecular" as much as the other way round. Yet archaeologists and anthropologists of premodern societies commonly reject the idea of a religious sphere. All of life was religious in the modern sense: but in that way it is hardly a differentiable category since it defines a way of life in the round. Indeed, that is what Max Weber meant in his ground-breaking conceptualization of world religions via his study of *Entzauberung* ("disenchantment").[11] Ewan Fernie, in his account of the demonic in *Macbeth*; Michael Witmore in his wide-ranging analysis of theological semiotics; Richard McCoy in his skeptical chapter on fideism, all show their sympathy with what is coming to be called "postsecular" (as well as "post-Christian") thought in the twenty-first century. Paul Stevens makes as the centerpiece of his argument the apostle of postsecularity, the Canadian philosopher Charles Taylor. Taylor's meditative work in modern apologetics, *A Secular Age*, provides an intriguing postscript to the travail of Shakespeare's latter-day existential religious crisis. Shakespeare has gone from being secular to being postsecular almost without catching breath. Taylor at once appeals to the grand narrative that once underpinned Shakespearean studies, and yet also undercuts this narrative in providing the outline of a countertheory. "Our age is very far from settling in to a comfortable unbelief," he says.[12] This melancholy apprehension of the "unquiet frontiers of modernity" (*Secular Age*, p. 711) is a far cry from the secular triumphalism of a previous generation. However, could it be that an understanding of religion as ideologically fragmentary and subjectively unpredictable is not exclusively modern, but also applicable to the early modern? Taylor's idea of the plurality of modern religious beliefs may yet allow for a new way of understanding the post-Reformation world of mixed and metamorphosing confessions, and of Shakespeare's ambivalent register within that world. What is obvious is that we can no longer do without early modern religion in thinking about Shakespeare.

[11] The phrase *Entzauberung der Welt* ("disenchantment of the world") originates in Weber's late lecture given in Munich in 1918 and published in 1919, "Wissenschaft als Beruf," in Johannes Winckelmann (ed.), *Gesammelte Aufsätze zur Wissenschaftslehre* (Tübingen: J.C.B. Mohr, 1985), p. 594.

[12] *A Secular Age* (Cambridge, MA: Harvard University Press/Belknap Press, 2007), p. 727.

# *Index*

**Notes:** Shakespeare's works are indexed by title. Other works, with the exception of *The Jew of Malta* and *Mansfield Park*, are indexed under the author's name (unless anonymous). Personal names refer to historical characters. References to stage characters appear at the play's title.

CPSIA information can be obtained
at www.ICGtesting.com
Printed in the USA
LVOW04*1913060516
487064LV00007B/84/P